Also by Jonathan Shay

ACHILLES IN VIETNAM
Combat Trauma and the Undoing of Character

Odysseus and the Sirens[1]

ODYSSEUS IN AMERICA

COMBAT TRAUMA
AND THE TRIALS OF HOMECOMING

Jonathan Shay, M.D., Ph.D.

FOREWORD BY U.S. SENATORS
MAX CLELAND and JOHN McCAIN

SCRIBNER
New York   London   Toronto   Sydney

FO Amaz. 6/08 15.00

SCRIBNER
1230 Avenue of the Americas
New York, NY 10020

SCRIBNER and design are trademarks of
Macmillan Library Reference USA, Inc., used under license
by Simon & Schuster, the publisher of this work.

For information about special discounts for bulk purchases,
please contact Simon & Schuster Special Sales:
1-800-465-6798 or business@simonandschuster.com

DESIGNED BY ERICH HOBBING

Text set in New Caledonia

Manufactured in the United States of America

3 5 7 9 10 8 6 4

The Library of Congress has cataloged the hardcover edition as follows:
Shay, Jonathan.
Odysseus in America : combat trauma and the trials of homecoming / Jonathan Shay ;
foreword by Max Cleland and John McCain.
p. cm.
Includes bibliographical references (p.) and index.
1. War neuroses. 2. Vietnamese Conflict, 1961–1975—Veterans—Mental health—United States.
3. Homer. Odyssey. 4. Post-traumatic stress disorder.
5. Vietnamese Conflict, 1961–1975—Psychological aspects.
6. Veterans—Mental health—United States. 7. War—Psychological aspects.
I. Title.
RC550 .S533 2002
616.85'212—dc21   2002075817
ISBN-13: 978-0-7432-1156-7
ISBN-10:   0-7432-1156-1
ISBN-13: 978-0-7432-1157-4 (Pbk)
ISBN-10:   0-7432-1157-X (Pbk)
Permissions acknowledgments appear on page 331.

CONTENTS

FOREWORD

BY U.S. SENATORS

MAX CLELAND and JOHN MCCAIN

Those of us who have witnessed, taken part in, and suffered the tragedies of war know that the ancient Greek epics offer compelling insights into our own experiences. In the *Iliad,* an epic of war, and the *Odyssey,* an epic of a veteran's attempt to get home, Homer speaks as one who has "been there." As veterans of the Vietnam War, we appreciated the clarity and utility of *Achilles in Vietnam,* Dr. Jonathan Shay's first book, which put into words what we as veterans have always known: Homer's story of Achilles matters.

Now Dr. Shay has done it again. In *Odysseus in America,* he uses the story of Odysseus to examine another layer, revealing what it means to return from war to a safe civilian society. Dr. Shay's call to protect our troops from injury, and make them more formidable to the nation's foes, takes his vision to another level. He hits the nail on the head by proposing to compel American military institutions to create and protect *trust,* and he sets forth certain key results that must be achieved: positive qualities of community in every service member's military unit; competent, ethical, and properly supported leadership; and progressive, realistic training for what military service members actually do. If we achieve such results within our military, we will prevent not only psychological injury, but physical casualties as well, because these three fundamentals are also *combat strength multipliers*.

As part of our work in the U.S. Senate, we both serve on the Armed Services Committee. Although we come from different parties, we are in agreement with the treatment outcomes that Dr. Shay seeks from the combat veterans he serves in the Department of Veterans Affairs. As veterans, we endorse the goal of trust he proposes for all service members. The laws of nature did not force our present military institutions on us. These institutions are man-made and can be transformed to better serve our nation and its military servicemen and -women.

ACKNOWLEDGMENTS

I thank the Rockefeller Foundation, Bellagio Study and Conference Center, for direct support for the early preparation of this book. I thank Marine Manpower and Reserve Affairs and the U.S. Naval War College for support of research that contributed substantially to the concepts in this book relating to prevention of psychological and moral injury in military service.

Four groups have been both my teachers and supportive community during all or part of the preparation of this book: the clinical team and veterans of the Veterans Improvement Program (VIP) of the Department of Veterans Affairs Outpatient Clinic, Boston; the VWAR-L internet discussion list; the CLASSICS-L internet discussion list; and the First Friday Defense Lunch, an entirely unofficial group that meets monthly in Washington to analyze and promote beneficial changes in the U.S. armed services.

The worldwide collegium of classical scholars has been large-spirited and kindly with this amateur beyond any call of duty. Perhaps their long experience in dealing with late adolescents has given them so much patience with me. Without their work collectively, and their help individually, this book could never have been. My debt can never be fully repaid.

Over the eight years of its preparation, an enormous number of people have helped me with expansive generosity. I can thank by name only a small fraction. My gratitude is not bounded by the list below. In keeping with the nature of this book, the list is alphabetical:

Karl Ackerman, Mark Adin, Gary Allord, Professor James Arieti, Colonel Carl Bernard, U.S. Army, retired, Nancy Bernhard, Major General Robert R. Blackman, Jr., USMC, Gillian Blake, William F. Boomhower, Mark Bowman, Mike Brittingham, Steven L. Canby, Professor Domenic Ciraulo, Michelle Citron, Vicki Citron, Corky Condon,

Professor Erwin F. Cook, Lieutenant General John H. Cushman, U.S. Army, retired, Colonel Charles J. Dunlap, Jr., USAF, W. T. Edmonds, Jr., Lieutenant General Bob Elton, U.S. Army, retired, Jack Farrell, Helmuts Feifs, Commander Rabbi Robert Feinberg, USN, William J. Filipowich, William J. Finch, Professor Lydia Fish, Lisa Fisher, Professor Henry Flores, Chaplain Donald R. Forden, Professor Eugene Garver, Mary Garvey, Professor Leon Golden, Rear Admiral Kevin P. Green, USN, Diana Gregory, Sally Griffis, Bruce I. Gudmundsson, Lieutenant General Michael W. Hagee, USMC, H. Palmer Hall, Donald Hines, Admiral James Hogg, USN, retired, Robert "Dr. Bob" Hsiung, Lieutenant Colonel William F. "Toby" Hughes, USAF, retired, General James L. Jones, USMC, Professor Terence Keane, Lieutenant Colonel Faris Kirkland, U.S. Army, retired (deceased), General Charles C. Krulak, USMC, retired, Colonel Robert E. Lee, Jr., USMC, retired, Mark Lewis, James Lynch, Jack Mallory, Jonathan Matson, Major General James N. Mattis, USMC, Bill McBride, General Edward C. "Shy" Meyer, U.S. Army, retired, Sue Michmerhuizen, Dr. Thomas L. Milbank, Captain Daniel E. Moore, Jr., USN, Professor William Mullen, James Munroe, Warren K. Murray, Professor Gregory Nagy, Lieutenant General Gregory S. Newbold, USMC, Monte Olson, Ed Palm, Perseus Digital Library, Ralph Peters, Dale Peterson, Major Greg Pickell, USANG, Colonel Mark Pizzo, USMC, retired, Gunnery Sergeant H. John Poole, USMC, retired, Captain Ike Puzon, USN, retired, John Rakes, Lieutenant General John E. Rhodes, USMC, retired, Chet and Ginger Richards, Tom Ricks, Roy Ringel, Michael W. Rodriguez, Professor Amélie O. Rorty, Joseph W. Saltzman, Major General Robert H. Scales, U.S. Army, retired, Alan Scheri, Jim Schueckler, Lieutenant General Terry Scott, U.S. Army, retired, Professor Stephen Scully, Hannah Yael Shay, Samuel Zvi Shay, Henri Shay-Tannas, Bruce Shirk, Dennis Spector, Franklin C. "Chuck" Spinney, General Donn Starry, U.S. Army, retired, Judee Strott, Reverend Ray Stubbe, Tom Sykes, Professor James Tatum, Richard K. Taylor, John Tegtmeier, Harry Thie, John C. F. Tillson, Edward "Ted" Toland, Vice Admiral Pat Tracey, USN, Lieutenant General Bernard "Mick" Trainor, USMC, retired, Lieutenant General Richard G. Trefry, U.S. Army, retired, Professor Lawrence Tritle, Lieutenant General Walter F. Ulmer, Jr., U.S. Army, retired, Major Donald Vandergriff, U.S. Army, Lieutenant General Paul Van Riper, USMC, retired, Michael and Michele Viehman, Professor David Sloan Wilson, Professor Donna Wilson, David Wood, Piers Wood, Colonel Mike Wyly, USMC, retired, Chris Yunker.

PREFACE

The *Iliad* may have been a fiction, but the bard sang the truth. By comparing veterans' stories to the story of Achilles, in *Achilles in Vietnam* I showed that what Homer sang about—particularly betrayal of "what's right" by a commander and the deep human attachment between battle comrades—cut close to the experiences of *real* soldiers in *real* war. I pointed out that the surface story of Achilles is about war itself, all war, and will be valid as long as we have war. The *Iliad* is a classic, not because it's on college reading lists, but because it is so vividly truthful about this persisting and terrible human practice. In fact the veterans' words have helped the professors hear the poet's words afresh.

The poet also taught those of us in psychiatry and psychology to hear things in the veterans' words that we had not previously attended to: the moral dimension of trauma and the dreadful, rabid state of the berserker, which Homer shows with such fidelity when Achilles "loses it" after Patroclus is killed.

This book is an obvious next step. Homer's *Odyssey* has sung of a veteran's struggles to get home for more than two and a half millennia. Let's take Homer at his word and see what we can make of it.[1] The *Odyssey* as a whole—but most vividly the fantastic adventures of Books 9–12—may profitably be read as a detailed allegory of many a real veteran's homecoming. Time and again Odysseus shows himself as a man who *does not trust anyone,* a man whose capacity for social trust has been destroyed. This is the central problem facing the most severely injured Vietnam veterans. Odysseus stands for the veterans, but as a deeply flawed military leader himself, he also stands for the destroyers of trust. Homer's Odysseus sheds light—not always flattering light—on today's veterans and today's military leaders.

I invite the reader to see that real veterans' psychological and social homecomings cast new light into the *Odyssey.* No single "true" interpretation of the *Odyssey* trumps all others. Here I expand the appeal that I first made with *Achilles in Vietnam:* that when reading Homer, we take seriously combat soldiers' and veterans' actual experience as an added source of interpretive insight.

I was completely surprised by the tide of support for *Achilles in Vietnam* among professional military people. The book made a strong pitch for the prevention of psychological and moral injury in military service, and for changes in U.S. military culture and practice that would promote prevention. As an unknown VA psychiatrist back in 1993, I had been unable to recruit a single active-duty military service member to comment on the manuscript before it was published. I figured I had no hope of getting a hearing from the people on the inside.

An early review of *Achilles in Vietnam* in the journal of the U.S. Army War College, *Parameters*, changed that: "Were it in the reviewer's power, no officer would be allowed to swear the oath of commission until he had read this book."[2] Two Commandants of the Marine Corps have put it on their professional reading programs for All Hands in the Marine Corps. I have met privately with two successive Marine Corps Commandants and an Air Force Chief of Staff; a Secretary of the Navy invited me to give his guest lecture in the Pentagon. Heady stuff! The invisible company of the combat veterans standing at my shoulder when I speak gives me missionary courage to address a roomful of generals and admirals. The veterans don't want other young kids wrecked the way they were wrecked. The fire in my belly for prevention burns hot and hopefully will shine light in every chapter of this book.

I cannot presume to speak for or about all veterans. But I do know that the veterans I have the privilege to serve in the Department of Veterans Affairs clinic in Boston want me to do this work. They remain, despite their terrible psychological injuries, proud Americans who want the armed services to attract the best young people in the country, and for those young people to flourish.

So this book comes into being as the first one did: a labor of love that joins Homer's great epic with the lives of American combat veterans to give them the chance to cast new light on each other. And it continues my missionary agenda to convince the American public to *care* about how military units are kept together, how they are led, and how they are trained.

So let us begin . . .

ODYSSEUS IN AMERICA

I

Introduction

"Must you have battle in your heart forever?
The bloody toil of combat? Old contender . . ."
—*Odyssey* 12:132f, Fitzgerald[1]

"I wish I had been *untrained* afterward . . . reintegrated and included. My regret is wasting the whole of my productive adult life as a lone wolf."
—Jim Shelby, Vietnam veteran[2]

"Doc, you're f——ing crazy."
—One of my patients, a former Army Airborne
sergeant, veteran of four Vietnam combat tours,
upon hearing that I was going to lecture
on prevention of psychological injury at the
United States Military Academy at West Point

Homer's *Odyssey* is the epic homecoming of a Greek fighter from the Trojan War. Odysseus' trick of the hollow horse got the Greeks inside the walls of Troy, a feat that ten-to-one superiority in troop strength had never achieved. He was the very last fighter to make it home from Troy and endured the most grueling travel, costing him a full decade on the way. Odysseus' return ended in a bloody, triumphant shoot-'em-up. It is now more than thirty years since the majority of American veterans of the Vietnam War have returned home—physically. Psychologically and socially, however, "many of us aren't home yet," in the words of one combat medic.[3] My portrait of the psychologically injured combat veteran is colored by respect and love. However, I shall conceal none of the ugly and hateful ways that war veterans have sometimes acted toward others and themselves during their attempts to come home and be at home. To the ancient Greeks, Odysseus' name *meant* "man of hate" or "he who sows trouble."[4] Indeed, some veterans have sown trouble in their families. No one should ever hear from his mother, "You're not my son!" or "Better you died over there than come home like *this*." Yet veterans with severe psychological injuries have sometimes heard these terrible words.

Odysseus, like Achilles, is remembered as a *hero* of Greek myth. Today we see our heroes as unmixed blessings, almost as though pure beneficence is part of the definition. When we call those firemen and police who rushed to the New York World Trade Center on September 11, 2001, heroes, we have reason to see them as intending only good and to an amazing degree accomplishing it, at the sacrifice of their lives. However, the ancient Greek idea of the hero was deeply mixed. As I just noted, Odysseus' name means "man of hate." Achilles' name means "he whose host of fighting men have grief"—referring to his own Greek troops as well as to the enemy![5] Ancient Greek heroes were men of pain who were both needed by their people and *dangerous* to them. Achilles' withdrawal resulted in numberless Greek deaths; Odysseus' long return home to Ithaca caused more than seven hundred Ithacan deaths on the way or when he got there. Achilles harmed the Greek army during the war; Odysseus harmed his people after the war. They were both heroes in the ancient Greek sense.[6]

Almost everyone has somehow heard of Odysseus—sometimes he's called by his Latin name, Ulysses—but not everyone has read the *Odyssey* or remembers the details. I have tried to write this book in a way that will allow those who have never read Homer's *Odyssey* to follow it and not feel lost. A brief pocket guide to the epic in the style of a movie synopsis is offered in Appendix One. It's a complex story, easily muddled in memory. So I urge readers who are not currently familiar with the *Odyssey* to give the synopsis a quick reading before they start. While I hope that this book will ignite a desire to read or reread the *Odyssey*, no one should think it's required beforehand.

Part One of this book invites the reader to hear the *Odyssey* as exactly what it says it is: the story of a soldier's wanderings and troubles as he tries to make it home. The first dozen or so chapters "decode" Odysseus' adventures in wonderland—the most famous part of the epic—as an *allegory for real problems of combat veterans* returning to civilian society.

These are adventures that Odysseus himself tells as a story-within-a-story, to people who resemble wealthy, complacent civilians. Reading the *Odyssey* as allegory is not new,[7] but I suspect and hope that this allegorical reading will carry a different emotional weight than those rendered in the past.

In Part One, Odysseus appears, so to speak, on a split screen. On one screen, Odysseus as a veteran, trying to come home. On the other screen, Odysseus as a military leader who shaped the experience of others—often in disastrous ways.

All of my current patients, except a single Gulf War vet, are Vietnam combat veterans, men in their early to mid-fifties. When I first started working with veterans, they were perhaps the same age as Odysseus, returning home to Ithaca from ten years fighting in the Trojan War and ten years trying—and not trying—to get home to his wife, Penelope, and son, Telemachus.

Television, not to mention schoolbooks and feature films such as *Ulysses*, have made Odysseus' encounter with the Cyclops, the Sirens, and episodes such as the contest of the bow familiar to even the smallest children. What adventures! How poignant the story of the old soldier struggling to get home to his family! How many trials and obstacles thrown in his way! Homer's epic is the earliest known and most famous account of a combat veteran trying to get home after the war, and of what he does after he gets there.

In the last chapter of Part One, the narrative shifts from the world of fabulous monsters, witches, and ghosts to Ithaca, the real world of Odysseus' farms, home, and hometown. When Odysseus arrives home at last, he is disoriented and does not recognize Ithaca. The fact that he doesn't recognize his own homeland is itself a metaphor that many veterans can understand. The first person Odysseus meets is an unknown youth who is the goddess Athena in disguise. The two exchange courtesies and Odysseus tells her a dazzling pack of lies. Dropping her disguise, the goddess teases him:

> A man would have to be cunning and thievish to surpass you
> in all your tricks—even if he were a god.
> Wretch, with the mind of a chameleon, master of tricks,
> not even in your own land will you leave off your deceptive
> and thievish tales—which you love from the bottom of your heart.
>
> (13:291ff, orig., Jenny Strauss Clay, trans.[8])

Odysseus thought he had duped a civilian, but he was speaking to his own guardian angel who knew his trials and his tricks better than anyone. Finally at home in Ithaca, he finds himself in danger from the young bucks trying to win his wife's favor—the suitors. He moves in disguise and concealment, surrounded by a bodyguard of lies. He is reunited with his wife, son, and father, but much of the time he is icy or cruel. And then he runs off again!

Looking beneath the surface to what Odysseus, the master of disguise, has hidden in the stories he tells the civilians, we see not only the "what" of real experiences, but the "why" of a veteran's need to disguise his experiences at all. What is "home" anyway?

Part Two explores recovery from psychological injuries. The basic message is that whether recovery occurs spontaneously or in a defined treatment setting, *recovery happens only in community*. We are habituated to the assumption that injuries or illnesses can only be treated one on one in a professional's office. I shall explain below that two people (no matter how well trained, well meaning, and caring one of them is) are not a community. I believe this one-on-one assumption is responsible for how frequently we have failed in the treatment of severe psychological injury, especially when it has damaged character.

The American Psychiatric Association has saddled us with the jargon "Post-Traumatic Stress *Disorder*" (PTSD)—which sounds like an ailment—even though it is evident from the definition that what we are dealing with is an *injury:* "The person experienced, witnessed or was confronted with an event or events that involved actual or threatened death or serious injury, or a threat to the physical integrity of self or others." We do not refer to a veteran who has had an arm blown off by a grenade as suffering from "Missing Arm Disorder." But I am not going to fight it. "PTSD" it is, even though I much prefer "psychological injury." Combat PTSD is a war injury. Veterans with combat PTSD are war wounded, carrying the burdens of sacrifice for the rest of us as surely as the amputees, the burned, the blind, and the paralyzed carry them.

Part Two explains the distinction between simple PTSD—the persistence into civilian life of adaptations necessary to survive battle—and complex PTSD, which is simple PTSD *plus the destruction of the capacity for social trust*. Then we shall come at recovery from two directions. The first, coming from the direction of organized health care, comprises the treatment concepts and practices of our small outpatient program in the Boston VA for Vietnam combat veterans with complex Post-Traumatic

Stress Disorder. The second approach spans the poorly understood "spontaneous," or "natural," processes of recovery that happen in the native soil of a veteran's own community. Picture these two recovery models converging, like the two polished granite surfaces of the Vietnam Veterans Memorial in Washington, D.C.—the Wall—and meeting at a sharp vertical line. Veterans in our VA program and members of the treatment team travel to the Wall together annually. This trip joins the universally human potential for spontaneous recovery with our intentional VA treatment program for complex combat PTSD.

The Wall itself is but one example of healing through community—self-organized Internet e-mail groups are another. In Part Two, with their permission, we shall listen in on one self-organized e-group as its members attempt to come to terms with the suicide of Lewis B. Puller, Jr., whom some knew personally, but most knew from his Pulitzer Prize autobiography, *Fortunate Son: The Healing of a Vietnam Vet*. His suicide turned this upbeat book title into a kick in the stomach. Here we are able to witness one example of the communalization of grief—no one in that Internet group had to go through it entirely alone. As a nation and as individuals we are still grappling with Vietnam, emotionally, philosophically, and spiritually. This is not a closed chapter.

Homer's lyre is silent in Part Two, but memories of ancient Greece and veterans' wisdom from the intervening centuries are not far away. Athenian war memorial practices, such as inscribing names of the dead in the *kerameikos*, classical Athens's military cemetery, are reflected on the polished surface of the Wall and of community memorials all over America.[9]

Part Three calls for *prevention* of psychological and moral injury in military service. The public needs to know not only what measures will prevent psychological and moral injury, but why, and also how these measures will affect the ability of our military services to do what we ask of them. In the course of my travels in the active duty armed services as a missionary on prevention, I have learned that the very same measures that prevent injury are also combat strength *multipliers*. So why aren't we doing them?

The leading preventive psychiatry recommendation is to *keep people together through training, into a fight, and home again*. Most citizens know very little about the administrative side of the military, but if they know *one* thing about personnel policy in the Vietnam War, they know that individual soldiers were rotated into the war zone with strangers and home again with strangers, to catastrophic effect. Yet with the partial exception of the Marine Corps, we are *still* shuffling and reshuffling our units like decks of cards, just as we did in Vietnam!

Army Major Donald Vandergriff's compelling and meticulously researched history of the American military personnel system, called *The Path to Victory: America's Army and the Revolution in Human Affairs*,[10] gives the full history of how we got where we are, shows the dangers and incredible human waste of the present system, and explains how the system can be renovated. The most compelling need for renovation comes from the mismatch between the units and leaders that the system creates and the changing face of warfare in the twenty-first century.

The most fervent wish of the veterans I serve is that future kids not be wrecked the way they were wrecked. The public must hear about matters of military personnel policy that are rarely discussed with outsiders. The most effective prevention lies almost entirely with better military practices, and does not place mental health professionals in center stage. Health professionals may often be able to stop injuries from becoming fatal, disabling, or permanent, once they've happened. Preventing the injuries in the first place is beyond their power. That is in the hands of the line leaders and trainers and of the policymakers. By the end of this book I hope every reader will know the mantra—*cohesion, leadership, training*—and demand policies that produce skilled, cohesive units and competent, ethical leaders. Since their voices were heard in *Achilles in Vietnam: Combat Trauma and the Undoing of Character*,[11] my patients are intensely proud of contributing to public knowledge about war, particularly the measures that can be taken to reduce and partially prevent psychological injury in war.

While Homer has little to contribute to our understanding of modern military training, the poet is brilliant on the subject of military cohesion[12] and leadership, two critical legs of the prevention tripod. Homeric scholar Johannes Haubold goes so far as to say that the relationship of leader and his people is the common theme linking the *Iliad* and *Odyssey*. Part Three compares Achilles and Odysseus as military leaders, and Odysseus comes off very badly. The details of Odysseus' performance as an officer read like the charge sheet for his court-martial.[13] The problem was not competence, but character. So even here, in the most improbable setting of a call to renovate modern military institutions, we shall discover new meanings in a poem more than twenty-five centuries old. The great scholar of the *Odyssey* W. B. Stanford wrote, "One must be prepared in advance for some remarkable differences of opinion on the moral worth of Ulysses. No

other classical hero has been the subject of so much moralistic controversy."[14]

I add to the "moralistic controversy" in this book, both because I see
the figure of Odysseus through the eyes of those who might have served
under him, but also of those officers today who are responsible for selecting, training, and promoting American military leaders. Their judgments
on his conduct are likely to be even harsher than my own.

You already know that this book is written in a "personal voice." I don't,
or won't, or can't hide behind an expressionless mask of professionalism.
But this personal voice is somewhat different in each of the three parts of
the book. The voice of the first part is the labor-of-love voice, telling readers about veterans, about the *Iliad* and the *Odyssey*.

In Part Two I notice that my voice changes because I am also trying to
persuade my professional colleagues in psychiatry to think differently
about what psychological injury is and how best to assist in recovery
from it. At the same time, I have seen the enormous value that basic education on trauma can have for veterans and their families. Part of my personal voice here is influenced by the immensely moving experience of
seeing a veteran or his wife grow visibly lighter as the burden of freakish
stigma lifts.

In Part Three, I address military professionals and the policymakers
who are their bosses, and, most important, the American people, who are
their boss's bosses. It is an effort in democratic persuasion—because I have
authority over *no one* but myself. Part of this effort stems from the soul satisfaction I get as a missionary for the veterans I serve, and part comes from
my determination to be a citizen, not an idiot. According to classical
scholar Tom Palaima, "Originally, the Greek word '*idiōtes*' meant 'a man
who attends to his own concerns.' The Athenian leader Pericles, according to Thucydides, used the term '*idiōtes*' of citizens who focused on their
own affairs and were ignorant of the important issues facing the city of
Athens."[15] All of these audiences—high school and college students,
teachers, combat veterans, veterans' families, mental health professionals,
and military professionals—are fellow citizens, vital parts of one another's
future.

PART I

Unhealed Wounds

2

Odysseus
Among the Rich Civilians

Further up the table the accountant has just been explaining how, if only we had held out a bit longer, the war would have been won. . . . Lower down, they are talking about stocks and bonds and peace terms, and all of them, of course, know much better what should be done. . . .

All the talk makes me stupid in the head, and I am soon unable to follow any longer. . . .

At this moment—God be praised!—crisp, grilled chops appear on the table. I sniff. Real pork chops they are, fried in real fat too. The sight of them consoles me for all the rest. I lean over and secure a good one and begin chewing with relish. It tastes marvelous. It's a power of time since I last ate a fresh chop. In Flanders. . . . I neither hear nor see anything now; I lose myself in memories—

A giggle awakens me. About the table is dead silence. Aunt Lina has a face like a bottle of acid. The girl beside me is stifling a laugh. Everybody is looking at me.

Sweat breaks out on me in streams. Here I sit, just as we did then out in Flanders, absent-minded, both elbows on the table, the bone in my two hands, my fingers covered in grease. . . . But the others are eating cleanly with knife and with fork.

Red as a beetroot, I look straight ahead and put down the bone. How could I have so forgotten myself? . . .

But there is anger too in my embarrassment,—anger against this Uncle Karl, now beginning to talk so loudly of war loans; anger against all these people here that think so much of themselves and their smart talk; anger against this whole world, living here so damned cocksure with their knickknacks and jiggery-pokery, as though the monstrous years had never been when one thing and one thing only mattered,—life or death, and beyond that nothing.

—Erich Maria Remarque, *The Road Back*[1]

Odysseus' return to "the world," the civilian world, has a very rough start. A storm has pounded his homemade raft to pieces, half drowned him, and washed him up literally naked on the shore of a strange land. He and we learn it is the Land of the Phaeacians. He is *not* home yet; he is alone; this isn't Ithaca. It's someplace else yet again, his fourteenth stop since Troy, which he departed ten years earlier commanding a squadron of twelve ships.

In addition to being Odysseus' last stop in the decade of wandering since Troy, this Land of the Phaeacians also brings a particular kind of encounter with civilians, with rich and complacent civilians. Ernst from *The Road Back,* sequel to *All Quiet on the Western Front,* has this kind of encounter at Uncle Karl's dinner party. Ernst can go home to his mother after the humiliation, but Odysseus is still on the knife edge of survival. He's a castaway on civilian shores, alone with his *gastēr,* his "ravenous stomach." Figuratively Odysseus' *gastēr* is his gluttonous will to acquire and control. *Gastēr* brings to mind stealing and lies, as well as hunger, greed, and compulsive self-gratification. What has happened to his noble fighting heart, his *thumos*?[2]

The opposition between *thumos* and *gastēr,* heart and belly, is also that between wartime and peacetime, between the different civilian perceptions of the men they send to fight for them and the men who return home to them. What in wartime is a heroic amphibious landing, is in peacetime a criminal pirate raid. What in war is bold and courageous, in peace is reckless and irresponsible; in wartime resourceful, in peace lawless. Achilles and Odysseus might have been the same person—Achilles *in* war, Odysseus *after* war.

We should also reflect that the difference Homer shows us between *thumos* and *gastēr* may be in ourselves—between what we as civilians, who are terrified and enraged by an enemy attack, *value* in soldiers, and what we *fear* in them when the enemy no longer scares us, and the soldiers come home as veterans. When we are in fear of the enemy, nothing is too much or too good for the "greathearted spirit" (*thumos*) of our fighting men; when they return as veterans we see their needs as greedy, demanding, uncultivated belly (*gastēr*).

When Odysseus crawls up on the Phaeacian beach, he has two urgent needs: first, his immediate safety—that he not starve or be killed by the natives as a dangerous intruder—and second, help to get home. With a hand from the goddess Athena (6:15ff, Fagles) he comes face-to-face with the king's beautiful young daughter. Odysseus charms Nausicaa, manipulates her to get past the rough sailors who would willingly snuff his life, and into the palace of her parents. Once safely inside and courteously granted asylum by the king and queen of the Land of the Phaeacians, Odysseus keeps his eyes and ears open. What sort of people are these?

> High rooms he saw . . .
> with lusters of the sun and moon . . .
> The doors were golden . . .
> (7.89ff, Fitzgerald)

The Phaeacians are rich and secure. Odysseus identifies himself as a "man of pain" without saying anything specific about his identity. His host shows him every Mediterranean courtesy and doesn't press on the details. Always alert, Odysseus learns a great deal more about the Phaeacians.

They are—in the manner of today's luxury health club habitués—avid athletes, but not in the combat sports. Odysseus finds them *not* serious. When he is pushed to compete with the sleek young runners and throwers, he says:

> I have more on my mind than track and field . . .
> hard days, and many, have I seen, and suffered.
> I sit here at your field meet, yes; but only
> as one who begs your king to send him home.
> (8:162ff, Fitzgerald)

Even more, Odysseus finds them self-indulgent, avid in the pursuit of luxury and entertainment. The king says:

> . . . we set great store by feasting,
> harpers, and the grace of dancing choirs,
> changes of dress, warm baths, and downy beds.
> (8:261ff, Fitzgerald)

They are also connoisseurs of the arts: the court boasts the services of the great minstrel Demodocus. The Phaeacians are, in a word, *civilians*.

The gulf between Odysseus and his civilian hosts is visible in their drastically different responses to the songs of Demodocus. This bard is the genuine article—the Muse whispers the truth of the war at Troy in his ear when he composes his songs. His songs, narrative poems like the *Iliad,* reduce Odysseus to tears, which he tries to hide. Afterward he proclaims that Demodocus sings with the truth of someone who was there himself. The Phaeacian civilians love these epic poems of war (8:98)—along with the harper's dance music (8:265ff) and his bedroom farces (8:280ff).[3] It's all the same to them. *It's all entertainment*. But for Odysseus, the truth-filled stories of the Trojan War open the gates of grief.

Demodocus sings of the clash between Achilles, the hero of the *Iliad*, who embodies *biē*—violent force—and Odysseus, the hero of the *Odyssey*, who embodies *mētis*—cunning tricks and strategy.[4] The bard sings about how their insecure and incompetent commander, Agamemnon, delights in this clash. This provokes Odysseus' reaction:

> [Odysseus] with massive hand drew his rich mantle down
> over his brow, cloaking his face with it,
> to make the Phaiacians miss the secret tears . . .
> (8:90ff, Fitzgerald)

Odysseus makes every effort to hide his anguish from the complacent audience. But every time the poet resumes, emotion overcomes Odysseus. Only the king at his elbow is aware. A tactful host, the king rescues Odysseus by interrupting the poet to suggest an athletic exhibition.

After athletics, the feasting and entertainment resume with dancing and comic poetry. Odysseus publicly praises the poet, sends him a splashy tip, and asks for a "request number." He tells Demodocus:

> Now . . . sing that wooden horse
> Epeios built, inspired by Athena—

> the ambuscade Odysseus filled with fighters
> and sent to take the inner town of Troy.
> (8:526ff, Fitzgerald)

Thus far, Odysseus has not told his hosts who he is, but he knows he must do it soon. Perhaps he wants the poet to sing this episode in which Odysseus himself is the star. This would set the stage for him to reveal himself in the most impressive light. Or perhaps Odysseus thinks the poet is a phony and wants to see if he really knows what he's talking about. But it is Odysseus himself who is tested—and ambushed by his own emotional reaction.[5] A surprising and powerful simile is the tip-off that he is not the master of this situation:

> . . . the famous harper sang
> but the great Odysseus melted into tears,
> running down from his eyes to wet his cheeks . . .
> *as a woman weeps, her arms flung round her darling husband,*
> *a man who fell in battle . . .*
> trying to beat the day of doom from home and children.
> Seeing the man go down, dying, gasping for breath,
> she clings for dear life . . .
> and the most heartbreaking torment wastes her cheeks.
> (8:585ff, Fagles; emphasis added)

Again the king interrupts the performance to spare his guest's feelings.

Homer makes the same point twice, as if to drive it home. These stories rip Odysseus' heart out, while for the Phaeacians, they are never more than entertainment. Homer doesn't show the king and his people as monsters; they are just limited, unable to offer Odysseus what he needs in his soul. They give what he needs physically—plenty of food for his belly, clothing, and a ship to take him home. But at this moment the most the king can offer him is courteous sympathy:

> . . . let Demodokos touch his harp no more.
> His theme has not been pleasing to all here.
> During the feast, since our fine poet sang,
> our guest has never left off weeping. *Grief*
> *seems fixed upon his heart.* Break off the song!
> (8:576ff, Fitzgerald; emphasis added)

King Alcinous now presses Odysseus to reveal his identity—which surely Odysseus saw coming, and for which he was perhaps preparing himself. Quite reasonably, his host asks him to explain his emotional reactions, the "grief . . . fixed upon his heart." But in the very next breath, he tells Odysseus what Odysseus' own experience means:

> *That was all gods' work,* weaving ruin there
> *so it should make a song for men to come!*
> (8: 619f, Fitzgerald; emphasis added)

The king asks Odysseus why he grieves, but then doesn't give him even a moment to answer before he negates Odysseus' grief by explaining that the "big picture" justifies the suffering—as entertainment! Granted, Homer's epics are more than just entertainment; they are art at its most enduring. To the ancient Greeks they were also Bible, history, and philosophy, all in one. But here Homer shows us the Phaeacians as rich tourists in the landscape of suffering.

Picture this scene: A Vietnam combat veteran goes to a family wedding some ten years after his service. (Odysseus is ten years out from Troy.) The band plays a Jimi Hendrix piece that reminds him of a dead friend, blindsiding him with emotion. He tries to conceal his tears, but a rich relative notices and says, "Why aren't you over that Vietnam stuff yet? Anyway, that war was all about oil—and damn right, too, or we'd be paying $5 a gallon for gas."

Saying that to one of the veterans I work with at such an emotional moment would provoke an explosion of rage. He might tip the table over in the man's lap. The veteran's relative is intimidated, stammers an inaudible apology, and rushes away. The veteran looks around feeling like someone has just peeled his skin and every nerve ending is naked and exposed. Everyone in the church social hall is silent; everyone is watching him, just as everyone stares at Ernst in Remarque's *The Road Back.* He walks slowly from the room and out of the church. His wife is weeping with mortification, fury, and self-blame that she didn't catch this in time. She is torn between her love for and loyalty to her husband and the ten-year family consensus that the veteran is a dangerous psycho.

Odysseus does not have the luxury of "losing it." He must keep a grip on his emotions to stay alive and must stay on the Phaeacians' good side to get home. Elsewhere, Homer describes Odysseus' capacity to suppress and conceal his emotions as a part of his guile, *dolos* (19:212, orig.).

Odysseus has also found he *cannot* talk about the war at Troy at this

moment—at least not to people who show themselves incapable of hearing the stories with their heart. The combat veterans I have known fly into
a rage when a civilian tries to tell them the meaning of their own experience. For Odysseus there can be no communalization of his experience
here—not with this audience.

Whether Odysseus made up his mind in an instant or over the thirty-six
hours of watching his hosts, he decides three things about revealing himself: First, he will not tell these civilians *anything* about Troy—although
his host, the king, has implicitly asked him to do just that, by inquiring
whether he weeps for a "comrade" (*hetairos*—8:584, orig.) who died at
Troy. Second, he will correct the implied civilians' misconception about
combat veterans—that once the war ends, the losses and suffering end,
too. The king assumes that Odysseus is tormented with grief only for
deaths that occurred during the war. And third, he decides that he will fully
satisfy the king's request to tell his story, "Where have your rovings forced
you?" (8:643, Fagles) and will tell it in the only form that they are capable
of taking it in: entertainment.

He reveals his identity: "I am Odysseus son of Laertes . . ."—his next
words are extraordinarily ambiguous and surprising: ". . . *who am a
worry* [or concern, or problem] *to all men by my wiles*" (9:19–20, orig.,
Segal, trans.).[8]

What a way to introduce himself to powerful strangers he desperately
needs! Odysseus is not quite so raw as this one line, taken out of context,
suggests. Nonetheless the first thing he declares about himself is the cunning, guile, and trickery that make him famous "to the sky's rim." Imagine you have taken in a complete stranger as a houseguest. He evades
identifying himself for a day and a half, and then he boasts that he is
famous the world over as a con man! What's more, you've heard of him,
and of some of his more spectacular scams.

Odysseus is not quite so "in control" as he is usually pictured. He
desperately manages his own emotions at the same time that he woos his
hosts to give him quick passage home. He cannot tell the truth about
"what it was really like" at Troy without risking his own composure.
Odysseus could have introduced himself in any of a hundred flattering
and safe ways, such as "architect of the Greek victory at Troy," or "courageous fighter and master bowman," or as the person to whom the Greek
army awarded Achilles' armor as a prize of honor, or simply "the best of
the Greeks." But none of these would have created the diversionary distraction of his boastful, somewhat off-color self-introduction. It allows
him the sleight-of-hand shift from the king's actual question about the war

to, "What of my sailing [*nostos* = homecoming], then, from Troy?" (9:41, Fitzgerald). Without missing a beat he launches into the adventures that will entertain, enchant, and dazzle his royal listeners for the rest of the night.

3

Pirate Raid:
Staying in Combat Mode

Just as some thieves are not bad soldiers, some soldiers turn out to be pretty good robbers, so nearly are these two ways of life related.

—Sir Thomas More, *Utopia*, published in 1516[1]

But will warriors lay down, together with the iron in which they are covered, their spirit nourished . . . by familiarity with danger? Will they don, together with civilian dress, that veneration for the laws and respect for protective forms . . . ? To them the unarmed class appears vulgar and ignoble, laws are superfluous subtleties, the forms of social life just so many insupportable delays.

—Benjamin Constant, Swiss, 1767–1830[2]

But all was not right with the spirit of the men who came back. Something was wrong. They put on civilian clothes again, looked to their mothers and wives very much like the young men who had gone. . . . But they had not come back the same men. Something had altered in them. They were subject to queer moods, queer tempers, fits of profound depression alternating with a restless desire for pleasure. Many of them were easily moved to passion when they lost control of themselves. Many were bitter in their speech, violent in opinion, frightening. For some time while they drew their unemployment pensions, they did not make any effort to get work for the future. . . . Young soldiers who had been very skilled with machine-guns, trench-mortars, hand-grenades, found that they were classed with the ranks of unskilled labor in civil life.

—Philip Gibbs, British, 1920[3]

Odysseus' first adventure after he leaves Troy with his squadron is the sack of Ismarus. It's a pirate raid—there's nothing particularly amazing or fairy-tale-like about it.[4] No one-eyed or six-headed monsters show up here, no witches, no gods either. The crews get drunk on captured wine and Odysseus loses control of them. They go wild and run riot in the town. This reflects no credit on the troops—they indulge themselves and put themselves in a weak position. The victims of this raid and their kin counterattack and inflict serious losses on the boat crews before they can escape out to sea.

Hardly what we expected! But here Homer shows us the first way that combat soldiers lose their homecoming, having left the war zone physically—they may simply *remain* in combat mode, although not necessarily against the original enemy.

Once discharged from the military, what civilian occupations are open to a veteran that employ the skills and capacities he has developed? While former military pilots may find civilian employment as airline, charter, or corporate pilots, what work does a combat infantryman look

for? In the course of my work I see many Vietnam War military discharge papers—Department of Defense Form 214—and always experience a sour amusement at item 23b, "RELATED CIVILIAN OCCUPATION." For every veteran with Military Occupation Specialty 11B, "Infantry light weapons specialist"—a "grunt" infantryman—the related civilian occupation is given as "Firearms Proof Technician," i.e., someone who test fires guns for their manufacturers. So just how many of the hundreds of thousands of infantry veterans were able to find employment in gun manufacturing? Very few, of course. And how much does this civilian occupation actually resemble the work of the combat infantryman?

A bitter joke.

For which civilian careers does prolonged combat prepare a person? Let's look at the strengths, skills, and capacities acquired during prolonged combat:

- Control of fear.
- Cunning, the arts of deception, the arts of the "mind-fuck."
- Control of violence against members of their own group.
- The capacity to respond skillfully and *instantly* with violent, lethal force.
- Vigilance, perpetual mobilization for danger.
- Regarding fixed rules as possible threats to their own and their comrades' survival.
- Regarding fixed "rules of war" as possible advantages to be gained over the enemy.
- Suppression of compassion, horror, guilt, tenderness, grief, disgust.
- The capacity to lie fluently and convincingly.
- Physical strength, quickness, endurance, stealth.
- Skill at locating and grabbing needed supplies, whether officially provided or not.
- Skill in the use of a variety of lethal weapons.
- Skill in adapting to harsh physical conditions.

This is a chilling picture. World War I veteran Willard Waller remembered what it was like on street corners after that war. In 1944 he wrote in anticipation of the return of the troops from World War II:

There is a core of anger in the soul of almost every veteran, and we are justified in calling it bitterness, but the bitterness of one man is not the same thing as the bitterness of another. In one man it becomes a consuming flame that sears his soul and burns his body. In another it is barely traceable. It leads one man to outbursts of temper, another to social radicalism, a third to excesses of conservatism.[5]

Most of the skills that soldiers acquire in their training for war are irrelevant to civilian life. . . . The picture is one of men who struggle very hard to learn certain things and to acquire certain distinctions, and then find that with the end of the war these things completely lose their utility. . . . Digging a fine fox-hole or throwing hand grenades with dexterity, they are entirely valueless. . . .

The boss, who hires and fires him, writes recommendations for him, raises or lowers his pay, and otherwise disposes of his destiny is nothing but a soft civilian. The foreman thinks he is tough. . . . While the veteran was risking his life for his country, the boss and the foreman were having an easy time of it. . . . The veteran cannot help reflecting that a smash of a gun-butt, or even a well-directed blow at the bridge of the nose . . . might easily dispose of such a man forever.[6]

Very few combat veterans have become mercenaries or "civilian defense contractors" who train, support, and/or fight for foreign governments or for insurgents at the behest of the U.S. government, such as for Afghan mujahedeen fighting the Soviets. These ways of staying in combat mode have captured the public imagination in film and pulp fiction, as well as magazines such as *Soldier of Fortune*. As sociologist James William Gibson has described in *Warrior Dreams: Violence and Manhood in Post-Vietnam America*,[7] this fascination with the mercenary shows us much more about ourselves as civilians than it tells us about veterans. I am less interested in the exotic and the glamorous than in what matters every day in South Boston, Somerville, or Quincy, Massachusetts.

Law enforcement in all its varieties has some military traits, and might seem most to resemble the occupation of the combat infantryman. Policemen carry guns. They wear uniforms. The images of the embattled inner-city cop whose precinct is a war zone, and of the specialized "tactical" unit, both suggest similarities. Many combat veterans have, in fact, joined the civilian uniformed services. Bear Mercer (a pseudonym) was one of these. He became an officer at a maximum-security prison.

Bear is the second son of a proud, hardworking family in a Boston multiethnic neighborhood. His father was a foreman, his mother, a health professional.

He joined the U.S. Army in December 1965, out of high school after learning that an older, admired friend in the ——— Airborne had been killed in Vietnam. Bear's father, a Silver Star honoree tank sergeant in Europe in World War II, opposed his enlistment, but acquiesced. His father was later to tell the Department of Defense official who [erroneously, as it turned out] notified him of Bear's death: "Go to hell! You got the wrong Mercer."

Bear served one combat tour in Vietnam as a "grunt" forward observer sergeant. He was honorably discharged in December 1968. He never missed time, was never subject to disciplinary action, and was eligible to reenlist. He was honored with the Combat Infantry Badge, the Air Medal, and the Army Commendation Medal for Valor with Oak Leaf Cluster, which denotes a second separate act of bravery.

After his first month as the radioman for the 81mm mortar at the center of the perimeter, Bear felt like he was simply a helpless target for enemy rockets and mortars that fell in the perimeter. He knew that in theory he was safer in the center than outside it patrolling and waiting in ambush, but he had come to fight, not to cower under bombardment. So he volunteered to serve as a forward observer, to patrol with the grunts and call in mortar, artillery, and air strikes in their support. He takes pride in the fact that he was never responsible for an artillery error that caused American casualties.

Sergeant Mercer did, however, see the results of the fires he called in on the enemy. His patrol found a Viet Cong, dying after his legs had been blown off by a strike Bear had called in. Over the radio, the CO refused to call a MedEvac for the enemy and ordered Bear to kill the wounded enemy soldier. Unwilling to order anyone in his squad to do it, he performed this mercy himself, and believes that the dying Vietnamese assented to it by gestures. Now in nightmares and flashbacks the color of his blood, changing from bright red to almost black after Bear cut his throat, comes back again and again, as does the evil grin of a man in his squad who crushed the dead man's chest with a boulder, drenching Bear with blood that squirted out of the severed neck arteries. Bear felt the enemy had "paid his dues" and is enraged at the disrespect shown by the other American soldier.

Four days later in the same patrol a friend named Kennedy, known for his joking and cheerful disposition, volunteered to throw the smoke grenade in a clearing to guide in a helicopter. He stepped out of the concealment of the jungle and Bear heard an "Uh!" sound and saw Kennedy fall back on a bush. "I ran over and took him off the bush. His front tooth was gone. I put my hand behind his head to lift him off the bush, and felt this warm sensation. I had part of his brain on my hand. I looked back and saw blood pouring down off the bush." This scene, too, repeats endlessly in Bear's nightmares. He knows there was nothing he could have done to save Kennedy.

Bear is also haunted by the death of a new forward observer, whom he had been breaking in for three months by going out on patrols with him. One night when Bear was "just so frigging tired" that he stayed behind, the new FO went out with a patrol on a night ambush. The ambushers were ambushed, and the men inside the perimeter could hear the wounded (including Bear's best friend) screaming all night. The next morning they found two dead with the wounded survivors, but two were missing. A distance away they found the headless bodies of the missing two. Following a blood trail, they came to a clearing where the two heads were set up on stakes, with their eyelids pinned back with vine thorns. One of these heads was that of the new FO. "I see the head just staring at us. If I hadn't been so frigging tired and gone myself, he wouldn't be dead." These dead eyes stared at Bear during the times he tried to kill himself by driving his car off the road in 1974 and 1975.

After this enemy atrocity Bear's platoon went berserk, "just went nuts—started cutting heads off, collecting ears. They called us the 'head hunters.'" The berserk state leaves a permanent imprint on the physiology of a person who has been in it—a permanent hyperarousal of the autonomic nervous system and adrenaline secretion. Mercer suffers repeated adrenaline storms, with racing heart, sweats, and most of all, rage.

He recalls that for six months, the captain who had ordered Bear to kill the wounded prisoner was the company commander. This captain was dangerously incompetent. During one operation he ordered the company to reconstruct an old night position abandoned by the ——— Infantry. All the seasoned NCOs told the captain not to do it, because GIs always left booby traps behind. One "chow hound" in the company nicknamed Teddy because of his size and hairiness, who always scarfed up any C rations that the other men did not eat, spotted a C ration can in the sump of the abandoned position. When he picked it up, an American grenade with its pin pulled fell out, releasing the safety spoon that had been tucked against the inside of the can—a classic GI booby trap. Teddy died instantly. This same captain, apparently motivated by no more than idle curiosity, ordered a man nicknamed the Italian Stallion to pull the pin on a found Chinese Communist–manufactured grenade and throw it so the captain could see what it was like. All the seasoned NCOs shouted at the man "You don't have to do it—some of them are rigged!" but the captain's insistence overcame his reluctance. He pulled the pin and it detonated instantaneously, blowing off both his arms. The Vietnamese enemy had removed its time-delay fuse. Bear recalls screaming in rage at this CO that he was an "incompetent son of a bitch—lucky to be alive [i.e., close to being fragged by his own men]."

Bear remembers one instance in which his lieutenant ordered him to take his squad into a senseless death trap in a rice paddy and he refused. The lieutenant found three other men more compliant and sent them across the rice paddy, rather than around as Bear had advised. All three died from mines. In another incident, after Bear heard sounds of heavy movement ahead and advised the officer to call in an air strike, the disbelieving lieutenant sent a squad to "make contact—if Charlie's there at all." The whole squad was wiped out and the platoon was pinned down on that hill, Hill ——— near ———, for two days.

Any incompetence Bear encounters in civilian life arouses the same feelings of fear, rage, and grief. When he yanked his general supervisor at the post office across his own desk and screamed at him, he screamed exactly the same words he screamed at his incompetent CO.

He feels profoundly tainted by the pointless risks and senseless cruelty he participated in while taking prisoners for interrogation. He received his Air Medal for highly dangerous "in and out" helicopter insertions to snatch prisoners for interrogation by U.S. Army intelligence. He particularly recalls that one Viet Cong "catch" his team had captured at great risk was refused as unneeded by Army intelligence. They were told to give him to the ARVN "Tigers" whose base adjoined that of the Airborne. Bear had witnessed these South Vietnamese "elite" troops behave with a contemptible blend of cowardice and sadism. After three hours of listening to the man's screams, Bear's whole team walked into the Tiger compound to find the man bleeding from hundreds of little cuts, particularly around the genitals. They shot him through the head, so enraging the Tigers that a firefight almost ensued.

Bear received his Army Commendation Medal for Valor for an action where he called in artillery on his own position (which necessarily was observation distance from the platoon he was working with), to permit the platoon he was serving as forward observer to escape encirclement. He received a second such award, but has complete amnesia for the action for which it was given.

Bear is a proud man. He is proud of supporting his family, but is profoundly apprehensive that he is "losing it," now more than thirty years after the war.

His wife has taken to sleeping on the sofa. Bear always sleeps with a knife under his pillow, despite her pleas not to. He lives a long way from Boston in a rural community where few people lock their houses, no one locks the car, and many leave the key in the ignition. Bear is fanatical about both—forcing his family to lower the blinds at sundown, and he "walks the perimeter" every night before bed looking for snipers and ambushes. He rarely gets more than two hours of sleep a night because of nightmares. Four hours sleep is a good night.

After Vietnam he took a job in the Department of Corrections as an officer in a maximum-security prison. Clearly his background as a combat sergeant in the Airborne made him appealing to the prison authorities. He says he was motivated by a desire to help the many incarcerated veterans. But he also loved the sense of being alive that came from being the only guard on a prison tier, where only his cunning, his will, his comprehension of the psychology of the moment stood between him and a shank (homemade knife blade) between the ribs. He reveled in his ability to "mind-fuck" the prison administration when they mistreated Vietnam vet inmates.

He recalls with relish various strategic deceptions that he pulled off against prisoners and administrators alike. In one episode, he feigned a regular, predictable pattern of sleeping while on duty in one of the prison towers, drawing a contraband operation to the apparently safe spot in plain view beneath his tower. He loved this job and only left it because he rebroke the ankle he had broken in a post-Vietnam parachute jump at Fort Bragg.

Now at work in the post office he feels he no longer is able to pick his targets, but rather engages in physical violence before he even knows he is doing it. This hurts his pride because he has always counted on his self-control and self-discipline. Along with his understanding of combat veterans, these were his major assets when he worked as a prison guard.

On one occasion Bear confused a Vietnamese co-worker at the post office with the Vietnamese enemy. He grabbed the man and told him he was going to cut his throat just like his comrades. Bear finds these episodes hateful, because he despises racism and recognizes that the man he terrorized is "a nice guy, by the way."

Co-workers say that sometimes he just stands and stares. No one dares to interrupt him at these moments, or to come up behind him unannounced.

Thirty years after military discharge he has in one year used up four weeks of vacation time, 150 hours of sick time, and 80 hours without pay, mainly having to leave work in order to prevent himself from killing somebody, but also to receive treatment at the VA.

Many, like Bear, who joined uniformed services quit or were fired after relatively short careers. Unlike Bear, some found civilian policing too boring, too dictated by rules that made them feel unsafe, too full of "chickenshit" authority relationships and apparently meaningless administrative tasks.

A career that war exactly prepares veterans for upon return to civilian life is a *criminal* career, symbolized here by Odysseus' pirate raid on Ismarus. Even though piracy had a certain cachet, even respectability, much as privateers, from Sir Francis Drake to the American brig *Yankee* in the War of 1812, have had in more recent times, I shall use it as a metaphor for a criminal career.[8] For obvious reasons, the veterans I work with do not tell me crimes they have committed for which they were never caught and punished. I wouldn't want to know. It would both impair my personal safety to know these things, as well as lower the level of safety felt by the veterans in the treatment program. One veteran, asked if he had ever "done time," replied without a flicker of emotion, "Not under this name." A significant number of the men I have worked with have been incarcerated, which is not statistically unusual. According to the massive, congressionally mandated *National Vietnam Veterans Readjustment Study*, 11.6 percent of Vietnam-theater veterans who still met criteria for PTSD in the mid-1980s when the interviews were done disclosed to the interviewer that they had been convicted of a felony.[9]

Active criminals live in a world that surrounds them with dangers, but even more so does *prison*. Combat veterans who are unable to leave combat mode are in a sense perfectly adapted to these hideous conditions. "They're fine there. They know *exactly* where they stand," says Navy veteran Wiry (a pseudonym), one of my patients who has been incarcerated repeatedly. He continues, "I sleep better there than I do here. You hear that door [to solitary confinement] close on you and you know you can't hurt anyone and nobody can get at you."

Veteran Wiry served twenty-two months in the United States Navy on assault support patrol boats (ASPBs), in the Mobile Riverine Force in the Mekong Delta. During this service his boat, including four sailors and the bosun's mate captain, received the Presidential Unit Citation. This unit citation is considered equal to the Distinguished Service Cross (second only to the Medal of Honor) for individuals.[10] He was also individually honored with the Bronze Star Medal, with V device for valor, and a cluster, denoting a second separate honor of the Bronze Star. He received one Purple Heart for combat wounds.

Wiry was born in a Boston Irish neighborhood to Roman Catholic parents. He joined the Navy out of his senior year in 1965 and completed his high school education in the Navy. The oldest of many siblings, he was the first person in his family to enter military service.

Initially Wiry was trained as a cook and served in this capacity during the unopposed Marine landing at Da Nang in 1965, but after his return, he volunteered for the newly forming Mobile Riverine Force to fight in the Mekong River Delta.

Training for this force was *very* rigorous. The men trained as five-man crews, where everyone was cross-trained in all the weapons and everyone else's specialties: in radio, in engine mechanics, in language and interrogation, in the tasks of the medic, and as steersmen. All were trained in counterinsurgency warfare, psychological warfare, hand-to-hand combat, and in the art of making and disarming booby traps. The climax of the training was the Survival, Evasion, Resistance, and Escape course (SERE) during which the trainees were persuaded that they never wanted to be taken alive, by being starved, beaten, subjected to mock executions with a gun in the mouth, kept naked in cold rain, being held upside down in a barrel of water. The training was also effective instruction in methods of torture—this is how you do it.

Wiry's specialty was weapons and explosives. After training, the five-man crews were introduced to their fifty-foot assault support patrol boats designed for river warfare, specifically to remain afloat after the most violent mine explosion. As Wiry recalls it, the boats were heavily armed with twin .50-caliber machine guns in the bow, a swivel-mounted M-60 in the driver's position, and a 20mm belt-fed cannon on the roof with an automatic grenade launcher. In the stern, the boat carried a .30-caliber machine gun and a belt-fed, hand-cranked 40mm grenade launcher ("Thumper"). In addition the crews carried on board an arsenal of individual weapons ranging from light antitank weapons (LAWs), M-16s and shotguns, to .38 Special Smith & Wessons in rib holsters.

The crews went over in March 1967, to be joined by their boats about a month later. Wiry's squadron of ten ASPBs were assigned to ———, on the ——— arm of the Mekong River as it forms its delta entering the South China Sea. The main arms of the river are connected by a maze of thousands of miles of natural and man-made waterways, which also extend away from the river in each direction as it flows south out of Cambodia. The area is the most productive rice-growing area in Vietnam and heavily populated along the banks of the waterways. It was a Viet Cong stronghold.

"Our job was to go in first to find the enemy, keep them busy, until the troops were landed to flush them out. . . . The rivers were our homes. Helicopters came out to fly orders to us. . . . We'd beach and take prisoners—we'd do our own interrogations." They patrolled in narrow waterways where the Viet Cong controlled both banks, and built dug-in, well-concealed ambush positions. Large command-detonated mines were placed underwater at the enemy's leisure, sometimes creating such large explosions that the bow or stern of the fifty-foot boat would be blown sideways onto the bank, immobilizing the boat and killing some or all of the crew.

"Every time we went out, five guys had to die—this was from four to six boats. . . . Out of the original fifty of us, seventeen are alive. Two or three are paraplegic and a couple others are in VAs all their life [psychiatric casualties]. . . . One shot from a village and we took *everybody* out. We'd go in and wipe out a fucking village—*completely*." Wiry served on two ASPBs in his time on riverboats in Vietnam. He is the sole survivor of the first crew, and only one other man is alive from the second. "Sometime we didn't have no MedEvac, we carried our own dead and our own wounded. . . . In my nightmares I can't stand the screaming." The screaming is sometimes that of wounded crewmates and sometimes of prisoners being tortured.

One particular incident figures strongly in Wiry's life since Vietnam: flashbacks, intrusive memories, and intrusive thoughts related to the twelve-day period during the Tet Offensive. On St. Patrick's Day, March 17, 1968, two direct hits from rocket propelled grenades (RPGs) separated by a brief time ambushed his boat in a narrow waterway in the Delta. The first rocket killed the other men in the boat and the second blew Wiry onto the riverbank, where, wounded and unconscious, he was apparently left for dead by the enemy. The Navy also apparently left him for dead, because there was no effort to rescue him. He feels deeply betrayed and enraged by this abandonment, and has lost control of his rage subsequently in civilian life under conditions that seem to repeat this abandonment. During the next twelve nights he made his way on foot through enemy territory, hiding during the day, putting maggots on his infected wounds to clean them, and killing everyone who spotted him or had food to be taken.

Other flashbacks and nightmares relate to the earlier deaths, one by one, of the crew he trained with. "One was an old-time bosun's mate who had been in the Navy sixteen years. He got hit, a direct hit with an RPG. I was holding a dressing on his stomach and I could feel the blood squishing under my hand every time he took a breath. . . . One guy lost his arm. He was screaming and screaming, and I picked up his arm and threw it at him—'Shut the fuck up!'

"We were there to die, and I *didn't* die. . . . I always have that thought, why am I alive? Look at what we did to them people. . . . Keeping me alive so they don't forget. . . . What happens is, I like pain. . . . Pain makes the nightmares go away. There's not enough pills or booze to make the nightmares go away, but pain. . . . In jail I *made* them do me [beat him]—grabbed a guard and beat him so they'd do me. . . . If I get hurt bad it helps the nightmares go away faster."

Wiry is an intelligent, capable man. After discharge from the Navy, between 1970 and 1985 he held himself together by being a workaholic, building up and repeatedly losing businesses, both legal and illegal. He started a successful delicatessen and then destroyed the business when his symptoms flared up. He describes "certain points where I get erratic—all fucked up—and whatever I have going at the time is irrelevant." He has worked as a caterer, as a tractor-trailer driving instructor, and as a trucker. Several of his businesses were criminal, "in the rackets," for which he has served prison terms.

One such criminal business involved stealing locked safes from business establishments and then expertly opening them elsewhere with explosives—a civilian application of his trained military skill. He informs me that an ordinary auto tow truck is quite up to the job of pulling a safe through the wall of a building with its cable and then driving away with it.

His first VA hospitalization occurred in January 1985 when he was employed as a trucker. His truck broke down in the cold, and he called in to his employer, who promised to send help. Wiry waited in the truck, but help never came, resulting in the development of hypothermia, for which he had to be hospitalized. He now understands that he experienced this as a replay of being abandoned in the Mekong Delta after being blown off his boat. At the time, however, he did not see this: "They left me. . . . [After release from the hospital] I went off and I shot up the warehouse. . . . I made the people who owned the company get down on their knees. . . . I treated them like [Vietnamese] prisoners."

Treatment in the VA since the mid-1980s has only partially stabilized Wiry. He remains highly symptomatic, highly mistrustful, and highly explosive. In the periods around Christmas and around the anniversary of Tet in March [that is, of a period of thirty-five consecutive days of fighting during the Tet Offensive], he has gotten himself beaten up almost every year. He does this by going into a bar and attacking the largest man in the place. Wiry weighs no more than 140 and is about five feet seven, and, of course, wiry in build.

Speaking of his criminal activities he says, "It's not the money, it's the *action.*" His skills, his cunning, his craft—a precise word, because it means both highly developed skill *and* cunning—all become valuable again in "action" in a way that they never are in civilian life. To my knowledge, he has never read Tennyson's poem *Ulysses,* but would readily subscribe to the following:

> How dull it is to pause, to make an end,
> To rust unburnish'd, not to shine in use!
> As tho' to breathe were life . . .

He shares the disdain that Tennyson's Odysseus has for the civilians: they merely "hoard, and sleep, and feed, *and know not me*."[11]

What kind of recognition and acknowledgment would have let Wiry feel he was "known," understood, and valued? Any kind? Would it have affected his need for "action"? I believe that a unit association of Riverine Force veterans, such as exists now thirty-plus years out, could have made this difference had it existed at the time.

Some readers will angrily accuse me of perpetuating the "crazed, criminal, out-of-control Vietnam Veteran Stereotype." *Absolutely nothing* I have to say here is distinctive to the Vietnam War. War itself does this. War itself creates situations that can wreck the mind. If Wiry has lost his reason at times, he had good reasons. I'll put it as bluntly as I can: combat service per se smoothes the way into criminal careers afterward in civilian life. Reread the list above on page 21 of capacities that combat cultivates. A criminal career allows a veteran to remain in combat mode, use his hard-earned skills, and even to relive aspects of his experience. In other words, he is doing exactly what Odysseus does in the sack of Ismarus.

Leban (another pseudonym), a now-deceased World War II veteran whom I treated in my early years at the VA, became a "leg breaker" for a criminal gang upon his return from Europe. He pursued this career of violence for about five years and then gradually became a recluse in the house owned by his immigrant mother. "I can't explain it—I just got afraid to go out." After she died, he continued to live there as it crumbled around him, with ceiling plaster falling due to unrepaired roof leaks.

Some years before I became his psychiatrist, a VA social worker who ran a therapy group for former POWs heard about him, went to his house, and persuaded him to come into the VA clinic for the group. Leban had been captured during the Battle of the Bulge—his unit was being rested, "the first time since I was in France that I undressed to go to sleep!"—and was a POW in Germany till war's end. During his years of solitude in his mother's house after his criminal career, he reinvented much of Stoic philosophy and Buddhist practice—neither of which he had ever read or heard about. I listened to his philosophic reflections with astonishment and admiration. With different luck in terms of resources and education, Leban could have become a noteworthy philosopher. British poet and novelist Robert Graves had that luck and became an international literary figure after World War I. An infantry officer in the trenches, Graves wrote of his rocky and scapegrace return to civilian life:

> I still had the Army Habit of commandeering anything of uncertain ownership that I found lying about; also a difficulty in telling the truth—it was always easier for me now, when charged with any fault, to lie my way out in Army style. I applied the technique of taking over billets or trenches to . . . my present situation.
>
> Other loose habits of wartime survived, such as stopping cars for a lift, and unbuttoning by the roadside without shame, whoever might be about.[12]

This is hardly a criminal career, and his social position as a decorated "officer and gentleman" and as a published poet shielded him from most of the legal complications of "commandeering anything of uncertain ownership that I found lying about." An American grunt veteran, especially if black or Hispanic, would not have been treated so tolerantly.

Graves was not violent. Leban was violent during his early postwar years. For many combat veterans, violence plays constantly in their heads, disrupting their ability to concentrate on and take pleasure in civilian pursuits.

Ernst, the main character in the celebrated World War I novel *All Quiet on the Western Front,* goes to work as a schoolteacher in *The Road Back,* which follows the survivors' lives after the war. The violence that intrudes into his thoughts mocks the civilizing and uplifting tasks of the elementary school teacher.

> There sit the little ones with folded arms. . . . They look at me so trustingly, so believingly—and suddenly I get a spasm over the heart. . . .
>
> What should I teach you? Should I tell you that in twenty years you will be dried-up and crippled, maimed in your freest impulses . . . ? Should I tell you that all learning, all culture, all science is nothing but hideous mockery . . . ?
>
> What am I able to teach you then? Should I tell you how to pull the string of a hand grenade, how best to throw it at a human being? Should I show you how to stab a man with a bayonet, how to fell him with a club, how to slaughter him with a spade? Should I demonstrate how best to aim a rifle at such an incomprehensible miracle as a breathing breast, a living heart? Should I explain to you what tetanus is, what a broken spine is, and what a shattered skull?[13]

Just imagine the consequences today to a newly hired American grade school teacher if he were to reveal such thoughts to his supervisor! It's not too much to guess that the police would be called.

Homer put *first* the pirate raid on Ismarus. I take this as a metaphor for all the ways a veteran may lose his homecoming by remaining in combat mode. Of these ways, taking up a criminal career is the most destructive to the veteran and to the civilian world around him. Everyone knows that war can wreck the body, but repeatedly forget that it can wreck the soul as well. The sacrifice that citizens make when they serve in their country's military is not simply the risk of death, dismemberment, disfigurement, and paralysis—as terrible as these realities are. They risk their peace of mind—please, hear this familiar phrase, "peace of mind," fresh again in all its richness! They risk losing their capacity to participate in democratic process. They risk losing the sense that human virtues are still possible. These are psychological and moral injuries—war wounds—that are no less of a sacrifice than the sacrifice of the armless, or legless, or sightless veteran. One of my former patients, a combat medic in Vietnam, has said, "Just acknowledge the sacrifice!"[14]

These veterans want acknowledgment; they want treatment; and when disabled, they want disability pensions. But they also want prevention. Are there helmets or flak jackets for the soul and for the character? Can combat veterans be kept away from criminal careers in civilian life? Can we *prevent* this damage to good character, which is so destructive to the veteran and to those around him? The alienation, bitterness, and boredom with civilian life cited by Waller in 1944, and that I have heard from many Vietnam veterans, contribute to a drift into criminal careers. Anything that pulls the plug on alienation, bitterness, and boredom will reduce the attraction of remaining in combat mode by criminal "action."

The answer does not lie in something that is new or expensive, or once it is said, surprising: it lies in *community*. Vietnam veterans came home *alone*. The most significant community for a combat veteran is that of his surviving comrades. Prevention of criminal deformity of returning veterans must start with the beginning of military service, not as an afterthought when the veteran is home and already in trouble. We shall go into this further in Part Three.

Let us go back to the scene in the Phaeacian court, where the king pressures Odysseus to reveal his identity. Odysseus' way of doing it is surprising and ironic under the circumstances. It seems more intimidating or off-putting than ingratiating:

> Men hold me
> *formidable for guile in peace and war:*
> this fame has gone abroad to the sky's rim . . .
> (9:20ff Fitzgerald; emphasis added)

Just twenty lines further he launches into the pillaging of Ismarus.

The questionable side of Odysseus' character, and how it came to be, is a thread that runs through this book, sometimes in the foreground, but always in the background. I hope that the sensationalism attaching to crime will not distract the reader from those losses that never make headlines, such as losing a great job because of making a mission out of it, or becoming almost fatally obsessed with "what really happened" in a certain battle. But the *Odyssey*'s most famous section, Books 9–12, Odysseus' adventures, does begin with *three* elements of the hated Vietnam Veteran Stereotype: violent crime, drug addiction, and irresponsible thrill and pleasure seeking.

4

Lotus Land:

The Flight from Pain

Throughout history, returning veterans have endured the pain of grief for dead comrades, along with the physical pain of war wounds. But there is a special pathos when comrades die *after* the war is over. In an epic that shows Odysseus losing *all* his comrades, the first winnowing of the crews at Ismarus is given a fuller appreciation than much greater losses later. Odysseus and his crew become progressively "numbed out" as these blows accumulate.

Odysseus and his squadron have taken heavy losses in their first postwar battle of homecoming, their plundering of Ismarus:

> Six benches were left empty in every ship
> that evening when we pulled away from death.
> And this new grief we bore with us to sea:
> our precious lives we had, but not our friends.
> No ship made sail next day until some shipmate
> had raised a cry, three times, for each poor ghost
> unfleshed . . .
> then two long days and nights we lay offshore
> worn out and sick at heart, tasting our grief . . .
> (9:67ff, Fitzgerald)

Ismarus was a real place, north-northeast of Troy on the Thracian coast.[1] But once the flotilla pulls away it is caught in a violent storm and driven completely off the map. Odysseus will not set foot again in the known world until the Phaeacian rowers put him down, sound asleep, on the beach at Ithaca.

Taking the *Odyssey* as an allegory of real homecomings from war, we should not be surprised that the next landfall is on the Land of the Lotus Eaters, who come across as stoned flower children:

> [they] showed no will to do us harm, only
> offering the sweet Lotos . . .
> *but those who ate this honeyed plant, the Lotos,*
> *never cared to report, nor to return:*
> *they longed to stay forever, browsing² on*
> *that native bloom, forgetful of their homeland.*
> (9:96ff, Fitzgerald; emphasis added)

Odysseus reacts with the moves of a tough disciplinarian, having possibly learned a lesson from letting wine flow at Ismarus:

> I drove them . . . wailing, to the ships,
> tied them down under their rowing benches,
> and called the rest: "All hands aboard;
> come, clear the beach and no one taste the Lotos,
> or you lose your hope of home."
> (9:105ff, Fitzgerald)

We shall never know if Homer had some particular narcotic plant in mind, and if so what plant this *"lotus"* was, but his description is clear enough: you get into *lotus* abuse and you lose your homecoming. Forget your pain—forget your homecoming! This is the path to destruction taken by a horrifyingly large number of Vietnam veterans. Chemical attempts to forget with alcohol or drugs—reaching the American Psychiatric Association criteria for dependence or abuse—were sought by 45.6 percent in alcohol and by 8.4 percent in drugs. If a veteran has current PTSD, these rates are higher still, 73.8 percent and 11.3 percent respectively. These data unfortunately lump together all in-country veterans, both combat and noncombat. It is shocking to realize that male civilian non-veterans who are demographically similar to Vietnam combat veterans have a 26 percent lifetime incidence of alcohol dependence or abuse and a 3.4 percent rate of drug dependence or abuse.[3]

The episode with the Lotus Eaters is actually the second time that Homer has suggested the complexity of combat veterans' "substance" use and chemically induced forgetting. We first encounter it during Telemachus' (Odysseus' son's) search for the truth of whether his father is alive or dead. He comes to the court of King Menelaus, one of Odysseus' fellow officers. Menelaus guesses that Telemachus is Odysseus' son and bursts into tears of grief:

> "His son, in my house! How I loved the man,
> And how he fought through hardship for my sake!
> I swore I'd cherish him above all others . . .
> And so we might have been together often . . .
> But God himself must have been envious,
> to batter the bruised man so that he alone
> should fail in his return."
>
> A twinging ache of grief rose up in everyone,
> and . . . Telemakhos and Menelaos wept . . .
>   (4:181ff, Fitzgerald)

There's no hint that Menelaus wants to forget Odysseus, nor that he finds the pain unmanageable, nor that he finds his own tears humiliating. But Menelaus' wife, Helen, the famous beauty, Helen of Troy, over whom the whole war was fought, apparently thinks "it'll be good for him" to forget:

> But now it entered Helen's mind
> to drop into the wine that they were drinking
> *an anodyne, mild magic of forgetfulness.*
> Whoever drank this mixture in the wine bowl
> would be incapable of tears that day—
> though he should lose mother and father both,
> or see, with his own eyes, a son or brother
> mauled by weapons of bronze at his own gate.
> The opiate of Zeus's daughter bore
> this canny power. . . .
> She drugged the wine, then, had it served . . .
>   (4:235ff, Fitzgerald; emphasis added)

While some veterans will say that they want to forget what they've seen, what they've been through, what they've done, they never say they want to forget the comrades they've lost. Veterans are more often distraught that they cannot remember the name of a friend who died or cannot envision his face, much as it's common for bereaved widows and widowers to go through agonizing periods when the pain is there but voluntary recall of the beloved's face is impossible. The veterans I have worked with regard forgetting dead comrades as dishonorable as forgetting dead parents.

A third time, when Odysseus' men fall into the clutches of the witch Circe, Homer connects drugs with forgetfulness:

> "[Circe] ushered them in to sit on high-backed chairs,
>
> then she mixed them a potion—cheese, barley
> and pale honey mulled in Pramnian wine—
> but into the brew *she stirred her wicked drugs*
> *to wipe from their memories any thoughts of home.*"
> (10:256ff, Fagles; emphasis added)

The drug turns the veterans from Odysseus' crew into pigs—a ripe metaphor for moralizing on what drug and alcohol addiction can do. But the core of what Homer shows us is that drugs cause veterans to lose their homecoming. The Lotus and Circe's drug both make them "forget" their home. The drunk may literally be unable to recall how to get home, and the crack cocaine addict may be unable to remember anything worth going home to at all. In the subtler sense, the drug- or alcohol-addicted veteran may be physically at home, but his cognitive and emotional resources are entirely consumed by the next drink or fix.

Sometimes a veteran's desire to "stop the screaming" or "stop the nightmares" gets framed as forgetting, "If only I could forget . . ." But the inability to remember things that the veteran longs to recover and the inability to feel safe from ambush by flashbacks and nightmares are two sides of the same coin. The veteran has lost *authority* over his own process of memory. Restoring that authority is one dimension of recovery from combat trauma. A veteran who is actively drinking or actively using drugs can never regain authority over the processes of memory. Sobriety is one of the three essential *starting points* for recovery from complex PTSD after combat, the other two being safety and self-care.[4]

Using drugs and alcohol for forgetting, to suppress nightmares, to get to sleep in the face of unbearable agitation, are examples of what has come to be called "self-medication." Legally and illegally, the civilian world offers a range of psychoactive substances, which street lingo divides broadly into "uppers" (stimulants such as amphetamines and cocaine) and "downers" (sedatives such as alcohol and barbiturates, anxiolytics such as Valium and other benzodiazepines, and opiate analgesics such as heroin).

With the story of the Lotus Eaters, echoing Helen's "anodyne, mild magic of forgetfulness," Homer suggests that if you forget your pain, you forget your homeland—you "lose your hope of home." To really *be home* means to be emotionally present and engaged. Even without alcohol, stimulants, opiates, or sedatives, some entirely clean and sober combat veterans endure civilian life with all of their emotions shut down, except for anger, the one emotion that promoted survival in battle. Homer seems to be saying that if you are too successful in forgetting pain, forgetting grief, fear, and disgust, you may dry up the springs of sweetness, enjoyment, and pleasure in another person's company. This fits our clinical experience.

Veterans use many strategies to numb their pain, to silence the nightmares, to quell guilt. Chemicals are only one such strategy, danger seeking is another, workaholism is another, sexaholism another still[5]—and it is not an exaggeration to say that Homer has seen it all (see Chapters 5, 6, and 14). These have in common that they cut the *emotion* out of the veteran's homecoming. Even when he's physically with his wife, his children, his parents, he's not *there*. Many men go through the motions, but emotionally speaking, they're like ice. The second chapter of Aphrodite Matsakis's *Vietnam Wives* carries the grim title, "Living with the Ice Man."[6]

Selective suppression of emotion is an essential adaptation to survive lethal settings such as battle, where numbing grief and suppressing fear and physical pain are lifesaving. Whatever the psychological and physiological machinery that produces this emotional shutdown, it appears to get jammed in the "on" position for some veterans. Do not imagine that this is a comfortable or pleasant state of being. Veterans in this state say they feel "dead" and that they watch life through a very dirty window. They are never *in* life. More than one has described it as like being wrapped in cotton wool. Such deadness prompts some who sufferer from this hateful numbness to self-medicate with "uppers."

In parallel, mobilization of the mind and body for danger, the vigilant sharpening of the senses, the tense readiness to kill an attacker, is also an obvious survival adaptation to combat. When this is stuck in the on position and persists into civilian life, the veteran may embark on a frenzied search for calm. Such a state directly interferes with sleep, often causing a vicious cycle, because of the physiological and psychological "jacking up" that comes from going completely without sleep. "I've got to get some sleep!" is a cry of many veterans. The easy, cheap, legal availability of the sedating drug alcohol has been irresistible to many veteran insomniacs. Most have learned, to their sorrow, that it is a poor choice, full of its own dangers and ambushes. The other downers have their own characteristic problems, some different from alcohol's, but problems no less.

I argued in *Achilles in Vietnam* that simple combat PTSD is best understood as the persistence into civilian life of valid survival adaptations to combat. Both hyperarousal and numbing may persist into civilian life, paradoxically coexisting as constantly inflamed anger, but numbing of everything else. Or they may alternate with one another, giving the veteran a history of "cycling" between overexcitement and numb withdrawal. No wonder many have been labeled "manic-depressive," or the more recent term "bipolar affective disorder." Combat veterans with PTSD sometimes come to our clinic dragging behind them a long history of alternately self-medicating *both* numbing and hyperarousal and carrying the dismal label of "polysubstance abuser."

Can drug and alcohol abuse among veterans be prevented? Clearly, when one in four *civilians*[7] meets the criteria for alcohol abuse or dependence currently or some time in their life, we are talking about something that no one has an easy answer to. There are many encouraging developments in today's U.S. military services in the form of alcohol awareness, the availability of treatment for alcoholism, reduction of the semiofficial practice of using alcohol as a reward for a unit's doing well at some challenge, considerable institutional discouragement of drunkenness—all of these may result in a future veteran population less inclined to alcoholism. What about the major role I advocated in the last chapter for unit associations in easing the transition back into civilian life? Were not American Legion and VFW posts mostly cut-rate bars and drinking clubs? I shall not address this prejudicial stereotype of these mass membership veterans service organizations, but rather describe my personal experience with one unit association with which I had a brief, but informative, contact.

In 1996, Lieutenant General John H. Cushman, U.S. Army, retired, invited me to attend the reunion of the 101st Airborne Division Association at Fort Campbell, Kentucky, after reading *Achilles in Vietnam*. He had commanded the 2d Brigade of the 101st in Vietnam, and had subsequently commanded the whole division. At the time of this invitation he was president of the 2d Brigade Association, which appeared to nest comfortably inside the larger 101st Airborne Division Association. I went with expectations based on the unexamined stereotypes of boozy, loud, and argumentative local VFW posts. When I arrived, somewhat late because of the vagaries of air travel, the banquet was already in progress in the Enlisted Men's Club. On a large-screen closed-circuit TV another event was in progress, a full-dress affair at the Officers' Club, which few seemed to be watching. What impressed me were the comfortable hum of conversation and an almost palpable atmosphere of mutual love. Yes, there were pitchers of beer on the tables, but the noise level was so quiet that I doubt that much of the beer had been consumed. People shout when they're drunk, in part because they themselves are somewhat deafened from the neurological effects of alcohol.

I found General Cushman among enlisted veterans from his brigade. He took me over to one of his aviation company commanders, who immediately wanted me to know about a former trooper who had been having a rough time with his memories and with alcohol. The local chapter of the 101st Airborne Association had recovered contact with him after many years of not knowing where he was or how he was doing. They had drawn him into their circle and persuaded him to join Alcoholics Anonymous, and were immensely proud of their continued ability to be a "Band of Brothers." Unit associations appear more capable of fostering this sense of mutual support and obligation than the mass-oriented veterans service organizations.

There are many other military unit associations—large, such as the First Marine Division Association, and small, comprising former members of a single company or even platoon. Prior to the twentieth century, each American military unit was raised from a specific geographic area, and usually bore the name of the place it was raised. This resulted almost automatically in every local veterans association, both formal and informal, being a unit association. The spectacular political power of the main mass membership veterans association in the nineteenth century, the Grand Army of the Republic, has obscured this history. The GAR was accused of raiding the U.S. Treasury for Civil War veterans' pensions.

Today, because of a conscious policy of both promoting national unity and protecting any single town from being bereaved of a whole generation of its young men, every unit is made up of recruits from anywhere in the country. However, modern technology, starting with the telephone, and now with the Internet, permits scattered veterans to form and maintain unit associations that are little impaired by geographic scatter. I have personally witnessed the beneficial, even lifesaving power of the social support that veterans can gain through Internet communities, and shall expand on this in Chapter 18.

So Captain Odysseus drives his men away from the silky embrace of the addicting Lotus, and gets his flotilla back out to sea. The sullen sailors pull away from Lotus Land, but they have no clue where they are. The dope dealers of Lotus Land were recognizably human, but on their next landfall, they encounter monsters.

5

Cyclops: The Flight from Boredom

After a mile or two I said to Boanerges ["Son of Thunder," the name Lawrence had given his motorcycle], "We are going to hurry" . . . and thereupon laid back my ears like a rabbit, and galloped down the road. . . . It seemed to me that sixty-five miles an hour was a fitting pace . . . but often we were ninety for two or three miles on end, with old B. trumpeting ha ha like a war horse. . . . [In Oxfordshire, where traffic moved at about thirty miles per hour] Boa and myself were pioneers of the new order, which will do seventy or more between point and point. . . . Boa was round the next corner, or over the next-hill-but-two while they were sputtering.

—T. E. Lawrence, "Lawrence of Arabia," 1926[1]

In popular culture the Cyclops is the part that stands for the whole of the *Odyssey*. It's what shows up in the Saturday morning cartoons. Oceans of ink have drowned continents of paper explaining this episode. Homer lays it on thick, with suspense, marvels, clever twists, gore, and gross-outs. Not only does the Cyclops snatch up pairs of Odysseus' shipmates, bash their brains out across the floor, and munch them down raw, but at one point he even barfs up undigested pieces of eaten Greek. Like a stage magician, Homer controls our gaze with stunning gestures of one hand, while the real action is in the other hand in plain sight. What mostly concerns us here is the conjurer's *other* hand.

"LAWLESS BRUTES"

The Cyclops is adventure number three that Odysseus recounts to the Phaeacian civilians. It comes after the plundering of Ismarus, where his flotilla lost about one man in ten when the natives counterattacked,[2] and as the end point of their flight from the sweet oblivion of Lotus addiction. These themes of random fighting, loss of friends (after the war is over!), and forgetfulness are fresh when the flotilla is carried by the winds to the "land of the high and mighty Cyclops, lawless brutes" (9:119f, Fagles). Odysseus tosses off a few more disparaging remarks about Cyclopes and then describes making camp on an island just offshore. He leaves his squadron and takes his own ship and crew across the narrow water to

> probe the natives over there.
> What are they—violent, savage, lawless?
> or friendly to strangers, god-fearing men?
> (9:194ff, Fagles)

At the time, Odysseus the naval officer had no reason to know anything about where the wind had blown him, even though as he relates the tale to the Phaeacians, Odysseus the storyteller knows exactly what he faces: giant cannibals. But in the context of the story, it would seem a reasonable reconnaissance that he hazards. Yet Odysseus goes on to tell us that his "bold heart" (*thumos*) prompted him to bring along a large skin of especially potent wine, because

> ... I'd soon come up against some giant ...
> a savage deaf to justice, blind to law.
> (9:239f, Fagles)

What's going on here? He's the captain of his own ship and commodore of a flotilla of twelve. He has told us repeatedly how sorry he is that not one of the six hundred or so men he was responsible for made it home alive, but it was their own damned fault . . . or so he says. And the narrator says. And the gods say. The families back at Ithaca reasonably will hold him responsible for all *six hundred* young men who shipped out with him, but here we are looking at Odysseus' conduct only with regard to the six men who get eaten by the monster.

The squadron has lost its bearings. Reconnaissance is called for, and any responsible commander would see it competently done. Odysseus and his crew cross the small stretch of water. Now closer, looking up from the shore, Odysseus can see that the cave is a giant's lair. This prompts him to take the skin of extra-potent wine, much as a modern commander might take extra, nonstandard weapons he thinks the mission requires.[3] Odysseus leaves most of his crew with the ship, and with twelve picked men climbs up to the giant-scale den. They enter it wide-eyed. The owner is not at home. Odysseus' men plead with him— This is bad shit, Cap'n! Let's grab what we can carry and get out of here! But Odysseus turns stubborn and says,

> But I would not give way—
> . . . not till I saw him, saw what [guest-]gifts he'd give [me].
> (9:256ff, Fagles)

This "curiosity" to see what *xeinia,* hospitality gifts, the giant would give him costs six men their lives. This is no ominous hunch. He knows that a giant inhabits this cave, but nevertheless he keeps his men there in danger!

One of the veterans I have worked with for many years once punched his sister's husband in the side of his head as he passed him in the back hall of their house. What happened in the ensuing fight matters less than why he did it: "I just wanted to see what happened." Another veteran says that a couple of years after returning from Vietnam he dove off a roof. Was he trying to commit suicide? No. "I wanted to see what would happen— sometimes you do that."

Commentators on Odysseus' behavior are divided between those who emphasize his "curiosity"—praising him as a sort of ancient proto-scientist—and those who emphasize his greed—that he hoped for a guest-gift of some immensely valuable item.[4] I see the adventure with the Cyclops as an emblem for combat veterans' attraction to danger, an attraction that has cost so many of them their lives *after returning home,* and tortured those who love them with untold hours of fear for their survival. To quote from a veteran's poem you will read later, in Chapter 18:

> I drive Chu Yen [the veteran's motorcycle] to the Wall in a Demon rage,
> we make the trip in eight minutes; if she'd been flesh and blood I would
> have ridden her to death.

Vietnam veteran bikers did not invent dangerously fast motorcycle riding, as we saw in this chapter's epigraph by the famous World War I combat veteran Lawrence of Arabia, who died from it.

Veterans' behavior has been variously called irresponsible, impulsive, judgment-impaired, thrill-seeking, and danger-seeking, but these adjectives don't quite get at the sense that the dice *must* be rolled. In addition to hungering to acquire the guest-gifts, Odysseus just wanted to "see what would happen" in the Cyclops' cave. Prolonged combat leaves some veterans with the need to "live on the edge" to pose the same question to the cosmos over and over again: yes or no? The veteran who dove off the roof was not "curious" about what broken bones feel like. Odysseus' irresponsible impulse to see "What *are* they—violent, savage, lawless? / or friendly to strangers, god-fearing men?" (9:195f, Fagles) and what guest-gift he would receive from the giant makes perfect sense, as something that veterans of much fighting simply *do*. It is as if, having lived in a world where the dice were constantly rolling, the calm, plan-filled responsibility of civilian life (or for that matter, of peacetime military service) is intolerable. They speak of it as a "boredom" that somehow grows to unendurable proportions. Tennyson captured this boredom in the opening lines of his poem *Ulysses:*

It *little profits* that an *idle* king
By this *still* hearth, among these *barren* crags,
Match'd with an aged wife, I *mete and dole*
Unequal laws unto a savage race,
That *hoard,* and *sleep,* and *feed,* and *know not me.* [Emphasis added.]

So, in part just to see what happens, Odysseus has his men settle down to dine on the giant's stored food and wait. Who are the "lawless brutes" here? Homer has made the point just a few dozen lines earlier that they have plenty of stores in their ships and have just gorged themselves on wild goats; these men are not starving. Necessity is not driving them. No learned commentator on the Cyclops episode has claimed that the customs of the ancient Mediterranean permit uninvited strangers to walk into someone's home in his absence and eat up his food. In fact, a refined version of this same misconduct has occurred earlier in the epic, in Books 1 and 2, when Penelope's infamous suitors back in Ithaca eat her, Telemachus, *and* Odysseus himself out of house and home. Over and over, we are given to understand that the suitors deserve the death that Odysseus rains down on them in the climactic Book 23 for eating his supplies uninvited.[5]

Polyphemus the Cyclops returns and tidies up some domestic chores, at first not noticing the intruders. And like a householder returning for the evening, he locks his front door: Odysseus and his men are trapped in the cave when Polyphemus deftly plugs its entrance with a rock so big that twenty-two wagon teams could not budge it. When finally he discovers them,

> '*Strangers!*' he thundered out, 'now who are you?
> Where did you sail from, over the running sea-lanes?
> Out on a trading spree or roving the waves like pirates,
> sea-wolves raiding at will, who risk their lives
> to plunder other men?'
>
> (9:284ff, Fagles)

Fitzgerald translates the last words even more bluntly: "Or are you wandering rogues, *who cast your lives like dice,* and ravage other folk by sea?"[6] [emphasis added]. Because Homer has put these words in the mouth of a brute, it is easy to overlook that this is *exactly* what Odysseus and his crews have become—men "who cast your lives like dice, and ravage other folk." Odysseus has indulged in *atasthaliai,* irresponsible, wanton recklessness, leading his men into it, rather than holding them back. We have already seen that war smoothes the way to criminal conduct after the war. One twentieth-century sociologist credits Erasmus of Rotterdam in the fifteenth century with being the first to notice this.[7] I'd say it was first shown by Homer in the *Odyssey.*

Cunning

They are well and truly caught. Odysseus, at least, "deserves" it within the moral code of the *Odyssey.* But two by two seized at random—supper, breakfast, and supper—six of his twelve men pay the price, brains dashed out like unwanted puppies, and eaten raw.

When the Cyclops falls asleep after his first meal of shipmates, Odysseus' great *thumos*, his fighting spirit prompts him to take his sharp sword and stab the sleeping giant in his liver. But he restrains himself when he realizes that heroic revenge for his eaten shipmates—the angry resort to *biē,* force—would leave him and his ten remaining men to starve and thirst to death behind the enormous door plug. When the path of force, *biē,* is blocked, Odysseus does what Achilles would never do in the *Iliad*: he calls upon *mētis,* craftiness. The tricks and deception he uses to get out of the monster's cave are as famous as they are entertaining:

His scheme is to blind the Cyclops with a fire-hardened stake, prepared while the giant is out with his flocks the next day, and to escape by clinging underneath the livestock when the blinded Cyclops lets them out to pasture the morning after that. To lull the giant before this attack, Odysseus offers the superpotent wine he had brought with him, presenting it as a gift to buy pity. The Cyclops loves the wine, demands more, and asks Odysseus his name so he can give him a gift in return. Odysseus pours out more wine and says his name is "Nobody" (*outis*). The Cyclops tosses off bowl after bowl of the wine and with loutish self-congratulation announces that his return gift will be to eat Nobody last of all the trapped men—and then falls down in a drunken stupor. Odysseus and four men drive the heated stake into his eye (which Homer describes in gross-out detail). The giant roars in pain and rage, attracting his neighbors, other Cyclopes. They call from outside his cave, "surely no one's (*mē tis*) trying to kill you now by fraud (*dolōᵃ*) or force!" To this he cries, "*Nobody* (*Outis*), friends, . . . Nobody's killing me now . . . !" (9:453ff, Fagles). The neighborly Cyclopes lumber off convinced their friend doesn't need help. At this point Homer's audience is elbowing each other in the ribs, not only because of the way Odysseus' tricky name, Nobody, has played out, but because the other Cyclopes have inadvertently made a pun: in Homer's Greek, "no one" (*mē tis*) is spoken aloud close enough to the word for "cunning" (*mētis*) for the audience to make the association.[9] The violently powerful Cyclops, the *biē*-monster in the cave, has been overcome by cunning intelligence, *mētis*.

I'm going to milk the one-eyed monster for one more metaphor: Odysseus has no hope against the Cyclops in a force-on-force match-up. This is the way some veterans I work with feel when they face the *government*. They see themselves as powerless, liable to be eaten alive. Cunning, they believe, is their only defense. Like any one-eyed creature, government bureaucracies lack depth perception. They tend to see only the one thing they were set up for, and are blind to how things interconnect. A bureaucracy set up for vocational training sees one thing, another set up for law enforcement sees another, and one set up for health care sees yet another. When dealing with government, the veterans I work with have frequently felt trapped and liable to be eaten alive. Odysseus has saved his skin by denying his identity, humbly making himself Nobody.

"And Know Not Me"—Loss of Identity and Boasting

Don't draw attention to yourself. Don't tell anyone who you are or your real name. When first discovered in the Cyclops' cave, Odysseus had nonspecifically identified himself and his men as Greeks from the army of famous Agamemnon. Now he's "not someone" (*mē tis*). Vietnam veterans who at the time they enlisted had imagined themselves marching down Main Street, head held high with people gesturing, "There! You see him? That's him!" found themselves keeping silent about their military service or lying outright that they had never served. Because of both the political climate of the early 1970s and the well-founded fears of job discrimination, many veterans made themselves "Nobody" on the job, in school, or in social situations at a time when every fiber in their bodies demanded that they be "known." Odysseus pursued an active strategy of Nobody-hood as a means to escape and revenge; veterans were galled by their "invisibility," the comprehensive indifference of the civilian world.

Fame (*kleos*) was what Homeric Greeks risked and often lost their lives for. *Kleos* is the exact opposite of being a nobody, of not being someone. A key element in Odysseus' trickery lay in his ability to suppress his warrior identity and go against what was crying out in him, to do what warriors do. Remember that he saved himself and his men from slow death trapped in the cave by *not* killing the sleeping Cyclops that first night. He has saved them again by telling the Cyclops his name is Nobody, rather than proudly identifying himself by his father's name and his given name—as the heroic code would lead him to do.

The trick works and Odysseus and his men ride to freedom slung underneath the giant's fat sheep. Once out, they drive the flock down to the shore, board, and pull their ship away from the beach. But now Odysseus' self-restraint gives way and he begins to vaunt, to boast his triumph over the monster's *biē*.

> 'So, Cyclops, no weak coward it was whose crew
> you bent to devour there in your vaulted cave—
> you with your brute force!
>
> (9:531ff, Fagles)

Throwing toward the sound, the blind Cyclops heaves a rock over them so huge that the backwash alone pushes them back to the beach. Frantically they pole and row themselves away, but again Odysseus taunts the giant. For a second time his shipmates beg him to be prudent and self-restrained, as they had when they first entered the cave of the absent Cyclops. Now, six grisly deaths later, he cannot resist arrogant taunting.

'So headstrong—why? Why rile the beast again?'
. . .
'Good god, the brute can throw!'
So they begged me
but they could not bring my fighting spirit round.
I called back with another burst of anger, 'Cyclops—
If any man on the face of the earth should ask you
who blinded you, shamed you so—say Odysseus,
raider of cities, *he* gouged out your eye,
Laertes' son who makes his home in Ithaca!'
(9:550ff, Fagles)

With this boast, he seals the fate of his shipmates. This Cyclops is the off-spring of the sea god, Poseidon, and Polyphemus prays to his Olympian father with this curse:

'Hear me—
Poseidon. . . .
Grant that Odysseus, raider of cities,
Laertes' son who makes his home in Ithaca,
never reaches home. Or if he's fated to . . . reach . . .
his own native country, let him come home late
and come a broken man—all shipmates lost . . . —
and let him find a world of pain at home!'
(9:586ff, Fagles)

Homer says that the god heard his prayer, and the rest of the story shows that Poseidon fulfilled the curse in the Cyclops' prayer.[10] Odysseus returns alive, alone of the six hundred or so from Ithaca and its environs who sailed with him. Odysseus has greatly underestimated the potency of his adversary, just as the Cyclops has underestimated this cunning mortal, Odysseus. The Cyclops lost his eye, and Odysseus lost all his men and almost ten years of his life. A modern parallel, where both sides bled and bled as a result of their mutual underestimation, can be found in the history of World War II: the Americans suffered for their underestimation of the Japanese capacity to build and fly modern combat aircraft, and the Japanese suffered for their underestimation of American fortitude in withstanding the rigors of long-range submarine patrols.

Odysseus *and* Homer-as-narrator *and* the gods blame Odysseus' comrades for their own deaths:

> Many were the pains at sea that he suffered in his heart
> striving to win his spirit, and the return of his companions.
> But not even so did he save his companions eager though he was,
> for they were destroyed by their very own reckless acts,
> fools, who devour the cattle of [the sun god],
> and he in turn took from them the day of their return.
>
> (1:5ff, orig., Erwin Cook, trans.)[11]

But his crew was not responsible for deciding to stay in the giant's cave and eat and await his return. They had pleaded with their captain to make it a straightforward pirate snatch-and-run:

> Why not take these cheeses . . .
> and make a run for it?
> We'll drive the kids and lambs aboard. We say
> put out again on good salt water!"
>
> (9:241ff, Fitzgerald)

And his vaunt after their escape provides target coordinates for the deadly curse that the Cyclops calls in like a cruise missile strike from his father, the sea god, Poseidon.[12] But Odysseus is determined to reclaim his warrior identity—is the need to "live on the edge" a psychological component of warrior identity?—with disastrous consequences for his people.[13]

Can the thrill seeking and danger seeking by combat veterans after their homecoming be prevented? Can they be induced to use prudent foresight about the consequences of their actions for themselves and their families? Among Israelis I have heard a widely circulated belief that Israel has escaped the worst effects of post-combat wildness by sending its young veterans abroad for novelty and adventure, before they settle down as sober civilians upon their return. If this is true, it deserves unprejudiced study. It would be unconscionable for any country simply to export its troubles. However, if the novelty and risk taking, for example, of going by foot along almost the whole west coast of South America (a post-combat adventure I have heard about from an Israeli veteran who is now a very sober citizen) harmlessly burned off what might otherwise have ended in death or jail, we ought to know about it, so that we can do right by our own combat veterans.

6

Odysseus Gets a Leg Up— and Falls on His Face: The Workplace

One of the most common stories by and about Vietnam veterans is their experience of being discriminated against in hiring: "Once I said I was a Nam vet, it was strictly, 'Don't call us. We'll call you.'" One marine veteran recalls applying for a manufacturing job. The personnel department interviewer asked him brightly, "What was your job in the military?" perhaps expecting a veteran trained in electronics, or helicopter maintenance. "Machine gunner," he replied. "We don't need many of those," she said, smiling at her own wit. The veteran, already on the verge of becoming what the Bureau of Labor Statistics calls a "discouraged worker," did not find it funny. He got up and walked out of the office and out of the building without saying another word.

In response to employment barriers for veterans, formal hiring (or rehiring) preferences were set up, or hiring preferences originally established for World War II veterans reactivated. These formal systems were put in place mainly in government or quasi-governmental organizations such as the post office, public utilities, and defense contractors. In some large corporations, several veterans I know were automatically rehired into the job where they had *last* worked before enlisting in the service. These might be called *public,* or at least publicly announced, veterans' preference in hiring.

States, corporations, even mom-and-pop grocery stores are modern inventions. In the blood-feuding honor culture of the Homeric poems, it is a stretch to say that government—in the sense of institutions that exist apart from the ad hoc creations of specific people who create them through conflict and coalition—existed at all.[1] But the ancient and eternal persist in the modern world: there has always been what might be called *private* veterans' preference, based on family or friendship networks, sentiment, and cultural ideals. Such networks allowed the returning Vietnam combat veteran to get in to see a "big man," who himself is often a veteran of an earlier war. Whether he was a veteran himself or not, the powerful person considered this a pleasurable exercise of patriotic responsibility. Usually this patron was a successful businessman, a union boss, a politician, or—there's a dark side here, too—maybe a mob boss.

Here is the pattern: A veteran tells his combat service story to the big man. I can't say how much and how often the story is embellished, as we may suspect Odysseus of embellishing. (Powerful men are widely believed to "check out" what they are told, so my guess is that usually the veteran's stories were told modestly, truthfully, and with self-deprecation.) And this powerful person responds with an offer of help, a leg up, an offer of "clear sailing." What the big man offers is a job, *not* charity. The vet will have to earn his pay. But the powerful patron offers a position far more desirable than any the vet could have found through the state unemployment office or newspaper want ads.

Yet combat veterans have ruined opportunities that their war service has earned them in a thousand different ways. Homer portrays some heartbreakingly characteristic pieces of the pattern in the episode of King Aeolus, the King of the Winds. After fleeing the Cyclops, Odysseus tells it straight to King Aeolus, as many veterans have done.

> To this city of theirs we came, their splendid palace,
> And Aeolus hosted me one entire month, he pressed me for the news
> of Troy and the [Greek] ships, and how we sailed for home,
> and *I told him the whole long story, first to last*.
> (10:16ff, Fagles; emphasis added)

Aeolus offers to help with an open hand, holding nothing back:

> And then, when I begged him to send me on my way,
> *He denied me nothing. . . .*
> He gave me a sack . . .
> binding inside the winds that howl from every quarter,
> for Zeus had made that king the master of all the winds . . .
> (10:20ff, Fagles; emphasis added)

The King of the Winds gives Odysseus a double benefit. He gives him a perfect following wind—a straight shot for home—and in a big bag that he stows on Odysseus' ship, Aeolus bottles up all the winds that can blow him off course. As a general metaphor Aeolus offers Odysseus an obstacle-free return, a "painless" (thus unheroic) return, a homecoming without personal tempests. Occupationally, it is clear sailing with a following wind—what a metaphor for opportunity!

> Nine whole days we sailed, nine nights, nonstop.
> On the tenth our own land hove into sight at last—
> We were so close we could see men tending fires.
> But now an enticing sleep came on me, *bone weary*
> *From working the vessel's sheet myself, no letup,*
> *Never trusting the ropes to any other mate,*
> The faster to journey back . . .
>   (10:32ff, Fagles; emphasis added)

Odysseus has stayed awake nine days and nights managing the sail! He doesn't *trust* anyone else to do it right, even though Aeolus has given him a perfect following wind.[2] Odysseus has, in the words of many veterans, made a "mission" out of it, and he didn't trust anyone else to do it right while he himself caught some sleep. Sailing directly downwind was probably within the skills of even the least capable of his crew, but he wouldn't "delegate."

One veteran in our program, an African-American man I shall call River, because he is intensely proud of his service in a riverine unit in Vietnam, got in to see the head of the authority that operates the toll bridges and tunnels in the Boston area. A job as a toll taker was regarded as a plum in his community at the time because of its good pay, stability, benefits, and relative protection from racial discrimination. After landing the job, River worked shift after shift without resting, until the police took him away after he assaulted a motorist as a result of his sleep-deprived irritation and confusion. He lost the plum job.

Odysseus had also not trusted his shipmates enough to tell them what was in the big bag under his bench. Woe to the leader who starts from the assumption that his men must be kept in the dark on everything except their orders. In the absence of trustworthy information from the leader, they fill in the blanks from their imagination, often imagining the worst. After Odysseus falls asleep, they begin to mutter among themselves,

> 'Look at our captain's luck—so loved by the world . . .'
> 'Heaps of lovely plunder he hauls home from Troy,
> while we who went through slogging just as hard,
> we go home empty-handed.'
> 'Now this Aeolous loads him
> down with treasure. . . .'
> 'Hurry, let's see what loot is in that sack,
> how much gold and silver. Break it open—now!'
>
> (10:43ff, Fagles)

The hurricane winds in the sack come roaring out and blow the ships back out to sea.

Odysseus awakens with a start and instantly realizes what has happened. For a moment, he bleakly thinks of suicide, the only time we hear Odysseus consider taking his own life. (In this Odysseus is very *unlike* the veterans I work with in the clinic. Almost every one thinks daily of suicide—it seems to sustain them as a bottom line of human freedom and dignity. Having touched that talisman each day, they continue the struggle.) The implied lesson that falling asleep is dangerous is a very common gut sense among combat veterans. Being able to stay awake is one of the fundamental survival adaptations of soldiers in modern war, and persistence of this survival adaptation into civilian life creates endless problems. Falling asleep while on bunker guard duty on the perimeter of a base could mean severe punishment if caught, but in a night defensive position while "humping the boonies"—long-distance combat patrols on foot—it could mean "waking up dead." Vietnam veteran folklore, very possibly based on truth, recounts the enemy "mind-fuck" of silently cutting the throats of every man sleeping in a position, *except* the one sleeping soldier who was supposed to have been alert.

The 101st Airborne reconnaissance sergeant with four combat tours in Vietnam, whose voice and narrative figured prominently in *Achilles in Vietnam,* developed his own personal aversion to sleep. He became suicidal and panicky when the medication I prescribed caused him to sleep soundly. Toward the end of his first combat tour in Vietnam as the sergeant in charge of a five-man reconnaissance team, he had contracted pneumonia and been hospitalized. While he was in the hospital, his team was sent out under another leader, and his closest friend on the team, the Patroclus to his Achilles, had been killed. He felt that he was to blame for his friend's death because he allowed himself to relax in the hospital—and to get one good night's sleep for the first and only time in Vietnam. He carries in his soul the guilty belief that had he not been sick, had he not *slept*, his friend would still be alive. He now cannot sleep. Whatever his reason may say, his heart tells him: "You let down, you go to sleep—people die."

Within sight of home, Odysseus' squadron is blown all the way back to Aeolia. Depressed, Odysseus drags himself from the beach to the palace and sits down on the threshold. Aeolus, the powerful patron, spots him and shouts,

> 'Back again, Odysseus—why? . . .
> Surely we launched you well. . . .'
> I replied in deep despair,
> 'A mutinous crew undid me—that and a cruel sleep.
> Set it to rights, my friends. You have the power!'
>   (10:70ff, Fagles)

Back again? Give me another chance. Back again? Give me another chance. How many times this has replayed itself in the lives of the veterans I work with. They have screwed up the golden opportunity that their war service has earned them and they go back, humble supplicants, to the big man.

Aeolus gives him only one bite at the apple, and harshly turns Odysseus away with words that ring like a curse:

> Away from my island—fast—most cursed man alive!
> It's a curse to . . . [help] a man . . .
> when the blessed deathless gods despise him so.
> Crawling back like *this*—
> It proves the immortals hate you! Out—get out!
>   (10:79ff, Fagles)

Hated by God—this is how many veterans feel.

Homer identifies some characteristic ways in which combat veterans blight valuable chances offered by influential benefactors:

- He turns it into a "combat mission," such as working the job for days and nights without sleeping.
- He doesn't trust anyone else to "do it right."
- He doesn't trust anyone with the facts they need to know to help him do the job.

Many a veteran has felt his "real homecoming" just within his grasp and then lost it, leading to despair, demoralization, and thoughts or attempts of suicide, whether before or after going back to the benefactor to beg for a second chance. The drama of homecoming is in part a drama of rejection or acceptance. Many a veteran has had the experience that people who formerly helped them "turn cold and still," and greet him with the question, "What, again?" They have been left feeling humiliated by their own pleading for another chance. They have been driven out of factory offices, union halls, government offices and felt "cursed by heaven."

In American culture, one's claim to automatic esteem, respect, and recognition is determined by having a "good" job. The generation of young men who grew up in households of World War II veterans believed that simply serving one's country, especially in war, established a claim to automatic esteem, respect, recognition, and employment. That was what they expected to come home to. To repeatedly lose jobs became a bitter way to lose their homecoming.

The experience of returning from war to civilian society is universal, something that's been with us as long as war has been a human practice. In the Homeric world, what a powerful man could do for a veteran was to offer material help of some sort, such as food, shelter, transportation on the way home, as King Aeolus does. Homer shows us several examples of exiles settling as dependent retainers in the household of the powerful man.[3] "Employment" as we know it hardly existed, although the bards appearing in the *Odyssey* and the heralds of the *Iliad* seem to be in some sense "employees" of the princes they are attached to. So could any of the singers known to tradition as Homer have "intended" this metaphor that I find in the story of Aeolus, King of the Winds—of ruining an opportunity from a powerful patron? Maybe not. But mistrusting others so much as not to let them help, or not to tell them what you know, and thus causing a disaster—these were not invented in the twentieth century.

A Vietnam veteran, who has never sought a VA disability pension or psychological treatment from the VA, contacted me by e-mail after reading *Achilles in Vietnam,* and we met when he moved to the Boston area for his wife's graduate studies. We talked about the King of the Winds chapter, and I sent him my first draft—resulting in e-mail with these reflections on his own work life:

> I've never screwed up a job because of sleep deprivation. I have however, screwed up my relationships on the job by making that job a mission.

More to the point, my life is a mission. I don't know how not to be on a "mission." Intellectually, it's not a problem. Emotionally, it is.

Insofar as employment, I've never been fired. Instead, I have pissed people off by making them look bad. I do this by working harder than anyone else, and I never stop. In more than one case, I've quit because none of my co-workers could stand to be around me, and I would end up hating all of them, fantasizing about killing them, etc., until I couldn't stand the idea of going there anymore. My wife calls it my obsessive mode. On the job, I don't know how to stop, and I'm nearly always on the job. . . .

Someday I'd like very much to rest, and feel rested. I think that that's got something to do with not having any real friends. I can't relax, and no one else seems to when they're around me. My wife's the exception, but even that's only sometimes. You know, those times when I'm absolutely clear that she needs me to be there for her, then I'm okay.

Nobody else has had the guts to be that way with me for twenty-five years. I respect her for that.

Dedication, sometimes going over the line into fanaticism, is normal for combat veterans in the workplace. It accounts for the success in the world that many do achieve. They typically work *much* more than forty hours a week. The truism "Money isn't everything" has an unusual application here. I have never known a group of people so little interested in money as the combat veterans I have worked with. If they have worked like madmen, like they are on a "mission," it is not for the money, but for the sake of having a mission that shuts everything else from their minds.

One veteran formerly in our treatment program—a giant of a man who left school in grade school—worked so much overtime as a stevedore on the docks that he was able to purchase a large house in an upscale suburb of Boston for his wife (now ex-wife) and children. They never saw him.

When I write these words, I have been working with Vietnam combat veterans for fourteen years. The veterans are now more than a decade older than when I started. While I have not attempted to go back to clinic records and do a count, my impression is that the typical civilian employment history of the veterans newly coming into the program a decade ago was fifty or more jobs since Vietnam, none longer than a year. Now the typical Vietnam veteran newly admitted to the program worked the same job for ten to thirty years making good money, and then "broke down," incapacitated by combat-related symptoms and emotions. The life courses of the veterans with fifty-plus jobs in twenty years and those who held a single job in that time are very different, with very different consequences for the veteran, his family, and society. But what impresses me most, having gotten to know veterans in both groups quite well, is not how different they are, but how *similar*.

The event triggering a "breakdown" from a long successful job history has usually been some external event that prevented the veteran from keeping the workaholic schedule he had followed. One veteran currently in the program worked his way to top site supervisor in a nationally prominent demolition firm. Arrest and incarceration for assault—probably facilitated by the amphetamines that he used to support his workaholism—led to his collapse. Another "broke down" when cardiac bypass surgery interrupted his fourteen-hour-a-day work habits.

Farmer (pseudonym), a Navy veteran of the vicious "brown water" war in the canals of the Mekong Delta, had worked well and happily (and for killingly long hours) for ten years in a high-tech company producing equipment for the pharmaceutical industry. His perfectionism was a highly valued trait in the custom manufacture of this equipment for ultra-pure chemical processes. He felt respected and valued, and the interpersonal conflicts in the workplace so prominent in the "Vietnam Vet Stereotype" were blessedly absent. Then the parent company, a huge international pharmaceutical firm, sold the business to its main competitor "for market share," and all ninety employees, including the president, lost their jobs. Destruction of his livelihood and work community by distant powers acting on highly abstract and—to him—unreal motives set off numerous traumatic triggers for this Navy veteran. But most of all, he lost the setting in which he could perform his "mission." He became depressed, suicidal, and flooded with intrusive symptoms related to the ambush of his assault support patrol boat in the Mekong Delta the night before Thanksgiving 1968.

Every one of the workaholic veterans with a "stable work history" would have responded with an abrasive comment like, "I'm all right. What the fuck's your problem?" if someone asked if there was any way his pattern of constant overtime or multiple jobs was related to his war experience. Their pattern of arriving at work earlier than anyone else is often in the service of avoiding contact: two veterans in our program have worked for different public utilities as solo service men or installers, and arrived earlier than anyone else so as to be in the truck and gone from the yard before others arrived. Both considered themselves very good at what they did and were openly contemptuous of the attitude, dedication, and competence of their fellow employees. The families of such veterans have often done quite well—financially—but frequently will tell you that the veterans never brought themselves home with their paychecks. They were absent, emotionally aloof, irritable, and perfectionistic as parents and husbands, with the marriages often ending in divorce.

After World War I and again after World War II, the German government's approach to post-combat readjustment to civilian life was work, work, and more work. There was little in the way of disability pensions, nothing in the way of treatment for combat trauma, but a great deal in the way of vocational training, job placement, and veterans' preferences. Even the most grievously wounded were trained to do *something* and put to work. From the point of view of economic reconstruction, this was a "success"—I find myself wondering how much of the German post–World War II "economic miracle" was the product of the convergence of government policy and the workaholic strategy to keep a lid on the memories and emotions of war. When it was published in the United States, *Achilles in Vietnam: Combat Trauma and the Undoing of Character* was just one of a full shelf of books on combat trauma. When it was translated into German[4] it was greeted with astonishment as something previously unheard of, a startling new perspective. Germans are just now beginning to wrap their minds around the idea of combat trauma, having suffered—as well as caused—so much of it in the first half of the twentieth century.

Workaholism is a *very* successful strategy for keeping a lid on things, for those whose luck and makeup permits it to function reliably. While the numbers for the economy may look good, the families and the veterans themselves bear hidden costs that economists measure very badly.[5]

I do not feel comfortable recommending efforts aimed at *preventing* workaholism, in the same way that I'd endorse any reasonable strategies to prevent alcoholism and drug abuse among returning war veterans. But to sanctify workaholism as an unmixed blessing, something to be encouraged or even somewhat coerced, as in the German rehabilitation practices, seems profoundly wrongheaded to me. My goal is a flourishing, good human life for veterans, their families, and their communities.

Odysseus has served us as a metaphor of the veteran—in this instance in the workplace, where by not trusting anyone, by trying to do it all himself, by making a mission out of it, he fails and loses the job. However, he also stands very well for exactly what he his, the commodore of a flotilla, who does not trust anyone beneath him to do anything right, and thus micromanages and fails to take care of himself. When this leader breaks, people often die. In the episode with the King of the Winds miraculously no ships are lost in the hurricane, but they easily could have been.

7

A Peaceful Harbor:
No Safe Place

Six men on each ship in Odysseus' flotilla have died in the pirate raid on Ismarus; the Cyclops ate six more from Odysseus' own vessel. Visits to the lands of the Lotus Eaters and the King of the Winds at least have cost no more lives. But now the twelve ships of despondent men pull their oars, clueless and chartless, away from the island of the wind king. They row for days and nights with no idea where they are. On the seventh day they find a steep-walled fjord with a narrow mouth that keeps out the ocean waves, wind, and currents. The tired sailors pull into the glassy-calm harbor and moor close together.

Only Odysseus ties up outside, on the seaward side of the headlands. Did he have another premonition, like the one that led him to take strong wine to the Cyclops' cave? He sends a small scouting party overland. Survivors rush back to warn that scouts have discovered and been eaten by the giant, cannibal Laestrygonians. The Laestrygonians swarm from their town to the top of the cliffs that hem the fjord and rain down boulders, smashing the fragile wooden hulls lashed below.

They speared the crews like fish
and whisked them away home to make their grisly meal.
But while they killed them off . . .
I pulled the sword from beside my hip and hacked away
at the ropes that moored my blue-prowed ship . . .
and shouted . . .
'Put your backs in the oars—now row or die!'
In terror of death they ripped the swells . . .

clear of those beetling cliffs . . . my ship alone.
But the rest went down en masse. Our squadron sank.
. . . we sailed on, glad to escape our death
yet sick at heart for the dear companions we had lost.
                                        (10:135ff, Fagles)

Eleven of twelve ships and crews are now lost.

We now look at Odysseus as a military leader. What can we say now
about this hero, Odysseus, their commander? What are we to believe
about the narrator in the first lines of the poem (1:5ff, Fagles), who,
announcing Odysseus as its subject, blames the men for their own deaths?
He says they ate the sun god's cattle. The men in these eleven ships who
drowned beneath the rocks rained down on them or were butchered for
the Laestrygonian meal had never even reached the island where the sun
god kept his cattle. Is Homer just careless, or is he saying that troops—as
a category, not individually—are always the cause of their own deaths,
never the commander?[1]

So far the portrait of Odysseus is complex and many-sided. We have
learned from the *Iliad* and the song of Demodocus about the Trojan Horse
that he is a brilliant planner and strategist—that counts for a lot—and he's
brave and effective in a fight. That counts for a lot, too. But we also know
that as an independent troop commander, he doesn't keep control of his
men (allowing them to get drunk and ignore his withdrawal order from
Ismarus), shows impulsiveness and poor judgment (entering and then
remaining in the Cyclops' cave, and perhaps attacking Ismarus to begin
with), unable to delegate authority (sole helmsman for the nine-day sail
home from Aeolia), and lacks consistent leadership backbone. While he
did not indulge his troops in the free and abundant narcotics in Lotus
Land, he lacked the leader's will to deny his men the comforts of the
Laestrygonian fjord, even though he apparently suspected it was a death
trap and moored his own ship outside. Odysseus and the rest of his own
crew might well have felt claustrophobic in the fjord, for what is a fjord if
not like a roofless marine cave. Now more than nine-tenths of his men, the
flower of the Ithacan region's youth that sailed with him ten years earlier,
are at the bottom of the fjord—or worse, at the bottom of a cannibal stew
pot. If I am unforgiving about Odysseus' failures as a leader that caused the
deaths of his men, I am mirroring not only the angry criticism of enlisted
soldiers who pay the butcher's bill, but also the demanding standards of the
current American officer corps. They make no allowances at all for fellow
officers who lose lives in their command out of self-serving or self-

protective motives. Some officers go beyond this to the extreme of strict liability—*any* operational failure is culpable in their eyes, even if no misconduct or negligence was involved.

Odysseus, who is telling his own story at this point, neither explains why he alone moored outside the fjord nor expresses any remorse at having allowed the rest of his squadron to tie up inside. He dismisses the deaths of about 550 men, all but a twelfth of his command, with the words

> So we fared onward and death fell behind,
> and we took breath to grieve for our companions.
>   (10:147f, Fitzgerald)

Not all translators are as terse as Fitzgerald is here, but the frigidity with which this holocaust is narrated gives us cause to wonder.[2] Some scholars have attributed this to the story line that Homer inherited. Homer was obliged, they say, to start with the twelve ships Odysseus had in the *Iliad*, weave them together with traditional sailor tales that are clearly about one ship and its crew, and finish up with *no* ship, with Odysseus arriving alone to face the suitors . . . mmm . . . How to get rid of all those ships?[3]

Yet we should not let either Odysseus or Homer get away with such frigidity without remarking upon it. Twelve boatloads of tired, scared, homesick war veterans trying to get home to their families die horribly in this fiction because of their leader's failings.

But it is fiction, after all. It's entertainment. So does it matter?

Yes. The heartlessness with which the poet treats the loss of these "nonheroic" lives is the first example in the Western narrative tradition treating the doings of the "great" as all that matters. Ever since, the lives of all those "little people" have been treated as just so many stage props, sometimes necessary, and sometimes clutter to be rid of because they're in the way of the Story.[4] We could easily charge this to an aristocratic bias, if it were not for the contrast offered by the *Iliad*, where there is a greater inclination to treat each and every death as significant, and not as a mere plot device.

What can we learn from this shocking episode as metaphor for the soldier's homecoming? The veterans I serve in the VA clinic are all former enlisted men, not the generals, cabinet secretaries, or presidents. Their sense of being playthings of distant, capricious gods was explored in *Achilles in Vietnam*. Instead, I want to focus on the poet's picture of the peaceful fjord as a death trap. Many times in the clinic, veterans have said that as much as they long for calm, peace, and safety, these conditions arouse a feeling of unbearable threat, a remnant of warfare in the Vietnamese countryside.

One veteran arrived for a weekly therapy group very agitated, trying to calm down after an encounter outside the commuter rail terminal with a panhandler. The beggar, evidently drunk and sitting propped up next to the exit, had growled,

"Gimme a buck, there."

"No!"

"Gimme a buck, shithead!"

The beggar was still sitting on the ground.

The veteran became panicked that he was not carrying a weapon, having spent the train ride in rare pleasure at the sunny day, enjoying the sense of peace in the almost empty railroad car, not preparing himself for danger. He somewhat regained his composure when he found a stick pen in his pocket and clutched it in his hand, intending to stab the beggar in the neck with it, if attacked.

"No, you're a shithead!" he shouted and walked quickly away, the drunk still on the sidewalk.

During the therapy group, he spoke about this incident as something that he "deserved" because he had gotten "too comfortable on the train." It was "too peaceful." To find safety in any place not specifically prepared for defense, especially an uncontrolled public space, is in this veteran's view "stupid." Veterans I have worked with scan the rooftops of the low-rise buildings near the clinic for snipers and look in the spaces between parked automobiles for people crouching for attack.

This is the combat veterans' metaphor I hear in the *Odyssey* episode of the Laestrygonians: *there is no safe place*. The more serene, the more peaceful the place, the surer they are that it's a death trap.

Where does this expectancy of attack come from? At the simplest level, it is the persistence into civilian life of *valid* adaptations to the lethal situation of battle. In Vietnam, patrols were put out around both fixed installations and temporary night defensive positions, because, factually, "the enemy is all around you." But in the apparent safety of civilian life, a person who believes he is surrounded by enemies is considered paranoid—mentally ill.

One veteran, who has never been my patient and asked not to be identified, wrote the following to me by e-mail:

> i live in scrub wood. in the florida panhandle. i cant stand crowds in—[a small city in northwest Florida]. it aint no cicago. but even out her[e] it's never rite. at nite i hav to check every sound i cant figgure out. when its

quite [quiet] its worst. in the central hilands was always sounds from liz-
erds and I dont no what in the dark. when it got quiet you [k]new them
nva [North Vietnamese Army] fuckers was on toppa you.

Another veteran described how he had spoiled a very pleasant outing in
the early autumn woods with his wife. When they stopped to picnic, she
wanted to sit in a sunny meadow so as not to get chilled. He insisted on
picnicking in deep shade "in the tree line," because the meadow was too
exposed. Exposed to what? To sniper and mortar rounds. In their argument over where to picnic, he agreed that it was chilly, but could not
explain to his wife the nonnegotiable fear he experienced in open places.
It's not that the fear was "unconscious." He knew he was afraid of snipers
and mortars but was embarrassed to admit that he was afraid of these
things in the pleasant woods of north coastal Massachusetts. This veteran
and his wife had a nasty fight. In the heat of anger she said to him, "Why
do you always spoil anything good? We were having such a nice day,"
which made him feel ashamed and then angry. Embarrassed by its "irra-
tionality," he had never explained his reaction to open spaces to his wife.
The near instantaneous replacement of the emotions of fear or embarrassment or shame with the emotion of anger does untold harm to veterans' lives in their families, jobs, and communities.

Continuous mental and physiological mobilization for attack is the
result of having learned *too well* how to survive in combat. When left unex-
plained, it becomes a burdensome and debilitating disability in life with
others, but does not inevitably wreck that life. The problem of recovery
from simple PTSD afterward in civilian life becomes a problem of
unlearning combat adaptations and particularly of educating those the veteran lives with. Just as with physical injuries such as the loss of a limb,
many veterans adapt to symptoms of simple PTSD, e.g., this veteran's fear
of open fields, without loss of the ability to have a good human quality of
life. But with unhealed *complex* PTSD, all chance of a flourishing life is
lost. We shall look at this more closely in Part Two.

At the Laestrygonian fjord, this "great man," Odysseus, does not trust
his subordinates with the insight he has into the dangers of the place. His
betrayal of responsibility could have caused lifelong mistrust in any sailors
who escaped this and later death traps. Odysseus has surely betrayed
what's right by protecting himself and doing nothing to protect his men.[5]
Many World War II vets see Douglas MacArthur at Corregidor in the
same light as I see Odysseus at the Laestrygonian fjord.

"I don't trust nobody," is the voice of complex PTSD.

8

Witches, Goddesses, Queens, Wives—
Dangerous Women

One of the ugliest characteristics of some psychologically injured Vietnam combat veterans we work with is their hostility and habitual disrespect toward women. They know that all members of the clinical team to which I belong, both men and women, find it hateful to hear them refer to women as "bitches," "roadkill," or "ho," or obscenely as "cunts," or condescendingly as "girls." During a therapy group devoted to relationships, one veteran advised another, with no apparent moral or psychological distress, "Why don't you just kill the bitch?" When called on it, he claimed to be joking. Not *all* these veterans are hostile to women; in fact, some of the most influential veterans in the program make their displeasure clear when there is such talk around them. Nevertheless, negative attitudes toward women are a continuing obstacle to veterans feeling at home.

Turning back to Odysseus as a veteran (rather than as a military leader), the *Odyssey* shows how dangerous a woman may be to returning veterans: she can trick you onto a fragile sea raft from the safety of dry land and then drown you (Calypso), she can betray you to assassins who lie in wait for you (Clytemnestra and—who knows?—maybe Penelope), she can see through and betray your disguise, getting you killed (Helen's chance to blow Odysseus' disguise to the Trojans), she can accidentally get you killed by seeing through your disguise (Odysseus' old childhood nurse, Eurycleia), she can hand you over to toughs who habitually kill strangers (Nausicaa), she can turn you into a caged pig eating acorns or castrate you in her bed (Circe), she can fill you with such obsession that you forget to eat and starve to death (Sirens), she can literally eat men alive (Scylla). She may have gotten you and your friends into the war to begin with, where most of them were killed (Helen).[1]

The cumulative impression of female dangerousness and untrustworthiness in the *Odyssey* is overwhelming.

Just two lines of the poem carry Odysseus' ship from the carnage in the fjord, to the island home of the witch-goddess Circe, "the nymph with lovely braids, an awesome power too . . . the true sister of murderous-minded Aeetes" (10:149ff, Fagles). Nymphs were minor goddesses, usually associated with wonder-arousing natural features, like caves, waters, forests.

The one remaining ship and its crew land on a wooded island, Circe's island, but they don't know that yet, being utterly lost. They grieve and panic for two days on the shore. On the third day Odysseus does a reconnaissance. From a lookout he sees smoke. Returning to the shore, he divides his crew in two and puts one platoon in the charge of Eurylochus, his kinsman. Everyone is scared that this is *another* death trap, and they cast lots to decide which of the two platoons will go inland to see where the smoke came from. Eurylochus loses the toss and heads inland with his platoon. They get to Circe's palace and find it surrounded by strangely tame lions and wolves. Quaking with fear, they make their way to the door, hear a woman's enchanting song, and call out. They are immediately admitted, but Eurylochus smells a trap and doesn't go in. The others enter and are treated to luscious mulled wine in royal style. It's a honey trap!—the men's wine has been drugged and she taps each with her magic wand, turning them into pigs. Eurylochus sees them being driven into sties and flung acorns by the contemptuous witch. He breaks for the ship and, speechless with terror, finally gets the story out. Odysseus puts on his armor, straps on his sword, and says, Lead me back there. Eurylochus is too scared. Odysseus shrugs and says, Never mind, I'll find my own way.

We already know that Odysseus has friends in high places, and one of these, the god Hermes, pops out of nowhere just short of Circe's palace.

> Where are you going now, my unlucky friend . . . ?
> And your men are all in there . . .
> cooped up like swine, hock by jowl in the sties.
> Have you come to set them free?

> Well, I warn you, you won't get home yourself,
> you'll stay right there, trapped with the rest.
> But wait, I can save you. . . .
> Look, here is a potent drug. Take it to Circe's halls . . .
> She'll mix you a potion, lace the brew with drugs
> but she'll be powerless to bewitch you, even so—
> this magic herb I give will fight her spells.
> Now here's your plan of action . . .
> The moment Circe strikes with her long thin wand,
> you draw your sharp sword . . .
> and rush her fast as if to run her through!
> She'll cower in fear and coax you to her bed—

Like a good fairy tale, the magic herb will counteract the magic spell. And Hermes warns of another peril, once the first is overcome:

> But don't refuse the goddess' bed . . .
> but have her swear the binding oath of the blessed gods
> she'll never plot . . . to harm you,
> once you lie there naked—
> never unman you . . .
>
> (10:310–34, Fagles)

What do these two dangers mean?

Circe has transformed Odysseus' crew into pigs. Pigs were an honorable form of wealth, second only to beef cattle and horses.[2] But still, calling someone a domestic pig was no flattery, in the sense that calling him a lion or wild boar might have been. Circe has destroyed the dignity of the crewmen she has transformed, made them her slaves, and caused them to eat animal fodder—utterly demeaning them. Who eats what is enormously important in the moral and social world of the *Odyssey*, marking the difference between animal and human, between god-fearing and sacrilegious.

One metaphorical reading of she-turns-men-into-pigs is this: if returning veterans behave like pigs to the hometown women, it must be—according to the veterans—the women's own doing. They turn men into mud-wallowing swine. As implausible as this may seem as an "eternal verity," first recorded by Homer, the beliefs that some veterans have about their womenfolk support this. The prejudicial stereotype of Vietnam veterans as chronically violent domestic tyrants turns out to have another side, the veteran who allows himself to be a doormat, a domestic slave to his wife or girlfriend. These overly compliant veterans hate their domestic lives, hate themselves, and often hate the partners whom they blame for their own passive slavishness in the home.

Wilson (pseudonym for a composite of several veterans) is a handsome, athletic man with thick black hair who was in our program at the time I joined it fourteen years ago. He had served two tours as an infantryman in Vietnam. His ex-wife (also a composite) refused while they were married ever to meet or speak with the treatment team. This is a normal part of our program, and rarely refused. She told the team members who called her that she was not going to waste her time "talking about that moron." Yet every day she would leave him a detailed written schedule of tasks, as if he were a domestic servant, and berate him if he failed to accomplish any of them. Their only child, a daughter, whom he now hardly ever sees because of the divorce, was the apple of his eye. For many years he daily made her lunch, took her to school, and picked her up each day, in between housework, yard work, and home repair. His wife did the family shopping, because he had panic attacks in public places such as the supermarket.

While the marriage lasted his wife treated him with open contempt in front of their daughter. His wife's mother would join her in verbal abuse of the veteran, switching off every so often with abuse of their daughter, who they said was "just like her father."

He struggled constantly against violent images of how he would make his wife beg for her life as he had with suspected Viet Cong during the war. When these impulses became overwhelming, he would ask our assistance to get him admitted to the VA hospital. Once, two years before he joined our program, he had lost control and beaten his wife unconscious and the police took him screaming in Vietnamese to the VA hospital. She refused to cooperate with the police in prosecuting him. Then she repeatedly threw this incident in his face over the years that followed. She once even had him taking phone messages from a man who turned out to be both her lover and her cocaine dealer.

For many years in the clinic he spilled torrents of what can only be called "hate speech" against women, blaming all women for his unhappy and demeaning home life. "All" women were "always" out to control, manipulate, rip off, and humiliate men. "That man-hating bitch" was his usual moniker for his wife.

Much of the treatment with veterans like Wilson consists in strengthening two sets of seemingly opposing mental muscles: strengthening control over impulses to violence, while at the same time strengthening their ability to assert their own need for respectful treatment in their own homes and to assert authority over their own time, rather than allowing their wives to schedule it entirely to suit their convenience. Unfortunately, sometimes their wives find their husbands' newly revealed personal dignity intolerable and file for divorce. In a number of cases they have successfully used police records of past violence toward them in court to paint the veterans as unfit to have visitation with their children.

Wilson grieves over the loss of contact with his daughter and tries to take solace in the other veterans' advice to be patient, that his daughter will return to him when she is no longer under her mother's thumb. He now has a new girlfriend with whom he has been able to negotiate a safe and mutually respectful partnership. While he still spews hatred of his ex-wife and her mother, he no longer speaks in violent or demeaning ways about women in general. Because he now has confidence in his own self-control, he no longer needs to be a compliant puppet to protect others from his own violence. His fear of his own violence had paralyzed his capacity for even dignified and nonviolent self-assertion. If Wilson was passive and overcompliant with his ex-wife it was because he feared himself, not her.

Homer seemed to understand men's capacity to blame women for everything. Unfortunately, he also seems to say that this blame is entirely justified. I cannot detect a shred of doubt or irony in his picture of Circe. Recall the god Hermes' instructions to Odysseus. If she turned into a tame sex kitten, it was only because Odysseus was ready to stab her with his sword. As a goddess, she could not be killed, but she could be temporarily hurt. Perhaps more important to her submission was Odysseus' demand for the magic oath Hermes had instructed him to exact. Presumably this oath is unknown to ordinary mortals and tipped off Circe that Odysseus had the backing of another, stronger god.[3]

The second half of Hermes' warnings and advice to Odysseus touches on a very different source of woman hating: fear that they conceal deadly weapons in their alluring beds and sexual parts. Hermes warns him of Circe's counterattack, once he defeats her drug and magic spell: she will lure him into her bed for sex and then cut off his sexual organs. In the world of fairy tales, we are willing to believe Hermes' instruction that Odysseus can protect himself from this second attack by exacting a special oath from Circe not to "unman" him.

American soldiers in Vietnam were in a world where such threats were thought to be real and the gods very far away and uncommunicative.

These soldiers could not protect themselves with words and oaths. One widely circulated rumor among American GIs in Vietnam was that prostitutes were Viet Cong cadres, who put razor blades or broken glass in their vaginas. A variant of this was the advice never to fall asleep after sex with a prostitute, because the VC would sneak in and cut off your balls. Similar to these rumors, but with more frequent basis in reality, was the fear that Vietnamese prostitutes harbored antibiotic-resistant strains of venereal diseases, known collectively as the "black syph."

The painful and destructive legacy that some veterans brought home with them from the Vietnam War was this visceral sense that women are dangerous. Remember that many young men had their first sustained experience with sex in the demeaning and dangerous context of prostitution in Vietnam. Veterans have told me that they always went armed to a "steam and cream," a brothel providing steam bath, massage, and ejaculation. Rapes and rape-murders of Vietnamese prostitutes were widely known. They were not investigated by either military police or South Vietnamese civilian police. Fear, anger, and violence do not lay groundwork for any postwar sexual life that deserves the name "intimacy," not to speak of sweetness or delight. Exactly the contrary.

Once Odysseus defeats Circe's plan to turn him into a pig like the rest of his crew (with a little assistance from the god Hermes), she enthusiastically pulls him to frolics in bed, punctuated only by daily feasts of meat and wine. Her words to him are like a combat veteran's wish-fulfillment dream:

> Royal . . . Odysseus, man of action,
> no more tears now, calm these tides of sorrow.
> Well I know what pains you bore on the swarming sea,
> what punishment you endured from hostile men on land.
> But come now, eat your food and drink your wine
> till the same courage fills your chests, now as then,
> when you first set sail from native land. . . .
> *Now you are burnt-out husks, your spirits haggard, sere,*
> *always brooding over your wanderings long and hard,*
> *your hearts never lifting with any joy—*
> *you've suffered far too much.*
>
> (10:502ff, Fagles; emphasis added)

Odysseus laps it up and apparently forgets all about his faithful wife, Penelope, and son and homecoming for a whole year, until his shipmates snap him out of it—"Captain, this is madness! / High time you thought of your own home at last" (10:520f, Fagles).

Circe's inviting bed would appear to need little decoding as an obstacle to returning home, but that appearance may be misleading. I wrote above about the danger and degradation that often permeated sex with prostitutes in Vietnam, as one obstacle. Another obstacle, the extreme opposite of danger and degradation, is described by a veteran, a former Airborne officer, who has never been my patient. His picture of sex with prostitutes in the midst of a war—a dreamlike, wonderland quality—created its own obstacle to homecoming. I shall omit explicit sexual detail:

FROM "LOVE AND WHORES" BY DENNIS SPECTOR[4]

What would the good mothers of the PTA say if they knew what type of sex their sons got off on in Vietnam? Those wonderful women who bake cookies and expect their boys to go off to war, with all the glory of the 4th of July and Memorial Day parades. . . .

[In Vietnam] you learn that the quickest way to a man's heart is through his cock. . . .

If it is your first time, getting your rocks off, it's even more believed. And, it was the first time for almost all of us in the 1960s. Mary Magdalene is part of our heritage of forgiveness and redemption. There was no redemption in our jungle of blood, redemption could be found in taking care of a vulnerable woman and being taken care of in return. A redeeming time of peace and care and passion. No killing, only female softness, femininity of giving totally in the care of a strong man.

These Vietnamese women were perfect beauties, small-boned, very delicate, petite beauties with soft, smooth olive-colored skin, and the gentle rounded curves of youth, girl-like in their beauty. The natural way they ply their trade created a perfectly good loving acceptance of these whores by a man. They needed us to care for them and protect them, that was the only way they could survive. The hardships and constant touch of death made this love right for us, for this moment it was love, all soft yielding, pleasing flesh. We begged for it. We knew that: "Hey, I could be dead tomorrow. So why not live every moment?" The insanity, lies, cruelty all around us, all of the time, made us want to run to the soft gentle flesh of a woman accepting, without any hint of danger, a respite from the killing to make life intimate and worth living again. . . . We needed nurturance so badly, they gave it to us so naturally. They needed a man to take care of and protect them. . . . These women had no choice, and that also made it right. . . .

These Asian whores treated an American like a king. Sather [the author's pseudonym for himself] had seen so many ladies get serious about a GI; believing he would really be allowed to bring her home, wanting his loving protection, falling so loyally in love with him. . . .

These women were all passion, it was their femininity, that was all that they knew. They wanted to make it real if they could.

In the U.S., Sather missed the passion.

Circe's offer—once Odysseus has intimidated her—of sex, baths, food, wine as therapy for a haggard, sere spirit appears to have played out in reality among some American combat soldiers in Vietnam. These Eurasian and Afro-Asian prostitutes, whom Spector describes as working in bar-whorehouses in "a boom boom village" at the crossing of two roads that Spector's unit was patrolling, were not free, self-determining sex workers. They had probably been sold to the brothels as children, or they had been born in the brothels, being outcasts because of their mixed race. They were, as most prostituted women in the world are, enslaved. Spector writes of this village among the rubber plantations, "Decades of French Foreign Legion assured this legacy of outcasts. The South Vietnamese hated the mixed races of Senegalese, Algerian, Moroccan, French. . . . The only living open to these women was the same as their mothers, as whores."

If homecoming means returning to the specific civilian world from which one departed for war, to its now boring job, to its now trivial social demands, to the annoying insistence that things be paid for, to an unsexy wife, and to a crowded and unglamorous neighborhood, then perhaps a life of limitless sex, food, and wine with a rich, bewitching nymph (and later with the another nymph, Calypso) sure could distract a guy from coming home! But two questions spring to mind: How real is this threat to a soldier's homecoming? Does Odysseus' affair with Circe shed any light on the mistrust and hostility toward women described in the earlier part of this chapter?

A minority of the men I work with today have active, let alone promiscuous, sexual lives—now. The rest are not celibate on principle, but are so socially isolated—even in their own homes, sometimes living on a different floor from their partner—that there is little occasion for sexual intimacy. However, many went through periods during the first decade after returning from Vietnam when they apparently did seek the solace that Circe specifically offers in wine, good food, and great sex. Veterans have described periods when they were wildly promiscuous, having sex with as many as three women a day over an extended period. We shall return to the subject of sexaholism in Chapter 14.

Perhaps it's the New England moralist in me speaking, but I do not believe there is salvation for a haggard, sere spirit in sex, or even romance. In fact, I speculate that the hostility toward women displayed by many veterans with PTSD stems from *disappointment* of the hope that "the love of a good woman" would be enough to heal the wounds of war: "If my wife (or wives) did not do that for me, it must be because they had some other agenda." Or to be more exact, if the momentary relief found in sex from the after-effects of combat did not last, then the woman must have taken that relief away from the veteran for some sinister or self-serving reason. A young man coming home to America hoping for, possibly expecting, the kind of wonderland dream-love-sex described above by Dennis Spector might well be bitterly disappointed. He might well conclude that women are to blame for his disappointment. Homer puts a similar wish-fulfillment dream into Circe's words with such beauty and understanding of what a returning war veteran wants that it's extremely painful to recall that it *is* a fiction, it *is* a dream, and she *is* a nymph, a demigoddess, and not a merely mortal woman.

A real-world woman, in America, meeting a haggard combat veteran, might have been as understanding as Circe, but unlike Circe had no staff of serving women, had to consider how to pay to keep up the household, had a life with her own family and friends apart from the veteran.

Dennis Spector writes the following about his experience when he returned:

> Coming home to women is very hard, it is impossible to reestablish an intimacy. They just can't relate. . . .
>
> Women are treated so well in our society, there life is so gentle. I'm glad that they are. I'm talking about the average American female. That is the good side of the double standard. . . .
>
> It's not because they don't have it, it's that we have changed. We can't share our inner self with them. We come home with the reality, there's blood on the risers, there's blood on our hands, there's friends we can't touch. What happened is scary, very scary. We have this reality, we know that it can happen again. . . .
>
> How can you come home to a woman and be yourself after combat? How can she even understand that? You can hardly be yourself again.
>
> I went to see that great movie *Born on the Fourth of July* with my wife. We went to a matinee, at a small theater. Only eight couples were there.

Born on the Fourth of July did something, it explained the death of a soul. . . . When you come back you find that they lied to you. It had the . . . analogy of the death of a spine with the hero. It was the first movie that captured the idea that you have to . . . have a rebirth, whatever it is, you have to have it.

I remembered looking around the theater and all the people were still sitting around, just like I was. You could tell they were all my age. I could hear the whispers. . . . I got out of there quickly because I was going to cry and I don't like to cry. They were hit by the story of a need for rebirth, just like I was hit.

My wife could not understand what I was talking about.

How do you bridge that gap? . . . I understood the need for a rebirth. She could not comprehend what happened to me, because she had never been beaten up. If she had been raped, abused, beaten, scared, or starved [like the mixed-race Vietnamese outcast prostitutes?], she could understand. I am glad that she wasn't.

And, I thought: "How many people have touched a dead person. Or have had to put their buddies in a bag, and made sure that you got all the parts. Or, stuffed their stomach back in so that you could get them out."

You have sex, but you don't have intimacy. We live in a hell that is ours alone and we don't want to drag her into it, so we live in there alone and cut off intimacy.

With a life partner you want to be able to share everything with her. You can't even come close, she has never experienced anything like that. Her image is the illusion that a man goes off to fight, you're strong, you come home and you build your life.

You have the reality. [5]

Here Spector emphasizes the chasm between the danger and horror of war and the safe complacency of civilian life and the chasm between veterans and women.

The theme that women are dangerous and untrustworthy because of their deceptive *mētis* and because they allure men with secret powers will haunt the rest of the *Odyssey*. The opening four books of the *Odyssey* concerning Odysseus' wife and son at home in Ithaca depict women in a generally favorable light, especially the faithful and long-suffering Penelope. As Odysseus is presented as a "man of pain," she is a woman of pain who *could* understand this husband. She also has plenty of *mētis* herself, including the famous trick of the shroud that she weaves each day, and unweaves every evening to deceive the suitors (2:100ff, Fitzgerald). But this *mētis* is apparently in the service of loyalty to her husband. Homer depicts females who are powerful, but not actively malevolent on their own account, such as Queen Arete. But early on, we hear about the scare-figure of Queen Clytemnestra, King Agamemnon's treacherous wife. Agamemnon's brother, Menelaus, says of her—

> A stranger killed my brother, in cold blood—
> Tricked blind, caught in the web of his deadly queen.
> (4:98f, Fitzgerald)

With the introduction of Circe in Book 10 the picture of women gets rapidly worse and more sinister as we encounter autonomously dangerous female beings who are *both* powerful *and* malevolent. Clytemnestra becomes Agamemnon's murderer, rather than merely an accomplice, says Agamemnon in the Underworld—

> There's nothing more deadly, bestial than a woman
> set on works like these—what a monstrous thing
> she plotted, slaughtered her own lawful husband
> (10:484ff, Fagles)

And it is impossible to avoid the emotional impact of the cosmic she-evil of Scylla, the six-headed man-eating monster in the narrow strait across from a giant whirlpool, Charybdis, also gendered female. When facing such powerful female malevolence, Circe says—run for your life:

> That nightmare [Scylla] cannot die, being eternal
> evil itself—horror, and pain, and chaos;
> there is no fighting her, no power can fight her,
> all that avails is flight.
> (12:139f, Fitzgerald)

Our encounter here with Circe merely opens a theme we shall meet again and again in the chapters that follow.

9

Among the Dead: Memory and Guilt

Veterans carry the weight of friends' deaths *in* war and *after* war, and the weight of all those irretrievable losses among the living that, like the dead, can never be brought back. When Circe tells Odysseus that their homeward route takes them through Hades, the House of Death, Odysseus says, "So she . . . crushed the heart inside me" (10:546, Fagles). Who has ever heard of anyone coming back alive from Death? It is his longest single "adventure."[1]

THE DEAD (TRY TO) REPROACH THE LIVING

Homer enlarges our understanding of what is conventionally called "survivor guilt "[2]—the lesson being in the contrast—Odysseus' almost complete *absence of moral pain, guilt, self-reproach, and self-criticism.*

His encounter in the Underworld with the great Ajax is particularly revealing. In courage, self-sacrifice, combat leadership, fighting skill, and fortitude, Ajax was second only to Achilles in the entire Greek army. His strength and giant stature were legendary, as was his unadorned, simple, and almost tongue-tied manner of speech. By contrast, Odysseus is glib and tricky-tongued. Ajax was a man of deeds, not words. When Achilles was killed, his corpse and armor were saved from the enemy. The armor was awarded during a grand assembly as a prize of honor to—honey-tongued Odysseus! Afterward, in humiliation and rejection, Ajax suffers a psychotic break in which a corral full of consecrated animals becomes—in his delusion—the hated top leadership, Agamemnon, Menelaus, and

their henchmen. He kills them all. When he snaps out of his delusion surrounded by the slaughtered sacred animals, he is doubly humiliated,
religiously defiled, and kills himself by falling on his sword.[3]

This is how Odysseus tells his encounter with Ajax, the suicide, in the
underworld:

> Only the ghost of Great Ajax . . .
> kept his distance, blazing with anger at me still
> for the victory I had won . . . that time
> I pressed my claim for the arms of Prince Achilles.
> . . .
> Would to god I'd never won such trophies!
> All for them the earth closed over Ajax,
> that proud hero Ajax . . .
> greatest in build, greatest in works of war. . . .
> I cried out to him now, I tried to win him over.
> 'Ajax . . . still determined,
> even in death, not once to forget that rage
> you train on me for those accursed arms?
> The Gods set up that prize to plague the [Greeks]—
> so great a tower of strength we lost when you went down!
> . . .
> Zeus sealed your doom.
> Come closer, king, and listen to my story.
> Conquer your rage, your blazing, headstrong pride!'
> So I cried out but Ajax answered not a word.
>   (11:620–43, Fagles)

In the value system of warrior heroism constructed by the *Iliad*—which
Achilles and Ajax embodied—there was only one choice for who should
receive the arms of the dead Achilles as the army's prize of honor, and
that was Ajax. Exactly how Odysseus weaseled it for himself doesn't matter. He never should have competed for them, and never should have
used his *mētis* to win them.[4] I hear his apparently large-spirited attempt
to make peace with the shade of Ajax—he cannot bring him back to
life!—as posturing for the Phaeacian audience to show his superiority to
Ajax. In the honor code of the *Iliad*, Odysseus' generosity to his defeated
rival is actually a kind of further put-down.

The lyric poet Pindar, who is closely associated with the pan-Hellenic
athletic "tour," of which the Olympic Games are the best known today,

composed the following bitter lines about Odysseus' "sophistry" in cheating Ajax out of his arms:

> Sophistry [lit., "persuasion with hostile intent"] was rank then too,
> Mongering fictions, two-hearted, cultivating its vile sleights.
> It desolates all splendor, then for obscurity
> Raises some hollow monument.
>
> (*Nemean* 8, lines 32–34, Mullen, trans.)[5]

The Olympics were contested with Achilles, so to speak, as their tutelary spirit. Professor Gregory Nagy writes,

> We know from ancient sources that the traditional ceremony inaugurating . . . [the Olympic Games] centers on Akhilleus: on the day before the Games are to begin, the local women of Elis, the place where the Olympics were held, fix their gaze on the sun as it sets into the Western horizon—and begin ceremonially to weep for the hero.[6]

Pindar glorifies Achilles and treats us to visions of Achilles running down deer and lions at age six, and enumerates his combat kills to glorify him.[7] Straightforward Achilles survived as the culture hero, not tricky-tongued Odysseus.

Sophocles, and the other Athenian tragic poets, detested Odysseus as a sleazy ass-kisser to the powerful Agamemnon and Menelaus, according to Homer scholar W. B. Stanford.[8] In the Athenian poets' eyes he is "quibbling, unscrupulous, corrupt, ambitious, self-serving, sophistic, rejoicing to make the worse argument appear the better."[9] Stanford's chapter title on how the Athenian tragic poets presented Odysseus says it all: "Stage Villain." Their hostility has been attributed variously to the politics of the day, pandering to popular prejudice, and dramatic utility. Euripides' portrait of Odysseus is "without a redeeming feature."[10] However, I believe much of this attitude is explained by the simple fact that *all* the practitioners of Athenian tragedy—as indeed was everyone in the audience—were themselves combat veterans. Aeschylus fought at Marathon (his brother was killed there), Plataea, and Salamis; Sophocles was elected general at least twice—and this was no mere popularity contest, slanted by his successful theater pieces. The voters' lives depended on his skill and leadership during the revolt of Samos in 441.[11]

Having rejected Odysseus' remorse over Ajax's suicide as insincere, I cannot use his visit to the Underworld as a metaphor for survivor guilt—

except by way of contrast. Typically, survivors of horrible trauma consider their *own* pain unworthy compared to that of others who "had it worse." According to Army veteran Mary Garvey, women who served in the Vietnam era, but who were never in country, include women who—

> are very very affected . . . and not just the women who were there . . . who are of course very very very affected . . . but women who weren't . . . and feel that therefore their feelings, in fact their PTSD, are not legitimate. . . ." I only was a nurse in a burn unit in Japan." I only was a nurse in a psychiatric ward in the States. I only met the coffins at the Air Force base. I only worked with the medical films taken of the wounded. I only was a stewardess and delivered them there. I only typed up the lists of the dead. Or from yours truly, I only sent them off to die.[12]

Placing one's self in a "hierarchy of suffering" to one's own disadvantage is widespread among trauma survivors. I have written about this phenomenon among Vietnam combat veterans in *Achilles in Vietnam*.[13]

"I WON'T FORGET A THING"—KEEPING FAITH

Elpenor, the most recently dead among Odysseus' crew, greets him in the Underworld. He has died unheroically the morning of Odysseus' departure from Circe's palace, snapping his neck in an accidental fall from the flat roof where he had been sleeping. Either Odysseus was unaware of his death, or after lingering a year at Circe's table and in her bed was suddenly in too much of a hurry to give him a proper cremation and burial.[14] The ghost of Elpenor begs Odysseus to give him these rites, which will allow him to rest in death, rather than wander painfully through all eternity:

> You and your ship will put ashore again
> . . . [at Circe's island] . . . then and there,
> my lord, *remember me*, I beg you! Don't sail off
> and desert me, left behind unwept, unburied, don't. . . .
> No, burn me in full armor, all my harness,
> heap my mound by the churning gray surf—
> a man whose luck ran out—
> so even men to come will learn my story.
> Perform my rites, and plant on my tomb that oar
> I swung with mates when I rowed among the living.
>   (11:77ff, Fagles; emphasis added)

Soldiers, sailors, marines, airmen, no matter how humble and undistinguished, abhor being *forgotten*. Elpenor wrests a promise from Odysseus to cremate and bury him with full military honors. Odysseus can't brush this aside, coming from a ghost:[15]

> 'All this, my unlucky friend,' I assured him,
> 'I will do for you. *I won't forget a thing.'*
> (11:87f, Fagles; emphasis added)

The families of combat veterans, and sometimes even their therapists, demand in frustration, "Why can't you put it behind you? *Why can't you just forget it?*" Odysseus' vow, "I won't forget a thing," is the vow of a combat soldier to his dead comrades to keep faith with them, to keep their memory alive. Bewildered families, hurt and feeling cheated by the amount of energy their veterans pour into dead comrades, apparently do not realize that to forget the dead dishonors the living veteran. In asking the veteran to forget, the family asks him to dishonor himself. For anyone, civilian or veteran, to be told to do something dishonorable usually evokes *anger*. Imagine, for example, that your mother has died within the last year or so, and your spouse or your employer says to you, "Just forget about her."

The resuscitative function of memory—bringing the dead back to life—takes many, often unrecognized forms. Intractable guilt, rage, or grief, sometimes serves this honorable purpose of keeping faith with the dead. Many a well-meaning therapist has stumbled onto an exploding land mine of rage from a veteran by making the well-intended, supportive remark, "You don't have to feel guilty about that."

One of the founders of the modern trauma field, Yael Danieli, who has worked mainly with Holocaust survivors and their children and grandchildren, observed the four "existential functions of guilt": to deny helplessness; to keep the dead alive by making them ever present in thought; to sustain loyalty to the dead; and to affirm that the world is still a just place where someone (even if only the guilt-ridden survivor alone) feels guilt at what was done.[16] Danieli's observations on guilt can equally be extended to grief and to rage. Grief rejects helpless acquiescence to the rupture of attachment and affirms that someone is still attached to the dead and still cares that they ever lived. Rage affirms that someone will still avenge the dead or at least never forgive those responsible. The other three functions are the same as for guilt.

Odysseus' encounter with dead comrades in Hades can be seen as a metaphor for the pervasive presence of the dead in the inner worlds of some combat veterans. They are truly "haunted." I have thought long and hard about how such haunting can be prevented, and now believe that the answer lies in changing the modern American military culture on grief. After battle, once it is safe enough for everyone to sleep, it's safe enough to grieve; and the unit should do this together, with the unit's direct leaders setting an example with their own tears.[17]

What follows is my own narrative of a recent encounter with a veteran I have known for all fourteen years I have been with the VA.

Timmy

The thirty-five-year-old flashbulb snap has a slightly greenish hue that makes the five young men look a bit sickly. In black-and-white photocopies that I make from it with the veteran's permission, the youth and health of these men is easier to see. They are unmarked, unscarred. It was taken five or so days before Christmas 1967 and a small plastic Christmas tree is just visible at the bottom of the photo like the trunk of a tree—the five young men arranged in a triangle above it are the tree's crown. The tropics—two of the five are not wearing shirts. The flash picture, indoors, washes out the youngster closest to the lens, so I have to make the photocopies darker to see the trooper in front and lighter to see the one in back.

"That's Timmy, two days before he died."

He points to another young man in the picture and tells me he went to Saigon shortly after the picture was taken. They never saw him again, never knew what happened to him.

I know how much Timmy meant to my patient. The picture was sent to him Christmas 2001 by Timmy's mother, who had received it thirty-five years ago from the young man closest to the lens in the lower right.

Until about five years ago my patient had—inexplicably to his family— refused to answer the telephone or to collect mail from the mailbox. He was terrified that the person calling or writing would be Timmy's mother, asking him how Timmy died. He was the only witness and had made the affidavit that allowed Timmy to be classified as KIA, rather than MIA.

A soldier not in the picture—these were members of my patient's tank platoon—tracked my patient down a few years ago to tell him that he had met Timmy's mother with another member of the platoon, and that she was the *nicest* person. Wouldn't he like to contact her? She remembered my patient very well and that Timmy and he had been closest friends on the tank together. Another member of the platoon had visited

Timmy's mother in her small farming community in Ohio, and the whole town turned out to welcome him and to honor Timmy—thirty years after his death.

In *Achilles in Vietnam,* this veteran remembered his friend:

> He wasn't a harmful person. He wasn't a dirty person. He had this head that was wide up at the top, and his chin come down to a point. He had this hair he used to comb to his right side and he always had this big cowlick in back. Big old cowlick. And when he smiled—you ever hear "ear to ear"?—it was almost a gooney-looking smile. You know, it was just WA-a-ay—it was huge. He just had this big, huge smile. He never said nothing bad about nobody. He was just . . . he was a caring person.
>
> And when you're on a tank, it's like a closeness you never had before. It's closer than your mother and father, closer than your brother or your sister, or whoever you're closest with in your family. . . . Because you get three guys that are on that tank, and you're just stuck together. You're there.
>
> It should've been me.
>
> I jumped first. It didn't blow me up. Sa-a-ame spot. Same spot. Same exact spot.[18]

I sit across from the veteran in my tiny VA office with this old photo in my hand and begin to weep. I have known him for fourteen years. I have known the story of Timmy's death in an antitank mine explosion and of its lifelong effects on my patient. These smooth, healthy, athletic young men in the long-ago picture remind me of my own son, who is now their age, and my teariness turns to uncontrollable sobbing. I think of the "grief fixed upon . . . [the] heart" of any parent who loses a child in war, *and* upon the hearts of their closest comrades.

After years of therapy, this veteran has worked through his fear that his story and his life will injure his therapists, and he waits tranquilly for my tears to stop. "It's okay, Doc," he says quietly. His native kindness and decency and sweetness—which war ripped out of him for a long time—are all in his voice.

He did visit Timmy's mother, and they now are in regular phone contact.

ANYONE CLOSE WILL BE HARMED

The death of close comrades received a great deal of attention in the *Iliad* as the source of unbearable grief, guilt, and a trigger for the berserk state. The *Odyssey* shows in metaphor that veterans carry guilt for deaths and losses that happened after the war's end. Odysseus' mother, Anticleia, is the next specter who comes to him out of the darkness. Odysseus has no idea until this moment that she has died! He must, following Circe's instructions, hold all the shades off until he has heard from the ghost of Teiresias, the great seer and prophet. But when that is done, his mother is the first ghost he reanimates with sacrificial blood, following Circe's magic ritual instructions.

She died, she says, because, "yearning for you . . . robbed me of my soul" (11:202–3, orig., Ahl and Roisman, trans.).[19] The word Homer uses for "yearning" is the same as Achilles used to describe his yearning for his dead comrade, Patroclus (*pothos/pothē*, *Iliad* 19:321, orig.). Because of this yearning Achilles can take neither food nor drink. Thus the text hints that Anticleia starved herself to death in a melancholic depression. In effect, she says to her son, "You killed me, that's why I'm here in Hades." When you add it up, nearly *everyone* who has anything to do with Odysseus gets hurt.[20] He lives up to his odious name, "he who sows trouble for others." If this is Odysseus' perspective on himself, the *Odyssey* certainly adopts his perspective.

The point of this for veterans is *not* that they "spoil everything they touch," but rather that many of the men I have worked with *believe this about themselves*. They see themselves as toxic because they expect to harm others with their knowledge of the hideousness of war—"if you knew what I know, it would fuck you up." Some feel this way because of the actual cruelty, violence, and coercion they have committed after returning from Vietnam. These veterans shun closeness with others, because they are certain that others will be harmed by the contact.

But while Odysseus' conscience was quite lethargic, but I can testify that some of the men I work with are profoundly troubled in their conscience by the harm they have done to others since returning to civilian life.[21] Many of my patients experience shame and remorse for how the lives of their wives, parents, and children have been deformed by the impact of their own psychological and moral injuries. This phenomenon of "secondary traumatization" in close relationships has been extensively studied and documented[22]—and the veterans themselves are vividly aware of it.

The *Odyssey*'s particularly poignant example that Odysseus can never hold his mother in his arms again, or be held by her, can stand as an emblem for a large, varied category of losses.

> How I longed
> to embrace my mother's spirit, dead as she was!

> Three times I rushed toward her, desperate to hold her,
> three times she fluttered through my fingers, sifting away
> like a shadow, dissolving like a dream, and each time
> the grief cut to the heart, sharper, yes, and I,
> I cried out to her. . . .
> 'Mother—why not wait for me? How I long to hold you!—'
> (11:233ff, Fagles)

The poignancy and anguish of this scene is true to the experience of real combat veterans with PTSD. Both the original traumas of war and the wreckage caused by their psychological injuries have caused irretrievable losses of this magnitude.

IRRETRIEVABLE LOSSES

When one's closest comrade dies in combat, his death is permanent and irreversible. This painful truth needs no explanation. Indeed it rivets our attention to such a degree that many combat veterans and those who want to understand them often overlook the many losses that occur *after* the war has ended. These irretrievable losses take many forms.

Men that I work with have children they have not seen in twenty years, parents who died while they were estranged, or who have been estranged for all but the last few years since Vietnam. Many have shared the same domicile with their wives and children but have been utterly detached from them, living on a separate floor. The overwhelming sense of futility and waste: "For fifteen years I was completely in*sane*, drinking and drugging and fucking people up, what do I got to show for it?" Our culture values occupational achievements almost to the exclusion of anything else, so it is not surprising that many of our patients have felt humiliated by their inability to be "successful" and prosperous. Others feel like the veteran whose words are an epigraph to the Introduction—"My regret is wasting the whole of my productive adult life as a lone wolf." He feels he has missed the sense of belonging, recognition, and mutual appreciation that his talents and hard work should have earned him. He has been reasonably successful in his profession, but he believes he is not nearly as successful as he would have been if he could trust other people enough to collaborate with them—instead of always being a "lone wolf." A lone wolf feels at home nowhere.

Odysseus' mother's death while he was absent is but one way to lose a mother. Others are no less painful: One of my patients, a marine veteran whose dignity and "command presence" are an important contribution to the veteran community—I tease him about being the colonel of the Southie [South Boston] Marine Regiment—returned home after his service in Vietnam in a state of boiling anger, overwhelmed by suffocating grief at so many killed and the sense that all ideas of "what's right" had been utterly discredited. He drank heavily and fell in with—or sought out—"bad company." He says he was in his room in the family home and overheard his mother say, "That's not my [his name]." He says, "I was so mad, I just walked out of the house and didn't come back for ten years." During those ten years he did a lot of harm to himself and to others. And those ten years are irretrievable.

Lawrence Tritle, a Vietnam veteran and professor of history at Loyola Marymount University in Los Angeles, recounts the following story, which links the haunting presence of the dead and the loss of a mother:

> This grip of the dead on the living was related to me . . . by Emma, the mother of a Vietnam combat veteran. She told me of talking with her son soon after his return from Vietnam, where he had once been the sole survivor of his ambushed platoon. As he recounted one horrific incident after another, sometimes confessing his own brutalities, Emma thought to herself, "This isn't my son." As he continued his confessions, she began to look for birthmarks and childhood scars, to prove to herself that the man sitting before her was an imposter. Quickly her son sensed what she was doing and, like many another veteran, "went off" as he realized that his own mother did not believe or trust him.[3]

Odysseus was absent from home for twenty years. Ten of those were the Trojan War itself. The remaining ten years were . . . what? The only account we have of them is Odysseus' fabulous tales told to the Phaeacian courtiers in Books 9–12. Might they have been ten years at home, but not home? Ten years of wildness, drinking, drugging, living on the edge, violence, sex addiction, not-so-petty crime, and of "bunkering in," becoming unapproachable and withdrawn? If so, would not Odysseus have been just as "absent" a son to Anticleia, just as "absent" a husband to Penelope, and "absent" a father to Telemachus as if he still had been overseas? Could not these ten years have been told in metaphor as the very same story told in the *Odyssey*?

10

What Was the Sirens' Song?:
Truth As Deadly Addiction

[After discharge in 1971] I spent a great deal of time in my old stomping grounds, Oceanside, home of Camp Pendelton Marine Base. . . . I rarely let on that I was a vet. I learned to enjoy hearing the stories told by vets to (what they thought) was a non-vet. A whole new genre emerged. . . .

When I entered the college classrooms in 1977, I met Vvets attending school under the GI Bill. Again, I kept a low profile. I can't believe Vvets say they couldn't talk about the war. That's all they talked about. It seemed that no matter what the subject being discussed, some clown in a boonie hat would throw his shit digger up in the air and somehow make a tie-in to the war. "Excuse me professor, but I was in the Nam, and I can assure you that you don't need a microscope to see amoeba. In the Delta, two of 'em carried off my buddy."

—George "Sonny" Hoffman,[1] "The War Story"

In the years I have been working on *Odysseus in America,* I have asked many people who claimed to have read and loved the *Odyssey* if they remembered what the Sirens were singing about. With the exception of professional classicists, I have never received a correct answer. The overwhelming majority of people incorrectly recall that their song was about sex,[2] with a smaller number saying it was about what was going on at home in Ithaca. Here, in Homer's words, is the answer:

Come this way, honored Odysseus, great glory of the [Greeks],
. . . so that you can listen here to our singing;

for no one else has ever sailed past this place in his black ship
until he has listened to the honey-sweet voice . . .
for we know everything that the [Greeks] and Trojans
did and suffered in wide Troy. . . .
Over all the generous earth we know everything that happens.

(12:184ff, orig., Pucci, trans.[3]; emphasis added)

The Sirens know the complete and final truth about what happened in the Trojan War! It is *the complete truth* that trapped Trojan War veterans on their way home like bees in syrup, and they died. Circe's advance warning about this peril allows Odysseus to stop the ears of his crew with wax and sail safely by:

. . . woe to the innocent who hears that sound!
He will not see his lady nor his children
in joy, crowding about him, home from [war];
the [Sirens] will sing his mind away
on their sweet meadow lolling. There are bones
of dead men rotting in a pile beside them
and flayed skins shrivel around the spot.

(12:50ff, Fitzgerald)

In the language of metaphor, Homer shows us that returning veterans face a characteristic peril, a risk of dying from the obsession to know the complete and final truth of what they and the enemy did and suffered in their war and why. In part, this may be another expression of the visceral commandment to keep faith with the dead. Complete and final truth is an unachievable, toxic quest, which is different from the quest to create meaning for one's experience in a coherent narrative. Veterans can and do achieve the latter.

Linc is a marine veteran of the Vietnam War, who has large gaps in his memory of what happened to his company and what they did during the summer–fall offensive of 1969. For several years— he has come out of it now—his life was organized around trips to the Marine Corps historical archives in Washington, D.C. He photocopied every After Action Report and every entry of the Company

Phaeacian Court
Raid on Ismarus
Lotus Land
Cyclops
King of the Winds
Deadly Fjord
Circe
Among the Dead
➤ **Sirens**
Scylla and Charybdis
Sun God's Cattle
Whirlpool
Calypso
At Home, Ithaca

Diary and Battalion Diary for his unit in the period in question. I can recall spans of months during which he came and went from the Clinic with a gym bag containing the photocopies, afraid to look at them, but unable to part with them even temporarily. He feared what he would find there, things that would inflame his rage, grief, or guilt to unmanageable intensity—but paradoxically, he was also terrified that he would discover that the things he did remember "for sure" were untrue. What if the marine who had died "for" him when the two had exchanged jobs at the last moment had actually died on a different day in different circumstances?

Linc no longer carries his gym bag of historical "truth" with him. He and his individual therapist slowly and patiently worked through its contents. It contained no disorienting surprises; he learned that he could master his emotions.

Nothing is simple, of course. Other things have contributed to his recovery. Linc's trips to obtain Marine Corps records coincided with visits that veterans in our program made to the Vietnam Veterans Memorial, the Wall. In the four years I had known him as a patient prior to this period of two or three years in which trips to the Wall and examination of records took place, he had inhabited only a very few moods or emotions. Sarcasm, cynicism, rage—these were easy and frequent when in the Clinic. Apathy, just staring into space, is how he described his mood at home. Alternations between apathy and rage were the rhythms of his life at the beginning of his participation in our program. But after a few months of contact with the other veterans, a new mood became more and more prevalent: worry about his physical health. Extensive medical workups and careful investigation of these worries failed to reassure him, and he would respond to any "How's things?" with a repetitive droning recitation of his ailments. Some mental health professionals would deny that this was "progress," calling it symptom substitution with hypochondria, but we defined it for ourselves and him as progress, if only because during the decades before he came to the VA, he was a severe, apparently intractable alcoholic—a dilapidated, sleeping-in-the-gutter drunk. This new preoccupation with bodily health was at least basic self-care. While never noted for his sense of humor, he was able to take some teasing about his bodily preoccupations. Even while I paid strict attention to his medical complaints, and referred him for medical evaluation to other physicians within the VA, I began to welcome his recitations of symptoms as musical performances, as "organ recitals," and he could see the humor in my response.

I conduct a monthly wellness and preventive medicine session with the veterans in our program. They are now in their fifties, never having expected to live to twenty-five! Past thirty? Past forty? "Neva happen!" When the future isn't real, why take care of your body? As one veteran put it, "This is the first time I have something to live for, and now—aw, shit!—I'm old and I'm gonna get sick before I can enjoy it." Transient but intense preoccupation with illness, what seems like hypochondria, is partly the utter newness of paying attention to body sensations that previously were numbed out or stoically ignored. It is as though all of the suppressed health worries of thirty years and what came to others as a gradual awareness of the threats of aging hit them all at once. Another veteran said, "After so many years of not feeling anything, this sucks!" Another, who spent many years in abandoned drugging and drinking, now lives in terror of irreversible harm he might have done to his organs, problems that have not yet announced themselves. "When you expect to be dead by next week, you just don't think about what you shoot in your vein or put down your throat," said this other veteran. Linc had been a *very* severe alcoholic, so his constant preoccupation with the state of his bodily organs was not entirely irrational or neurotic.

Photos of Linc from his first trip to the Wall show emotions that he had never allowed. One photo shows his face as a mask of sorrow and grief—emotions he never gave voice to in the Clinic. Another shows him with a grin so big even his eyes are smiling. I had never seen this smile in the years I had worked with him, only an occasional wry, cynical, knowing, they-may-be-trying-to-fuck-me-over-but-I'm-smarter smirk. Apparently the human heart works this way: shut down the pain of grief and you lose the capacity for joy as well. Helen's "anodyne, mild magic of forgetfulness," seems quite sinister in this light.

THE LANGUAGE OF TIMES THAT MAKE A WORLD

As often with great poetry, language carries much that cannot be reduced to the factual or narrative content of the words. Because Homer sang in a special dialect of archaic Greek, we need the help of scholars to "hear" it. The language of the Sirens episode in Odysseus' yarn does more than reinforce the content—the potentially life-sapping snare of obsession with finding the absolute, complete, and final truth—it draws our attention to one aspect of the workings of that obsession. The "voice" of the Sirens, scholars tell us, is the "voice" of the *Iliad*,[4] the voice of a wartime past experienced as more real and meaningful than the present. One veteran speaks of his most painful war memories as "sacred stuff."

There is also a pleasurable[5] side to the use of jargon, speech rhythms, tones of voice that combat veterans take in talking to each other about their experiences. Civilian friends and family members may be by turns bewildered, amazed, bored, and then annoyed by veterans' ability to talk with each other for hours on end about details of weapons that they used, of the contents and texture of different C rations. This is what it sounds like: You never carried a Thumper? I once used a Willy Peter round to fire up a hooch / Bull-sheeet, there wasn't no Willy Peter[6] for the Thumper, you musta put a flare into it, you fucking turkey / Ever see a belt-fed Thumper? That musta been something / Yeah, on our boats it was hand-cranked, but I heard they were putting the automatic ones on the boats, too, but I never saw one, I think they were trying to use the same kind as on the Cobras, but like I said, I never saw one . . . and on, and on.

The speech rhythms, the jargon, the technical minutiae are sometimes the only doorway a veteran finds into the rooms full of pain that they carry: Farmer, the veteran of the brown water Navy we met above in Chapter 6, once spoke at length in group therapy about the 20mm cannon in the turret of his boat. This powerful weapon helped Farmer and his comrades survive. The cannon had originally been designed as a World War II aircraft dogfighting and ground attack weapon, to function in the well-cooled setting of an aircraft in flight. (Years later he and I stood silently together, in the World War II museum in the Marine base at Quantico, staring at a display of this weapon and the entire aircraft in which it had been so successfully used.)

However, the riverine model could also kill or maim the sailor using it. These guns were not suited to steamy tropical rivers where they overheated and jammed. When they jammed, they had to be cleared by hand by the gunner in the turret. The heat of the gun barrel added to the extreme environmental heat, for which the ammunition had never been designed, causing jammed rounds to "cook off," i.e., to explode. A friend of Farmer's named ———, "the nicest guy in the whole division," had requested transfer from the flamethrower on his boat to the 20mm cannon, because the flame weapon horrified him.

Farmer's personal log notes the visit of Secretary of Defense Melvin Laird around Christmas. A weapons demonstration—a show—was put on for the secretary, during which ———'s cannon jammed. He cleared the weapon, and as he held the round up to throw it out the turret hatch, it exploded, blowing all the fingers off his right hand and destroying the right side of his face and right eye. Farmer carried this needless waste in his belly like something curdled, until he was able to talk about it to his brother veterans. The language of weapons, of the military setting, was his doorway into the traumatic material of his friend's maiming, and his sense of betrayal that it was not in battle against the enemy, but as part of a show for a dignitary.

MEMORY UNCONNECTED TO COMMUNITY

One of the good things that marine veteran Linc did for himself (with our vigorous encouragement) was to start attending ———— Marine Division Association reunions, attempting to find people from his unit. He has become progressively more engaged with the unit association. The social nourishment it gives him has eroded much of his habitual bitterness and expanded the scope of his life. The absolute truth of the Trojan War that the Sirens sang was utterly detached from any community that remembers and retells it. Instead of nourishing and sustaining, it killed—much like crack cocaine sometimes kills—by starvation.

One source of obsessive attraction to the Sirens could be their appeal to the veteran's vanity. Certainly, the Sirens are blowing smoke when they address Odysseus as the "great glory of the [Greeks]." At this point after the fall of Troy, and considering how and why Troy fell, Odysseus certainly deserves this greeting. But the flattery of it is what scholars Frederick Ahl and Hanna Roisman have in mind when they write that the seductive power of the Sirens' song was "the musical reenactment of his own past, his own self, his own reflection, his own narcissism."[7] However, another scholar, Pietro Pucci, offers a different slant, which I have sometimes heard confirmed in the veterans' words. Pucci writes: "The Siren's invitation and promise . . . is 'written' in strictly Iliadic diction. . . . The paralyzing effects . . . [are] because their song binds its listeners obsessively to the fascination of death."[8]

I have heard a marine veteran of Vietnam say, "I never expected to come home alive. We were marines. Marines die. That's what we do. *I think I failed.*" What this marine veteran refers to is the sacrificial cult of the "beautiful death" that is part of the Marine Corps culture. Marines give their lives willingly, it says, so that the battle and the war can be won quickly, sparing so many more lives that would be lost in a slow slugging match of attrition. In some settings, especially in wartime, this has blurred over into a cult of death, akin to Japanese *bushido*. Some readers of the *Iliad* come away with the idea that it is the original militaristic document praising the "beautiful death" of the hero in battle and thus praising war itself, totally missing its antiwar, tragic message.[9] But as a portrait of how the story of a war can "bind its [veteran] listeners obsessively to the fascination of death," Professor Pucci's observation is on the mark.

TOTAL CERTAINTY IS JUST AS DAMAGING

Linc's obsession was to *find* the absolute, complete, and final truth. He did not find it. But he now has his own narrative, his own understanding of what he was part of. He is intensely interested when he meets someone from his company who remembers something he has forgotten or never knew or even contradicts some aspect of his own narrative. His life-sapping obsession to fill a void of forgotten experience with absolute truth has moderated to a life-sustaining sense of belonging to a community with a meaningful history, his friends in the ———— Marine Division Association. Human memory is physical in the brain, psychological, social, and cultural—it is all of these things at every moment.

The Greek word for truth, *alēthea,* means literally that which is unforgotten (*a*—not + *lēthe*—forgetting). Homer's near contemporary Hesiod represents *Lēthe* as a divine personification of forgetfulness. The word *lēthe* appears at *Iliad* 2:33 meaning forgetfulness, but never appears as a goddess or a river. Remembering that Odysseus has just come from Hades when he encounters the Sirens, we can see an intriguing interpretation—he just escaped the land of Death and its river *Lēthe* and the very next mortal danger he faces is *alēthea* so seductive he risks death hearing it. First he escapes forgetfulness and then he escapes its opposite, absolute truth. We do not know if Homer believed *Lēthe* was around Hades, as is familiar to us from Plato's *Republic,*[10] hundreds of years after Homer, and from Milton's geography of Hell in *Paradise Lost:* "*Lēthe* the River of Oblivion."[11] According to a study by the French scholar Marcel Detienne, called *The Masters of Truth in Archaic Greece,* "*Alēthea* is . . . structured around the major opposition between memory and oblivion."[12] Particular types of men—the seer, the bard, and the "king of justice"—were "masters of truth." Curiously, the Sirens only "speak of 'knowing,'" as scholar Charles Segal has observed, never "of 'memory' or of 'remembering.'"[13]

This is no small distinction, because much still hinges today upon whose understanding of the war and its consequences becomes generally accepted Truth. Who are the masters of truth on the Vietnam War? This war lies in our midst like a dead elephant being torn apart by hyenas—

who then fight viciously among themselves for control of the nutrient-rich carcass.

The modern world has its own masters of truth, some of them very public and visible, like judges and broadcast media commentators. Others are faceless, anonymous bureaucrats who "adjudicate"[14] veterans' disability claims.

Doc, both a conventional nickname for a medic and here a pseudonym, was one of two suicides "on my watch" during the fourteen years I have been the psychiatrist for our specialized intensive outpatient treatment program for Vietnam combat veterans with PTSD.

Doc volunteered for the U.S. Army in 1964, and trained at Fort Sam Houston as a medical corpsman. He then served in Germany and upon reenlistment in 1967 volunteered for duty in Vietnam. Doc arrived in Vietnam in June 1967, and was assigned to the Military Assistance Command as a medical adviser, based in a military compound in Hue City. The five-man advisory unit traveled with an ARVN (South Vietnamese Army) unit up and down Highway 1 as far as the DMZ in the north and Phu Loc in the south. These movements along Highway 1 invited repeated ambushes, mortar attacks, and mine explosions. The American advisory unit became extremely close-knit, because they found that in a firefight the ARVN abandoned them and that they could only rely on themselves. During one such ambush four of the five men on the team were hit, two died immediately and two survived, but Doc, the only one not hit, felt then and until he killed himself, that he should have kept his two dead buddies alive.

The Tet Offensive started in Hue City on January 31, 1968, with heavy rocket and mortar barrages followed by ground assaults on their compound within the city. At first light the American soldiers in the compound could see numerous Viet Cong and NVA (North Vietnamese Army) flags surrounding it. The next six days, surrounded and cut off, they went utterly without sleep under constant rocket and mortar bombardment and repeated ground assault. The incoming rounds formed the content of Doc's hallucinatory reliving experiences ("flashbacks"), triggered by firecrackers or other sharp loud noises. Three of the five U.S. medics in the compound were killed, two of them close friends. Doc recalled feeling overwhelmed by the number of casualties, and his inability to evacuate them. In particular, he was torn up by the number who died under his care, who would have lived had it been possible to evacuate them.

During the six days of encirclement, before the Americans in the compound were relieved by the marines, an episode happened that formed the basis of the veteran's most frequent repetitive traumatic dream: He was standing next to the captain, when within a second both he and the captain were hit by snipers' bullets. Both went down together. The side of the captain's neck was ripped open and the blood spurted in Doc's face and drenched his shirt. Though wounded himself (he received the Purple Heart for this occasion), Doc carried on his duties as a medic. When the marines broke through, he refused to be evacuated and accompanied a Marine unit whose medic had been killed. This led to twelve days of house-to-house combat as the marines retook the city. There were heavy marine casualties, to whom Doc ministered under fire. He was present at the discovery of mass graves of those executed by the VC and NVA. These masses of dead and mutilated bodies also figure in his repetitive nightmares.

Doc was honored with two Bronze Stars, with the Vietnamese Cross for Gallantry, and the Army Commendation Medal for Valor, in addition to receiving a Purple Heart and the Combat Medic Badge.

Prior to Vietnam, Doc didn't drink and had never experimented with drugs, but after Tet, while still in the service, he became a heavy drinker and a steady user of marijuana and heroin to shut out grief and suppress flashbacks and nightmares. When he was honorably discharged from the Army in June 1969, he was heavily addicted to alcohol and heroin.

After discharge, Doc drifted from one menial job to another, holding and losing over fifty in twenty years. He married three times, each marriage ending because of PTSD and substance abuse. His self-medication of PTSD with alcohol, heroin, and then IV cocaine was partially successful, especially in controlling nightmares and flashbacks. Starting in 1975, he repeatedly sought treatment, with numerous hospitalizations and detox. On every occasion, withdrawal from alcohol and drugs was followed by a resurgence of PTSD symptoms. After completion of the most recent hospital drug abuse treatment, starting in May of 1988, he was transferred to a psychiatry unit, because of reemergence of PTSD symptoms. Previously he had been discharged with no PTSD treatment, only further drug abuse treatment. He was discharged from the psychiatry ward to a halfway house and referred to our specialized outpatient combat PTSD program. Following this final hospital admission Doc remained sober and "clean" for the next three years, until a single, fatal heroin overdose, shortly after his claim for a disability pension for combat PTSD was rejected.

The coroner signed off the overdose death as accidental, but I believe Doc was too sophisticated, both as a heroin addict and as a paramedic, not

to know that he had lost his drug tolerance during the long period of absti-
nence. His "normal" dose as a hard-core, daily IV heroin addict was a lethal
dose to the recovered addict without a tolerance. I believe he intentionally killed himself in despair, anger, and humiliation after the value of his
service was—in his eyes—"officially" rejected by the VA.

The masters of truth in the government bureaucracy followed "objective" procedures and observed "objective" criteria that led them to conclude that he had been disabled by his own "willful misconduct" in drug
and alcohol abuse, not by psychological injury in the line of duty in service to his country and fellow soldiers. Whereas Linc died figuratively for
a few years in quest of the absolute truth, Doc literally died by his own
hand in response to what he apparently experienced as others' possession of the absolute truth—that his war service had not injured him, only
his own misbehavior. He was humiliated and dishonored by the official
action. The "masters of truth" had found him unworthy.

German veterans after defeat in World War I, who inhabited the
absolute truth of the *"Dolchstoss von hinten"*—the "stab in the back" by
traitors inside the government and the army—were willing to kill someone who said that Germany had been beaten fair and square by the
British, French, and their late-coming allies, the Americans. They felt
personally attacked and dishonored by the suggestion that they had been
bested, rather than betrayed.[15]

Dishonor arouses the desire to kill—self or others, sometimes both.
Honor and dishonor are social processes, which declares "the truth " of a
person's or group's worth. What kind of truth is it that induces an addict's
craving for it when absent, as if for cocaine, and produces an arrogant, violent, paranoid state when possessed? I wish I could answer this question.
It goes to the heart of extremist religious and political movements. We can
recognize this lethal intoxication with absolute truth in Timothy McVeigh,
Osama bin Laden, and Jewish law student Yigal Amir, the assassin of Prime
Minister Yitzhak Rabin. Veterans' tragic experiences render their own
reckonings of ultimate truth and worth so very hard for them and so explosive. People will kill for it, and will die for it, as the metaphor of the bodies moldering in the Sirens' meadow shows.

11

Scylla and Charybdis:
Dangers Up, Down, and Sideways

Recall that Odysseus vowed to return to Circe's island to give Elpenor a proper burial. Circe wines and dines the crew and pulls Odysseus aside to give him more sailing instructions. She tells him about the Sirens' trap, and how to waltz past it using wax earplugs. Then she warns him of the narrow strait beyond: on the left are breakers, hull-tearing rocks, and a fearsome whirlpool called Charybdis; on the right is a sheer cliff, home to the cave-dwelling six-headed monster Scylla. The two deadly hazards are "side-by-side, an arrow-shot apart"[1] across the strait. She advises him to make a dash for it under Scylla's lair, instead of losing the whole ship in the whirlpool. If he makes it through the strait, the next landfall is the sun god's cattle ranch on the island of Thrinacia. She repeats the warning Teiresias had given Odysseus in the Underworld not to touch the god's fat beef cattle.

Americans in Vietnam fought against the "finest light infantry in the world."[2] A part of what made them the finest was their mastery—even within their limited technologies and resources—of what is known as "combined arms." This is the military competence and mental discipline to create a Scylla and Charybdis for the enemy, and doing it so fast or so unpredictably that the enemy loses his grip on the situation and freezes or panics and the attacked unit comes apart. It's no exaggeration to say that persistent, skillful use of combined arms drives the enemy insane. An

American column of half-tracks on a road encounters mines—slow down and sweep the mines!—and at the same time a barrage of rocket-propelled grenades—speed through the killing zone as fast as you can! These two tactical responses, slowing down and speeding up, are incompatible, and both bad, Scylla and Charybdis. American infantry patrols encountered ambush sites where the vegetation on either side of the trail was prepared with punji stakes—concealed needle-sharp bamboo or metal stakes set in the ground or wooden planks pointing up—for the soldiers or marines to impale themselves on when they dove for cover to avoid rifle fire from their front. Scylla and Charybdis.

Some veterans I work with never allow themselves a moment of satisfied relaxation after successfully meeting any challenge, such as making the car payments, or fixing a burst washing machine hose, because, they say, there is always something more they have to prepare themselves to meet. Here again is the persistence into civilian life of adaptations that allowed the veteran to survive in battle.

As usual, Homer's gold is to be mined from details of the text. Circe counsels Odysseus—

> Hug Scylla's crag—sail on past her—top speed!
> Better by far to lose six men and keep your ship
> Than lose your entire crew.
>
> (12:118ff, Fagles)

Odysseus bridles at this coward's dash and asks her if he can't just steer away from the whirlpool and fight off the monster. To this she replies—

> Must you have battle in your heart forever?
> The bloody toil of combat? Old Contender,
> will you not yield to the immortal gods?
> That nightmare cannot die, being eternal
> Evil itself—horror, and pain, and chaos;
> there is no fighting her . . .
> all that avails is flight.
> *Lose headway there*
> *. . . while you break out arms,*
> and she'll swoop over you . . .
> taking one man for every gullet.
>
> (12:136–45, Fitzgerald; emphasis added)

Circe tells Odysseus that apart from headlong flight, there is no chance of surviving an encounter with "eternal Evil itself." She asks him if he must have battle in his heart forever, responding to *every* danger that the world presents with resort to heroic feats of arms. Even though Odysseus responds to her advice—remember, she is a minor goddess and knows what she's talking about—with a salute and a "Yes, Ma'am," when he actually reaches the spot, he ignores her advice. His answer to her question whether he'll have battle in his heart forever is—yes. This quotation, along with Circe's perceptive picture of the veteran's "haggard spirit," brings together so many elements of combat PTSD—battle forever, nightmare, eternal evil, the sense of helplessness—that I am tempted to smirk like the cat that swallowed the canary. After this, how can anyone *not* see the connection with combat veterans?

But like Odysseus, I go forward . . . Odysseus reaches the narrows,

> *But now I cleared my mind of Circe's orders—*
> *Cramping my style, urging me not to arm at all.*
> *I donned my heroic armor.*
>
> . . .
>
> Now wailing in fear, we rowed up these straits,
> Scylla to starboard, dreaded Charybdis off to port. . . .
> When she[3] swallowed the sea surge down her gaping maw
> the whole abyss lay bare and the rocks around her roared . . .
> bedrock showed down deep, boiling
> black with sand—
> and ashen terror gripped the men.
> But now, fearing death, all eyes fixed on Charybdis—
> now Scylla snatched six men from our hollow ship.
>
> (12:245ff, Fagles; emphasis added)

Odysseus is the only one who knows the danger of Scylla, having decided not to mention her to his men. This means that he alone can be on the lookout against her sudden appearance. But along with everyone else on board he becomes riveted by the sucking vortex below and to the left and misses Scylla's first attack. Odysseus only turns in time to see six of his crewmen drawn upward, writhing like hooked fish at the ends of the monster's six long necks.

The poet throws dangers at this terrified crew from left and right, above and below. Veterans have described their own need to "wail in fear" when ambushed in a particularly skillful way, using combined arms: mortars and grenades from above, mines and punji stakes below, and automatic fire from the side and front. I've already commented above in Chapter 7 on some veterans' expectancy of attack from any direction, or as with Odysseus' ship, *all* directions.

As a metaphor for some combat veterans' response to the civilian world, this episode has a number of unfortunate echoes. Various powers in the civilian world—the police, the IRS, an employer's personnel department, the Department of Social Services, the Social Security Administration, the Veterans Administration, the gas company, the electric company, the telephone company, the Department of Motor Vehicles, the criminal courts, the divorce courts, the bank that financed the pickup, the company that insured it, the agency that financed the college loan, the collection agency, the ex-wife's lawyer—these all seem to have the capacity to swoop out of the sky and snatch the veteran, writhing, and carry him to some dark place to devour him. In such a state of vulnerability, they often want to do what Odysseus did, to arm themselves and fight the foe the only way they know how. Direct, courageous, armed action that we associate with military heroism is wildly out of place. There is literally no place for it.[4]

Scholars have debated whether six more of his men die horrible deaths because Odysseus cannot take Circe's instruction, or whether the first six were unavoidable. Her advice runs counter to *his* way of doing things.[5] Does he risk his life for them when he dons his armor, or risk *their* lives? Possibly he will lose six *no matter what* he does (12:109f, orig.). Scholar Alfred Heubeck clucks his tongue at Odysseus as if to say, "heroes will be heroes"—

His heroic stature is no more diminished by his ignoring of a warning . . . than by his clever tactics towards his own men [i.e., keeping them in the dark]. Ignoring all that he knows of [Scylla], Odysseus attempts the impossible and foolish because it is also the heroic. He must be true to his own nature, and, faced with a hopeless situation, nevertheless risks his own life for the sake of his men.

The heroic gesture of arming against an [unpreventable disaster] in a world where there is no place for the heroic, is here almost grotesque, but it also vividly illustrates the tragedy of the hero with his limited outlook.[6]

12

The Sun God's Beef: The Blame Game

Six shipmates lost at Ismarus, six more to the Cyclops, then eleven entire ships and crews destroyed in the fjord, now six more shipmates snatched by Scylla. More than 550 deaths have occurred before the remaining ship reaches the island where the sun god keeps his cattle. Recall that the narrator has blamed Odysseus' men—all of them—for their own destruction, because they had transgressed by eating the god's sacred beef:

> But [Odysseus] could not save them from disaster, hard as he strove—
> the recklessness of their own ways destroyed them all,
> the blind fools, they devoured the cattle of the Sun
> and the Sun god blotted out the day of their return.
>
> (1:7–10, Fagles)

Odysseus has been warned authoritatively, warned twice (by both Teiresias and Circe) not to molest the herds belonging to the sun god on the island of Thrinacia, which now heaves into sight after the horrors of the strait. True to form, Odysseus has not shared this knowledge with his crew and only tells them in general terms—forcefully to be sure—"the worst disaster awaits us."[1] He orders them to just row right on by.

He says nothing about the sun god's cattle, even though the sailors can hear them mooing across the water. The men are exhausted, strung out from their latest near-death experience, and they see nothing wrong with camping for the night on this green shore. They have food, but these men *love* beef.[2] Even though he knows how his men are drooling at the thought of spitted roast, Odysseus doesn't tell his men not to touch the cattle or the reason why—don't mess with a god! His kinsman Eurylochus[3] complains about their fatigue and the risks of sailing at night in stormy unknown waters:

> Night falling fast, you'd have us desert
> this haven and blunder off into the mist-bound seas?
> Out of the night come winds that shatter vessels.
>
> (12:308ff, Fagles)

Now Odysseus finally mentions the cattle—he makes his men take an oath not to kill them—but without explaining the prophecy from Teiresias and Circe that the sun god will slaughter all the men if they take any of his cattle. Why does he not tell them the most important, life-or-death facts? The text gives no explanation. It appears to be part of Odysseus' leadership philosophy to be an information miser, disclosing to his subordinates only what he absolutely must, and sometimes not even that.

Odysseus relents, and they land on Thrinacia, but he has set up Eurylochus to take the blame from his audience and from "history." He has warned the men not to land there, "But Eurylochus waded in at once— with mutiny on his mind" (12:301, Fagles). What Eurylochus said was hardly mutinous, it's simply stating the facts: the crew is half dead with fatigue and sleep deprivation, night is falling, and storms can wreck ships in the dark (12:305ff, Fagles). It is typical Homeric irony that we have been led to see Eurylochus as a whiner who just wants to bed down, but we learn a few lines later that during the night, just as Eurylochus had warned, "Zeus . . . loosed a ripping wind, a howling demonic gale"[4] (12:138f, Fagles).

Previously, in Book 10 (line 437, orig.), Homer again put the truth in the mouth of the same low-prestige player, when the not-very-heroic Eurylochus blurted out that Odysseus' calling his crew to feast in Circe's palace was leading them into another death trap like the Cyclops' cave. He explicitly blames the deaths in the cave on Odysseus' *atasthaliai*—wanton recklessness. This is more vintage Homeric irony, because this same word, *atasthaliai*, is used in the prologue to explain that the death of Odysseus' men was their own fault, thereby acquitting him of any blame. We shall see below that Homer has a discredited voice speak the truth again near the end of the epic when he has the father of Antinous, the most despicable suitor, say that Odysseus has killed two generations of the town's youth.[5] He has!

The next morning, finally, Odysseus tells his men that the cattle belong to Helios, the sun god. But now begins a solid month of powerful, non-stop southwest winds that lock them against the shore. Homer's audience would have been reminded of the horror that *opened* the Trojan War, Agamemnon's sacrifice of his daughter Iphigenia to free the wind-locked fleet at Aulis, allowing them to begin their amphibious operation against Troy.

The ship's company begins to run out of the food that Circe had given them, and they have to hunt birds, small game, and fish for their food. Apparently they do not have enough; hunger is getting to them, but the text is a bit unclear as to whether the main problem is that their food is not to their taste, or that there is not enough of it.[6] Odysseus picks this moment, when he knows full well that they are getting desperate—to take a long walk in the countryside to find a quiet place to pray! On top of that he takes a quiet nap, blaming that on the gods.[7] Again scholars Ahl and Roisman are skeptical:

> Under the pretext of piety, Odysseus seeks to absolve himself of responsibility for his comrades' act. . . . Yet the nap he takes . . . lasts long enough not only for Eurylochus to make a subversive speech to the crew . . . to kill the cattle, but long enough to allow for the killing, flaying, roasting, and consuming.[8]

These scholars conclude that "the whole point of the story is that Odysseus will remain guiltless. . . . In the course of his self-exculpation, elements show through which cast doubt on his pose of guiltlessness."[9] The biblical book Exodus contains an intriguing parallel. While Moses is away from the people on Mount Sinai, his kinsman, Aaron, leads the people into trouble with another form of sacred beef, the Golden Calf.[10] However, there is no irony in the biblical account, and no doubt that Moses' hands are clean.

Odysseus speaks to the Phaeacian court in his own voice, saying in effect that there is no reason for them to think less of him, arriving there, his entire command lost. It was his companions' fault, not his! But why does the *narrator*, the poet himself, single out felonious feasting on Sun-brand beef as the cause of six hundred deaths, when at least 550 are already dead? Why does the narrator transfer blame for the catastrophic Ithacan losses after the war was already over?

The men I work with in the VA Clinic have vast stores of bitterness over being blamed for the U.S. defeat in Vietnam. They feel that those really responsible have weaseled out of taking responsibility and the blame—people such as Secretary of Defense Robert McNamara, President Lyndon Johnson, and National Security Adviser/Secretary of State Henry Kissinger, as well as the spineless senior military leadership.[11] Veterans were confronted with intergenerational blame when World War II veterans crudely spurned them with taunts that, unlike themselves, Vietnam soldiers had lost their war. The prejudicial doped-up, violent, crazy "Vietnam Vet Stereotype" further created the idea that the men who fought in Vietnam were themselves solely responsible for how badly it turned out.

WHY ODYSSEUS' ADVENTURES ARE AN IRONIC ALLEGORY

The tension between the life experience of Odysseus, a veteran of prolonged heavy combat, and the pampered lives of safe, complacent civilian Phaeacians gives rise to the fairy-tale atmosphere and content of *Odyssey* Books 9–12. I have made this case from the text alone, without reference to any speculations on the Homeric poets' own ways of making a living and being influenced by what their customers wanted to hear.

Up to this point I have spoken of "Homer" as if there were a single person, like Shakespeare, who created these massive epics. The consensus of scholars is that the epics were originally *oral* narratives composed in performance by traditional bards using a store of traditional stories, stock scenes, stock lines, and groups of lines ("formulae"). While there might have been one or more Shakespeare-class towering geniuses among them, there was no single Homer, and he never wrote either the *Iliad* or the *Odyssey*. There were no audio recordings—*somebody* wrote them down. The written epics as we have them were the product of cultural-political editing during the seventh and sixth centuries B.C.E.—with bards continuing to perform them all the while. In Athens this culminated in an official text that became part of the religious life of the city. Homer's epics were performed to crowds in the thousands during the main summer festival, the Panathenaea, by professional Homeric singers known as rhapsodes. Plato's short dialogue *Ion* gives a sketch portrait of a rhapsode and a public festival performance. The epic texts we have are canonical in the same way and from the same kind of official editing as the written books of the Old Testament were edited by high-level committees over a couple hundred years. To avoid the clumsy wording "Homeric poets" in this book, I've referred to "Homer" as if I were speaking of a single artist. But the reader should understand this to mean the whole class of performers who gave rise to our written texts.

To return to my speculations on how the interaction between the Homeric poets and their customers shaped the two epics—even though

we're unlikely ever to have evidence to disprove or prove any of them—
here is my just-so story[12]:

The *Iliad* was a masterpiece by artists who themselves personally had
"been there, done that" in war and sang about it for their comrades. I
believe that the first customers or audience for the *Iliad* were other
combat veterans whose wealth and political legitimacy as leaders of an
emerging *polis* ("city-state") were based on their *personal* accomplish-
ments in military prowess and "counsel"—i.e., good tactical and strategic
advice. These leaders also had the resources to pay the bards. In this sce-
nario, the audience for the *Iliad* was both the product of and advocate for
meritocracy. The people in charge, those getting the most honor and most
rewards, had gotten there by showing themselves to be "the best" through
their own achievements.

However, an alternative system of fixed, inherited[13] status hierarchy
was known and available in the world of the *Iliad*'s performers and audiences. That's what Agamemnon stood for and embodied as the king of
Mycenae. It is reasonable to expect that they were also aware of hereditary monarchies in Egypt and Asia Minor.[14] Agamemnon and his brother
Menelaus were not only "old money" and "royals," their supporters such
as Odysseus also proclaimed divine sanction for their preeminence (e.g.,
Iliad 2:214ff and 236ff, Fagles). These two settings, *polis* and aristocratic
court, shaped the *Iliad* and *Odyssey* respectively, according to my spec-
ulation, and both poems were performed in both settings by the same
itinerant combat-veteran bards.

The *Iliad* painted a very unflattering portrait of Agamemnon and the
fixed aristocratic hierarchy.[15] I imagine the meritocrats lapping it up.
Achilles, with whom the meritocrats identified, shines by comparison. In
the *Iliad*, Odysseus is Agamemnon's lapdog, carrying out, justifying, and
when possible repairing the damage from his boss's caprices. Neither
epic shows much interest in a nonelite *dēmos*, the tensions being played
out between two competing elites. Members of the meritocratic elite
saw themselves as fundamentally one another's equals, who struggled
among themselves for *timē*, that is, for status or honor.[16]

However, from roughly 800 to 500 B.C.E., the bards who performed the
Iliad had a *second* customer base made up of those very royals who
looked so bad in the *Iliad*. The *Odyssey*'s Phaeacian court may be an ide-
alized picture of these royals.[17] Greece and the Ionian coast were a patch-
work of *polis* and monarchy, constantly at war with each other in constantly
shifting alliances, with city-states and monarchies sometimes experiencing revolutions from one form into the other.

What's missing from the courtly picture of the make-believe Land of the Phaeacians in *Odyssey* 6–13 is the high-performance soldiers who in the real world would have fought its battles and kept it in power.[18] These same soldiers, fifty miles away, could have been meritocratic leaders of a *polis,* or formerly were such, but had hired out to a king. My just-so story has the same bards circulating between *both* settings. The same seen-the-elephant veterans were present in both settings—as the leaders and bill payers in the *polis,* and as subordinate retainers to the bill-paying kings in the courts. (A veteran who has actually been in combat, not having served only in peacetime or only in the rear during war, is said to have "seen the elephant.") The great performers played both venues.

This just-so story relates to the present allegorical reading of the *Odyssey* in the following way: in the kings' courts I imagine the bards playing to *two* audiences—the paying audience of rich, Phaeacian-like royals and a wink-and-a-nod audience of former or current fighters in their court who *have* seen the elephant. I imagine a poet winking at some of the grizzled veterans in the course of a performance, much like the veteran in Sonny Hoffman's "The War Story" (quoted above at the beginning of the Sirens chapter) might have winked at another G.I. Bill veteran in the classroom when he said that two amoebae had carried off his buddy in Vietnam. I believe the dual audience for the *Odyssey* gives it its distinctive character.

In the *Iliad,* the gods are arbitrary, heartless, capricious, and unconcerned with justice. The combat vets of the Homeric poets' original audience had no need or desire to justify the ways of the All-Powerful, or the very powerful, to man. To them, the idea of divine justice was a joke. In my clinical practice, veterans of prolonged combat mostly found that the chaos and rolling dice of war made such an idea absurd. However, in a royal court, I speculate that the bards (like Odysseus among the Phaeacians) had to watch their step and play to the ideological self-justification of the kings and their gods. The *Odyssey* proclaims the justice of the gods (and by association the kings who claimed divine descent or saction), and proclaims that if anything went wrong in one of the king's wars, the enlisted men were to blame.[19]

When the bards sang in court, the royals would not have noticed that the bards *showed* Odysseus to be at fault, as long as they loudly and repeatedly proclaimed that someone else was to blame. For this audience, Homer adopts Odysseus' perspective, which is that of the kings. But the old veterans would have noticed and smiled their wry smiles.

If we accept this tension between the powerful paying audience of complacent hereditary kings and the wink-and-a-nod audience of old veterans listening in the shadows of the great hall, the *Odyssey* can be seen as an *ironic* allegory of exactly what it says it is, a veteran's homecoming. It is entertainment for the royals, and communalization for the veterans.

13

Above the Whirlpool

Odysseus awakes from his pious nap with a sense of dread and hurries back to the sun god's beach where the ship is hauled up. He can smell roasting beef even before he sights the ship. He scolds and upbraids his crew, but the damage is done. The god's sacred cattle lie dead next to the roasting pit. The cuts of meat sizzling on the spit moo spooky reproaches at them all.

Meanwhile on Mount Olympus, the sun god rants and threatens Zeus with cosmic consequences if he doesn't take action. A week later, Zeus quiets the winds that pin Odysseus and his crew to the shore. Like a shot, the men get the boat launched, rigged, and out to sea toward home.

Once they're beyond sight of land, Zeus makes good on his promise to the sun god and builds a giant thunderhead above the ship. The squall hits, shredding the sail and rigging, toppling the mast, then blasting the hull with a giant thunderbolt. Everyone who is not killed out-right is drowned in the waves—except for Odysseus. He improvises a life raft from the mast and keel, hanging on till the squall passes. But a powerful wind springs up blowing him back, back—to the narrows between Scylla and Charybdis! Just as the giant whirlpool seizes his raft, Odysseus grabs for the branch of an ancient fig tree overhanging the strait.

> like a bat I clung . . . for dear life—not a chance
> for a good firm foothold. . . .
> But I held on, dead set . . .
>
> (12:467ff, Fagles)

There's the image that interests me: the veteran clinging to sanity above the sucking whirlpool of rage and grief, fear, guilt, and despair—*and* of all the destructive ways that humans act on these vehement emotions. What's at the bottom of that vortex? Death by suicide, death from the myriad ways that drugs and alcohol can kill, death from risks gone bad—in fights, crashes, shootouts, falls, death from neglect of self-care, death as the end of a prison life sentence. Yet most of the veterans I have worked with have hung on, or they wouldn't be alive to be my patients thirty-plus years later. Like Odysseus, they are survivors.

I believe that nearly every veteran who returns to civilian life after a long time in combat has moments in which he is afraid he is losing his mind. Let me be clear: not everyone carries permanent psychological injuries from combat, but I believe that everyone who makes the transition from battle to home—especially if the transition is made quickly—fears for his sanity at some point. This may only be when he awakens from a nightmare, or when he notices that he senses danger around every corner.

The World War II generation is famous for its stoical silence on post-combat thoughts and emotions, a silence that has only recently begun to thaw. There are many reasons for the World War II veterans' spirit of stiff upper lip, or only-tell-the-funny-or-uplifting stories. That generation had spent their formative years in the Great Depression. Their generational experience taught them what Woody Guthrie gave voice in his mistrustful "Dodger Song," which rings the changes through candidates, lawyers, preachers, farmers, and generals, calling them all dodgers.[1] This bleak song not only doubts the goodwill and good intentions of society's power holders, but with the words "and I'm a dodger, too," acknowledges the thousand little and large betrayals of "what's right" that poverty tortures out of the desperately poor. If Woody Guthrie reports truthfully on the Depression, the World War II generation did not go to war thinking itself all that righteous and pure, thinking that it had upheld every word of the Boy Scout Law, "Trustworthy, Loyal, Helpful, Friendly, Courteous, Kind, Obedient, Cheerful, Thrifty, Brave, Clean, Reverent." The World War II generation didn't expect as much fairness, rationality, or honesty as their children who went to Vietnam did. It's my impression that the films of the 1930s are full of crooked cops and corrupt public officials who mysteriously disappear from the films and television series of the 1950s that the Vietnam generation grew up watching.

The culture of the post–World War II period also conferred enormous prestige on the model of rationality recommended by the ancient Greek and Roman Stoics: *any* emotion weakens reason and virtue, so root out emotion from your soul. A story is told about General George C. Marshall, possibly the most admired American of his generation. It goes like this: After some big news (perhaps it was the Berlin Blockade) a reporter asked General Marshall what his feelings were, to which the general is said to have replied, "You ask me about my feelings. I can tell you that I have no feelings on this or any other matter, except for those I reserve for Mrs. Marshall, which I shall not discuss." I have been unable to verify this possibly apocryphal story, yet I tell it because it distills the Stoic posture toward emotion that ruled the imagination of American elites of that period. Veterans of the time were much more willing to embrace the norms of the elites than their sons were upon return from Vietnam. I speculate that the reasons for this are multiple. The fathers' generation found themselves getting richer in the 1950s than their youth had led them to expect and credited the elites for it; the sons got poorer than they expected and blamed the elites for it. The fathers feared being labeled Commies if they disagreed with the elites and self-censored; the sons had lost their fear and criticized freely.

A major unwritten chapter of the American history of World War II represents another factor silencing its veterans. I believe that the huge "neuropsychiatric" hospitals built by the Veterans Administration after that war loomed as a warning in the minds of World War II combat veterans: "If you talk about what's going on in your head, tell anyone the anger seething in your belly, or what's in your dreams, they'll put you away and you'll never come out." Most of the story of these multi-thousand-bed hospitals, and particularly their impact on veterans who were *not* hospitalized there, has never been told.

By 1970, when the bulk of Vietnam veterans had already returned from the war, the situation for them was worse than it had been for their fathers, in terms of a supportive community in which to digest their experiences, because of the intense struggle over the wisdom and legitimacy of the war itself and how it was being conducted. So most veterans had to face their nightmares, their storms of fear and rage, their visitations by the dead, their lacerating guilt, alone. Many doubted their sanity and hung solitary above the whirlpool.

GUILT AND GOOD CHARACTER[2]

Much of what I have reported about veterans' guilt, both here and in *Achilles in Vietnam,* has pertained to veterans' moral anguish over what they did or did not do with regard to their American comrades. Horrific things done to enemy soldiers and civilians have great power to injure the mind and spirit of those who have done them. The recent controversy concerning former U.S. Senator Bob Kerrey's Vietnam service as a Navy SEAL brings many important aspects of this into focus.

In the spring of 2001, *The New York Times Magazine* broke the story of the 1969 killing of at least thirteen unarmed Vietnamese women and children in Thanh Phong, in the Mekong River Delta in Vietnam.[3] The article and the news coverage that followed over the next weeks and months gave Bob Kerrey's pain-filled account, and the competing narrative by fellow squad member Gerhard Klann. Kerrey's team was inserted near this hamlet (from just such riverboats as the veterans Wiry and Farmer served on) to kill or capture an important Viet Cong commander. Here are the two competing accounts of what happened: Kerrey says the team was fired on in the dark. He says they returned the fire, and when they came forward to look, they found numerous dead women and children. Klann says that they got into the hamlet, didn't find their target, but did find a dozen or so women and children. Klann is quoted as saying, "Our chances would have been slim to none to get out alive"[4] if they had let the villagers live to call in their own forces to kill or capture the Americans during their retreat. Kerrey tells it as a horrible accident in the dark; Klann frames it as "us-or-them," and says that Kerrey gave the order, "them."

It would be no exaggeration to say that the guilt and remorse of such acts of war can drive veterans insane after they get home. A number of veterans I work with have suffered greatly in this regard. When other people hear these veterans speak of it—and most veterans with such things on their souls keep silent, both for fear of condemnation and fear of hurting others with their terrible knowledge—they usually get one of the following black-or-white responses:

1. War is hell. There are no "rules of war" other than kill or be killed any way you can. All's fair, and anything goes as long as you win.
2. Killing innocents is always a war crime. Better to die yourself than to kill innocents. If you did kill innocents, you are guilty.

The Viet Cong commander who was the target of Kerrey's team's mission was a "lawful combatant." The hamlet where he was headquartered (or merely sleeping) was deep in enemy territory. It is morally irrelevant whether this enemy leader was attacked by airplanes, artillery, or a small deep-penetration infantry team. It *was* morally relevant for the Viet Cong commander to situate his headquarters in a civilian hamlet, because to do so compromised the villagers' protected-person status. Bombs and shells were then and still are crude ways of attacking a legal combatant and much more likely to cause innocent deaths than a sniper's bullet or commando's knife. The concept of Kerrey's mission had much to recommend it from an ethical standpoint—the much sought after "surgical strike." Had it gone off successfully, as conceived, there would have been no civilian deaths.

Kerrey was in country about a month at the time this disastrous mission took place. He understood himself to be responsible not only for carrying out the mission, but also for the lives of the seven other members of the team. At the time, it was universally believed among American ground forces that the enemy kept no enlisted prisoners alive and very few officer prisoners. The rank makeup of the small number of prisoners eventually repatriated bears out this belief. So even if Kerrey had been of the saintly disposition that said, "Better I should die than shed innocent blood," what was his moral position regarding the members of his team? Would he have been blameless making the decision for them that it was morally preferable that they should die? Could he, or anyone in that position, have known the right thing to do? Even if we accept Klann's version, Kerrey's decision was not an uncoerced choice to do evil. The situation was evil. Kerrey now finds the whole incident tainting, even though in his version it was utterly an accident.

One does not have to be Aristotle to see that both Kerrey's and Klann's accounts cannot be true simultaneously. Most people will then conclude that one of the two narrators, Kerrey or Klann, is lying. I confess that I am not enormously interested in this question, which is separate from the question of culpability for the actual act of killing the civilians. Can Klann and Kerrey both be telling the truth? Factually, no, but psychologically, yes. The returned-fire-in-the-dark narrative may well have been created in the riverboat returning the team to base and repeated by everyone thereafter, becoming implanted as sincerely remembered "truth" by all concerned. Here is my conjecture: as the most experienced person on the team, Klann himself may well have been the one to say, "Now listen up. This is what happened tonight . . . Got it?" Memory has a large component of social construction. Klann's greater experience at the time and (in my conjecture here) his greater role in constructing the group narrative may have contributed to his being able to recall it differently than Kerrey and the other five team members whose memories correspond with Kerrey's and not Klann's.[5] It is possible, given the way memory works, that none of them is lying, in the usual sense of knowingly telling a falsehood about what they remember from that night more than thirty years ago.

Innocents died, and apparently everyone involved that night feels anguished by it. Those "gotcha!" journalists, who seem to believe that because Kerrey admits to feeling guilty, he must be guilty, are completely wrong. A person of good character feels moral pain—call it guilt, shame, anguish, remorse—after doing something that caused another person suffering, injury, or death, even if entirely accidental or unavoidable. Ethics philosopher Martha Nussbaum has made that point in her commentary on Aeschylus' *Agamemnon,* pointing out that the chorus—the voice of the moral consensus, of "what's right"—condemns King Agamemnon for his lack of anguish at having been forced to sacrifice his daughter Iphigenia, not for the fact of doing it. Even if Klann's account were correct, it would mean only that Kerrey had bad moral luck in being faced, like Agamemnon, with a choice between two courses of action, both disastrous.

At last, the giant whirlpool finishes the sucking down part of its cycle and vomits back up Odysseus' pathetic life raft. He gratefully eases his cramped muscles and drops to it. As fast as he can, he paddles out of the strait, casting fearful glances over his shoulder at Scylla's cave in the cliff. After ten days of drifting, he makes landfall on the island of the nymph Calypso, another honey trap, and the last stop in wonderland before the Land of the Phaeacians, where we started.

14

Calypso: Odysseus the Sexaholic

Some veterans report turning from one sex affair to another, trying, no doubt, to discover in the relationship of the sexes the meanings that war and army life had taken from their lives. . . . And so they go about . . . forever knocking at all the doors of their youth, hoping they may be admitted because they are still so young and wish so much to forget.
—World War I veteran Willard Waller[1]

The narrator, not Odysseus, tells us that the goddess Calypso kept Odysseus as a sex slave for seven years. The narrator pictures him daily

> . . . on the headland, sitting, still,
> weeping, his eyes never dry, his sweet life flowing away
> with his tears he wept for his foiled journey home,
> since the nymph no longer pleased. In the nights, true,
> he'd sleep with her in the arching cave—he had no choice—
> unwilling lover alongside lover all too willing . . .
> (5:167ff, Fagles)

We learned above that Circe's sex-food-and-wine cure to restore Odysseus' "haggard spirits" did not lose its charm in one year, and that his shipmates had to get him moving. But seven years cooped up alone with a nymphomaniac? The eighteenth- and nineteenth-century physicians who coined this word probably had Calypso specifically in mind.

Only a direct order from Zeus springs Odysseus from captivity.[2] Calypso submits to orders and tells Odysseus she's letting him go. His first reaction is to suspect a trap:

Long-enduring Odysseus shuddered at that . . .
"Passage home? Never. Surely you're plotting
something else, goddess, urging me—in a raft—
to cross the ocean's mighty gulfs. So vast, so full
of danger not even deep-sea ships can make it through . . .
I won't set foot on a raft until you *show* good faith,
until you consent to swear, goddess, a binding oath
you'll never plot some new intrigue to harm me!"

(5:190ff, Fagles)

Although many of my current patients have withdrawn from sex as part of withdrawing from social contacts altogether, some went through periods during the first decade after returning from Vietnam when they sought out the solace that Circe and Calypso offered in sex. A few of my patients have described extended periods when they were promiscuous. For them it did not provide long-term healing. I have no way of knowing how often the sex-food-and-wine cure worked to restore "haggard spirits." I never see the successful cures, because by definition they don't come to the VA for help.

We met Wiry, the Navy veteran of the riverine forces in the Mekong Delta, in Chapter 3. Wiry served on the sort of boat that inserted Bob Kerrey's SEAL team and recalls many such insertions and pickups. The civilian occupation Wiry pursued upon his return was a criminal career; he relished the "action." He also craved sex with women, lots and lots of them.

When I realized that I had only heard about this part of his life from scattered, indirect references, I asked him to give me a taped interview about his experience. The following are Wiry's words:

You know, the difference between your wife and other women. Your wife is—that's not sex, that's something that you hold for when you need someone who will hold you. It was a different kind of sex, it wasn't rough, it wasn't—you know we had a hard time with that *because* it wasn't rough. Frustration, release—I wouldn't call it lust, just plain outright fucking, you know, that you *can* do it. I think when we came back we had such a hard time with intimacy, okay?, a whore, we were more comfortable with some slut than we were with our wives. We were afraid to do that with our wives. I think that's an important point. You know some of the guys here, we've all been married for thirty years.

In Nam you just grabbed some broad and you fucked them. It was to let you know you're still a human being. The women probably didn't like it. We fucked anything that walked. Over there it wasn't wining and dining, it was get over here and [sexually explicit material omitted]. Sex proves you're not a fucking animal. Picture this—you come in off an operation, you just killed some people, some of your friends are dead. You helped put them together, you helped take some of them apart, you cut somebody's throat, okay? What do you do? There ain't enough booze in the world. You're fucked.

I remember in ———, it was our home base, they had a perimeter, which was a good-sized perimeter, trip flares, the whole fucking bit. We'd go through this perimeter to get to the fucking village, under the fucking trip wires, two hundred yards, to get laid. Mama-san had a whorehouse the other side of the perimeter. We're tripping flares, they're throwing grenades, we didn't give a fuck, we're going to get laid.

I remember one specific incident coming back from ——— we got the shit knocked out of us anyways, and half my boat got blowed off [killed or wounded], I was on this other fucking boat, we had the troops with us, and I remember we had the chaplain with us, guys were fucking dying, and we had the chaplain with us on the boat going back after we got the wounded into the helos. And I remember just before pulling into the base and I remembered that fucking whorehouse, and I turned that fucking boat and rammed that boat right up on the beach and dropped the fucking ramp and said, "Everybody gets laid!" [Holding his head in his hands,] the chaplain said, "Uhhhh!" All the guys went, "All *right!*" You know you stunk of fear, from sweat and fucking tension, and you had to get laid. I just ran the fucking boat right up there with everybody on it. Booze wouldn't do it all the time.

We used to have a beer bust after an operation. Pallets of fucking beer. I have it in the movie [an 8mm movie that the veteran shot while in Vietnam, which I have seen]: Black Label, Schlitz, Ballantine, all the beer you could drink. Because they knew—I don't think they know what we would do. They knew they did well with the beer bust. Get drunk, pass out, briefing tomorrow, time to go back out again. All the beer you could drink, whole pallets on the pontoon. Take all you want and get fucking drunk. You went on your boat and went to sleep, and started all over the next day.

VD was rampant. We all knew it. You'd get the shots. And there was the black syph, incurable syph, I knew a couple guys with it. They was shipped to the Philippines to die, and reported KIA. We all knew this shit, but we still fucked. Talking razor blades and all kinds of crazy shit. Just heard it, I never actually knew anyone who encountered it. Snakes, none of that shit scared us.

I remember when I got out, man, I, I, all I did was look for some relief, some release and the only release was fucking. I'd fuck anything, fat, tall, that wasn't the point.

[After returning, but while still in the service,] we were sent to Nantucket Island, a bunch of guys, I think there were 110 of them. I went to Nantucket Island—what in the *fuck* am I doing on Nantucket Island?—and that was to study us, to give us our medication, whatever the fuck they were giving us, we didn't know. . . . We were on Nantucket, fucking everything that walks, drinking and fucking and here we are in the service on this island. It was mixed forces [not all Navy], Green Berets, a lot of us was shell shocked. They didn't know what the fuck to do with us. They just kinda kept us there. You could not leave the island for the first six months. I was there for a year. They was giving us medication. They had a thing called the pill line. I couldn't tell you what they gave us. . . .

It is evident that *someone* in the military at the time recognized that personnel in units actively engaged in counterinsurgency warfare, such as Wiry and the counterinsurgency teams he inserted and extracted, could neither be turned loose on the American public nor simply given other noncombat military assignments—without some intervening "treatment."

Nantucket in the summertime was a fucking playground. You meet broads, we're stationed there, we don't know what the fuck we're stationed there for. A different broad every night, twosomes, threesomes, it was a liberal fucking place. It was just fucking crazy, but it was a relief for a short period of time. It worked better than booze. In my mind it had intimacy. With booze I didn't have intimacy. You're fucking someone you don't know, but you know that *you're* fucking. I wouldn't even call it lust. It's what I'm supposed to do and I feel good doing it, but then you get up and leave. After you're done you couldn't wait to get the fuck outta there. Also on Nantucket. Once you're done everything popped back up [i.e., intrusive memories and emotions related to Vietnam]. But for that five minutes you forget everything. Then you get up and leave.

You know you're walking down the street [today] and you see a guy with his wife, holding hands, and you wonder "why can't I do that? Why can't I hold hands like that?" I want to, but I don't know how. It seems like there's a process to it, but we don't know the process. You know, people hugging and shit like that? We do it in different ways. We take care of our wives, we give them what they want. We make sure they're not afraid of anyone—we're there if anything fucking happens. We have intimacy in *that* way.

You're drunk, you're slobbering over some broad—I touched it [intimacy]. I didn't touch it with the person I *want* to [i.e., his wife], but I touched it. Back then I didn't know what it was for. It felt good, and not too many things felt good lately and this is one of them. You know I can drink till I drop. Booze and fucking has a lot to do with all our scenarios, booze would lead to sex. Half of us don't drink anymore. The pact between booze and sex fucking ended.

And when I went home—you know, I think I still have a problem, I still have a problem today, approaching my wife for sex. I don't know if she wants me to approach her. I don't know the steps. Every once in a while it's okay, but most of the time it ain't. I won't say it's the punishment, but I'd say for us it's the way it's supposed to be. We don't put a lot of stock in it.

You got a wife and a family, and you can't abandon them, so, you just fuck. There's nights you don't come home. The wife, she figures you're out on a drunk again. And most of us did weird things, really, but we always left the money at home. Like, "That's for you, because this part of me isn't good." [I would] fuck nasty, but you couldn't do that kind of thing to your wife. That's a whole different thing. That's the woman that nurtures you, and puts you back together and puts up with your bullshit.

If you look at a lot of us, we had solid women, the women were strong, they were solid. That's what we lost. We were in the fucking jungle while they were going to their prom, the holding hands. You know, the high school sweetheart, we gave that up. Willingly, we gave it up. We didn't know it. But we gave it up willingly and said "I'm going to do *this* [fight a war]," so we can't capture [what was lost], don't know how to. Before Nam, I remember going out with girls in high school, not fuck or anything, but making out all night, kissing and—I remember doing that. [Before Vietnam] not really fucking. It was that time in the early 1960s, you went home and took a cold shower half the time. But the intimacy was there, the hugging and the kissing and you could put your arm around the girl you went out with. These weren't sluts. . . .

Wiry was conscious that prostituted women are in fact enslaved.

You don't want to degrade your wife to that level. [Like a slave?] Yes. There's times when she approaches me, and you know what? You're very careful making love. You're very careful in your mind. In your mind you don't want to get dog-fucking-dirty. This is my wife, the mother of my kids. She's the one who holds the family together. I supply [the family's livelihood]. That's a whole different thing. I don't have a word for it.

It has a type of relief that's good for a while, sure as hell better than any booze. Some of us ain't drinking anymore so it's harder.

The way we, amongst ourselves, look at it is it's just another price we pay.

This very sad narrative is a remarkable example of persistence into the modern world of very ancient patterns of citizen-wife contrasted to slave-prostitute. The emotional distinction Wiry makes has been extensively discussed in terms of "the Madonna and the whore," missing, I think, "the citizen and the slave." Wiry was as addicted to sex as any alcoholic to alcohol or heroin addict to opiates. I do not use the term "sexaholic" as a metaphor.

The veterans' counselor and prolific author on trauma Aphrodite Matsakis, now retired from the Vet Center system, wrote on this subject in her book *Vietnam Wives,* where she devoted a whole chapter to "PTSD and Sex." She writes,

> For some vets, sex is more than sex. It is a form of tranquillizer or sedative for their anxieties and other tensions. Not only does sex provide a sense of physical peace, but emotional peace as well. "Sex takes away my anger," explains Tom. "After satisfying sex, for a few moments at least, all seems well, both within and without." . . . Furthermore, for some vets, orgasm functions as a form of "shock treatment" for their depression. "If I don't have at least three orgasms a day, I get so blue I can't stand it. The minute I start feeling down, I reach for my wife . . ." [said another veteran]. When his wife refuses him sexually, it is not just sexual frustration which he suffers, but the full weight of some of his symptoms of PTSD.[3]

Homer, it could be said, thought that Odysseus spent eight of the ten years getting home taking the sex cure, one year for Circe and seven for Calypso. The Circe and Calypso episodes in the *Odyssey* may be interpreted as real attempts at calming the violent blowback of war with sex—lots of it.

Calypso, under Zeus' orders, helps Odysseus build a large, seaworthy raft, provisions it, and sees him off. Twenty days later, nearly drowned and stripped naked by the storms that Poseidon sent to torment him, Odysseus washes up on the shores of the Land of the Phaeacians, bringing us to where we first met him at the beginning of Chapter 2.

From the Phaeacians he has succeeded in winning a wealth of guest-gifts and a swift ride home to Ithaca. We now turn to what he does and what kind of person he shows himself to be when he gets home. Homer isn't through with us.

15

Odysseus at Home

By now you must wonder if I have not so turned against Odysseus as a military leader that I cannot rejoice in his long-sought reunion with son and wife as a veteran. Indeed, it is hard to warm to someone who has done so much harm. The portrait Homer gives us of his doings once actually at home on the island of Ithaca is hardly more endearing than the one painted by his adventures on the way. Constant lying, coldness toward his wife, cruelty toward his aged father, killing off more than a hundred townsmen, and ordering the extermination of a dozen of his women servants, and then after all that—he takes off again! The only thing that stands in the way of finally and completely writing him off as a stage villain is the rich and humanizing relationship revealed with his wife, Penelope—who amazingly turns out to be his equal and "better half."[1] For all the terrible things he has done to others, Odysseus emerges not as a monster, but as human like ourselves. The *Odyssey* shows us ugly deformities of character that trauma can cause, but these deformities are fully human such as might happen to ourselves, and, in fact, did happen to many of the veterans I work with.

Odysseus speeds home to Ithaca on the automated ship (it reads the minds of the Phaeacian sailors) belonging to King Alcinous and Queen Arete. For a third time in the *Odyssey*, he falls asleep, but this time without a bad outcome. The crew puts him ashore in a cove, still sleeping, with his treasure hoard of guest-gifts, and they leave.

> Great Odysseus woke from sleep on native ground at last—
> he'd been away for years—but failed to know the land.
>
> (13:213f, Fagles)

Many veterans experienced that disorienting bewilderment. This wasn't the place they left. The rapid pace of social and cultural change in

America, starting in the early 1960s, has been often remarked and often blamed by Vietnam veterans themselves for their sense of estrangement. But for a returning combat veteran to "fail to know the land" is typical for the return to civilian society. The whole middle third of Willard Waller's 1944 *The Veteran Comes Back* is titled "The Soldier-Turned-Veteran Comes Back to an Alien Homeland." Homer saw this first, and what he saw wasn't pretty.

LIES, TESTS, DISGUISES

After stomping around in a rage at the deceit of the Phaeacians in marooning him (he thinks) on yet another foreign shore, Odysseus consoles himself by checking his treasure and finding it intact. This done, he wanders homesick and aimless by the shore and encounters an elegant youth   resembling the scion of a local noble's house—who the poet tells us is the goddess Athena, Odysseus' patroness, in disguise. He asks for sanctuary, for guest-protection and . . . what land is this anyway? With a flowery buildup, the youth replies, Ithaca.

> *Ithaca* . . . Heart racing, Odysseus that great exile
> filled with joy. . . .
> He stood on native ground at last
> and he replied with a winging word to [Athena],
> not with a word of truth . . .
> always invoking the cunning in his heart:
> "Ithaca . . . yes, I seem to have heard of Ithaca,
> even . . . far across the sea . . ."
> (13:284ff, Fagles)

And then for another thirty lines he spins a fluent stream of lies about who he is, where he comes from, and how he has landed here. This self-introduction is surprising in the same unsettling way that his self-introduction to the Phaeacians as master of cunning was surprising. He tells this utter stranger, who is armed, and from whom he is asking safe sanctuary, that he is a fugitive murderer from Crete. Is this aimed at intimidating the noble youth? I killed him, I could just as easily kill you, if you don't give me what I want—all told in a breezy, confident, here's-my-story-because-I-trust-you tone. Odysseus chatters on in this confidential way, mixing momentous revelation with trivial fictitious details about the boat and crew that provided his getaway. In the course of these thirty or so lines Odysseus spins a verbal web that says, I can kill you if I want; I am noble like you; I have reinforcements; I'm willing to bribe you; there's lot's more where that came from; and where's my food, anyway. All of this was already recognized by ancient commentators, known as scholiasts, and the twelfth-century Greek churchman Eustathius.[2]

I have encountered this sort of threat by indirection in the VA Clinic. One veteran told me offhandedly about another psychiatrist he had choked—his tone suggested that I was not to worry, because I'm smarter and more understanding than the other psychiatrist was and that the veteran trusted me already. That was in the other building. This is a fresh start in a new building . . . and other easygoing and reassuring details.

Unlike a merely mortal VA psychiatrist, the goddess Athena doesn't even break a sweat. With a big grin she drops her disguise and says,

> Any man—any god who met you—would have to be
> some champion lying cheat to get past *you*
> for all-round craft and guile! You terrible man,
> foxy, ingenious, never tired of twists and tricks—
> those wily tales that warm the cockles of your heart!
> Come, enough of this now. We're both old hands
> at the arts of intrigue. Here among mortal men
> you're far the best at tactics, spinning yarns,
> and I am famous among the gods for wisdom,
> cunning wiles, too.
>
> (13:329ff, Fagles)

This is one of several deliciously comic scenes in the *Odyssey*. But it is also a scene that waves like a banner at the top of the narrative hill, in the middle of the epic, announcing "disguise, deception, and misrecognition" as the dominant themes of the 12,110-line poem.[3]

Without missing a beat, Odysseus chides the goddess for making herself scarce during the ten years of his wandering abroad.[4] She ducks this, again strokes him for being so enchantingly devious, and turns Odysseus' (and our) attention to his wife:

> Anyone else, coming back from wandering long and hard,
> would have hurried home at once, delighted to see

his children and his wife. Oh, but not you,
it's not your pleasure to probe for news of them—
you must put your wife to the proof yourself!

                          (13:379ff, Fagles)

Recall that Agamemnon—as a ghost in the Underworld—had warned Odysseus not to trust any woman. Agamemnon's own wife had conspired at his murder on the day of his return from Troy. Athena certifies Penelope's fidelity, saying, "She waits in your halls, as always, her life an endless hardship. . . . Weeping away the days" (13:383ff, Fagles). But then when she says, "We'll make plans so we can win the day" (417), she alludes for the first time to the suitors. Odysseus has heard about them from Teiresias in the Underworld,[5] but Homer has not made us privy to his reactions, if any, to this information until Athena goads him on:

Think how to lay hands on all those brazen suitors,
lording it over your house now, three whole years,
courting your noble wife, offering gifts to win her.
But she, forever broken-hearted for your return,
builds up each man's hopes—
dangling promises, dropping hints to each—
but all the while with something else in mind.

                          (13:430ff, Fagles)

This second, even stronger assurance of Penelope's fidelity doesn't stave off Odysseus' rush of fear that he was walking into a trap.

"God help me!" the man of intrigue broke out:
"Clearly I might have died the same ignoble death
as Agamemnon, bled white in my own house too,
if you had never revealed this to me now. . . .
Come, weave us a scheme so I can pay them back!
. . . Stand by me . . .
and I would fight three hundred men, great goddess,
with you to brace me."

                          (13:437ff, Fagles)

While he doesn't say it outright, to my ear he doesn't take Athena's word for Penelope's faithfulness.

Using her powers, the goddess now disguises Odysseus by withering

him to a shriveled, thin-haired graybeard beggar, and instructs him to
make his way to the pig farm in the hills, managed by his loyal retainer,
Eumaeus, there to gather intelligence. She herself, she says, will fly off
to Sparta to call Telemachus home.

Let's take Athena's display of god powers to think for a moment about
divine justice and peace—and how Homer might have told it differently.
Recall that Odysseus has landed on Ithaca with not one of the six-hundred-plus fellow citizens he led abroad to Troy. The goddess greets him
with words about the Jodies—Vietnam slang for civilians back home
who had taken the GIs' girls—words that "push all his buttons" and get
him enraged. Athena promises her assistance in the slaughter of these
further 108 Ithacans and Ithacan neighbors, gloating that their blood
and brains will splatter his floors (13:453f, Fagles).

For the moment, let's imagine a different ending. For example, when
Athena reveals herself to Odysseus on the beach and tells him of the villainous suitors, why could a war-weary Odysseus not have responded that
he's sick of death and bloodshed? She's a goddess, after all, and has the
power. If the gods are so interested in justice, let them see to it. She wears
(or carries) the aegis, mere sight of which makes strong men's knees go
slack from terror—can't she just go to his house and shake the aegis at the
suitors? Or she could ask her dad to land a thunderbolt in front of the door
every time one of the suitors approaches. They'll get the idea . . . If this
seems too far-fetched, remember the *Odyssey* ends *exactly* this way,
with Athena and Zeus stopping the townsmen of Ithaca from getting blood
revenge on Odysseus for their 108 newly dead sons and six-hundred-plus
brothers who died on the way home from Troy. Aegis and thunderbolt—
works every time. Or the poet could have come down somewhere in
between, such as killing the ringleader Antinous with one shot, and then,
again with Athena's help, wresting blood money (*poinē*) from all the others. He'd be ahead of the game.

As I pointed out above, the *Odyssey* was originally performed by generations of improvisational singers who may have bound each other to the
traditional "fact" of Odysseus' bloody revenge on the suitors. I am not saying that a poetic genius could not have gained acceptance for a different
set of "facts." By the time we get to the Athenian tragic theater in the fifth
and fourth centuries B.C.E., artists had "poetic license" to change the
"facts," so for example, Aeschylus' Agamemnon is the king of Argos, not
Mycenae, as Homer has it. It is impossible to tell how much poetic
license the Homeric poets had.[6]

When thinking why Athena could not just have "brought him home" we need to consider Homer's famous habit of showing every important turn in the plot as equally and convincingly motivated by both divine agendas and human aims.[7] It is simply not in Odysseus' character to make peace with anyone who has stolen his victuals and tried to steal his wife. He is implacable, but patient, self-disciplined, and cunning in his revenge. If character is destiny, the Homeric world saw character as formed by divine influence, symbolized by the patronage of the god or goddess who exemplified the leading trait of character. For Odysseus and Athena this trait is *mētis.*

The three-combat-tour tank veteran whose voice is heard often in *Achilles in Vietnam* limited his revenge:

> I had a picture of her I wrapped in plastic and kept in an ammo box. Every day I would take the picture out and look at it and write her a letter. An' every day, sometimes two or three the same day, she'd write to me. 'Course they didn't come every day, but in big bunches when they brought the mail out to us.
>
> Well, the letters just stopped. I wrote to her an' wrote to her, pleading with her to tell me how I hurt her, how I made her mad at me. Not a word. No letters. Nothin'.
>
> I guess I went a little crazy. That was when I started seeing mass wave attacks that wasn't there. I was firing and firing and . . . I guess I was becoming a danger—I mean to us, not the enemy, and that's when they tied me up and put pills in my mouth an' put me in the bustle rack behind the [tank] turret, till they got back and they sent me home because my tour and enlistment were up anyway. I don't remember much of that.
>
> I get back home and find out what happened. She was at a party and drank too much and this guy rapes her, actually I knew the guy. An' she gets pregnant and thinks she has to marry him because it's his baby and he asks her to marry him.
>
> When she heard I was home she threw him out and had me come over. She said, you're the only man I've ever loved and I love you now. I remember it so clear. I had a glass of beer in my hand. I threw it in her face and walked out of that house. I never saw her again.
>
> That's just what happened.

This man grew up in an American Roman Catholic family and community very different from the zero-sum honor culture of the Homeric world. He killed neither her nor her rapist husband. The anguish and abandonment that he felt when her sustaining letters stopped mattered more to him than current sexual jealousy that another man had taken his girl. His mind and emotions were still in Vietnam, and in Vietnam she had severed the life-line of the warm-hearted and high-minded youth who had gone to war. The "animal" who came home—the "animal" he became as a berserker[8] after Timmy's death (see page 81, above)—no longer cared about the girl or their love. I doubt that the likelihood of being caught and imprisoned restrained his hand. His heart was too deadened to care one way or another.

To be fair, Odysseus' life is in serious danger from the suitors, regard-less of Penelope's fidelity, despite his boast to Athena on the beach that he could kill off twice their number with her at his side (13:447, Fagles). His danger is greater if Penelope *has* been cheating on him, but usurpation is definitely in the wind—possibly in the suitors' minds as just vengeance for the dead crews of his flotilla. The suitors plan to murder Telemachus on his way back from his visit to Pylos and Sparta. Odysseus *must* keep secret his solitary, unarmed, unsupported presence in Ithaca if he hopes to survive. The situation demands that he lie and dissemble to everyone, with the exception of his son, Telemachus, before he springs his ambush on the suitors—the situation motivates this as much as his devious char-acter.[9]

The only real question now is whether Penelope will also end up among the dead.

Odysseus makes his way to the loyal swineherd's hut, tells him a detailed and entertaining pack of lies. For his trouble, the swineherd calls him a liar on the one true thing he's said: that Odysseus is alive and nearby. The swineherd's skepticism is not without foundation. A proces-sion of scammers has passed through Ithaca selling phony information on Odysseus' whereabouts. Odysseus is now on notice that he will have to convince Penelope that he is genuine. However, we begin to suspect that loyal Eumaeus, the swineherd, has already guessed who this wizened beg-gar is, because he not only orders the fattest boar killed for their supper, but also presents Odysseus with the choicest cut from the loin.

Homer cuts to Sparta where Athena appears to Telemachus and advises him to hightail it for home, but to come in the back door to Ithaca, to avoid the assassins laying for him. At the same time, she plants a doubt in Telemachus' mind (and ours) about the depth of Penelope's loy-alty. With this chilling thought about his mother, Athena tells him to hurry back:

Be careful lest she carry from your halls some treasure against your will.
For you know what sort of spirit there is in a woman's breast; she wishes to

increase the house of the man who marries her, but of her former children and staunch spouse she takes no thought.

(15:19ff orig., Dimock, prose trans.)

She tells him to head for the swineherd's hut and send the servant into town to tell Penelope that he's safe. This will set up the reunion of father and son and get Eumaeus out of the way for a while. Meanwhile back at the farm, Odysseus tells the swineherd more entertaining lies, and hears the latter's sad life story.

The youth arrives, Eumaeus goes off, and Athena undoes Odysseus' disguise, so he now appears tall, clean, ruddy, and dark-bearded. Telemachus is staggered, disbelieving, and he wonders if this shape-changer is a god. Odysseus straightens him out saying,

> No other Odysseus will ever return to you.
> That man and I are one, the man you see . . .
> here after many hardships,
> endless wanderings, after twenty years
> I have come to native ground at last.
> My changing so? Athena's work, the Fighter's Queen—
> she has that power, she makes me look as she likes,
> now the beggar, the next moment a young man. . . .
> It's light work for the gods who rule the skies.

(16:232ff, Fagles)

Father and son weep together, "Both men so filled with compassion, eyes streaming with tears" (16:249, Fagles).

With but one or two lines about how he got from Troy to Ithaca, Odysseus launches into strategy planning with his son, giving him various practical instructions for "prepping the battlefield," and telling him to expect a switch back to the old beggar disguise. Telemachus gives him the "order of battle," the size and makeup of the forces arrayed against them. But Odysseus will do his own reconnaissance in disguise and warns Telemachus not to react when the impious, overweening suitors mistreat the apparently helpless old man. And Telemachus is to maintain *complete* secrecy, even from his mother and grandfather and the most trusted servants, such as Eumaeus.

Telemachus is mostly on the receiving end of instructions, plans, and warnings, but when Odysseus says he plans to assess the strength of his support among his own retainers, Telemachus says this will be a waste of time, "probing the fieldhands man by man." He knows these men well and can give his father the rundown. The women, however, are another story, "But I advise you to sound the women out: who are disloyal to you, who are guiltless?" (16: 347ff, Fagles). This outspoken breach of youthful humility—advising his father to take the measure of the women—must refer indirectly to Penelope. Remember that Telemachus still has Athena's cynical warning in his head about his mother's possible defection. And despite Athena's apparent endorsement of Penelope's loyalty, Odysseus still has Agamemnon's warning in mind.

So when Odysseus, now magically reshriveled, makes his way with the swineherd to his great hall, the listener is in suspense about both how this lone man will survive the encounter with more than a hundred young lions, and whether the lioness around which they gather will eat him alive also.

Just by the front door Homer brings Odysseus to one of the great sentimental tear-jerks of all literature:

> Now . . . a dog that lay there
> lifted up his muzzle, pricked his ears. . . .
> It was Argos, long-enduring Odysseus' dog
> he trained as a puppy once. . . .
> But now with his master gone he lay there, castaway,
> on piles of dung . . . heaps collecting
> out before the gates till Odysseus' serving-men
> could cart it off to manure the king's estates.
> Infested with ticks, half-dead from neglect,
> here lay the hound, old Argos.
> But the moment he sensed Odysseus standing by
> he thumped his tail, nuzzling low, and his ears dropped,
> though he had no strength to drag himself an inch
> toward his master. Odysseus glanced to the side
> and flicked away a tear, hiding it from Eumaeus.
>
> (17:317ff, Fagles)

Odysseus pretends to see in this decrepit wreck—much like he himself appears to be—the fine lines of the once strong, once swift tracker. To this Eumaeus replies that

> "He's run out of luck poor fellow . . .
> his master's dead and gone, so far from home,

and the heartless women tend him not at all."

. . .

With that he entered the well-constructed palace.[10] . . .
But the dark shadow of death closed down on Argos' eyes
the instant he saw Odysseus, twenty years away.

(17:349ff, Fagles)

Recall that at this point Eumaeus doesn't know, or pretends not to know, the identity of this beggarman.

What follows is a long and entertaining scene of Odysseus' first encounter with the villainous suitors and their ringleader, the archvillain Antinous. Odysseus baits the suitors to the extent he can without blowing his disguise. He supplicates them for donations—of his own victuals! He fits himself into the cultural theme of the indigent stranger who is maybe a god in disguise, but under the gods' protection at the very least. This theme, that the gods visit mortals to test their hospitality and their generosity to the helpless, is widespread in myth, literature, and sacred writings.[11] It is the poet's opportunity to display the suitors' sacrilegious disregard of "what's right," their arrogant hubris. This culminates in Antinous throwing his footstool at Odysseus. This attack is an affront to the nominal master of the house, Telemachus, who has extended guest-protection to this beggar and given him permission to beg among the other "guests," the suitors. It also affronts the gods, under whose protection the beggar stands, and, of course, Odysseus personally.

Penelope in her upstairs apartment overhears the commotion. But always the master of the tantalizing delay, Homer inserts a further scene in which the suitors attempt to abuse Odysseus.[12] They pit him against an overweight local scrounger who has staked out the suitors' feasting as his turf, and gotten fat on the droppings as they stuff themselves with Odysseus' food and wine. With sadistic humor, the suitors set up a mock-heroic single combat between the young but flabby moocher and the seemingly aged and broken-down stranger. Amid great hilarity—which distracts the suitors' attention from the subtle chill they get when they see what a powerful and efficient fighter this old hulk is—Odysseus trounces and ejects the former beggar-king of the suitors' feasts.

Something—vibrations in the ether? inspiration from the goddess Athena?—prompts Penelope to pick this evening to tease and flirt with the suitors. She bathes and naps before showing herself to them. Ever ready with the makeup, Athena transforms Penelope from a grief-worn middle-aged widow to a young Grace touched by Aphrodite, the love goddess.

Veiled, with modest escort of two handmaids, she descends the steps to the hall where the suitors go weak-kneed with lust. The language Homer uses for weak-kneed here is the same used in the *Iliad* for a warrior collapsing from a wound—and thus foreshadows the suitors' deaths. This word-play identifies her as another potential Helen, another cause of many deaths. The same train of associations raises questions about her fidelity. Whether from instinct or cunning, she knows she needs a diversion, an excuse to let her allure build up. She scolds Telemachus for permitting the stranger to be abused, and he answers her, further extending the pause to admire. Of course, Odysseus is in the room, too! This is the first time he has seen his wife in twenty years.

Eurymachus, the most respectable of the suitors, bursts out in a babble of praise of her beauty, refinement, and steadiness of mind. This gives her the opening to say—contrary to the testimony of all their senses—that all her beauty and all her other merit were destroyed the day her husband took ship for Troy, that she is nothing without him, her life a torment without him. Then, almost as though she knows he is there listening and might have forgotten, she repeats his departing instructions that if he has not returned by the time their son, Telemachus, sprouts a beard—which has now happened—she is free to remarry. She then chides them for eating her food, rather than bringing her gifts to court her favor.

Her appearance among them in this manner, her recitation of her absent husband's terms of release, and the mention of courting gifts is tantamount to declaring a gift-contest for her hand. The suitors instantly get the message.

> "Gifts?"
> . . . Antinous took her point at once.
> ". . . Sensible Penelope,
> whatever gifts your suitors would like to bring,
> accept them. How ungracious to turn those gifts away!
> We won't go back to our own estates, or anywhere else,
> till you have wed the man you find the best."
>
> (18:319ff, Fagles)

This contest of the courting gifts—which the suitors *all* lose—is often forgotten in the later, more famous contest of the bow. But Odysseus "glowed with joy . . . to hear his wife's trickery luring gifts from her suitors now" (18:316f, Fagles).

Antinous is thinking, after three years of frustrated courting—caught at last! Odysseus is thinking, you're all dead meat, and whatever you bring to her is *mine!* All the suitors send retainers home to fetch courting gifts,[13] and they return with ultra-high-value goods of the sort readers have already encountered as guest-gifts: embroidered robes festooned with gold clasps, gold necklaces, bejeweled chokers, and so on. These prestige goods were so valuable, that even three years of supplying food and wine for a hundred young men might have been more than made up for. The courting gifts arrive and Penelope, now with all her maids as bearers, returns to her apartment above with the loot parading behind her.

The scene closes with further demonstration of the suitors' arrogance and disorder, finally causing Telemachus to tell them all to drink up the last round and go home to bed. When they clear out, leaving Odysseus behind, he sees that the big battle is coming soon and prepares the battlefield by helping his son stow all the arms that decorate the great hall. These are real, functional, deadly weapons—but also trophies of Odysseus' and his father's military victories as well as gifts, a store of wealth, and emblems of political legitimacy. In any case, Odysseus has no interest in fighting 108 men armed with *his* weapons, grabbed from the walls and weapon racks of *his* great hall.[14]

Odysseus' astute foresight generates a painful historical irony for us. Odysseus is partially successful at denying the enemy a chance to arm from his own resources. In Vietnam, during the first years of American involvement, the enemy was armed largely, not with Russian, Chinese, Japanese, or French weapons, but with *American* weapons that the Viet Minh bought, stole, or captured from the South Vietnamese Civil Guard, Self-Defense Corps, and Army to whom we had given them![15]

The weapons stowed, the stage is set, finally, for the long-suspended first meeting of Odysseus and Penelope. He dismisses his son to bed with the words, "Off you to bed. I'll stay here behind to test the women, test your mother too" (19:47f, Fagles). Odysseus is still not sure about Penelope's loyalty, whatever Athena has said about it, and whatever Odysseus himself supposedly thought about it ("Staunch Odysseus glowed . . . to hear . . . his wife's trickery . . . enchanting [the suitors'] hearts . . . but all the while with something else in mind" 18:316ff, Fagles).

The interview opens without privacy, Penelope surrounded by her maids. These include at least one, Melantho, whom the narrator has already revealed as in bed with the suitors. This maid and Odysseus bandy words. Penelope tongue-lashes her, calling her a "brazen, shame-less bitch . . . you will pay for it with your life, you will!" and then contin-ues that she wants to know what this stranger knows "about my husband . . . my heart breaks for *him*" (18:99f, Fagles).

Penelope asks him to give his origins, and like the scene in the palace of the Phaeacians, Odysseus evades the question with many elegant words. Penelope again declares how much she yearns for Odysseus and tells him about the delaying trick of the shroud that she wove each day for her father-in-law, Laertes—the pious duty of a good daughter-in-law while the old man still lives—but unwove in secret each night. The same maids that now surround her revealed her deception to the suitors, and so now she is up against it and has to pick one of the suitors to marry. And again she presses the beggar to identify himself. She says, in effect, my pain is as great as yours. You speak to one who understands.

Odysseus then launches into another of his colorful, fictitious autobi-ographies—saying his name is Aethon from Crete—this time weaving details of an encounter with Odysseus into it.

> Falsehoods all,
> but he gave his falsehoods all the ring of truth.
> As [Penelope] listened on, her tears flowed and soaked her cheeks . . .
> so she dissolved in tears . . .
> weeping for him, her husband, sitting there beside her.
> *Odysseus' heart went out to his grief-stricken wife*
> *but under his lids his eyes remained stock-still—*
> *they might have been made of horn or iron—*
> *his guile fought back his tears.*
>
> (19:234ff, Fagles; emphasis added)

We shall come back to Homer's amazing portrait of Odysseus' emotional blankness in the face of his wife's anguish, and to Homer's insight that it was his *dolos*, his guile, that strategically suppresses his emotions. Viet-nam veterans' wives have endured such blankness.

He meets with her to test her, but she tells him,

> Now, stranger, I think I'll test you, just to see
> if . . .
> you actually entertained my husband as you say.
>
> (19:248ff, Fagles)

Because Odysseus' fiction claimed a meeting on the outward voyage to Troy, she asks him what Odysseus was wearing. The beggar feigns difficulty remembering from twenty years ago and proceeds to describe every detail of the clothing, including the golden brooch, that Penelope had herself given him on his departure. He throws in the extra detail of the name and physical description of Odysseus' herald, Eurybates.[16]

This sends Penelope into further agonies of weeping—during which the beggar sits as expressionless as a block of stone—prompting him to repeat what he has said to Eumaeus, that he has heard that Odysseus is alive, nearby, and on his way home, and tells her a quick, partial summary of the adventures he told to the Phaeacians. He repeats the blame-casting story that all Odysseus' men-at-arms were drowned because they had killed the cattle of the sun god (19:318), and describes the mass of treasure Odysseus is bringing home. Penelope has heard much like this before from other travelers and is not willing to expose herself yet again to the pain of hope. She says, "Odysseus, I tell you, is never coming back" (19:358, Fagles). She instructs her maids to make up a luxury bed for the stranger, bathe him and rub him down. He demurs, saying that living rough for so long, he's not used to such things, but if there were an old sufferer like himself among her household, he would let that servant minister to him.

The stage directions are not clear on how the spying maids (plural, at line 19:317, orig.) exit and the single aged retainer Eurycleia enters. Penelope seems to flirt with recognition herself, saying that the beggar's hands and feet must resemble those of Odysseus, now twenty years after she has seen him last (19:408, Fagles). But by the time Eurycleia, who was Odysseus' wet-nurse when he was a baby, bathes his feet, only Odysseus, Penelope, and the old nurse are present. The famous recognition scene between Eurycleia and Odysseus follows, in which the old nurse recognizes him by the scar on his thigh, plowed there by the tusk of a wild boar. This scene is unthinkable as presented, with even *one* of the other maids present.

Despite the flowery words and fine emotions that flow between the disguised Odysseus and his wife, a tremendous atmosphere of threat hangs over the scene. One wrong step and he is a dead man. Within the frame of the epic fiction, Odysseus' mortal danger is a reality, a "fact." This in itself is something worth taking in as a metaphor of the sense of vulnerability that some combat veterans feel even in the most intimate, apparently safe settings. Although we work constantly to discourage it, many of the veterans we work with—even if they share a bed with their wives—sleep within a hand's reach of weapons.

During the long, dramatic exchange with Eurycleia, the goddess Athena puts Penelope into a trance, or so the narrator tells us. The trance ended, Penelope takes the beggar to an even deeper level of her private confidence. She tells him a dream she had of an eagle swooping in on her flock of domestic geese, snapping all their necks and leaving them dead in heaps about the hall. She wails for her dead geese in the dream, but the eagle returns and tells her to rejoice that he, the eagle, is Odysseus and the geese are her suitors.[17]

Perhaps Penelope was not in such a deep trance as we were told during Eurycleia's recognition scene, because immediately after telling this dream of the Odysseus-eagle and hearing the beggar pronounce it a true portent of mayhem to come, she tells him that tomorrow she will announce the contest of the bow and twelve axe heads. If she has recognized Odysseus, she knows that he can pull this off. She knows that he is a master bowman and that the "contest" would position him to be powerfully armed when the suitors would not be. Her plan, in effect sets the suitors up to face Odysseus as the only man in the hall already "locked and loaded." She says,

> I mean to announce a contest with those axes,
> the ones [Odysseus] would often line up here inside the hall,
> twelve in a straight unbroken row . . .
> then stand well back and whip an arrow through the lot.
> Now I will bring them on as a trial for my suitors.
> The hand that can string the bow with greatest ease,
> that shoots an arrow clean through all twelve axes—
> he's the man I follow, yes, forsaking this house
> where I was once a bride.
>
> (19:644ff, Fagles)

To this the beggar replies, don't put it off, "royal wife of Laertes' son," Odysseus himself will be here before the contest.

SLAUGHTER OF THE INFAMOUS SUITORS

The preceding chapters asked the reader to view Odysseus' adventures in wonderland as metaphors for generic experiences of real combat veterans. The contest of the bow, which Odysseus uses to ambush, rout, and slaughter the suitors, connects to real veterans in a different way: it is a fictional rendition of real fantasies, real wishes to seek revenge upon various classes of civilians back home for the veterans' damaged honor. We get a multifaceted picture of ways that civilians bruise the honor of veterans and arouse the growling, bristling rage that Odysseus finally puts into action.

The very first time Odysseus hears about the suitors—from Teiresias in the Underworld—two major themes are set. Teiresias says:

> You will find a world of pain at home,
> crude, arrogant men devouring all your goods,
> courting your noble wife, offering gifts to win her.
>
> (11:133ff, Fagles)

Eating up his food is put first! Because most Americans alive today have never experienced starvation or even persistent hunger—and many have had parents and even grandparents who were spared this also—it is hard to grasp the significance of being "eaten out of house and home" in a world of constant shortage. We tend to blow past it to the more accessible theme of sexual rivalry.

But the sense of some Vietnam veterans that civilians have been eating their lunch is a powerful source of resentment, even hatred. This takes the form of viewing civilians as having advanced educationally and occupationally while the infantryman "humping the boonies" stood still or lost ground because of discrimination against veterans in hiring and promotion. World War I veteran Willard Waller wrote the following about how this feels to the veteran:

> It is easy to understand why the soldier hates the young man of his own age who manages somehow to escape military service. The draft board in its wisdom decides that Tom Jones must go to war, and off goes Tom to be a soldier. But Henry Smith next door, has had the foresight to get entrenched in a necessary industry; he stays home, works for high wages, wins a promotion, gets married, and buys a little home in the suburbs. When Tom returns, Henry is still a necessary man in industry, still entrenched; he keeps his job and Tom goes on relief.[18]

The GI Bill was created at the end of World War II to address this very concern, with historically generous educational benefits, home mortgage assistance, and so forth. Despite the erosion of the value of Vietnam veterans' benefits by inflation, the raw lumped statistics on household incomes of Vietnam veterans do *not* support the idea that veterans as a whole got the short end of the stick, financially. In 1986, when the *National Vietnam Veterans Readjustment Study* was done, 17.4 percent of male in-country Vietnam veterans had family incomes below $20,000 a year, compared to 40 percent in the country as a whole. On the high end, 25.2 percent of male in-country Vietnam vets had incomes of $50,000 or more, compared to 17 percent in the country as a whole.[19] However, the point of this section is to understand the *beliefs* that some Vietnam veterans have about their homecoming experience that led them to hate civilians. Homer's Odysseus saw it in very concrete terms: "They're eating my food!" Vietnam veterans I have worked with saw it as "They took my job!" Women in the workplace compounded economic competition with the misogyny described above. Women were, after all, mostly civilians.

The more familiar theme of the suitors trying to steal Odysseus' wife needs little further comment as a cause for his vengeance. Despite the prominence in folklore of the Jody who steals the Vietnam soldier's girl, this theme has been notable by its *absence* as a general source of hatred against civilians among the veterans I have known. If general misogyny originated in women's supposed readiness to be seduced by Jody, I have not heard this from my patients decades later.

However, many other causes for veterans' hatred and resentment toward civilians emerge from the encounters between Odysseus and the suitors, once we begin to look for them.

I have already described the hurt and bitterness that a skilled infantryman encounters in civilian life when he is defined by the state employment bureau as "unskilled laborer." The skills of a truly expert ground warfare fighter are of a very high order, analogous to an NBA basketball player or professional musician. Imagine a world-class musician being dropped into the land of the deaf, where people shrug and say, "unskilled laborer." This lack of social acknowledgment of the value of a person's hard-won skill is a great blow to his self-respect, regardless of what social class he comes from and regardless of personal wealth. Most returning infantrymen did *not* have personal wealth, so the layering of the humiliations of poverty and low social class on top of disvaluing their skills was a potent and dangerously explosive combination.

Odysseus returns to his house and hometown disguised as a destitute beggar. Much of the dramatic spice of *Odyssey* 14–23 comes from the tension between his apparent position at the bottom of the social hierarchy and real position at its top. The audience and Odysseus know who's who, but the characters in action around him do not. The suitors treat Odysseus in a demeaning and dishonoring way, *because he is poor.* Many Vietnam vets felt that they experienced just such treatment in their first years of reassimilation.

COLDNESS AND CRUELTY TO NEAREST AND DEAREST

Let us return to the remarkable picture of Odysseus being as still and cold as a block of stone while his wife wept so piteously.

> Odysseus' heart went out to his grief-stricken wife
> but under his lids his eyes remained stock-still—
> they might have been made of horn or iron—
> his guile fought back his tears.
>
> (19:242ff, Fagles)

In a chapter that Vet Center counselor Aphrodite Matsakis tellingly titles "Living with the Ice Man" she describes wives of Vietnam veterans whose husbands are emotionally blank. One such wife said, "He doesn't want to talk that much and when we're in bed, he's like an ice man. He says he doesn't care whether we have sex or not, doesn't care whether we stay married or not. If I start crying, he'll tell me he loves me, but he just can't help it, he doesn't care about anything."[20] Unlike this veteran who will not talk to his wife, Odysseus and Penelope talk to each other in their olive tree-founded bed at such length that the gods have to miraculously lengthen the night to give them their fill. As I said at the beginning of this chapter, to me Odysseus' relationship with his wife is his most human feature.

Patience Mason, the wife of Vietnam helicopter pilot Robert Mason, writes, "Maybe you can't understand why your vet feels nothing when his mother dies."[21] She explains such suppression of emotion as the persistence of a valid adaptation to combat. "He's cold and unresponsive because he learned to be that way as a survival tactic in Vietnam. It's more than a habit. It's how he stays alive."[22] Mason quotes World War I poet Wilfred Owen's crushing "Insensibility":

> Happy are men who yet before they are killed
> Can let their veins run cold.
> Whom no compassion fleers.
>
> . . .
>
> And some cease feeling
> Even themselves or for themselves.

> Dullness best solves
> The tease and doubt of shelling
>   . . .
> Their hearts remain small-drawn.[23]

Now we have two different reasons for combat veterans to be emotionally distant, emotionally unresponsive: The first picture is given by Homer, calling Odysseus' nonresponse to his wife's anguish a result of his "guile." That is, Homer says his coldness is intentional, a strategic withholding of emotional expression, but says explicitly that "his heart went out to her"—i.e., he did feel it.[24] The second picture is given by Owen, who tells us that insensibility, numbing, feeling nothing is an adaptation to the pain, fear, and grief of combat. Which is true?

I am inclined to say that both are true. Odysseus is not yet in a safe, civilian setting. His life is as much on the line as it was on the plains of Troy. It *is* strategic for him to show no emotion. But he is as entitled to this emotional coldness as Wilfred Owen's "happy" ice man in the trenches. He is still in combat mode.

However, Homer complicates our understanding of Odysseus' character by a second scene of emotional withholding that strikes most readers as gratuitous cruelty—his reunion with his father, Laertes, at the very end of the epic in Book 24.

The suitors are all dead now. Odysseus, Telemachus, the swineherd, and another loyal retainer all slip out of town at first light before the cry for revenge has been raised. They head for Laertes' farm, where he has been living in seclusion since his wife's death. The picture is of a sorrowing old man, who keeps a lid on his grief for son and wife by constant hard work, clearing land and planting vineyards and orchards. The group arrives at the farmhouse—his father is already out in the orchard. Odysseus is no longer in disguise and has no need of any. He orders the others to prepare food while he finds his father, saying,

> And I will put my father to the test,
>   see if the old man knows me now, on sight,
>   or fails to, after twenty years apart.
>   (24: 238ff, Fagles)

What need does he have to test his father? For what? If this is a practical joke, Odysseus has a perverted sense of humor. He spies his father at a distance,

> spading soil around a sapling—clad in filthy rags,
> in a patched, unseemly shirt . . .
> and on his head he wore a goatskin skullcap
> to cultivate his misery that much more. . . .
> Long-enduring Odysseus, catching sight of him now—
> A man worn down with years, his heart racked with sorrow—
> Halted under a branching pear-tree, paused and wept.

Now it seems he is warmhearted toward his old father, but then, inexplicably, he holds a debate with himself:

> Debating, head and heart, what should he do now?
> Kiss and embrace his father, pour out the long tale—
> . . .
> or probe him first to test him every way?
> Torn, mulling it over, this seemed better:
> test the man first,
> reproach him with words that cut him to the core.
>
> (24:260ff, Fagles)

The scene is too painful to spin out. His father does not recognize him. Odysseus approaches Laertes, his father, with breezy sarcasm about the old man's dilapidated appearance and—lying as usual—says he's looking for Odysseus, whom he entertained abroad and sent off with lavish guest-gifts. His father begins to weep, saying Odysseus is dead. The unrecognized stranger then piles it on, essentially shaming Laertes with the gay words that, "We had high hopes we'd meet again as guests, as old friends, and trade some shining gifts" (24:350ff, Fagles). Laertes knows he cannot discharge his son's obligation to reciprocate and thus is *shamed* on top of his grief. He is completely undone and begins to soil his hair and beard with dirt.

This finally brings Odysseus to his senses and he reveals himself. Laertes demands proof of identity—he, too, has had his hopes raised by scammers. Odysseus' first sign of his identity is the same wound on his thigh, by which his old wet-nurse Eurycleia had recognized him. And Odysseus reminds his father of the specific kinds and numbers of fruit trees his father had given him in this very orchard as a child. When the proofs sink in, Laertes throws his arms around his son's neck and his knees go weak. We now return to the boar-tusk scar as we consider the whole question of what pathogenic burden of trauma Odysseus has carried.

Trauma and Odysseus' Character

I imagine myself locking eyes with Odysseus, perhaps in my office in the VA, perhaps across the table in the room where the veterans meet for their groups. I'm asking myself, how did this level of mistrust and manipulativeness come to be? So much wildness and so much violence, what am I missing?

I review his combat history in my mind . . . Homer tells us that Odysseus was in on the Trojan War from the beginning; that means ten years of fighting, right through and beyond the war's end. The *Iliad* mentions Odysseus more than 120 times, but by comparison mentions the great Ajax about twice as often and young Diomedes more than 150 times. He shares the highly dangerous night reconnaissance with Diomedes in *Iliad* 10. In *Odyssey* 4, Helen recalls that Odysseus scarred "his own body with mortifying strokes," to disguise himself before infiltrating Troy on an even more dangerous spy mission into the heart of the enemy city (4:274, Fagles). Agamemnon relies on him when a job needs doing that requires brains and diplomacy. Although he is noteworthy for the staff jobs he does for the commander in chief, Agamemnon, he's no rear-echelon pogue. He'd seen plenty of front line fighting, killed many men, seen many Greek fighters die, during heavy combat in *Iliad* 4, 5, 8, 11, and 14. One of those killed, Leukos, is called Odysseus' *hetairon*, someone who followed Odysseus as his military chief (4:491, orig.). Homer tells us that Leukos was *esthlos*, brave and stout.[25] Odysseus cared enough about him to fly into a rage at his death and kill his killer in the battle. He does not, however, go berserk.

Did he experience any betrayal by his boss, Agamemnon, whom he served so loyally and so well? We don't know, but there's a hint that something went sour between Odysseus and Agamemnon after the fall of Troy, but before the fleet departed for home. Did Odysseus feel cheated in the division of the spoils? He was every bit as greedy for gain as his boss.[26] We have to put two and two together ourselves. Here are the pieces:

In *Odyssey* Book 3, when Telemachus visits Nestor, we learn that a great split developed in the army after the fall of Troy over when to leave for home. Half, including Nestor and Odysseus, said, "We're outta here!" and sailed away, with Menelaus and Diomedes joining them. The other half stayed behind with Agamemnon to perform further sacrifices to Athena. The group that had headed home got only as far as Tenedos—an island about two and a half miles off the coast—before this group started to argue among themselves, too. Nestor speaking:

> But Zeus, not willing yet,
> now cruelly set us at odds a second time,
> and one lot turned, put back in the rolling ships,
> *under command of the subtle captain, Odysseus;*
> *their notion was to please Lord Agamemnon.*
>
> (3:173ff, Fitzgerald; emphasis added)

We don't know what happened when Odysseus and the others who followed him got back to Troy, but *something* happened, because Odysseus leaves Troy a second time with only the ships of his own flotilla from Ithaca (9:44, Fagles). No other contingent leaves Troy with him, nor does Odysseus himself ever mention the contretemps with Agamemnon that Nestor recalls ten years later. Considering Odysseus' unswerving loyalty to Agamemnon throughout the *Iliad*, something very serious must have blown up between them before Odysseus' first departure from Troy. His final attempt to patch it up apparently failed.

To summarize the Trojan War–related "exposures" that Odysseus experienced that might plague him later as the constellation of symptoms designated by the American Psychiatric Association (APA) as Post-Traumatic Stress Disorder, or PTSD:

- Many firefights involving both killing the enemy and witnessing combat deaths on his own side.
- One combat death of someone described as close.
- Two high-risk "special ops," one involving his murdering a disarmed prisoner during interrogation behind enemy lines, and the other involving his self-injury to evade detection.
- An unclear history of being betrayed by his own commander after the fighting was over.
- After demobilization, but before reaching home, many personal close brushes with death, during which he witnessed the grisly end of more than six hundred men of his own squadron, some of whom were relatives. He inconsistently acknowledges and denies command responsibility in these deaths.

This litany of death could produce full-blown PTSD, as defined by the American Psychiatric Association, in just about anyone.

Did Odysseus have PTSD as the APA defines it? The simple answer to the question is—no. Neither the text of the *Iliad* nor of the *Odyssey* gives us evidence that Odysseus is having *symptoms* related to any of the above experiences. Nor do we have evidence that, despite these terrible experiences, he responded to them with "intense fear, helplessness or horror."²⁷ Nor is it clear that the official definition of PTSD sheds much light on how horrible experience can deform character. In the Introduction I voiced my dissatisfaction with the official terminology.

I don't pretend to have infallible intuition about people, but sitting across from Odysseus in the VA Clinic, knowing his war history and his life afterward as a veteran, I have a whiff of something else, of pre-military trauma that settled him firmly in an I'll-get-them-before-they-get-me mentality before he even left for Troy. The most violent and intractable cases of combat trauma we have worked with in the VA Clinic have frequently experienced rapes or other severe abuse and neglect in childhood and/or adolescence prior to military service.

The scar on Odysseus' thigh, by which Eurycleia penetrates his cover, and by which he identifies himself to his father, strikes me as central to understanding Odysseus.

The recognition between the nurse and Odysseus is one of the great dramatic scenes in all of literature. It also gives us, with considerable detail, essential family and childhood background for Odysseus.²⁸

Homer builds the suspense—will she? won't she recognize him?—she comments on his build, voice, and his feet, and says, "You're like Odysseus to the life!" as she adjusts the temperature of the foot bath. Odysseus has sudden misgivings about the risk of exposure and twists his body away from the firelight.

> Bending closer
> she started to bathe her master . . . then,
> in a flash, she knew the scar—
>
>   that old wound
> made years ago by a boar's white tusk when Odysseus
> went . . . to see Autolycus. . . .
> The man was his mother's noble father, one who excelled
> the world in thievery, that and subtle, shifty oaths. . . .
> [The god] Hermes the ready partner in his crimes.
>
>   (19:443ff, Fagles)

In a feat of dramatic chutzpah, Homer suspends the action for almost seventy lines in the original poem to tell the story of Odysseus' naming by his career-criminal grandfather Autolycus, and Odysseus' puberty (*hēbēsas*, 410, orig.) visit with this same grandfather who nearly gets him killed on a boar hunt.²⁹ Autolycus' name means "Lone Wolf" or "the Wolf Himself,"³⁰ and as I pointed out above in the Introduction, the name that he gave the baby *means* "man of hate" or "he who sows trouble," or simply "hate."[31] The alternate name, Ulysses (in Greek, Oulixes), comes from his scar, *oule,* so he also has the name "scar." Scholar Nancy Felson-Rubin calls the wild boar wounding episode as "the transformative moment in Odysseus' life-history," relating it to culturally mandated rites of passage, and thus—we want to believe—essentially benign. The text supports this benign spin by reporting the splendid gifts showered on Odysseus afterward by his grandfather and the jolly celebration that his "happy parents" made when he got home. While I agree with Felson-Rubin that this episode was trans-formative, I see it as a darker transformation, when Odysseus concluded that *no one* is to be trusted, when he concluded that unless you beat them to it or get over on them first, other people only want to hurt, exploit, or humiliate you. Scholar Nancy Sultan frames it in a manner closer to how the ancient Greeks considered such things, as a matter of inheritance:

> Indeed, Odysseus has acquired his thirst for "all kinds of *dolos* [cunning]" directly from his divine ancestors. He is descended from Hermes, the god of thieves, being born the grandson of Autolykos, the one who surpassed all men in the art of thievery (*Od.* 19.394–397). In fact it would not be too dif-ficult to see Odysseus as many of the *lēistores,* "pirates, robbers" we find in Homer. Telemachos tells us that Odysseus procured his entire estate by "raiding" (*lēissato Od.* 1.397–398). In the male heroic society of Homeric poetry, it is expected and accepted to obtain anything, including women, by raiding.[32]

Scholar Erwin Cook ties it all together by pointing out that the darkly ambiguous "man of pain" designation for a hero crystallizes in the scar-name Oulixes. He is named and defined by this scar. Cook proposes that we hear the name Ulysses as "He who was permanently scarred in youth."[33]

The story of the scar may finally provide the answer to the much vexed question of Odysseus' cruelty to his father, Laertes, which seems completely unmotivated to many scholars and readers. A surprising, but extremely common, phenomenon arising from childhood trauma is the misdirection—or so it seems to most outside observers—of the most intense anger at the ineffectual bystander, rather than at the perpetrator of the trauma. Thus a woman who as a child was the target of incest by her father may hate her *mother* who failed to protect her with more vitriol than the father who raped her. Some Vietnam veterans, who volunteered to return to Vietnam after their first, not-voluntary combat tour, have told me that they hated American civilians after their initial return far more fiercely than they hated the Vietnamese enemy in the war zone. The scar on Odysseus' thigh by which he identifies himself to his father *explains* his cruelty to his father. The scar is the lifelong and to him still valid token of his rage that his father failed to protect him from his villainous maternal grandfather.

The impact of these childhood experiences, and of the family system that produced them, was evident even before Odysseus left for Troy. There are dark shadows even then in his character. The opening scene of the *Odyssey* has the goddess Athena visit Telemachus disguised as Mentes, the lord of a nearby island. Mentes offers the boy advice and cheerful reminiscences of his father, including this one of Mentes' first meeting with Odysseus more than twenty years before:

> [Odysseus had] just come in from . . . visiting Ilus . . .
> hunting deadly poison to smear on his arrows' bronze heads.
> Ilus refused—*he feared the wrath of the everlasting gods*—
> but [Mentes' own] father . . . gave him all he wanted.
> (1:302ff, Fagles; emphasis added)

This passage is loaded with puzzles and ironies. The goddess, who has a special soft spot for Odysseus, tells this story about Odysseus doing something that is anathema to the gods, poisoning his arrows. What's more the story is told to Telemachus his son as an example of how praiseworthy his father is.

In this book and in *Achilles in Vietnam,* I have been far more interested in the effect of trauma on character and on the capacity for social trust than in lists of symptoms. The American Psychiatric Association has held out against the idea that horrible experience, especially caused by other people's betrayal, coercion, cruelty, or injustice, can wreck good character or produce bad character. If the expectation that other people plan only harm, exploitation, and humiliation produces a cynical "strike first" attitude, trauma can produce an active, self-starting predator. Odysseus' scar alerts us to the interconnection of childhood trauma, combat trauma, and a veteran's adult character.

HE LEAVES—AGAIN!

The poem as we have it ends in Book 24 with the face-off between the posse of townsmen looking to carve up Odysseus for the two generations of youth he has killed off or let die. They are roused by Eupithes, the father of the most vicious suitor, Antinous. His appeal to the townsmen is this:

> My friends, what a mortal blow this man has dealt
> to all our island people! Those fighters, many and brave,
> he led away to his curved ships—he lost the ships
> and he lost the men and back he comes again
> to kill the best of our princes.
> Quick, after him! . . .
> Up, attack! Or we'll hang our heads forever,
> all disgraced, even by generations down the years,
> if we don't punish the murderers of our brothers and sons!
>   (24:471ff, Fagles)

He speaks the simple truth about the facts, and his appeal is to *tisis*, blood vengeance.[31]

On Mount Olympus, Zeus tells Athena, enough is enough, wipe everyone's memory and "Let them be friends. . . . Let peace and wealth come cresting through the land" (24:536ff, Fagles).

Against the posse three generations—Laertes, Odysseus, and Telemachus—stand shoulder to shoulder, with a few loyal retainers to back them up. Athena, of course, is on the scene in the guise of Mentor, but Odysseus recognizes her immediately. Despite Zeus' orders to her to force the two sides to make peace and an amnesty (amnesty literally means "forgetting"), Athena pumps up old Laertes to get off one shot that takes down Eupithes—"brandish your long spear and wing it fast" (24:572, Fagles). Odysseus and Telemachus charge, but now Athena uses her 250-decibel voice to stop everyone cold. The posse turns tail and runs. When Odysseus charges after them Zeus lands a lightning bolt and he stops. The last few lines tell us that peace reigns for years to come.

But the attentive listener/reader still remembers that in the Underworld, Teiresias had told Odysseus that he must leave again once he gets home, to tramp inland till he finds a place where the sea is unknown to perform sacrifices to his god-enemy, the sea god Poseidon. Odysseus has somberly repeated this to Penelope the previous night—their first and only night together in the whole epic. What a heartbreaking insight! After so much struggle, suffering, and loss to *get home,* he cannot *be home.*

The prophet Teiresias has promised that the final trial done, he will enjoy a "ripe old age, with all your people there in blessed peace around you" (11:155f, Fagles). Some of the men I work with, astonished to be alive now in their early to mid-fifties seem on the verge of finding this ability to be at home, here, now, with their partners, their grown children, and especially *grandchildren*.

PART II

RESTORATION

16

Introduction[1]

Odysseus has shown us how *not* to return home from war. It's been a grim picture with all the worst elements of the prejudiced Vietnam veteran stereotype. In this part of the book I will introduce two pictures of how those veterans who have been psychologically injured in combat can recover from those injuries.

The symptoms caused by psychological injury that the American Psychiatric Association calls PTSD[2] in its *Diagnostic and Statistical Manual of Mental Disorders* (DSM) can be understood in one clear and simple concept: persistence of *valid adaptations to danger* into a time of safety afterward. Reexperiencing symptoms of PTSD are varied outcomes of the capacity to learn about danger, so as to be able to anticipate it, to prepare for it, or to avoid it. The mobilization of the mind and body to meet danger, *and* the shutting down of mental and bodily functions not required to survive in mortal danger, become harmful and dysfunctional if they persist long after danger has passed. I invite the reader to look up this list of symptoms in the light of the simple concept I offer here, to see for themselves that these represent the persistence of no longer needed adaptations. Almost all of them fit this simple concept.

Despite our proud boast to be at the top of the animal kingdom, we are not the only species that has ever responded to great danger and then failed to unlearn those responses after the danger has passed. Our vulnerability to being injured in this way goes very far back into evolutionary history. What the APA calls PTSD (and I shall call "simple PTSD") is probably rooted in an array of changes in the physiology and anatomy of the central nervous system[3]—and may be irreversible. An injury, not a disorder! As with any injury, the symptoms can range from mild to devastating, depending on the severity of the wound, the robustness of health at the time of the injury, and the conditions—especially nutrition—under which recovery occurred. In the case of a physical wound what counts is physical nutrition; in the case of a psychological injury what counts is *social* nutrition.

Like physical injuries, simple PTSD can lead to specific disabilities. For example, an infantryman may learn from horrible experience that any bunching up or dense gathering of soldiers, particularly in the open, offers a too tempting target to enemy mortarmen and snipers. Later, in peacetime, this same infantryman may have an unshakable and non-negotiable fear of crowds and open spaces. In civilian life this is a disability. It interferes with various social, economic, and political functions that the veteran may want to take part in. The collision between the old combat adaptation, such as fear of crowds, and the requirements of a current civilian activity, may cause him to engage in *further* adaptations to his disability that allow him to salvage something. For example, in order to avoid crowds, but still be able cast his vote in elections, this infantry vet may show up at the polls before they open in the morning, may urgently insist on being the first one in the door, and be almost frenzied, possibly rude in his haste to be out again. His family and the poll workers probably view his behavior as annoying or even deranged. However, the resiliency, energy, and will he puts into such adaptations are of the same species as the amputee puts into playing ice hockey.

We all know or know of people with physical injuries who nonetheless have been able to make a flourishing human life, despite their specific disabilities. There are many famous heroic examples of this, such as Helen Keller. I have the privilege of knowing United States Senator Max Cleland of Georgia, an Army veteran who lost two legs and one arm from a Vietnam War grenade explosion. My impression is that, despite his specific disabilities, he has a flourishing life. We can only guess at and admire the personal strength, resiliency, and struggle that enabled him to achieve this, and do not fault others with similarly terrible injuries who have been laid low by them. Not everyone is a Helen Keller or Max Cleland, nor should we require them to be.

Depending on their severity and the resources and resiliency of the survivor, simple PTSD injuries can be disabling in the same sense that physical injuries are. But they do not *necessarily* blight the whole life of the person that bears them. Some combat veterans shrug off their nightmares, startle reactions, avoidances, and so forth as things to adapt to and live with, again akin to physical injuries. Their life is changed, to be sure, and often limited in specific ways, but the possibility of it being a good human life is not destroyed.

However, when the injury invades character, and the capacity for social trust is destroyed, all possibility of a flourishing human life is lost. I (and many others) call this "complex PTSD."[4] Social trust is *the expectation that power will be used in accordance with "what's right."* When social trust is destroyed, it is not replaced by a vacuum, but rather by a perpetual mobilization to fend off attack, humiliation, or exploitation, and to figure out other people's trickery. Veterans with complex PTSD see the civilian world in the same two dimensions as Homer's warriors saw warfare, *biē,* violent force, and *mētis,* cunning. Civil society, the world of the civilian at peace, is founded in a third dimension of trust that power will be used in accordance with "what's right." In actuality, both *biē* and *mētis* play significant roles in the modern state. However, no *legitimate* government anywhere in the world or in any historical era has ruled purely by armed might and deceit alone. Trust that power will be used in accordance with "what's right," however locally understood, is a key component of state legitimacy. This third dimension is invisible to veterans with complex PTSD, or they deny its existence. Claims of trustworthiness by any institutions of power—whether governments, employers, economic or educational institutions—seem to these veterans to be a deceptive veneer hiding a violent and exploitive reality.

Complex PTSD veterans usually suffer this along with their adaptations to war, so complex PTSD usually includes simple PTSD. At least this is true of the veterans we see in the VA clinic. Possibly a veteran like Odysseus with no simple PTSD, only injuries to good character, would never come to the VA. In *Achilles in Vietnam,* I observed that the World Health Organization (ICD-9/10) diagnosis "Enduring Personality Change After Catastrophic Experience" yields complex PTSD when added to the DSM diagnosis of (simple) PTSD. However, I was baffled by the WHO assertion that "Enduring Personality Change After Catastrophic Experience" *excludes* PTSD. This diagnosis fits Homer's Odysseus quite well, but in our clinical experience, symptoms of simple PTSD are present even in the most Odyssean veterans we work with.

Lying and deceit are valuable military skills, for which Odysseus boasted, "Men hold me formidable for guile."[5] In war, "they"—the enemy—really are out to kill you. The modern soldier's own military organization propels the soldier into the presence of that enemy and holds him captive in the war zone. This happens in all modern wars. Added to that in the Vietnam era were multiple violations of good military practice and betrayals of "what's right." After such experience, any friendliness and cooperation may only look like manipulations to trick innocents into a position where they can be exploited or hurt. One often hears veterans describe themselves as "paranoid" when speaking of their vigilance against harm, humiliation, or exploitation. Mental health professionals frequently agree with this label, although I believe that nothing is added to our knowledge about the veteran by using this psychiatric jargon, and much is lost in prejudicial stigmatization. It suffices to say that a given veteran does not trust anyone.

AVERSION TO RETURNING VETERANS IS AN OLD STORY

Acts of war generate a profound gulf between the combatant and the community he left behind. The veteran carries the taint of a killer, of blood pollution (perhaps what Dennis Spector described above as a need for rebirth) that many cultures respond to with purification rituals. Our culture today denies the need for purification and provides none, even though in the past it has done so. Both the veteran and his community may question the wisdom of return. The community worries about the veteran's self-control. The veteran, knowing what he is capable of, may also fear losing control. He may fear that if people knew what he has done, they would reject him or lock him up in a prison or mental hospital. Both the veteran and the community collude in the belief that he is "no longer one of us." Many Vietnam combat veterans with complex PTSD express the feeling that they died in Vietnam and should not have returned.

The anguish of guilt drives some away from life with others, but some, like former Senator Bob Kerrey, seem motivated by it to devote their lives to the service of others. The next chapter presents a good deal about what might be called medical-psychological therapies. They often help manage guilt, but they are not, and should not be, the only therapies available for moral pain. Religious and cultural therapies are not only possible, but may well be superior to what mental health professionals conventionally offer.

In the medieval Christian church, everyone who shed blood in war had to do penance. If you committed atrocities, you had to do more penance, but even if you wore a white hat and were a perfect model of proper conduct, you had to do penance. Most warrior societies, as well as many not dominated by warfare, have historically had communal rites of purification of the returning fighter after battle—the purifications in Numbers 31:19ff, for example, in the Hebrew Bible.[6]

The performances of the Athenian tragic theater—which was a theater of combat veterans, by combat veterans, and for combat veterans—

offered cultural therapy, including purification. Aristotle famously said that tragedy provides *"katharsis."* Scholars tell us that three meanings of *katharsis* circulated in Aristotle's time and were used by him at various places in his work: (1) religious purification of a ritual taint and expiation of a religious sin; (2) medicinal purgation of something unhealthy, poisonous, or impure; (3) mental clarification, removing obstacles to understanding, the psychological equivalent of producing clear water from muddy.[7] The ancient Athenians had a distinctive therapy of purification, healing, and reintegration of returning soldiers that was undertaken as a whole political community. Sacred theater was one of its primary means of reintegrating the returning veteran into the social sphere as "citizen."

The early Romans had a ceremony of purification for returning armies, the details of which we know little. It apparently involved passing under a beam erected across a street, with head covered, as well as other ceremonies, purifications, and sacrifices. The French scholar Georges Dumézil writes,

> The legend of Horace—victorious, furious, criminal, and purified—served as myth at the annual ceremony which marked the end of the military season, in which the warriors of primitive Rome passed over from the domain of Mars [the Roman god of war] unleashed to that of *"Mars qui praeest paci"* [Mars who is in charge of peace] thus . . . thereby desacralizing themselves, and also cleansing themselves for their acts of violence in battle which, if not "involuntary," were at least necessary.[8]

One of my patients, a Vietnam vet, was greeted by his father, who was torpedoed in the World War II Merchant Marine, with a $50 bill on his return from Vietnam and the words, "Here. Get drunk. Get laid. And I want you at the union hall on Monday morning." *That* is not purification after battle.

Over the years, I have said to my patients (who are almost entirely Roman Catholic because of the demography of the local veteran population), "If the Church's ideas on sin, penitence, forgiveness of sin, and redemption are about anything, they're about the real stuff. What the Church offers is about cruelty, violence, murder—not just the sins you confessed in parochial school." My clinical team has encouraged many of the veterans we work with to avail themselves of the sacrament of penance. When a veteran does not already know a priest he trusts to hear his confession, we have suggested priests who understand enough about combat neither to deny that he has anything to feel guilty about nor to recoil in revulsion and send him away without the sacrament. We also recommend service to others and the doing (not simply passive consumption) of the arts as ways of living with guilt.

Have we learned nothing about the importance of judging separately a war and the people who fight it? Yes, the Nuremberg Principles on war crimes are crucial. But do we condemn the inexperienced young Navy lieutenant Bob Kerrey for not refusing an order because it *could* lead him into the illegal act of killing unarmed women and children if the mission failed in some specific way, but not if it went off as conceived?[9]

While it is true that rapid social changes took place while many Vietnam veterans were in the military and away in Vietnam, I have pointed out repeatedly that this gulf between veteran and civilian is generic, and was experienced by returning combat veterans of prior wars. It is historically typical for returning American war veterans throughout our history to be ignored by the communities they returned to, rather than to be celebrated and cherished by them.[10] The experience of the World War II veterans—the fathers of the Vietnam veterans—is the historical *anomaly*. Toward the end of World War II, politicians with fresh memories of the Bonus Army of World War I veterans worried about so many returning soldiers looking for jobs. Willard Waller, the World War I veteran whom I have quoted so many times in this book, did his best to see that they *were* worried, warning of the social and political nitroglycerine that millions of returning veterans could present to civilian society. Congress appropriated unprecedented benefits.

Farmers from the Revolutionary War returned to find banks foreclosing their farms because the money the government gave them was no good. These first American veterans encountered a Platonic/Stoic/Puritan view that yes, what they had done in the Continental Army was virtuous, but virtue itself is sufficient to well-being[11]—so why are they asking for money? Implicit in this philosophic position is the reasoning that if the veteran does *not* have well-being, his virtue is somehow defective. Therefore, logically, misery and disability must be his own fault, his own deficiency of virtue, and therefore unworthy of compassion.

Sound familiar?

Only in the period after the War of 1812 did the nation awaken to its duty toward the veterans of the War of Independence. In his 1999 book, *Suffering Soldiers,* historian John Resch examined wealth and number of children for all the men of a single New Hampshire town from 1792 to 1823. He found that on the average, those who never served, or who joined the short-service militia, held their own economically, and had stable economic success and that the reproductive success of the two groups was similar. However, during the same period, the long-service Continental Army veterans got poorer. On average, the long-service veterans had started out the beginning of the period 11 percent poorer than the militia vets or never-served, but ended up a startling 66 percent poorer than the other groups thirty years later.[12] The number of living children in the household, which in that era was strongly influenced by the quality of year-round nutrition, and thus dependent on wealth, shows an average of 6.5 children for Continental Army veterans, 7.5 for militia veterans, and 9.4 for those who never served.

Civil War veterans had trouble finding employment and were accused of being drug addicts. Our word "hobo" supposedly comes from homeless Civil War veterans—called "hoe boys"—who roamed the lanes of rural America with hoes on their shoulders, looking for work. World War I Bonus Army veterans marched on Washington in 1932, the summer before FDR's election, and camped on the Mall. They demanded that they be paid the bonus that Congress had voted them in 1924. President Hoover had them driven out with tanks and bayonets and their camp burned. Korean War veterans were accused of being too weak to win. In that era of McCarthyism, repatriated POWs were suspected of Communist sympathies from brainwashing.

With increasing polarization over the Vietnam War, veterans returned home to protesters who accused them of being torturers, perpetrators of atrocities, and baby killers. For every returning veteran who encountered this personally, there were many more who saw scenes selected for their dramatic and/or outrageous qualities in the TV news or heard nth-hand stories. The media presented a barrage of images portraying the Vietnam veteran as crazy, drug-addicted, and violent. For many veterans who had joined up because they thought it was their duty as citizens, who had grown up on John Wayne and Audie Murphy, rejection by the community was infuriating. And then in their fathers' VFW and Legion posts, some were greeted with derision even more devastating than taunts by war protesters: "We won our war. What the fuck's wrong with you?"

Those Vietnam-era civilians inclined to show honor to returning veterans ran afoul of deep divisions over the wisdom of making this war at all (e.g., if Chinese expansionism was the threat, wouldn't Ho and the Viet Minh be our natural allies?), and over the justice of how it was prosecuted (e.g., "free fire zones"), making it appear that honoring the veterans endorsed both. From the hawks on the political right to the doves on the political left, the nation as a whole lost sight of the fundamental importance of social esteem in rebuilding the capacity for social trust within a person who has come home from war. Social esteem is embodied no less in private gestures of respect than in public rituals of honor and recognition. Vietnam veterans often received neither.

DAMAGE TO CHARACTER—INJURED *THUMOS*

Professor Amélie Rorty of Brandeis defines the Homeric word *thumos* as "the energy of spirited honor."[13] It is closely allied to the English word "character," but adds some important extra dimensions. I want to put *thumos* back into current use, and am not alone in this. As Professor Francis Fukuyama, an economic historian has pointed out, modern democracies often fail to recognize honor and the desire for recognition as part of the *universal and normal* makeup of humans, noticing it only in its pathological and deformed states.[14]

According to the German Idealist philosopher Hegel, all human warfare originates in a fight to the death over honor, a fight for unconditional recognition and acknowledgment by an equal, which only one combatant can win. Hegel says that there are two ways to lose: death with honor, or the all-encompassing dishonor—the social death—of enslavement.[15] Honor is a social phenomenon; its interior psychic mirror is *thumos*. Current psychiatric terminology calls *thumos* "narcissism." "Narcissism" is simply a new word for an old concept: *"thumos"* from Homer; *"thumoeides"* from Plato; "pride or vainglory" from Hobbes; *"amour-propre"* from Rousseau; "desire for recognition (*Anerkennung*)" from Hegel; "narcissism"[16] from psychoanalyst Heinz Kohut, who developed and modified Freud's ideas. I much prefer Homer's term *thumos* to the modern psychojargon, narcissism, because of the ways the latter term has been pathologized and turned into a general-purpose blame word. These thinkers, over thousands of years from Homer to Kohut, have seen this feature of mental life as normal and universal, even if it can develop dangerous excesses, deficiencies, or deformities. I believe that *thumos* is a human universal that evolved out of war in our ancestral evolutionary past and still explodes in killing rage, when violated.[17] Many cultural, legal, and social changes have removed these reactions from the *individual* realm, so we no longer teach our children that a man of honor must kill someone who makes a joke at his expense, or who steals food from his freezer, but such reactions are very much alive at the *collective* level.

The normal adult's cloak of safety and guarantor of his or her narcissistic stability is the society's image of "what's right" and the implementation of "what's right" by power holders, along with concrete social support of a face-to-face community to whom one is attached. Narcissism, allegedly the most "primitive" of psychological phenomena, is much entwined with the body, but it is just as deeply enmeshed in the social, moral, and political worlds.

The features of the normal adult world that control thumotic emotions and moods are *attachments, ideals,* and *ambitions.* Their good-enough realization in the world is the foundation of ordinary self-respect and of the sense of self-worth that we expect in the normal adult. *Thumos,* then, can be practically defined as

- The historically and socioculturally constructed *content* embodied in ideals, ambitions, and attachments.
- The intensity with which these are energized.
- The emotions aroused by cognitive appraisal of their condition (particularly improvement or deterioration) in the world.

Thumos is thus a container for the English word "character." Character exists in dynamic relation to the ecology of social power, modeled and remodeled throughout life by how well or badly those who hold power fulfill the culture's moral order. The shattering impact on character of mortal-stakes misuse of power was a major theme of my previous book, *Achilles in Vietnam: Combat Trauma and the Undoing of Character.*

Aristotle's explanation of *thumos* in the *Politics* (VII.6.1327b39ff.) surprises the modern mind. He starts by picking an argument with his teacher, Plato, over the character of the "Guardians" of the state:

> For as to what [Plato] said . . . about the character that should belong to . . . Guardians—they should be affectionate to their friends but fierce toward strangers—it is [*thumos*] that causes affectionateness, for [*thumos*] is the capacity of the soul whereby we love. A sign of this is that [*thumos*] is more roused against associates and friends than against strangers, when it thinks itself slighted. . . . Moreover it is from this faculty that power to command and love of freedom are in all cases derived; for [*thumos*] is a commanding and indomitable element. But it is a mistake to describe the Guardians as cruel toward strangers; it is not right to be cruel towards anybody, and men of great-souled nature [*megalopsukhoi*] are not fierce, except against wrongdoers, and their anger is still fiercer against their companions if they think that these are wronging them . . . Hence the saying "For brothers' wars are cruel."
>
> (VII.6.1327b39ff., Rackham, trans.)

This passage is remarkable for the way it draws together these apparently different threads: killing rage, love, the capacity to command, and feeling for freedom. This is exactly the kind of freight the concept of "character" should carry. It must have energy. It must be passionate. It must connect with other people and have an active commitment to right and wrong in the world, however right and wrong are locally constructed. Aristotle's account focuses on people and social groups to whom we are attached, on *philoi* (plural of *philos*). He explains compactly: a *philos* is "another myself." "The excellent person is related to his [*philos*] in the same way as he is related to himself, since a [*philos*] is another himself."[18] Obviously, there is the altruistic impulse of wishing the *philos* well, but there is also an element of narcissism here that I want to bring into the foreground and use in a positive way.

Attachment implicates us in the acts and fate of a *philos,* influencing mood and emotion and touching our sense of our own value. When a *philos* does something magnificent, we feel pride; when he does something vicious, we feel shame. If I am depressed because my daughter is doing badly in school, it is not because I have made a utilitarian calculation of how this will affect her lifetime earnings and ability to support me in my old age. No, it will be because of my attachment to her, her quality as "another myself." Threat to a *philos* arouses fear and rage, and the death or injury of a *philos* hurts and grieves us. The loving recognition and attachment by a *philos* sustains and nourishes.

Attachment to *philoi* inspires altruistic readiness to take risks and to resort to violence on their behalf against outsiders, both defensively and offensively. Betrayal of trust or a breach of "what's right" among *philoi* can wreck *thumos.* At the least, it results in withdrawal of emotional commitment and energy. But it may also produce anger and violence within the group, either directed against those *philoi* responsible for the betrayal-breach, or in more extreme cases directed against all *philoi,* against the entire community.

In *Achilles in Vietnam* (pp. 40–41) I wrote the following about the *philia* that arises between combat comrades:

> Modern American English makes soldiers' love for special comrades into a problem, because the word "love" evokes sexual and romantic associations. But "friendship" seems too bland for the passion of care that arises between soldiers in combat. Achilles laments to his mother [the goddess Thetis] that his *philos,* his "greatest friend is gone" (18:89f). Much ink has been spilled over whether this word (and the abstract noun *philia*) and all

its linguistic relatives should be translated under the rubric of "friend, friendship," etc. or of "love, beloved," etc. However, the difficulty of finding the right word reflects differences between ancient Greek and modern American culture that need to be made clear. "*Philia* includes many relationships that would not be classified as friendships. The love of mother and child is a paradigmatic case of *philia;* all close family relations, including the relation of husband and wife, are so characterized. Furthermore, our [word] 'friendship' can suggest a relationship that is weak in affect . . . as in the expression 'just friends.' . . . [*Philia*] includes the very strongest affective relationships that human beings form . . . [including, but not limited to] relationships that have a passionate sexual component. For both these reasons, English 'love' seems more appropriately wide-ranging. . . . [The] emphasis of *philia* is less on intensely passionate longing than on . . . benefit, sharing, and mutuality. . . ."[19] Many individuals who experience friendship as one of the central goods in their lives find that their employers will not recognize *philia* between people whose relationship is not familial. Veterans have lost their jobs because they left work to aid another veteran, in circumstances where the same absence would have been "understandable" and charged against sick or vacation time—had the other been a spouse, parent, or child. The social relationship of steady, paid employment was virtually unknown in ancient Greece. This relationship has come to so dominate our modern consciousness that many people view friendship purely as a leisure activity, or a sweetener that with luck arises among co-workers, neighbors, or members of a voluntary association such as a church or club, but will be put aside if it gives rise to any conflicting claims at work. Many veterans have also alienated their spouses, because they would leave home to rescue fellow veterans. The ancient Greeks, perhaps because their societies were so highly militarized (every male citizen was also a soldier), simply assumed the centrality of *philia.*

The formula that *philos* is "another myself" is the key to most socially organized human violence. In the modern world, the nation-state has appropriated the status of *philos*, along with other groups such as armies, religions, and professions. Today, except in our deteriorated inner cities, we no longer fight to the death in the streets for recognition as individuals, but nations continue to compel deference with violence, to demand acknowledgment with violence. If your *philos* is threatened or demeaned it arouses killing rage. Witness the primal rage of Americans after September 11, 2001.

As Aristotle pointed out in the passage above, *thumos* or narcissism is not exclusively an infantile or pathological phenomenon, but infuses essential elements in human flourishing. Narcissism is a part of the psychic economy of the healthy adult that is intimately bound up *with the moral and social world that the adult inhabits*.

The social conditions that cause complex PTSD—persistent human betrayal and rupture of community in mortal-stakes situations of captivity—destroy *thumos,* destroy normal narcissism, and undo character. Modern battle is a condition of captivity (even when it has been entered voluntarily), a fact that has escaped notice because the captives move about in the open carrying powerful weapons, and because the role of captor is cooperatively shared by the two enemy military organizations—which are presumed to cooperate in nothing.[20] "Primitive" warfare, of which Iliadic warfare is an example, is and was voluntary—Achilles really could say, "I quit." Modern combat is a condition of enslavement and torture. I am not demonizing the U.S. Armed Services when I say that. Modern war itself makes it so. Until we end the practice of war itself, this will continue.

What happens to normal adult narcissism—or *thumos* or character—when it is damaged? The list that follows is a spectrum of manifestations of injury to *thumos.* While they cannot all happen at the same time, we often see them succeeding each other over time in the same veteran, sometime cyclically.

- Demoralization (*athumia*), death to the world, apathy, ennui, and *aboulia* (no will), *anhedonia* (no pleasure),[21] and in its most extreme form: literally fatal collapse of self-care, as in military "nostalgia" and concentration camp "Musselman."[22]
- Self-loathing, a sense of unworthiness.
- Loss of self-respect and initiative.
- Pervasive "raw" vulnerability and feeling conspicuous.
- Social withdrawal, irritability.
- Hypochondriacal preoccupations, alternating with neglect of real ill health and injuries.
- Suggestibility and blind obedience, which may turn into a fanatical "mission."
- Mortal risk taking to divine the status of one's "luck."
- Danger seeking, fight seeking.
- Claims to having been players in the single most important event in human history.
- Grandiosity and entitlement.

- Coercive demands for respect, honor, acknowledgment.
- Rage at small slights, disappointment, lapses.
- Coercive attempts to establish power dominance.
- "Global" destructiveness of their fantasies, wishes, and, occasionally, behavior.
- Apocalyptic ecstasy.

Mental health professionals who have casually encountered combat veterans with complex PTSD often react negatively to the second half of this list and call it "narcissism." They are frustrated and offended by such veterans' insistence that they will deal only with "the head of the snake," e.g., chief of service or medical center director. When clinicians use the term "narcissistic" to damn veterans who present themselves this way, it is as though the clinicians have utterly forgotten the importance of narcissism in any good life. The first half of the list is no less involved with narcissism (its deflation) than the second half (its inflation), but deflated narcissism generally draws more sympathetic labels, such as depression.

Does Homer's Odysseus give us a portrait of a pure form of post-traumatic character damage that is neither simple PTSD nor complex PTSD? Some political tyrants, some criminals, some artists, some religious leaders, appear to have only a giant *thumos*, with no symptoms of PTSD. Trauma can crush *thumos* or inflame it and cause it to swell into giant, tyrannical *thumos*. In the same person, deflated and inflated *thumos* can alternate, giving the appearance, descriptively, of bipolar affective disorder. In a fixed inflated state, giant *thumos* can produce a ranting megalomaniac such as Adolf Hitler or a quiet megalomaniac such as Osama bin Laden.[23]

The earliest inventors of democratic politics invented equal citizen honor—*isothumos*—as the necessary psychological and social substructure for democracy.[24] With it they built laws into their *polis* to provide trustworthy restraints on *biē* and *mētis*, violence and fraud. The former was restrained by the law on *hubris*, and the latter by the strict accountability of magistrates, which made deceptive speech in public office very costly.[25] Either extreme, *thumos* too weak to imagine a future, or bloated, violently or deceptively subjugating all to its concept of the future, is destructive to the democratic process. Severe trauma can produce both extremes. Severe trauma destroys democratic *isothumos*.

Descriptively, the phenomena of damaged *thumos* draw in symptoms of many diagnoses in the DSM.[26] The symptoms of PTSD have been called "protean." Menelaus' battle with the god Proteus, as told in the *Odyssey*, is an excellent metaphor for the veteran's struggle with the symptoms of PTSD:

> But [Proteus']
> tricks were not knocked out of him; far from it.
> First he took on a whiskered lion's shape,
> a serpent then; a leopard; a great boar;
> then sousing water; then a tall green tree.
> Still we hung on, by hook or crook, through everything.
> until . . . [Proteus] saw defeat,
>
> (4:485ff, Fitzgerald)

ARISTOTLE AGAIN—HUMAN IS *POLITIKON ZŌON*

The human being is a bio-psycho-socio-cultural whole *at every moment*. This restates Aristotle's zoological observation (*Politics* I:1:1252a3) that the human is the *animal* of the political community. Body, mind, society, culture are not separate "realities," even less are they hierarchical "levels." Our physical brains are biologically evolved to make us culture bearers and users; it is our biological nature to live in relation to culturally constructed moral codes; our social lives remodel our brains; cognitive assessments and their related emotional states influence bodily health; and so on. The very fact that we speak in terms of body, mind, society, and culture is only a reflection of the methodological and institutional history of the Western world. These terms are temporary guides to perception and communication. They are throwaways, not eternal realities existing beyond the Platonic veil. What I do at this moment of writing and what you do at this moment of reading is at one and the same instant, physiological, psychological, social, and cultural.

Restoration of *thumos* and of the capacity for social trust happens only in community.

This simple and seemingly innocent statement is actually quite subversive, because it casts doubt upon a great deal of what mental health professionals do (following the cultural and economic model of medicine), how they find their value in the world, how the mental health workplace is organized, and how power is used there. In fact, the overall effect of this simple statement is to push mental health professionals off of center stage in the drama of recovery from trauma, and to place them in the wings as stagehands.

The next two chapters take us to two apparently unconnected settings: to the Department of Veterans Affairs outpatient clinic where I and my colleagues do our work, and to the Vietnam Veterans Memorial in Washington—known to many as the Vietnam Wall, or simply the Wall. We arrive at the Wall twice—once physically with the veterans in our program and once electronically via an Internet discussion group of Vietnam veterans and others as they communalize the shock of Lewis Puller's suicide.

17

From the Clinic to the Wall

Fourteen years ago, in another lifetime, I went to work for the Veterans Administration in Boston, hoping to restart my neuroscience lab research. I had never served in the military and knew virtually nothing about veterans. I do not believe I had even heard the words PTSD or combat neurosis in the course of my clinical psychiatry training. I had completed that training in June 1980, with my mind already preoccupied with worries about a troubled family business, and was unaware of the publication that year of the third edition of the DSM, which reintroduced psychological injury into the diagnostic vocabulary of American psychiatry as Post-Traumatic Stress Disorder. For most of the decade I gave no thought to psychiatry and certainly none to the newly coined diagnosis of PTSD.[1]

I started work as a general psychiatrist at the Day Treatment Center of the VA Clinic in Boston in November 1987, with my head full of research plans. Talk about being thrown into the deep end of the pool! Day Treatment was where chronically, severely ill veterans were offered support and intensive outpatient treatment, usually between hospitalizations. Out of the corner of my eye, so to speak, I became aware that within the Day Treatment Center was a specialized program for Vietnam combat veterans whom nobody else in the VA wanted anything to do with. Many had histories of violence—some had assaulted clinicians in the VA—and of incarceration. In mid-December, the Argentine psychiatrist and co-founder of this Vietnam combat vet program, Dr. Lillian Rodríguez, asked me to cover for her while she returned to Argentina for a long Christmas and New Year's holiday with her family. I gulped anxiously and said sure. I joined the team meetings and community meetings of the Veterans Improvement Program—VIP, as it is called—and tried to make myself useful. January came and went and we received word that she was ill and that her return would be delayed. Over the weeks a steady stream of veterans in the program came down the hall to my office (a converted storage room) with what were purported to be medication questions or problems, and only in retrospect did I realize that I was being interviewed by these very intimidating men.

Another month or so passed, and word came that Dr. Rodríguez had died at home of a recurrence of the breast cancer that had been treated some years before. My boss then (who is still my boss now) asked me if I would be willing to split coverage of the VIP with another psychiatrist, seeing it as a hardship to be equitably shared. By this time, after those few months of training by the VIP team (three of whom are still on the team fourteen years later), I was astute enough to say no. Either I am the psychiatrist for all of VIP or for none of it. My boss looked ready to faint from relief that I was willing to take on the most intimidating patients[2] in the whole clinic.

These veterans saw something in me that I did not see in myself. I think initially it was the willingness to listen and to learn from them, and not to think I *knew* already. And listen I did, and listen, and listen. I also listened to the rest of the VIP team, which was then ten years old, and absorbed their experience and philosophy across the chasm of different disciplines and less fancy credentials. But it is mainly the veterans who have been my teachers. They have redirected my life, and I thank them for it. It has been a privilege to know many of them, men of very high rank in being, even if gaining little success in the civilian world. We devote ourselves to helping them achieve a better human life than before they came to us, and in this we generally succeed.[3]

Not long after settling into VIP I noticed that I was hearing elements in the story that Homer told of Achilles in the *Iliad.* Over and over these elements recurred. I wrote a little paper for the *Journal of Traumatic Stress* pointing this out, thinking it was just a neat teaching piece: You want to take a combat history? Remember the story of Achilles and you'll touch all the bases. I've told the story of how this paper got turned into *Achilles in Vietnam: Combat Trauma and the Undoing of Character* at the request of Harvard's professor of Classical Greek literature, Greg Nagy, in the Introduction to that book.

Most of what I know about trauma I have learned from the veterans. However, most of what I know about the *treatment* of trauma, I have learned from one of the founders of VIP, Dr. James Munroe.[4] Anyone interested in the details of the VIP approach should consult our textbook chapter referred to in the notes. I only want to highlight a few points of our method here to set the scene for the annual VIP trip to the Vietnam Veterans Memorial.

We foster and protect the conditions under which veterans can heal themselves and each other. The heart of our program is this understanding that veterans heal each other. Because we move mental health professionals off of center stage, veterans can bypass many of the obstacles blocking those with complex combat PTSD from getting help.

If the stakes weren't so serious, the usual collision between a combat veteran with complex PTSD and a mental health professional could be like the raunchy, cynical, irreverent soldier's humor of Aristophanes' Greek comic theater:

> VA *Doctor (singing)*: See my certificates, degrees, an' diplomas— Look at every one, up to the last.
> *Veteran*: Trust you? Trust them! Stick 'em up your ass!

Because their psychological injuries have destroyed social trust, the most severely injured veterans are least able to get and retain access to treatment. Complex PTSD destroys the key resource—trust—necessary for its successful treatment.[5] So we have a paradox, or at least an impasse. The very thing that constitutes the difference between simple and complex PTSD—destruction of social trust—blocks the treatment of complex PTSD.

The veterans have reason, based on their experience, to distrust credentials, institutional position, and abstract, universally applied procedures. These veterans have had the real experience of lives lost and people maimed when a person in a position of power "went by the book," rather than first looking sharply at the particulars, and then applying the book to them with flexibility and good sense. (Aristotle: "The doctor cures a particular [i.e., not abstractly universal] man," *EN* I.6, 1097a13.) Most veterans will not insist that a therapist be a subject matter expert on every technical detail of the Vietnam War, but only that the therapist be willing to "listen."

During the Vietnam War, company and battalion commanders who resisted rotation out of dangerous command billets at the end of their six months were labeled as having "gone native," that is, having developed more commitment to the troops than to the officer corps and to personal career advancement. This label was a career-ending stigma. Ironically, many instances that were called "going native" were efforts to fulfill ideals of military competence. Such officers would show reluctance to rotate to a rear area staff billet, because the six-month rotation policy *guaranteed* that no one in command of a company or battalion had the time to learn what they had to know to do the job well—in purely professional military terms.

The veterans we treat, who were all enlisted men, treasure the memories of the officers who were more devoted to their substantive military tasks and to the men under their command than to the career system. More to the point clinically, any sign of careerism by a clinician is liable to be a traumatic trigger, bringing back memories of having been put in lethal danger to get body count—or worse, to fill out the denominator of a kill ratio, where the *presence* of American casualties was rated as positive evidence of the commander's "aggressiveness" and "balls."

These veterans' worldview is based on an expectancy of *exploitation for other people's advancement*. The urgency of fear lies behind the veterans' need to know that we are working in VIP because we want to, because it gives us personal pleasure and satisfaction for its own sake.

Expectancy of exploitation leads veterans to assume that we are only interested in them as vehicles to get a graduate degree, to write a book, or to earn VA salary money. In the last fourteen years, James Munroe *did* earn his doctorate,[6] and I *did* publish a book—periods of intense anxiety followed both of these events, while veterans watched to see if we each would leave, having accomplished our "real" purpose in being there.

Vietnam veterans experienced lethal incompetence at the hands of officers and bureaucrats who had all the right credentials but whose competency in passing through career progression schools did not equip them for the reality of war against an observant and resourceful human enemy who figured out how to turn every school solution into a death trap. The veterans insist that there is something *personal* that makes someone trustworthy as a combat leader or as a clinician. Our institutions treat professionals who have the same credentials as fungible—absolutely substitutable—for one another. The veterans reject this. Their trust is personal, nontransferable.

Essential to this trust is the clinician's willingness to listen to the particularity of the veteran's own experience, and not treat them as subsumable examples of an abstract category of psychiatric or even PTSD patients.[7] They don't ask us to be universal experts, and will not trust a widely read clinician who is smug about his knowledge, and neither listens nor learns.

Trust can only be earned, never assumed from job titles or degrees. In VIP we *assume* that veterans must test the trustworthiness of anyone claiming good intentions, particularly where power is involved. We don't take offense when they test us.

VIP has taught me how to work with crisis-ridden patients who have learned to survive through violence and intimidation. Amazingly, the veteran community in the Clinic provides both physical safety—the VIP veterans do not tolerate even the smallest threat against the team—as well as psychological safety.

STAGES OF RECOVERY

Among ourselves and in speaking with veterans we use the three-stage description of recovery developed by Judith Herman:[8] Stage One, establishment of safety, sobriety, and self-care; Stage Two, trauma-centered work of constructing a personal narrative and of grieving; Stage Three, reconnecting with people, communities, ideals, and ambitions. Although we think and speak of these stages, the VIP is not programmatically built around them, and each veteran progresses at his own pace.

I cannot emphasize too strongly that safety, sobriety, and self-care are the essential foundation upon which recovery is built. We are not an any-thing-goes therapeutic community that is infinitely "understanding" of drinking and drugging and wild behavior. There's no way to skip safety, sobriety, and self-care and go right to the trauma, no matter how logical the veteran's claim: "Doc, Vietnam *caused* all that drinking, and drugging, and fucking people up. You fix the Vietnam stuff and I can stop all the rest."[9] Never happen, soldier!

We work with the veteran, in Judith Herman's words, starting with the body and moving outward, to help him lay down weapons, maintain sobriety, meet health and nutritional needs, terminate current violence as perpetrator and/or victim, and eliminate danger-seeking behaviors.

While most VIP veterans are also in individual psychotherapy and request medications,[10] the heart and soul of the program is its group therapies and the ideas and rituals of the VIP veteran community. The core idea is "You are not alone; you don't have to go through it alone." From the beginning, other veterans provide what military social scientist and his-torian Faris Kirkland and his Army colleagues[11] called "substantive vali-dation," a knowledgeable audience (even if they were not in the same specific units or operations), to whom the veteran's experience matters, and who are able to support him through the confusion, doubt, and self-criticism that seem intrinsic to having survived the chaos of battle. The team provides practical support for veterans to obtain their military records, unit diaries, and after-action reports when the situation demands. Surprisingly, this often provides the first "institutional validation" that the veterans have had, sometimes learning for the first time of awards and decorations for valor that they had earned, but had never been presented to them. In group therapies with Stage One veterans, we are active and educational as group leaders, assisting members in gaining authority over the pace of trauma disclosure, so it is safe. We seek the delicate balance between silencing the veteran and allowing him to become flooded with bodily sensations, emotions, and images by reliving the trauma, which only retraumatizes him. There are no theatrical cures where the veteran screams, vomits, bleeds, dies, and is reborn cleansed of the war. Recovery is much more like training for a marathon than a miracle faith healing.

From the beginning we establish the VIP culture of mutual respect for all veterans. No individual's branch of service, military function, battles, or suffering is more "significant" than any other's. With one another's support the veterans finally, decades late, experience the three forms of validation—substantive, institutional, and memorial—that every soldier, sailor, marine, and airman should receive after combat.[12]

Stage Two of recovery calls for the veteran to construct a cohesive narrative of his war experience in the context of his whole life—and to grieve.

VIP makes an annual trip to the Vietnam Veterans Memorial in Washington, which provides a locus for "memorial validation." This is an opportunity for those veterans ready for it to grieve for and commune with dead comrades in a safe and sober fellowship. In this group there is no need to explain or justify the importance of keeping faith with the dead through authentic emotion, respectful remembrance, and honor.

A TRIP TO THE WALL WITH VIP

Three A.M. in the spring it is still very dark in Washington. The line of lights embedded in the walk along the Wall casts a soft glow. The brightest feature in the landscape is the floodlit obelisk of the Washington Monument, which reflects off the polished black surface of the granite panels, slightly blurred by the thousands of names incised in the panels' surfaces. At this hour, with veterans who fought in Vietnam, one understands that this *is* a shrine in the full sense of a sacred precinct, where the power—the fascination and dangerousness—of the holy is present.[13] The living and the dead meet here.

No veteran in VIP is required to go to the Wall, and no veteran who wants to go on the VIP trip can do so until he has firmly established his connection to the community, has safety, sobriety, and self-care firmly in hand. Prior to the trip he has also worked on enough of his own traumatic history to have a good idea what demons he might meet at the Wall. If a veteran is simply flooded with the trauma and drowns in reexperiencing, it does him no good—it retraumatizes. Obviously, we cannot forbid veterans to go to the Wall alone apart from the scheduled trip. However, we strongly advise any Vietnam veteran not to go alone, especially the first time, to go sober, and to go with people he or she trusts. We hold a series of group meetings in the weeks prior to the trip, during which each veteran is invited to talk about what he expects, what he's heard from other veterans, and to hear from VIP vets who are going for their second or third time. We also obtain their agreement to the basic ground rules of the trip: strict sobriety, staying with the group, participation in the meetings while on the trip to process the repeated visits to the Wall during the two days in Washington. They also have the opportunity in advance of the trip to look up the locations on the Memorial's panels of the names of their dead comrades, so that they don't have to struggle to do this in the dark under the enormous emotional pressure of the visit. There is no haste or time pressure. We generally arrive at the Wall, for the first visit of the trip, at three A.M. and stay as long as anyone wishes and needs to.

For many the first visits are pure grieving. Some of the veterans are physically very large men. A six-foot-three Marine Corps veteran weeping his heart out in the dark, hugged by other veterans, is a profound thing to witness. The supportive presence of the trusted other veterans eliminates embarrassment. They do not have to go through it alone.

Some veterans fear the Wall because they fear the dead will reproach them—for having not done enough, for having survived when the man on the Wall—"in the Wall"—did not. The polished stone reflects the movements of the veterans along its surface giving sensory credence to the sensation that the dead are present.

Some do not feel worthy to be there.

For some, the only emotion is anger.

One veteran exclaimed, "It's a grave!" There have been times I have walked down the slope toward the apex of the Wall and had difficulty breathing, as though the rising tide of names on my left was rising water and I was drowning.

Some ask forgiveness for something they did, or didn't do.

For some, it is a sad, quiet chat and visit with the dead, with love as the predominant emotion.

The names—all 58,226 of them[14]—are a very powerful statement: each of these was a whole life.[15] There are no et ceteras on the Wall.

Sometimes difficulty remembering a name, or enough of a name to find its location on the Wall, torments a veteran. People were often known by nicknames conferred before the young man—who decades later is our patient—arrived at his unit. The veteran may never once have heard his battle comrade's given name, even after several months. This is where unit associations provide irreplaceable assistance, when the veteran is able to find others who were there at the same time as he, who might recall both the nickname and the man's right name. Unit diaries and after-action reports record deaths day by day, so that if the date is known, the number of possible names can be greatly narrowed.

The agony of not knowing or not being able to remember names is captured in this poem, "Remembrance," by Joan Duffy Newberry, a veteran of the Air Force nursing corps:

> How is it possible that I remember
>   not one name on this tragic wall?
> How is it possible?
> After all, there are ten tall panels
>   that represent the year I spent in Nam.
>
> Too many names . . . names like Smith
>   and Herman and O'Brien and Siciliano . . .
> I know you   your faces are forever
>   seared into my brain.
>
> You were little more than children
>   when you came under my care,
> With wounds and illnesses that
>   no human should ever endure,
>
> My God, I hated to see you so hurt,
>   so frightened and so sick.
> How is it possible that I cannot
>   remember any of you dying?
>
> In nightmares you reproach me
>   for making you live when you were
>   determined to die . . .
> And you curse me for being so slow
>   to help your best buddy . . .

"There are others I must tend
　　to before him," I say in my dream . . .
Sweat covered, I awake and wonder just
　　how far my mind will go to absolve
　　me of your buddy's death.

My God, it was terrible to be so responsible . . .
I was too young and too inexperienced a nurse
　　to make such wrenching decisions.

No matter what I did it was never enough . . .
　　and no matter what I did, it will never
　　have been enough,
For there are too many names forever etched
　　on this wailing wall.

I grieve for you my nameless patients.
　　and I grieve as well for your loved ones.
I also grieve for myself, for I will
　　never be free of tormenting uncertainty . . .

What should I have done
　　and what could I have done
To keep you from joining
　　this heart-breaking roster of the dead?
　　　　　—Duff, 1/Lt USAF NC RVN 69–70
　　　　　Left at panel 24W, Memorial Day 1987[16]

In the very early morning—"0-dark-30"—the veterans have the Wall
entirely to themselves, which is the main reason that we go at that hour.
The intimate presence of the dead—for those who are well prepared for
it and meet the dead with the support of a community—has been paradoxically a breath of life for many. The famous line by Wilfred Owen,
"These are the men whose minds the Dead have ravished,"[17] seems relevant here, although his experience was in the Craiglockhart military psychiatric hospital while World War I still raged in France. The dead have
pursued the men we work with for thirty years. Actively going to meet
them in their sacred space, with living brothers at their shoulder, seems to
make a great and positive change in their relationship to the dead.[18]

　After the sun rises (often a wonderful moment standing on the steps of the Lincoln Memorial facing east up the Mall), we go to breakfast, go back to our billet on whatever military base has offered us hospitality. We hold a therapy group to encourage the veterans to talk about what they have just done and what it was like. After a nap, we return to the Wall in the early afternoon.

Talk about different!

The Vietnam Veterans Memorial is the single most frequently visited monument in the capital. On a spring afternoon this is very easy to believe. However, the sense of sacred ground is still palpable and takes hold of the crowds of tourists and schoolchildren. They walk and talk quietly—probably more quietly than in their own churches. I think they know they're in someone else's church.

VIP veterans, if they go to the Wall at all, generally go more than once over the years. We encourage this for several reasons, the most important being that they report that they get something different out of each visit. The presence of veterans who have been to the Wall before is also enormously valuable to the veterans going for their first time. And on a second or third visit, the veteran is much more likely to engage with the schoolchildren or other visitors at the Wall. On a spring afternoon, standing still for an hour at the far edge of the walk, they become aware of parents, brothers and sisters, wives, children, cousins, aunts and uncles, school friends, neighbors of the people on the Wall. This has an oddly consoling effect on many veterans. It is another previously unfelt dimension of knowing that they are not alone, not freaks. A second- or third-time veteran may offer to help these other mourners find the names or make rubbings of them on the strips of paper that the Park Service provides.

Other veterans have found great solace in watching groups of schoolchildren, and sometimes speaking with them. The children's "Thank you" and the poems and stories they leave at the Wall do not provoke any of the bitter reactions that the same words from adults sometimes bring: "Where the fuck were you thirty years ago?"

Adult tourists who are unconnected with anyone on the Wall sometimes bring out that bitterness and generate a raw, unpleasantly conspicuous feeling of being gawked at, "What are we, zoo animals?" Fortunately, these reactions are rarely intense enough to disrupt the veteran's purpose in being there or to spoil the trip for him. The same can be said for xenophobic reactions to the foreign tourists who come to the Wall. The reactions occur but they don't ruin things, because of the opportunity to talk about them and to have support from the other veterans.

While reactions to the Wall trip are many and varied, the predominant theme is grieving. This is an essential element in the second stage of recovery from complex PTSD after combat. When a member of VIP has tested the trustworthiness of the community and of the team sufficiently, he is often able to venture beyond the safety of we-all-went-through-the-same-thing into the particularity of his own experience, and *his* contribution to both events and to the course that his life has taken. The process of constructing a narrative invariably arouses intense emotions, particularly of grief. They grieve not only for comrades lost during and since the war, but almost always for irretrievable losses of prewar relationships, with parents, siblings, wives, and children. They mourn:

- Relationships, ideals, and ambitions blighted by alcohol and drug abuse, and its consequences.
- Relationships, ideals, and ambitions blighted by violence and its consequences.
- Relationships, ideals, and ambitions blighted by the avoidance symptoms of PTSD.
- Lost innocence.
- Lost youth and health.
- Waste.

Ruptured relationships are sometimes irretrievable, or have been made so by death. As we saw in Chapter 9, when Odysseus meets the ghost of his dead mother in the Underworld, he learns she died of grief during his long inexplicable vagrancy after the end of the Trojan War.[19] This can be taken as a metaphor of all such irretrievable losses that veterans must now face after their protracted, tormented *nostoi,* "homecomings." Grieving and constructing a narrative is not a smooth process. It often cycles through periods of renewed testing, sometimes with breaks in safety, sobriety, and self-care, which must then be restored.

In the group therapies, leaders serve to assure "airtime" and to safeguard the VIP value that every person's suffering is significant and cannot be measured against any other person's suffering. VIP tradition strongly discourages "pissing contests" over whose misery is worse. We monitor the emotional state of the veteran making the disclosure, as well as that of other veterans who may be triggered by it, or may be dissociating. Very often, the disclosure of traumatic material occurs first in individual therapy, and is only later taken into a group. In imparting fragments of trauma narrative to the group, veterans can start to believe that, for example, "My story has meaning and value to others. I can trust them to understand and remember it. They are trustworthy witnesses to my grief, rage, and guilt and they experience enough of these emotions with me that I know I am understood."

The first two stages of recovery turn the veterans inward both toward themselves and toward the other veterans in VIP. In the third stage, veterans selectively reconnect with people, activities, ideals, ambitions, and group identities from which they had become isolated, and make new connections. The core of this is the negotiation of safe, nonviolent attachments in the family. This often entails reunion with, or renegotiation of relationships with, long-estranged children and now elderly parents. The veterans of VIP strongly support a therapeutic culture in the program aimed at *preventing* the intergenerational transmission of trauma[20]—support born of guilt and sorrow at the damage that they did in past years to parents, spouses, and children.

Some veterans, by no means all, have taken satisfaction in educating youngsters on war, or in active peace advocacy. Several engage in regular volunteer work with homeless veterans, particularly those who have recently been homeless themselves. A great many have participated in educational activities for mental health professionals at various levels, as well as for medical students and psychology interns.

Stage Three of recovery starts with the small community of veterans in VIP and works outward to the veteran's family, military unit associations, church, neighborhood, and nation.

Dr. Mary Harvey's account of the dimensions of recovery[21] has influenced ours:

- Authority over the remembering process.
- Integration of memory and affect.
- Affect tolerance.
- Symptom mastery.
- Self-esteem and self-cohesion.
- Safe attachment.
- Meaning making.

We speak to the veterans of these dimensions as expected results of treatment. All of our patients struggle against chronic despair. There is no way to "give hope" of recovery without giving understandable *content* to that hope, and over time veterans readily understand Dr. Harvey's dimensions of recovery.

Social trust requires at least *three* people. Dyadic trust between two people, no matter how many times it is pair-wise created, does not make community. A community begins with the addition of the third person, and with all three trusting that the other two when alone together will continue to safeguard the interests of the person who is absent.[22] The trauma world assumption is that they will plot some exploitation or attack, or utterly forget the third person's existence. Good-enough nurturance in childhood produces social trust as a matter of course; bad-enough trauma at *any* age destroys it. Our task is its restoration.[23]

It is not enough to talk about trust and tell patients verbally what they need to do. Vietnam combat veterans, like veterans of many other wars and other traumatized populations, have great suspicion of words. They were deceived by words as part of their trauma. Our patients were told many idealistic things about war service, but were not told of its sorrows and suffering or that the personal cost could be so high. They were told about codes of conduct, but they then saw that the rules did not apply. They were told the enemy was weak and ill equipped, but then they saw how skillful the enemy's tactics and how well suited their weapons were. They were told in many voices that it was noble to be a warrior and that they would come home as heroes, but then they learned they were not wanted. Veterans learned not to trust words, but to observe behavior. They observe the behavior of mental health professionals who profess to offer treatment. They constantly observe us and test us for trustworthiness.[24]

The VIP veterans now have evolved a strong system of rules, devoted primarily to safety, sobriety, and self-care, developed over many years by the veterans, and mainly enforced by them in cooperation with the treatment team. The community rules are continuously a work in progress.

What we do is political in the richest senses of the word. Our patients all took part in the exercise of state military power in and around Vietnam between 1965 and 1972, and their injuries trace to this participation and to how power was used in military institutions. The dominating element of power makes the *cause of injury* political; the *forms of injury* are in part political; and you have seen here how the *treatment of injury* we provide is political—we foster an empowered community among the veterans that we work with. The task is to create *trust.* In a fundamental sense, our treatment is a form of democratic persuasion. We are in this together and are parts of each other's future as fellow citizens.[25]

We foster community among the veterans and join that community to the community of the treatment team. In doing so we establish the possibility of attachment to the larger social world because we (the treatment team) sincerely believe in that larger world and show that it is possible to participate in it with perceptive good judgment. We must do this as *rhētor*—a citizen openly and undeceptively seeking the trust of fellow citizens and sharing in their fate—not as hireling-sophist or as a slave of the institution and its rules and its institutional agendas. We speak to the veterans as free fellow citizens, not hired agents of social control or slaves of the state. This is our idea of ourselves.

During the first five or so years I was in VIP, I encountered numerous worries and angry denunciations to the effect that everything said in a VA therapy group or office was "reported to the government," that we were doing experiments on the veterans, that VA staff was specially selected to carry out the government's need to geld or defang the veteran. I cannot explain why such talk has disappeared. It has been years since I have heard any of it.

Our work is political also in the sense that we vigorously encourage the veterans to participate in the democratic political life of the country that they fought for. Unhealed combat trauma disables the basic social and cognitive capacities required for democratic participation:[26]

- Being able to show up at an appointed time and place, possibly in a crowd of strangers.
- Being able to experience words as trustworthy.
- Seeing the possibility of persuasion, negotiation, compromise, concession.
- Seeing the possibility of winning without killing, of losing without dying.
- Seeing the future as real and meaningful.

For any mental health professional to work with American combat veterans injured in the service of their country, and *not* to find incapacity for democratic participation to be a meaningful clinical issue, strikes me as odd, to say the least.

In various ways and with varying intensity, members of the VIP team role-model participation in public life. We are active in education of other mental health professionals on trauma treatment in general, and on combat veterans in particular. The veterans participated with great satisfaction in video education projects for mental health professionals—two such videos formed presentations at professional meetings. As a team we have presented at professional meetings and published in professional books and journals, with full knowledge of the veteran community. I have publicly testified on veterans' concerns at congressional hearings, done media appearances on the themes of combat trauma and on prevention of psychological injury in military service, written for the trade press (this book, for example, and *Achilles in Vietnam*), and lectured or organized conference panels on prevention of psychological injury for many active duty military audiences. The VIP veterans are particularly supportive of these "missionary" activities to the active military. They don't want other young kids to be wrecked the way they were wrecked.

In the traditional world of the health professional, such activities are regarded as a hobby, or a distraction from the "real" work of seeing patients one at a time in a health care institution. I believe that these public and political activities are integral to the treatment of complex PTSD after combat. That's my view, at least; not everyone in the VIP team agrees. As a team we earn trust on the basis of our character, and our public activities are *evidence* of our character.[27]

I have attempted here to sketch a portrait of an intentionally created and mindfully maintained community of combat veterans within a Department of Veterans Affairs clinic. The health professions in general have a long history of acting like the rooster who claims to raise the sun above the horizon each morning with its crowing. Much recovery from injury or illness is the body's own work, which the skilled physician can only cooperate with. Likewise, recovery from complex PTSD sometimes happens "spontaneously." I contend that self-organized or preexisting communities—that we have not yet found a way to notice and encourage—nourish such "spontaneous" recovery. Whether intentionally constructed or self-organized, the conditions required for recovery are the same: a trustworthy community.

One kind of self-organized community is the Internet discussion group. As a segue to the next chapter, I reproduce here an e-mail message to the VWAR discussion group. It describes the experience of Army veteran Michael Viehman at the Wall with another veteran and the latter's wife:

I went to the Wall—once . . .

Terminator [pen name of a discussion member who lives in the Washington area] and some other friends took me. I was in shock on the walk to my panel. I'm not used to pullin' point . . . I had my boots with a medal wired to them and with a copy of "Helmets" [a poem] inside. I wouldn't approach for a bit . . . I wanted to die . . . Finally I got the guts to go on up to the panel and stand there with my measly offering in my hand. There was a deep reason, to me, for each of the things I carried . . . I walked over III Corp and into Cambodia in those boots with my Brothers. That medal which I received, I never felt I deserved. You see . . . so many of my Brothers died—or worse . . . and never got one. I was nobody . . . nuthin' . . . and

I was NOT deserving. Others died and I got their medal. . . . I was afraid
to go to the Wall 'cause I was afraid that my emotional numbing would
come back as it overwhelmed me. I tell people that I don't remember the
names of my dead Brothers—I lie . . . As I ran across each name, they
jumped out of the Wall, down my throat past the lump and back into my
soul. I began to go numb and I just stood there with my boots an' shit in
my hands. ALL feeling left me as I stood there. THEN, one over-riding
feeling washed over me—THIS IS A SACRED PLACE OF HEROES—
I DO NOT BELONG HERE . . .

I'm a little unclear about what happened next but I remember this
much. . . . I turned, in shock, and began to move quickly away from the
Wall—towards the chain. I would've gone through it but for strong hands
stopping me. . . . A voice whispered in my ear something like "It's OK, it's
OK" and "Talk—say it . . ." I heard a voice from somewhere say these
words . . . "My stuff doesn't deserve to be here—not the boots, not the
Star, not the writing . . ." Some big burly, mean, son-of-a-bitch hugged me
and first a quiver from deep within my soul escaped after 24 years . . . then
a sob . . . The dam broke. I was wracked with deep gut-wrenching sobs as
my soul was torn out and cast across the clear, starlit sky. Term, . . . EtN
[Terminator's wife], an' others held me up. My dead Brothers watched
and I could feel their concern—for me. . . . I finally took my boots an' stuff
and placed them at the panel with respect and tried to lay part of my life
to rest. Never to forget . . . but, perchance, to move forward . . . I could
feel my Brothers watching—I shit you not.[28]

In the next chapter we hear some members of the VWAR Internet
community begin to talk through and communalize the suicide of Marine
Corps veteran and multiple amputee, Lewis B. Puller, Jr., the author of
the 1992 Pulitzer Prize for Biography, *Fortunate Son: The Healing of a
Vietnam Vet.* This autobiography was in large part a tribute to his father,
Marine Corps Lieutenant General "Chesty" Puller, who was probably the
most admired marine of the twentieth century. Lewis Puller's grit and
courage inspired many; the shock and prostration from learning of his suicide were deepened by the prior uplift.

18

Lew Puller Ain't on the Wall

Lydia Fish is not a veteran. She is a professor of anthropology at Buffalo State College, and a scholar of the American folklore of war, particularly of the songs of the Vietnam War. When she created VWAR, "an Internet discussion list set up to facilitate communication among veterans, teachers, scholars and students of the Vietnam War,"[1] she did not think she was creating a community. Even less did she think she was saving anyone's life—yet over the few years that I was active in this Internet discussion, several veterans expressed their belief that they would have died by their own hand were it not for the social support that this cyber-community provided. Veterans in VIP have said the same about our program.

I joined VWAR as one of the "scholars and students," not as a clinician. While I freely expressed my beliefs (particularly in the value of such communities) I stayed clear of anything resembling therapy or medical advice. I hoped to learn and to gain critical feedback on my ideas and writings. Like any ordinary member, I exchanged information and opinions, got into arguments, made friends, learned a lot, and was addicted to my e-mail. About five years ago, when my "missionary work" on prevention of psychological and moral injury in military service was taking off, I could no longer put in the time. I decided that dropping out of the discussion would be better than being inattentive and superficial.

What follows is an edited and abbreviated transcript of the first couple days' responses by members of this community to news that Lewis Puller had killed himself, and—most important—of their responses to one another. All messages are used by permission of their authors, none of whom have ever been my patients.[2] Most, not all, members of this discussion use nicknames. The discussion's roughly two hundred members came from all over the country, from Florida to Puget Sound, from Massachusetts to California, from the inner city to almost "off the grid" in the mountains of New Mexico or upper New York State.

Date: Wed, 11 May 1994 17:45:14 EDT
From: Corkster
Subject: Lewis Puller
X-To: Multiple recipients of list VWAR-L

A sad sad day—Lew Puller committed suicide today—of course I can't find Lola's number—tried to call Cap'n Jack since I hope Lola didn't have to hear it on the news . . . and the toll rises yet again.

Corkster

Corky Condon described herself this way: "Developer/Director of In Touch program—Incorporator of Sons & Daughters In Touch, a non-profit organization for family members of VN KIA/MIA. Wall and Moving Wall volunteer, daughter of Robert E. Condon KIA 1/18/68, wife of a combat wounded (disabled physical and PTSD) veteran (LRRP, 25th DIV—RVN 1967–1968)."

———

Ah, shit! Just shit!
Druid

———

LEWIS PULLER AIN'T ON THE WALL

News of Puller's suicide is painful, then tearful.

I drive ChuYen to the Wall in a Demon rage, we make the trip in eight minutes; if she'd been flesh and blood I would have ridden her to death.

There are many kids at the wall, tour groups on a deadline. I walk the Wall to the Three Doods, waiting for kids and big-assed tourists to disperse

Alone at last, I light my candle; cupping the guttering flame in my right palm. Staring at the flame I clear my mind of all but the death of Puller.

"God! God I'm tired of this shit! This is enough! No more! Please God! no more . . ."

But God doesn't answer, he never did; not then, not now.

I cry again, not for Lew Puller, but for me. If he can do it, so can I. My acknowledgment of that fact scares the hell out of me.

Walking down to the apex of the Wall I stand before the Ockham edge; 1975 on my left and 1959 on my right. Candle flame reflected in the beginning and the end equally. Lights from the walkway glowing upward on to each panel; joining as a single light in the edge, level with the flame.

I see Puller, and many others, there in the mix of flame and lights.

Not on the Wall . . .

But they should be . . .

Leaving the candle jammed in between two cobble stones I walk away to ChuYen.

The candle guttering low and blue in the breeze.

Tom Edmonds writes the following about himself: "William T. Edmonds, Jr. Born Nov 1944. Both parents were WWII veterans. Raised in a tough blue-collar neighborhood in Houston Texas. First in my family to graduate from college although it took almost 15 years to get it done. Drafted in 1965, re-enlisted after Vietnam and spent a total of 10 years on active duty. After the Army I worked twenty years in data processing and computer security in the US and Saudi Arabia. Retired in 1992. Currently living in Falls Church Virginia in genteel poverty with my second wife Marybeth, a former Army nurse and Vietnam veteran, and our daughter (the youngest of 5 kids between us.) 'Lewis Puller Ain't on the Wall' is from my unpublished manuscript THE WAY OF BAMBOO. I still write and make presentations to colleges and high schools about the war; and own and run several Internet discussion lists about the Vietnam War for veterans."[4]

Lola tried to encourage Puller to join the Mayday gathering— He didn't come.

Some writing is on the Wall. Some of it is between the lines.

Corkster

Nice obituary on "Morning Edition" (National Public Radio) this morning. They played excerpts from a reading he had given on "Fresh Air" a few years ago.

May he rest in peace.

Lydia

Lydia Fish, the list owner

One of the members had asked if Lew Puller was the same person as Chesty Puller.

Monte,

Lewis B. Puller, aged 48, lost his legs in Vietnam after stepping on a mine while leading a marine combat platoon.

His book, *Fortunate Son* (Grove Weidenfield, 1991) was written as a tribute to his father, Gen. Lewis B. (Chesty) Puller, the most decorated marine in the history of the Corps. The book won the Pulitzer Prize for biography in 1992. He was planning to write a second book about Sen. Kerrey who he met while they were recovering from their wounds at the Philadelphia Naval Hospital in 1968.

Says Kerrey after learning of Puller's death, "Tragically, in the end he was not able to give himself the lift he gave to all those who read his book."

His wife Linda is currently a member of the Virginia House of Delegates. He's survived by a son, Lewis 3d and a daughter, Margaret.

A man not to be forgotten. This is a classic example of the old statement, "do as I say not as I do" if one is to honor what Puller wrote about in his book. I know it's a hell of a lot easier said than done but it can be done.

He may not be "on the Wall" but he is certainly "of the Wall" and "in the Wall" as we all are.

dog handler

Dog Handler is the Net moniker for Tom Sykes, who is Director of Media Services at Lawrence University in Appleton, Wisconsin; he is active with the Vietnam Dog Handlers Association.[5] According to Harry G. Summers's Vietnam War Almanac, dogs were used by American forces in Vietnam for "scouting, mine detecting, tracking, sentry duty, flushing out tunnels, and drug detecting . . . ambush avoidance and detection of sampan movement at night."[6]

Tears flow freely onto the keyboard today. I didn't know Lewis Puller personally but he was a brother of mine. His visible scars were so terrible that maybe I just forgot that, of course, he would have the emotional ones too—like the rest of us.

Michele called me at the Fire Department this AM before I got relieved to tell me of Corky's post. I had to get off the phone quickly before I cried. I could feel the old sorrow, rage and frustration anew. I took one of the detectives (a fellow Redcatcher) outside and told him. Made his day too.

It was in the morning paper on the table. Shit. One of the guys, not a vet, made some kind of derogatory remark about it. Not trusting my voice or my temper, I simply gave him "a look," my eyes red with held-back tears. My anger must have been evident since he spilled his coffee on himself and went away. I saw another vvet explain things to him outside. I'm the in-house crazed nam vet and they are afraid of me. Good. I am too.

So why am I so upset by this death of a brother? It's not like it's the first—or the last. Maybe because I admired his strength. Maybe 'cause I fear my lack of it will come home to roost. Maybe because we worked another suicide at the FD yesterday. 48 yo woman with both ventricles pierced by an 8 inch butcher knife sunk in her chest past the hilt (121) or the "sudden death" (122) that came later yesterday or the heart attack this AM about 0200 or the heart attack about 0600. I do know—Death stalked the land yesterday.

What about today? Maybe the woods. Maybe the chair in the corner. Maybe the highway. Was gonna drive the chevy/dodge truck today but it doesn't go fast enough—the Supra does—I hope. I get real tired of hidin' an' runnin' from the demons. Am I the only one? Has it crossed anyone else's mind?

You think maybe Lew was right? Is it the only real escape? I got questions. I'm out of answers.

Lewis Puller—you have my utmost respect and admiration. I don't drink anymore but today I will smoke one in honor of your Spirit. May you, at last, be at peace. I hope to see you when I get there.

Peace,
V-man

Michael Viehman is also the author of the message that concluded the previous chapter. In e-mail to me on December 4, 2001, he wrote of himself, "Mike Viehman served in Vietnam as a Chaplain's Assistant in War Zones C & D in the Iron Triangle region of III Corp out of firebases Libby, Gladys and Nancy while assigned to the 199th Light Infantry Brigade in 1970 and, later, with 3rd Ord Bn. He received the Bronze Star Medal and returned CONUS to work for over 20 years as a firefighter/paramedic before retiring on duty disability after breaking his back on his last fire call

*in 1995. He is now embarking on a second career in knifemaking. He has
been married to his second wife and helpmate, Michele, since 1975." My
wife and I met Mike and Michele at a VWAR camp-in in the Adirondack
Mountains.*

———

hey. puller lives on. It's up to us to keep him alive. through the
tears, fears and pain. it goes on until we're all gone and then, like all
those who have gone before us, we belong to the great river. so it is,
so it goes, one day at a time.

voodoo chile

*Marc B. Adin, Fourth Infantry Division, Central Highlands, RVN,
1968–1969. He writes that he is now in end-stage liver disease, contracted from a blood transfusion in Vietnam.*[7]

———

i for one ask the same question everyday.
am i the only one?
lt puller wasn't alone
i tried and failed a couple times
next time i may succeed
who knows
the big question is when is the struggle
no longer worth the effort
when does the pain overwhelm the desire to live

murray the k

*Warren Murray writes: "I was commissioned an 18 year old second lt. and
turned 20 in Vietnam. It remains to this day the most defining and debilitating experience of my life. I am ashamed of my PTSD diagnosis and feel
somehow I have failed all those soldiers who served with honor."*[8]

———

murray—
i only tried once although i probably was trying more than once
when it came to the way i lived my life for so many years. but for me
living is for my family, my little girl and my wonderful wife, and my
mom, and my brother who still lives with the horrors of Con Thien.
i live for my cousin who is dying of aids, my aunt who is dying of

alcoholism, my cousin who is dying of hate left over from the Ashau.

i live to see the smiles on their faces when i tell them that i love them, cant live without them, and want to see them all the time. the pain, the pain is part of me, you, all of us and is never bigger than everyone we need and who need us.

pohenry, #83

Henry Flores is professor of political science at St. Mary's University in San Antonio, Texas. He writes, "I teach statistics, research methods and elections and voting behavior. I'm 57 years of age, am married to a literary critic and am the father of a brilliant, athletic, and highly creative 15 year old daughter. Oh yeah, we have a great dog—a dachshund named Caramelo."[9]

Got ahold of Rod [Lola] last night. Rod already knew about it; he'd called Puller yesterday, got the brother-in-law who told him. No surprise to Rod.

Peg pointed out something worth noting after reading the newspaper article this morning. While a lot of response focuses on Lew's being defeated by depression, failing to survive in the long term his injuries, being unable to deal with it all, in fact he was a survivor for 20-odd years. He parlayed a shitty hand into a lot of success, and that's what he should be remembered for, not his final act. That act tells us just how fucked that war left him, but his life tells us what kind of man he was.

Cap'n Jack

Jack Mallory is a former captain in the 11th Armored Cavalry Regiment and Vietnam Veterans Against the War member, now a high school teacher, counselor, and father of two young boys.[10]

V-Man,

Here's what happened to me day before yesterday. Being a Vvet helped me help somebody then. I don't know if this means anything.

A guy people would consider a "bum" was down on the sidewalk. His face was white, he had cold sweat running through his clothes, which were a rag tag collection. He had a beautiful set of Nikes on his feet. An ultimate incongruity.

He was shaking and looking up and down, holding the back of his neck. His hair, an oily mess—remember that?—was pasted to his scalp so I could see completely through to his pate. One person had stopped, but others were afraid to look at him or acknowledge his presence. I stopped, not because I'm a good guy by any means, but because I felt "there but for the grace of God go I." With my head problems, we could have been bros. There are a lot of bros out there.

We started talking and he shook some more. He was scared because his chest was giving him pain. He was scared because he was having a hard time breathing. He shook some more.

Theresa was standing off to the side concerned about the gentleman.

I tried to have him lay down on his side but he couldn't do it. He didn't want an ambulance, but I winked at the other guy (about my age) and he left to make the call. I put my hand on this guy's shoulder and we started to talk.

His sister had given him his new Nikes. She worked at Nike in Portland. He shook some more and said he'd been having seizures lately. Said he might need some medication. I didn't think he was strung out. He didn't look like it. He was down and out.

Who among us hasn't been at one time or another, whether it was in Nam or here after we got back?

People continued passing at a distance and we talked some more. We talked about what this guy wanted to do. His needs were simple. He just wanted to stop shaking and feel good. (Remember feeling like that?) He tried to breathe more slowly. We breathed together.

Within an instant the sirens slowly approached. A huge fire truck drove up. I was proud to see Eugene's finest respond so quickly. Three guys jumped out and walked slowly. I told them what I knew. They took over and put a hand on his shoulder. He couldn't look up. They were good to this guy. They treated him with dignity (remember when people didn't treat you with dignity? remember those officers who did? Bet Puller was one of those, eh?)

He didn't want to go to the hospital, but these firefighters treated him with the kind of care I would like to extend to others if I could. Some people I just don't give a damn about.

I cared about this guy, too. One of the firefighters looked about my age. He may have been a little older. I thought of you Vman. He started talking to this guy again and put his hand on the person's shoulder. He brought out some tubes and put some in his nose, while another person took this guy's blood pressure.

I left, but seeing these guys work with this person with such humanity brought back all of the posts you've made to this list, Vman. You're one special dude. A lot of folks need ya. I hope you hang around.

Monte

MtK,

I don't know when that happens (when the hurt gets too much), but I know what I said for Vman goes for you, too, bro. There are a few other folks on this list who keep me going everyday. Without em, I don't know.

I can only say I'm glad you're there. I don't want you taking no trips. I would be royally pissed and come back to haunt your ass.

Your bud,
Montster [Monte]

MtK,

Doan know, bro. I suspect the answer is highly variable, on a scale we don't even know the measurement units on.

I know I hang around 'cause I wanna see Weet[11] and if I off myself there's a chance I won't get the opportunity. I've waited too many years to waste that chance now. Works for me, won't for anyone else. *)shrug(*

You ain't alone in the question, Murray. And whatever the answer is for you, you won't be alone in that either. I think there's a helluva lot of folk like you, with the same damn answer every morning.

As long as you keep answering every morning, it's the right one.

McMike

Mike McCombs, Sr., died of breast cancer about two years after this message. Breast cancer is usually extremely rare among men, but is not rare among those exposed to Agent Orange. McMike, a veteran of the 5th Special Forces Group in Vietnam, wrote about his experiences with great eloquence.[12]

As I read the posts about Lew Puller, I thought about a recent thread on this list . . . the daily decisions being made about whether to go or to stay. Although this poem is written with masculine pronouns, it is meant for each of you who make these daily decisions . . . you know who you are.

A PRAYER FOR DEATH AND LIFE

By Judee Strott

For one I pray that Death will come to take him in the night,
for he no longer wants to live, he's given up the fight.
I pray for Death to take him, and yet he still lives on
while others only half his age have died and now are gone.

He's so old, he's lived his life, he's nearly 90 now,
he's weak and frail, he cannot walk, his back is bent, head bowed.
His wife has gone before him, and he cannot figure why
God makes him keep on living, and will not let him die.

For one I pray that Death will come; for one I pray for Life.

For one I pray he overcomes the demons and the dreams
that haunt his sleep and torment him with silent deadly screams;
the memories he can't forget that fill him with such dread,
that daily he decides between the living and the dead.

For one I pray that something can entreat him to remain
to try again for one more day, to live with all his pain;
'till all the sufferings of the past can finally fade away,
and a sweet peace overflows his cup, Lord help him decide to stay.

Judee

Judee Strott is neither a veteran nor a teacher or scholar of the Vietnam War. She and her husband, Jerry, are retired and devote enormous time and energy to the support of Vietnam veterans. She wrote in her VWAR address list profile, "Jerry and I provide information from data bases and various printed records related to POW/MIA, Names on The Wall, DoD Combat Casualty Files, etc. to anyone who requests it. We attend meetings of organizations to demonstrate what these data bases contain; provide information to assist organizations with special events such as stand downs, organizing POW/MIA recognition day ceremonies, etc.; participate in Friends of the Vietnam Veterans Memorial's programs (In Touch, In Memory, etc.) and distribute FVVM literature at events (Moving Wall, county fair, etc.).

"We do not charge for any information we provide . . . to borrow a phrase from a friend . . . VN Veterans have already paid the price."

Despite the derision that members of the discussion sometimes heaped upon "ReallyCares™"—the sarcastic label hung on civilians who seem mostly interested in their own self-images as compassionate and deep, and in their own touristic avidity in interesting and intense emotional experiences (much like the Phaeacian courtiers for whom the Trojan War was pure entertainment)—this motherly presence seemed to be accepted as genuine.[13]

I don't know what the demons all were but I think that Lew did what most Marines do when their gear wears out . . . they survey it. I think he realized that his body and his life had just worn out and it was time. I know his father will understand. We all wish him well and we will miss him.

Semper Fi.
Helmuts

Helmuts Feifs has an excruciatingly—I mean that modifier to be taken literally—funny imaginary business firm called Weptronics and mock advice column called "Ask Mr. Guilt."[14]

---

pain slips away in the dark of night
demons are put to rest

no more!
no more
pain

guilt
rage
no more
what if

home lt puller
home at last

peace
mtk

Warren Murray moniker

———

I am reminded of the apocryphal joke about the lady caught in the flood; convinced that God will save her, she refuses help from two rowboats and a helicopter, and drowns.

Arriving in heaven, she rails at God for not saving her.

"Lady," God says, "I sent two rowboats and a helicopter. How much more did you want?"

Lewis Puller could or would no longer reach out to grasp that skid. If you live for another and they are removed, you may not be able to see the true answer to your prayers.

As MaryBeth [the writer's wife] once told me with some surprize in her voice. You seem to be the answer to my prayers, not exactly what I was praying for; but apparently the answer."

For many of the vets on this list, Vwar-l is the helicopter, and we are the crewchiefs.

And I, for one, intend to grasp every hand that reaches for the skids; even if I have to slap the owner of that hand upside their heads to make them look up at the rotor noise.

Terminator

W. T. Edmonds is the author of the poem "Lewis Puller Ain't on the Wall," near the beginning of this chapter. He is the person mentioned by Mike Viehman at the end of the previous chapter as having taken him to the Wall for the first time.

———

>and then just put all of Vietnam behind me. [Excerpt from a posting by another list member.]

Forget it, Steve. Nevah hoppen, GI. Best you can do is live with it, and plan on continuing to live with it. I spent a long time waiting for "it" to go away. Finally realized that "it" was me, and I wasn't going away.

>(I have never believed that I suffer from post traumatic stress. I honestly wasn't exposed to that much trauma.) [A further excerpt from the earlier posting.]

I don't know how many times I've said this to myself and others. I don't know what you saw; I know what Rod and Lew and Jay-Bird and lots of others saw and experienced was far worse than what I went through. But, if you accept Jonathan's thesis, there are two things that combine to produce PTSD: a sense of deep moral betrayal, and experiencing the death of close friends. Many of us felt the moral betrayal, either through a conviction that the entire war was wrong, and/or through a sense that, regardless of the justification for the war, the government wasted our lives and society didn't give a shit about us. That, combined with the deaths of those we knew, even if not close friends, with viewing the death and dismemberment of other human beings, may bring to all of us a degree of post-traumatic stress. Such stress must be a matter of degree, rather than something you either "have" or don't "have."

Cap'n Jack

This message responds to one that I have not included here.

Tracey,

Thanks for saying this . . . it's what I've been thinking all day as I've read the messages from other vwar-l folks responding to Lewis Puller's death. It's especially meaningful since I took Jay to the VA hospital last Friday to seek help with his VN demons. You really have said it well.

Suezq

A number of members of VWAR were spouses or siblings, or like the author of the next message, siblings-in-law of Vietnam veterans.

Disclaimer—I'm not a vet, and I haven't yet had to ask these questions.

What I *did* have was many nights, 11 years ago, listening to my brother-in-law ask the same question. And many more nights wondering what else I could have done, and explaining to my husband what I didn't really understand myself—that there *was nothing* else that we could have done.

That said—I don't think the answer is "when is the struggle no longer worth the effort," but rather "when do you stop asking the question."

As long as you're still asking, you're still hanging on.

Catwoman

Catwoman writes that she "grew up in the 60's with a WWII vet father who came back from WWII swearing that he never wanted anyone else to go through that again, and therefore at an early age was taken along to activities that included WWII vets against the [Vietnam] war."[15]

———

Veewees,

I second all the good stuff that everybody said about Lew, I also was moved by his book.

In addition to all his other fine attributes, his writing showed a deep love for his Dad, his wife, and his country. He gave tribute to them and the nurses, doctors, and physical therapists that were involved in his recovery.

He did an *awful lot* for vets, with his book, his job as a lawyer with the VA, and many other ways.

We lost a good friend.

Polecat (aka Jim Schueckler)

Jim "Polecat" Schueckler writes that he is the "founder of the (original) Virtual Wall at www.VirtualWall.org." He volunteers as a National Park Service "Yellow Hat" docent and visitors' aide at the Wall.[16]

———

I guess I was the ultimate REMF [Vietnam vet slang for "rear echelon motherfucker," in this instance meaning noncombat support personnel], but Puller's death did hurt, reminds of all those others who don't make the news. His death and the coverage is for them, too.

"THE FORTUNATE SON"[17]

For Lewis Puller, d. 1994, from a festering wound

They shouldn't call it suicide,
this self-inflicted gunshot wound—
the trigger squeezed so many years ago—
day by day, the fragment slipped inside.
His name won't be chiseled on the Wall.
He won't reflect your face for you.
He doesn't qualify. He missed
the cut-off date. He died too late.

Lewis Puller? You'll find him on the Wall.
He's always been there. Chesty's son,
Marine lieutenant, tripped a mine, lost
his legs, made his hero daddy proud, wrote
a book, held firm the lives of all of us,
but, finally, could not hold his own.

—Palmer © 1994

H. Palmer Hall is a poet and editor of A Measured Response *(San Antonio: Pecan Grove Press, 1993) and author of* From the Periphery: Poems and Essays *(San Antonio: Chili Verde Press, 1994), in which this poem appeared. His fourth book is* Deep Thicket and Still Waters *(Chili Verde Press, 2000), a collection of poems dealing primarily with the murder of James Byrd, Jr.*[18]

––––––––––

Palmer,

Well, you did it. Thus far in these days since Puller's death I've been beleaguered by it, a bit obsessed with it, but hadn't actually reached the point of tears for him and all those who've gone before, and will go after, by their own hand. Your poem broke open the floodgates.

Thank you for a thoughtful contribution, a painful truth in a lovely package.

Michele

Michele is Michael Viehman's wife.

I did not know Puller. I have not read his book. I am saddened by his passing, as I have been saddened by the passing of others, but life does go on.

――――― was a friend of mine. ――――― had a wife and three daughters, all of who adored the man. ――――― also had his demons which, although he put in his tour in VN, had little to do with that. We knew about ―――――'s demons before he went. In 1971, the demons won. ―――――, with his 15-year old daughter in the next room, ate a .357, doing grievous damage to himself and the wallpaper.

What he accomplished for himself I do not know, other than the fact that for one brief nanosecond he must have realized that the pain was ending. For him. It was just starting for his family and friends, who were left to clean up the mess, literally and figuratively.

A friend of mine called me this morning, disturbed by Puller's death and worried about me. I'm not sure why he was worried about me. He need not have been.

'Tis indeed, at least in my tired old mind, better to endure the slings and arrows of outrageous fortune than to end it with a bare bodkin or anything else. I believe that, like ―――――, there would be only a hint of relief, satisfaction, revenge, self-pity, or whatever else I might have chosen as the reason, and then there would be nothing. I would not be here to revel in the result of the action. The only consequence would be the lifetime of recrimination and wondering why by friends, and a new set of problems for family and loved ones, far more serious than the ones I fled from. I'm not that selfish. I've devoted most of my adult life to making those I love comfortable and secure. The fact that I have not always succeeded in this will not deter me from continuing to try so long as I can still draw a breath.

And like Term, I'm willing to grab the hand of anyone else who is reaching for the skids or scrambling over the gunwale.

sharkbait

Dear All,

When I was in DC and met Corkster, I learned from her that the Friends of the Vietnam Veterans Memorial have a program called IN MEMORY devoted to Vietnam veterans who have "died prematurely" as a result of their service in and around Vietnam. My impression is that the program has just started. I looked through the IN MEMORY book, and about two-thirds of the men remembered in there died of Agent Orange related illnesses and most of the remaining third had killed themselves.

You've all heard me rant and rave about how we should regard combat veterans who suicide as "died of wounds" and I'll spare you a repetition. However, I shall repeat my impression that the *families* of veterans who have killed themselves are mostly sitting alone with this in pain and shame and the cruel notion that they themselves have fucked up or their son or daughter has fucked up—no other choices. Their surviving comrades sometimes find themselves in the same box. The IN TOUCH program is up and running and I believe is superbly suited to helping the families of these veterans to be in contact with each other if they are willing (IN TOUCH is *always* extremely protective of everyone's right to be in control of who they speak to).

I am sending a check for $200 to the Friends of the Vietnam Veterans' Memorial today, earmarked for IN MEMORY/IN TOUCH—as soon as Corkster posts the address (I have handed out the hundred or so fliers she sent me and forgot to keep one for myself!). I'll also spare you ranting and raving about the importance of *prevention* in general—but I must remind everyone that the children of a veteran who kills him or herself are at *greatly* increased risk of suicide themselves, so keep in mind that fostering systems of mutual support among the families of veterans who have died of wounds by suicide is crucially important "secondary prevention" (please forgive the public health jargon) of suicide in their children.

> *Much* love to you all,
> Jonathan

I first developed the habit of signing my correspondence with veterans "Much love," while active on VWAR, without understanding why I was doing it. I have continued this habit—with more self-awareness and mindfulness—when corresponding today with active duty military service members (only after we have developed a relationship of trust and friendship, of course), knowing that it pushes the envelope of their culture. In Part Three, I address the importance of the love that military people develop for each other in protecting them from psychological injury.[19]

Partners have their demons too. Bailing out may have felt like their kind of suicide . . . couldn't do it anymore. I still say God bless Toddy. She did hang in there for 25 or so years. Lew made a choice about his life just as Toddy did. Who are we to say what was highest and best for each of them.

Sally

Sally Griffis is a Vietnam War widow.[20]

I read the book the way you did, Polecat.

It could be that after all those years she left him—someone said they read/heard that. It could be that that was a final wound that Lewis Puller couldn't deal with; I don't think anyone can know that. Even if that's true, the guy whose book I read would take responsibility for her departure and not lay the blame on the woman who kept him going for so long.

But what do I know, anyhow? (ans.: As much as the rest of you.)

FNG

Jim Lynch writes, "Jim Lynch served as a platoon leader and company commander with the 48th Transportation Group from early February, 1969–early February, 1970. His units ran line-haul truck convoys throughout III and IV Corps; the southern half of South Viet Nam."[21]

Veewees,

I didn't see the NightLine program, but even the *suggestion* that Lew Puller's suicide is Toddy's fault is disgusting.

In Lew's own words, in his book "Fortunate Son," his wife is the hero. She is the one who suffered with him every day. She also came from a military family, and married him in spite of knowing that he would be going to Vietnam, and what could happen. What did happen.

She was the faithful wife who got into the hospital bed with him when he needed to affirm his masculinity after his terrible injuries. She bore his children facing an uncertain future.

She stuck with him for 25 years, most filled with turmoil and pain;

some filled with the joy and excitement of winning a Pulitzer Prize. She drove him to hospitals hundreds of times: for surgery, physical therapy, counseling, or alcohol addiction.

She raised the kids during the years that he was depressed and went into rage and self-pity. I have no doubt that there were times that Toddy felt that she should leave him in order to save the children. She was probably frequently torn by having to consider that decision.

Toddy remained sober, facing the problems alone, while Lew drank to escape. I think Lew intended to show that alcoholism was his problem; it pervades his book, from times before he went to Vietnam. One review that I read said that Puller may have been saying that alcoholism was a bigger problem than the loss of his limbs.

If you disagree with what I have said, but have not yet read his book, please go read it.

I am not trying to degrade Lew Puller's memory, but Toddy went through a hell that she could have escaped from for 25 years.

But she stayed with him all those years. Now she has even more pain to carry. She has my deepest respect and sympathy.

for Lew:

> Day is done,
> Gone the sun,
> From the land,
> From the sea,
> From the sky.
>
> All is well,
> Rest in peace,
> God is nigh.

> Much love,
> Polecat (aka Jim Schueckler)

You can see even from this fragment, edited from a much longer dialogue, that extremely important themes came up in this discussion, including veterans' suicides,[22] veterans' spouses and the toll exacted from them, the relationship of veterans to nonveterans, and the Wall. It is immediately evident that this cybercommunity's members were already doing many of the things that veterans do with and for each other in our VIP community-building treatment program. VWAR veterans provided each other with the various forms of validation. They expressed a wide range of emotions that relate complexly to their military traumas, to the aftermath, and to other people's reactions to their emotions. They realized that they have something to give to others. And while they discovered that others are enough like themselves that they have no reason to feel like freaks, they also discovered that other respect-worthy veterans hold disparate and even contradictory views on many things.[23] They created all of these benefits for themselves, without mental health professionals. They were doing this before I came and continued to do so after I left.

The veterans in the group unquestionably grieved together and helped each other construct cohesive narratives of what they had experienced. Safety and self-care were openly supported. Sobriety was another matter. I recall on and off discussions about whether the bar and lounge metaphor for VWAR was a healthy one. Occasionally, messages had a strong smell of liquor on their breath, as though the writer was sitting at his computer getting progressively drunker as the message traffic passed back and forth on the screen.

One member of VWAR voiced the sense of merging of place and identity,

> . . . We be here for the duration, a period of existence.
> Our existence.
> We will stay for as long as Lydia keeps the doors to the bar open.
> I ain't goin' nowhere.
> Got nowhere else to go.
>
> . . . You fuckers ain't much, but I know every one of you.
> You be my Bros.
> I shared your chow and my last cigarette;
> You called in my medevac,
> And I helped burn your "Dear John" letter.
> . . . We can never leave.
>> "The Lounge: We Can Never Leave," by Michael W. Rodriguez.[24]
>> (Michael Rodriguez is a Marine Corps combat veteran of
>> the Vietnam War. He has an eloquent Web site called *Humidity
>> Moon*: mikerod.home.texas.net/. His collection of short narratives
>> is published under the same name by Pecan Grove Press,
>> San Antonio.)

I was witness to a number of occasions when the social contract of VWAR was debated or was severely tested by threats of violence or by abuse. In the social contract debates, Lydia Fish, the list owner, acted much like a constitutional monarch and aimed to make VWAR a safe place to struggle over these perennial questions. When violence was threatened, she moved swiftly and firmly like an absolute monarch to exile any member who compromised safety. As list owner, she had the power to cut someone off from receiving e-mail from the community or from sending messages to it. The social contract established by the VIP veterans is much stricter than that of "Lydia's Lounge," but on the point of safety, they were in accord.

"Pissing contests"—denigration of the importance of others' experience compared to one's own—were perennial problems. At one point a schism took place, and a group of combat veterans who were dissatisfied with the presence of nonveterans and noncombat veterans on VWAR left to form a combat-veterans-only "closed" discussion list. The "bar and lounge" metaphor for VWAR captured its openness—anyone could walk in and pull up a stool at the bar—but also captured the necessity for the newcomer to get comfortable and establish himself or herself with the regulars, to learn its customs and mores. The breakaway group established something along the lines of a members-only private club. A stranger would find the door locked. However, many members of this private club continued to belong to VWAR in addition.

The Internet discussion technology has certain advantages over traditional face-to-face group therapy or support group. Among these are the obvious ones: it's open 24/7, which no group therapy is; you can think about what something means and what you want to say at your own pace—you don't lose out to members with a quicker tongue; several people can talk at once without interfering with each other; if you raise an issue or mention something that's bothering you, you don't have to worry about whether it's off the theme that the group is pursuing at this moment—there's likely to be someone else who wants to respond.[25]

In a certain sense, VIP's veteran community is open 24/7. The veterans in it have each other's telephone numbers and most know where the others live. There is a fair amount of visiting back and forth by phone and in person—and increasingly via e-mail—and they do call upon each other when they feel desperate. Among the team members, I am the only one who has given them my home telephone number.[26] I do this with the periodic reminder that they are not only permitted, but also invited, to call me if they need assistance in getting into a hospital because they are in danger of hurting themselves or someone else. I make it clear that calls at home for other purposes are not welcome, because I need my sleep, my time with my family, and for the missionary work that I do on their behalf to the armed services. In fourteen years as the psychiatrist for VIP, not one veteran has abused my privacy. I am certain that if anyone did the other veterans would not tolerate it.

From time to time, the VWAR cybercommunity seemed sorely in need of the VIP rules that work together to prevent the veterans from wearing each other out or bringing each other down:

> Any vet who is jeopardizing his or her own health and safety, or that of others, authorizes other vets to bring this to the Team, rather than be burdened by it. Any vet who is suicidal or homicidal authorizes anyone in the VIP to take emergency measures to prevent this from occurring.

> No bringing other vets down. Some examples are: calling for rescue when none is needed, borrowing money from another vet beyond the lender's means, offering street drugs or alcohol to someone who is trying to stay clean, involving other VIP vets in illegal activities, or making excessive phone calls.

> Whoever feels they are being taken advantage of should speak up. Don't get carried away rescuing others.

Lydia Fish neither wished, nor had the resources, to play the role toward the VWAR community that the VIP clinical team does toward its veterans.

I have been away from VWAR for about five years. No doubt it is very different today than it was then, if only because every human community changes constantly, even when it has a strong commitment to imagining itself eternally the same. I am almost afraid to rejoin it for fear that it no longer offers its members what it did when I happened to be there to witness it in the mid-1990s.

However, I never worry that the Vietnam Veterans Memorial—the Wall—is morphing into something less profound. Like Homer's great poems, every truly great work of art, which the Wall is, constantly refreshes itself, goes on giving and giving as circumstances change.

PART III

PREVENTION

19

Introduction

In Part One we saw the enormous price that veterans and those around them pay when their capacity for social trust has been diminished or destroyed. In Part Two we examined various spontaneous and intentional practices that can restore social trust. In this section I address those things that our armed services can do to protect the capacity for social trust and to *prevent* psychological and moral injury in military service. This is the fire in my belly stemming from a passionate commitment of the men that I work with as patients in the VA. They don't want other kids to be wrecked the way they were wrecked. My passion about this comes from theirs.

The best approach is to reduce *all* casualties, not just psychiatric casualties. Psychiatric and physical battle casualties rise and fall together. The more war wounds in the body, the more mind wounds. This has been observed among American troops in World War II and among Israelis in the Yom Kippur War.[1] Reducing casualties overall will reduce psychiatric casualties. Is there any way to do this? The answer is neither new nor surprising: the surest path to casualty reduction is swiftly and skillfully to *win* the fights that the nation sends our troops into. The three protective factors that this section emphasizes—cohesion, leadership, and training—are combat strength multipliers that produce this outcome.[2]

Combat soldiers at war struggle with the enemy in a two-dimensional world. Those two dimensions are *biē*, violent force, and *mētis*, cunning tricks and strategy. The *Iliad* and the *Odyssey* are equally powerful and equally convincing accounts of which of these military capacities is most important to vanquish the enemy, and to win the war. Achilles, the hero of the *Iliad*, embodies *biē*, while Odysseus, the hero of the *Odyssey*, embodies *mētis*. When I finish reading the *Iliad*, I am certain that the superiority of Achilles' straight-up-the-middle fighting strength has won the

Trojan War for the Greeks by bringing down the Trojans' main man, Hector. And when I have finished reading the *Odyssey* I am equally certain that Odysseus won the war by pulling off the trick of the hollow Horse, filled with elite fighters.

Biē or *mētis*, which is more important in war? This is not an academic question about long-dead antiquity. It is a subject of ongoing struggle within our own armed services today. What is more important, fire superiority or information dominance? Attrition or maneuver? "Heavy" armored forces or "light" infantry? Huge, survivable-through-redundancy air and missile fleets, or stealth technology? Crushing the enemy or surprising the enemy? Read *both* of Homer's epics and you'll find that the answer to this generic military question, "*biē* or *mētis*, which one?" is "Uh—yes! Both!"

For things to go well for a soldier, a third dimension must be added to his own army's *biē* and *mētis*: trust that those people who wield official power will do it in accordance with *themis*, "what's right." The catastrophic operational failure that the Greek army suffered in the *Iliad* flowed directly from betrayal of "what's right" by its commander, Agamemnon. *The trustworthy structure of "what's right" in a military organization—horizontally with peers, vertically in the chain of command, and personally in the training and equipment the military service has supplied—is what allows that armed service's force and cunning strategy to be put into effect against the enemy.*[3]

The keys to preventing psychological and moral injury are in the hands of uniformed and civilian military leaders and of their civilian bosses in the executive branch and the Congress. In this section I shall explain the measures that can protect our troops, in the hope that readers of this book will intelligently and passionately support reforms. First and foremost, I will argue that we must demand that our top military and civilian policymakers replace the existing institutional ethos of "scientific management" with a new military ethic that creates and maintains well-founded *trust*.

Every year the Department of Defense distributes posters in honor of Armed Forces Day. Look at this image and answer the question, "What's wrong with this picture?" Uniformed and civilian defense leaders consistently say that people are the Defense Department's top priority, but in 1997, 1998, 1999, and again in 2002, the Department approved Armed Forces Day posters that celebrated only *weapons*.[4] The retired officer who sent me this poster called it "an insult [to] the valor, sacrifices, and patriotism of the American soldiers, sailors, and airmen who have spilled blood in the service of our country since the American Revolution."

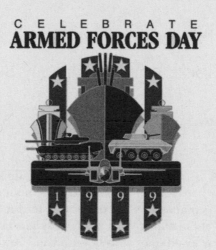

20

Preventing Psychological and Moral Injury in Military Service[1]

> "Mom. Dad, Brother, Sister, Grandma, Grandpa, you've seen and felt how hard it is for a soldier to come home. If even one man goes to combat why not make it easier for him to come home? And at the same time make our soldiers better. After all they are your loved ones and they are you." And, to the men and women who have fought in Vietnam, Korea, and WW II, "What did you experience—Don't you want to change it? Write to your Congressman about what you think."
>
> —Dennis Spector,
> 101st Airborne and 1st Infantry Division
> veteran of Vietnam, 1968[2]

Try to imagine going to war with strangers at your side! Do they know what they're doing? Can you trust them? Will they care what happens to you? Do you speak the same language, figuratively speaking, or even literally?[3]

COHESION—THE HUMAN ELEMENT IN COMBAT[4]

In a famous and oft-quoted passage, the nineteenth-century French infantry colonel Ardant du Picq wrote:

> Four brave men who do not know each other will not dare to attack a lion. Four less brave, but knowing each other well, sure of their reliability and consequently of mutual aid, will attack resolutely.[5]

And yet, American military culture, policy, and habit since World War I—with a few noteworthy exceptions—has treated the connectedness of soldiers to one another as irrelevant. Instead, soldiers with the same MOS (military occupation specialty) and training credentials are as fungible as dollar bills—utterly equivalent, substitutable, and replaceable. When first introduced into the U.S. Army in World War I by followers of the industrial efficiency expert Fredrick Winslow Taylor and his disciple Elihu Root,[6] this turning of soldiers into replaceable parts was regarded as rational and efficient. Many people still think that way.

But from a military point of view, it is *not* rational. Soldiers who know each other only slightly or not at all fight badly, regardless of their individual skills, training, and bravery. The great Israeli military historian Martin van Creveld blames the poor combat performance of American troops against their World War II German army adversaries on the individual replacement system:

> The U.S. Army . . . put technical and administrative efficiency at the head of its list of priorities, disregarding other considerations, and produced a [replacement] system that possessed a strong inherent tendency to turn men into nervous wrecks. *Perhaps more than any other single factor, it was this system that was responsible for the weaknesses displayed by the U.S. Army during World War II.*[7] [Emphasis added.]

Stephen E. Ambrose, the American historian of World War II, wrote:

> *The replacements paid the price for a criminally wasteful Replacement System that chose to put quantity ahead of quality . . . . It was paying lives but getting no return. It was just pure waste and the commanders should have done something about it.*
>
> Example: in January 1945, Capt. Belton Cooper of the 3rd Armored Division got thirty-five [individual] replacements to help crew the seventeen new tanks the division had received. . . .
>
> The previous night, the thirty-five replacements had been in Antwerp. At 1500 they lumbered off in a convoy of seventeen tanks headed for the front. Two hours later, fifteen of the seventeen were knocked out by German panzers.[8] [Emphasis added.]

Ambrose does not tell us how many of the thirty-five individual replacements survived. Many that did survive undoubtedly took horrible physical wounds and burns; and those lucky enough to escape unmarked were probably shattered psychologically. The rates of physical wounds and psychological casualties track each other very closely: what spills blood spills spirit.[9]

During the Korean War, the individual replacement system continued its lethal work, according to retired U.S. Army four-star General Donn A. Starry, who fought in both Korea and Vietnam and became one of the leaders of the military reform movement of the 1970s and 1980s:

> Many commanders [in Korea] would remark that the new replacements would arrive with dinner, and after a night of contact with the Chinese, they would leave in *body bags* as breakfast arrived.[10]

Social cohesion—from having trained together and traveled to the war zone together—is what keeps people physically alive and mentally sane when faced with a human enemy who *really is trying to kill them.* The malignity of the armed human enemy is not a psychological figment. Only the support of others makes it possible to face armed killers. Professional military literature on the combat strength multiplier effect of unit cohesion has been thoroughly reviewed by Nora Kinzer Stewart, a principal scientist with the U.S. Army Institute for Behavioral and Social Sciences.[11] The idea that the social connectedness and esteem of the soldier's unit are psychologically protective is *not* new, and is found in the lessons learned in World War II (but then forgotten):

> Repeated observations indicated that the absence or inadequacy of such sustaining influences or their disruption during combat was mainly responsible for psychiatric breakdown in battle.[12]

This has been confirmed by subsequent research that troubled to look at the qualities of community of the unit, rather than solely the traits of the individual soldier.[13] Most U.S. military studies do *not* look—their individual-focused culture blinds them to community phenomena.

Why Does Cohesion Matter?

A cohesive unit creates courage by reducing fear.[14] The *human brain codes social recognition, support, and attachment as physical safety.* Cohesion both increases the ability to overcome fear (we call that courage) and reduces fear. The fictional Spartan platoon commander named Dienikes, in the acclaimed novel *Gates of Fire,* puts it very compactly: "The opposite of fear . . . is love."[15]

One would think that the profession of arms would make the deepest study imaginable of the topics of courage and fear. Yet according to General Starry, "There is no course in any Army school today that teaches anything about fear in battle, how a leader copes with his own fear, how a leader talks about it to his subordinates and helps them cope with their fear."[16] Given current American military culture, General Starry's observation is not surprising. In a discussion on cohesion and love in the *Commandant of the Marine Corps Trust Study*, I wrote:

> When you talk to active American military officers and Non-Commissioned Officers (NCOs) about love—they squirm. They are embarrassed. On the one had, their organizational culture highly values rationality, which has been packaged to them as emotion-free[17]—and love is clearly emotional. On the other hand, they instantly start worrying about sex, which in modern forces is *always* prohibited within a unit, whether heterosexual or homosexual. In present-day America, the ideas of love and sex have gotten mashed together. The two notions of rationality-*contra*-emotion and love-is-sex give a one-two punch to clear thinking and discussion of mutual love among military professionals. *Of all groups in America today, military people have the greatest right to, and will benefit most, if they reclaim the word "love" as a part of what they are and what they do.*[18]

The courage-creating aspect of good leadership loses out in this cultural blind spot on love and the institutional practices, such as too-rapid turnover of leaders, which inhibits the growth of mutual love between leader and led. A leader's love *for* his troops reduces that leader's level of fear in the face of danger. The leader's lowered or absent fear—here usually called "confidence"—communicates itself to the troops, thus reducing *their* fear. But beyond an imitative or contagion effect of the leader's confidence, fear is directly alleviated when troops can *feel* the leader's love for them. But current American military culture runs the other way.

Those who have experienced good military training might object to my comments on cohesion: "but tough, realistic training reduces fear and bonds the unit together!" We must expect many circularities: cohesion reduces fear in the face of real danger, *and* going through danger together increases cohesion. Here are several more of these circularities:

- Cohesion increases success in acquiring difficult military skills; *and* success in executing difficult military skills increases cohesion of the unit.
- Cohesion can become portable from unit to unit as esprit de corps and increases esprit de corps,[19] *and* esprit de corps encourages cohesion among thrown-together service members who are strangers to each other.
- Trust makes consistent truthfulness possible, *and* consistent truthfulness makes well-founded trust possible.

These circularities are rising (or falling!) social and psychological spirals in time, not signs of logical failure or empty identities. The art of military trainers and leaders is to create and harness rising spirals for constructive ends.

Note that Ardant du Picq's rational expectation arising from mutual familiarity, quoted at the beginning of this section, and the nonrational effect of mutual love work together. They require the same conditions for their creation.

It is a common tenet of religious thought that awareness of God's love *reduces fear*. This is one of their major themes of the biblical Psalms—hardly an accident, because a fighting man, King David, composed them. Christian scripture continues the same theme: "There is no fear in love; but perfect love casteth out fear."[20] It is also widely observed that aware-ness of the love of one's parents, children, and spouse can control both physical fear, when confronting physical danger, and social fear when con-fronting moral danger. Religiosity and family support as sources of courage are forms of what could be called the "right stuff" theory of good military performance. According to this theory, some people have the "right stuff" in their character, and all you have to do is sift them out of the population. Proponents of this theory will say that high-performing units can instantly be built on the fly from people with good individual training, esprit de corps, and the "the right (individual) stuff."[21] I would not attempt to disprove this assertion as stated, but only point out that it cannot reli-ably be put into practice in the real world for whole American military services, whereas the alternative, creation of cohesive units of unselected ordinary Americans, *can* be put into practice.

The militarily strengthening and psychologically protective effect of stable, socially cohesive units is neither scientifically speculative, ambigu-ous, nor uncertain. But as Professor van Creveld noted above, the U.S. Army placed administrative "rationality" above the human powers of social cohesion. American military historian Gerald Linderman notes about World War II that

> *Almost all other armies established systems of rotating units out of the line.* Even the Wehrmacht, with enemy armies pressing on the homeland from east and west, *managed practically to the war's end to withdraw combat formations for days and weeks of refitting* [integrating cohesive subunit packets of replacements].[22]

Whatever the Germans did, they did by units. Surely, the Germans loved efficiency every bit as much as we Americans do, and yet they *never* adopted an individual replacement or rotation policy for their troops. The inconveniences of managing units, rather than individuals, were something that the Germans took in stride, according to Israeli military historian van Creveld.

Twenty years later, the North Vietnamese Army placed enormous emphasis on the maintenance of unit integrity, according to Colonel William D. Henderson, the author of *Cohesion: The Human Element in Combat*, who commanded an infantry company in Vietnam.[23]

In World War II, we "lost" so many of our battles against the Germans at the tactical level, but at the theater and strategic levels of war, we and our allies won it. In Vietnam, we "won" almost all of our battles with the North Vietnamese and Viet Cong at the tactical level—at least in the sense of being in momentary possession of the ground when the firing stopped—but at the operational and strategic level of war, we lost. The enemy had figured out how to use his advantage in the human factors of war to nullify our stupendous advantage in high-tech weaponry.[24]

Because we still seem enchanted by our own size, wealth, and technological inventiveness, it may help to point out that there is no necessary connection between the fighting strength conferred by an abundance of powerful weapons and the fighting strength conferred by the human factors of cohesion, leadership, and training. These factors vary independently of each other. Attempts to substitute the former for the latter sometimes fail in the short run, and always fail in the long term, because of the dynamic nature of war as a human struggle in which skill trumps technology—in time.[25] The Israel Defense Force (IDF) is as high-tech as Israel's economic resources and American aid permit, which is to say, *very* high. In some important areas, the IDF is technologically ahead of the United States. But just as the IDF is high-tech, it is also high-skill and extremely cohesive at the small-unit level. I mention this example, because I have heard American officers state as obvious truth that the complexity and educational requirements of a high-tech military are incompatible with the social creation of cohesion in its units. The IDF shows that they are not incompatible.

Nor is a loathing for American deaths and wounds a sign of weakness or deterioration in the American military. Currently some commentators worry about what they say is a growing national aversion to military casualties. Yet while no nation in the world is more averse to military casualties than Israel, where single deaths have been treated as national tragedies, no one takes this as a sign of weakness or timidity in the IDF. Do Americans cherish their children in the service less than Israelis? Should we, as a matter of national strength, be instructing American wives to stop caring if their husbands are killed or maimed in the nation's defense? Yes, I am mocking those who equate aversion to casualties with military weakness. Nothing protects the safety of troops—reduces casualties—like military excellence in cohesion, leadership, and training, and wisdom in the political leaders who commit the troops. Aversion to casualties—we should *all* be for it!

In World War II the United States made a Herculean effort to "screen" recruits for psychological fitness, based on the "right stuff" notion—this idea dies hard—that the individual character of the soldier primarily determines how he holds up under fire. Confidence in screening seemed to absolve the American leadership of any responsibility for protection of the troops through policy or organization, according to van Creveld.[26]

During the 1980s the U.S. Army instituted a program called COHORT,[27] an acronym for "Cohesion, Operational Readiness, Training," that kept soldiers together in their squads, platoons, companies, from the beginning of recruit training, right through to the end of their first term of enlistment. This hardly sounds like a revolution. Many civilian readers are probably making a mental shrug—because they are unaware of how radically different this was from the prevailing practices of individual-by-individual manning, individual casualty replacement, and individual rotation. Before COHORT, recruits would go through Basic Training with one group of recruits, then—shuffle the deck—with another group through Advanced Infantry Training—then shuffle again—assigned as an individual to an operational unit. In a three-year first term of enlistment, the average peacetime U.S. Army soldier made and broke the small-unit face-to-face social bonds *five times!* In peacetime this leads to low-skill units, enormous waste, rampant dissatisfaction, and the creation of the bored, resistant, negativistic enlisted-man stereotype. In war, it means that a soldier arrives in the battle zone with strangers. In Vietnam, this was the overwhelmingly predominant experience, with some few exceptions. In World War II, a shockingly large number of troops stripped out of reserve units were used to "fill" divisions embarking for overseas, and virtually all replacements of battle casualties and other attrition were made on an individual basis, not a unit basis.

In the modern Army (or Navy, Marine Corps, or Air Force), the entry-level training only begins the acquisition of military skills. The training that actually qualifies a soldier to fight effectively takes place in the operational unit. In general, soldiers love their first year of training, because they are constantly learning new and interesting skills, lore, and knowledge. However, when the deck is shuffled, typically the whole freshly shuffled unit is held back, like being held back in school. Before COHORT the average three-year enlisted Army soldier enjoyed freshman year, and then repeated freshman year, and then repeated it again![28] This was considered normal; things that are habitual over time come to be accepted as the way they *must* be according to human nature or the laws of nature. If enlisted men had a negative, bored, resistant attitude, that is the nature of enlisted men. What do you expect?

The individual-based American military personnel system inadvertently creates this recalcitrant enlisted man—it is not built into human nature. The Unit Manning System Field Evaluation by the Walter Reed Army Institute of Research (WRAIR) observes:

> The spontaneous motivation of the first-term [COHORT] soldiers played an important role in their achievements. . . . Senior commanders and NCOs were unanimous in their opinion that their privates were exceptionally intelligent, eager to learn, interested in the Army, and dedicated. . . . One NCO said, "These young soldiers will do anything we ask of them. So you have to be careful. . . ." Very few leaders understood as well as this sergeant that they were dealing with a new and unfamiliar phenomenon—soldiers who were self-motivated, who needed and wanted to be taught and guided, not driven.[29]

The soldiers in the units studied by WRAIR were *not* specially selected for high intelligence—what their leaders witnessed was the intelligence that is always there and which standard manning, training, and leadership practices had stifled. In fact, these COHORT soldiers had not been specially selected for any traits.

John C. F. Tillson, who commanded a troop of the famous 11th Armored Cavalry Regiment[30] (Blackhorse) in Vietnam, and military analyst Steven Canby[31] have written trenchantly about this in the unclassified report of study for the Pentagon by the Institute for Defense Analyses, a nonprofit think tank established by the Department of Defense:

> The replacement system forces combat units to devote a major portion of available training time to training . . . the most basic unit skills. . . . Because the unit loses large numbers of people upon completing training at a Combat Training Center, it must begin its training cycle over again, or, at least, retrain the new members in the skills that the departed members had already acquired. With high levels of turbulence [personnel turnover], the unit must continually train new members and never has the

opportunity to develop higher-level skills whose attainment requires soldiers and marines to stay together for long periods of time.[32]

When the Army instituted COHORT, soldiers finished freshman year and then—what a concept!—graduated to sophomore year, and then to junior year. They kept on getting better—nobody then in the U.S. Army had ever seen such a thing. COHORT units developed spontaneous practices of cooperative learning, where the soldiers taught each other, and made sure that the slowest and least skilled were brought along, rather than left behind. Men in these units believed that they would be going to war together—some of them did in Panama and the Gulf—and felt in their guts that their survival would depend on each other.

The Vietnam veteran and military social scientist whose memory inspires this chapter, the late Faris Kirkland (lieutenant colonel, U.S. Army), was a senior member of the team that evaluated COHORT for the Walter Reed Army Institute of Research. He observed the 7th Infantry Division (Light), the first all-COHORT division, over an extended period for the Department of the Army in the early 1980s. He estimated that the *least* capable COHORT unit was three times more skilled and effective than the *most* capable standard, individual replacement, shuffle-the-deck unit in the research comparison group. The best COHORT units took people's breath away. The troops assigned to these COHORT units were the ordinary, average cross section of American military recruits, not in any way specially screened or selected. This lack of special selection was intentional. When I speak of cohesion as a combat strength *multiplier*, this is not hyperbole. Many currently serving officers and NCOs who led COHORT units in the 1980s and early 1990s often say that this was the high point of their military career.

The unit stabilization policies of COHORT (and the related programs) are now *gone* from the U.S. Army. I repeat, COHORT is gone. It was killed by the personnel bureaucracy, both civilian and military, and by the line officers. The personnel men found it contrary to their concept of rationality and too inconvenient to administer. Their systems and their computer programs were all organized around numbers of individuals ("faces") and the "percent fill" of the units' table of organization ("places"). "Do we have the numbers?" was, and still is, the focus of the individual manning/replacement/rotation system.[33] Numerical "fill" is something that the existing computer programs were (and are) good at. Assignment of personnel in COHORT units had to be done by hand, because the computer programs had not been revised to focus on managing units rather than managing individuals.

The line officers found that COHORT's three-year (rather than one-year) training cycle made their "readiness " statistics look bad. And looking bad in those statistics meant no promotion; under "up-or-out," no promotion meant the end of an officer's career. During the first year of any COHORT unit, it was classified as "not ready," reflecting badly on the parent unit's commander. He knew he would be rated for promotion on the readiness of his subordinate units in competition with commanders of non-COHORT outfits. For example, a COHORT brigade with three infantry battalions would always have one battalion "not ready," compared to standard individual replacement brigades where all three battalions would always be rated as ready, no matter how mediocre.[34]

COHORT units progressed very rapidly and sometimes outstripped the habitual practices and expectations of their leaders. These leaders found themselves stretched by their trainees to provide more and more challenging, demanding, and interesting training exercises and situations. What should have been an occasion for pride and a call for the leaders' self-improvement was experienced as a humiliation—another reason COHORT was killed.

If we take Faris Kirkland's multiplier at face value, the fighting power of two officially ready COHORT battalions in a three-battalion brigade was worth the fighting power of six ordinary individual replacement battalions. So by this arithmetic, the administrative rigidity and career fears that killed COHORT chose a total fighting power of three over a fighting power of six. Where's the rationality in that?[35]

The metaphor of interchangeable parts has had a powerful and pervasive grip on American organizational culture. The military occupational specialty and training credentials of a soldier are treated like the physical dimensions, mechanical and electrical design specs of a carburetor. However, an automobile's carburetor and brake cylinders do not have to practice together in order to operate. They don't have to get to know each other, and it makes no sense to speak of the brake cylinder needing to trust the carburetor. A machine like an automobile has no "unit skills." Put in a working replacement carburetor of the right model, and the car will run like new; replace it again, and again, and again, and it will still run like new. *Not so* with a military unit, especially in conditions of danger and privation.

Military training *always* contains a significant component of retraining. This is inevitable because combat (actual or simulated) is a practice, like a sport, surgery, or music, not a science.[36] Its skills are perishable and have to be constantly retrained. Studies of the decay and restoration of the tank crew skills associated with tank gunnery have shown that retraining happened much faster when done in the same crew that the skills were originally trained in, compared to a crew of strangers who on paper were just as proficient as the original one. For example, tank crews lose 25 percent of their speed and accuracy in only three months, according to Tillson and Canby, who explain:

> First, unit members forget the details of complex tasks and lose their edge over time. Second, unit members may be replaced with new people who do not know their jobs. The latter factor is clearly the most important. While unit members do forget the specifics of tasks they may have learned some time ago, in general they can restore their skills relatively quickly with retraining, especially when they are with people they know. When untrained individuals are placed in a unit, they must be taught both individual and collective skills and the unit must stop or slow its own training to conduct this new training.[37]

Excellence in many domains of professional practice is not something that, once acquired, becomes a permanent possession, like riding a bicycle, never lost by turning to other things. Collective skills are no less important in an Army tank crew or a Marine Corps fire team than in a string quartet or cardiac transplant team.

This factor alone accounts for much of the learning gain realized by stable units, where faster retraining frees up the time saved for new, more advanced training. Similarly, because newly assigned soldiers have to be "brought up to speed," reducing the drain caused by "newbies" also increases available training time. This arithmetic is painfully simple. Our failures to reap the benefits of this arithmetic are self-inflicted. When there is too much shuffling of the personnel in units and of their leaders, everyone may be going through the motions of training, but the cognitive and emotional resources that should go into learning, go instead into figuring out the new people. A major outcome of excellent training is confidence in one's own military skills. Researchers in the Israel Defense Force after the Yom Kippur War found that paratroopers who broke down during or after the battles were eight times more likely to lack confidence in their skills than a random sample of those who did not break down.[38]

People are familiar with team skills (as contrasted to individual skills) from other complex, cooperative performance in real time. The performance of a basketball team or a string quartet is such a cooperative performance. Different positions on the team have different "jobs" but the team begins to cook when the players have practiced together and played together enough to develop what current Marine Corps doctrine calls "implicit understanding and communication." Of course individual skills are important, but our administrative practices make them the *only* skills. If you then add the element of mortal danger, which is not found even in the most competitive basketball league, the element of trust must be added to the picture. The only sure way to create trust among a group of unrelated strangers is time doing demanding, difficult, worthwhile, and sometimes dangerous things—together.

The American public understands the importance of keeping people together before, during, and after danger. Since the publication of *Achilles in Vietnam* I have spoken ten or so times a year to public audiences at colleges and universities. Even though my host is often the Classics department—not ROTC—and they want me to talk about Homer's *Iliad,* I always give my prevention message that the single most important preventive psychiatry move for the military is to keep people together: train them together, send them into danger together, and bring them home together. The audience response is—you mean we're *still* moving people around like we did in Vietnam! The public is not much interested in internal military administration. But the single administrative fact they are likely to know about the U.S. forces in Vietnam is the fixed tour, individual rotation policy that had men go over with strangers, work their way into a fighting unit of strangers, and then come home with strangers.

This practice of individual manning, replacement, and rotation would strike us as bizarre if it were not so familiar from practice over a century. Not only do cohesive units fight more successfully, thus reducing *all* casualties, but also they directly protect their members from psychological injury. This is not speculative. The evidence is in hand.

The heaviest weight of battle borne by Israelis in the Yom Kippur War fell on the armored units meeting the massive Syrian tank attack in the north and units rushing to block the Egyptian penetration in the south. After the war, researchers examined two levels of social connectedness that are present in all fighting units but especially clear in tank units: the level of the tank crew and the level of the unit to which the tank belonged. The Israel Defense Force prizes cohesion and normally keeps crews and units together for all purposes, even mess hall duty, "KP." However, the Yom Kippur attack came as a complete surprise. Men rushed directly from their prayers to the bases and were thrown into tanks and toward the front willy-nilly. Tankers who fought the Syrians or Egyptians with a crew of strangers (even though equally well trained) were four times more likely to break down during or after combat, and three times more likely if thrown into a strange unit.[39]

The inevitable reduction in the size of the U.S. armed services after the end of the Cold War does not have to be accompanied by deterioration in quality.[40] One goal of this chapter is to provide a clear and positive picture of the qualities we want a smaller twenty-first-century military to have.

My agenda is to prevent casualties, not to arouse apocalyptic fears that the United States faces destruction. In the new world after the Cold War, our forces can be both smaller *and* better, intelligently prepared for whatever we have to face. As a nation we have a painful history of having suffered monstrous bloodletting in the "first battle" of every war.[41] I am deeply worried by the triumphalism that took hold after the military victory against Iraq in the Persian Gulf War. As philosopher Friedrich Nietzsche wrote, success "makes the victor stupid."[42]

These criticisms of our forces as they stand today may strike readers as too harsh, especially when we seem to win our fights so handily, such as in the Gulf War and at the time I am writing these words, apparently in Afghanistan. My answer is that our performance in these two conflicts proves the point, rather than refutes it. In the Gulf an incompetent foe allowed us to train up with stable units for months before we attacked in the time, place, and manner of our choosing. By the time of the attack our forces had created the basis of cohesion, leadership, and training that would have been lacking had we had to fight our way into the Arabian Peninsula. In Afghanistan as of December 2001, we are using that relatively tiny fraction of our forces, which already gets the good resources of cohesion, leadership, and training. Army Special Forces certainly do.[43] The Marine Expeditionary Units (Special Operations Capable) have a very firm and successful policy of unit stabilization during the long and rigorous train-up prior to deployments. The 10th Mountain Division is similarly "regimental" in its ethos and practices.

Cohesion, from the Point of View of Ethics . . .

You don't have to be Saint Thomas Aquinas or Immanuel Kant to see that there is an ethical side to what I have presented above as matters of policy. If *you* are in the position to set policy on how other people are ordered into danger, and you know that sending them into harm's way with strangers greatly increases their chances of dying, you have an ethical duty *not* to make personnel policies that have that result. Better alternatives are available. It's simple "do unto others."

Policy and ethics should converge on the subject of keeping people together through training, into danger, out the other side, and home again—together. In the event, God forbid, of war, units should be rotated in and out of combat *as units, not as individuals*, and not kept permanently in contact with the enemy. When enemy action has caused operationally significant casualties, the unit should be pulled out of combat to the rear to reconstitute—i.e., to recadre, retrain, reequip, and establish social bonds with the replacement subunits. We must *never, never again* practice the individual replacement of casualties and individual rotation of troops that we practiced in Vietnam!

Unit Associations—A Neglected Resource

Many of the derailed lives of veterans and their families would have been preserved, I believe, if every service member going into harm's way *and his or her family* had enjoyed the social support and resources of a good military unit association. At every step—adjustment to military life, the family's experience of the service member's deployment, the service member's own and the family's experience of return from deployment (especially if it's been a dangerous one), recognizing and coping with psychological and physical injury, making the transition to civilian life, networking in civilian life and educating employers, again, recognizing and coping with psychological and physical injuries, practical assistance in obtaining health and governmental services—every one of these would benefit from a vibrant military unit association.

Unit associations could enter into seamless partnership with the family support programs on our military bases, thus taking advantage of the added wisdom from the families of former members of the unit who still live nearby. Members of the unit association could receive training as peer counselors. This would both help destigmatize psychological injury and provide a confidential and knowledgeable source for treatment referrals, if needed. It would also reduce the sense of isolation that psychologically injured service members and recently separated veterans often suffer.

While the mass membership veterans' service organizations have many advantages that come from their size alone, I believe that they have not been as effective as unit associations can be in providing continuity of support during the transition from active duty to veteran status. For combat veterans, generalized fellowship does not easily substitute for the shared experience and shared narrative of the unit association—common identity. But there is no need for unit associations and mass membership veterans service organizations to be adversarial. They can and should be synergistic and mutually supporting.

Thus, sound unit associations can be an effective and efficient means of delivering *both prevention and restoration.*

In the wake of any war, these unit associations will be noisy, demanding, and make themselves a thorn in the side of bureaucrats and politicians. Many civilian bureaucrats nervously view these groups as nearly criminal gangs because of their lack of docile gratitude. But the peer acknowledgment, social recognition, and practical support that unit associations provide should be treasured, not feared.

Historically minded readers may remember with a shudder the proto-Nazi Freikorps death squads, which destabilized the Weimar Republic in Germany after World War I, and may wonder how I could be advocating the encouragement of military unit associations. Historical research indicates that it was precisely those German World War I veterans who were demobilized *as individuals*, not as units, who gravitated to the Freikorps.[44] Their alienation, bitterness, and boredom crystallized into street violence, extortion, murder, and political terrorism.

Unit associations are no single magic bullet. The reception of returning veterans by the local community, abundant and combat-trauma-aware vocational and educational programs, employer education and support, and community-based, veteran-based treatment programs with early, assertive, and persistent outreach to psychologically injured veterans, all form part of the complete picture. What I am saying is hardly more than a restatement of what World War I veteran Waller said near the close of World War II.[45] Will we never put into practice what we learn from our own experience?

TRAINING

There is relatively little public awareness of the extent to which the U.S. armed services reformed themselves in the wake of the Vietnam War. Journalist James Kitfield devoted his 1995 book to this story: *Prodigal Soldiers: How the Generation of Officers Born of Vietnam Revolutionized the American Style of War.*[46] The Army's COHORT program was a direct product of this self-reform process—now undone. But something that so far has largely *not* been undone is the revolution in training made by the generation of officers who stayed in after the Vietnam War.[47] The most visible legacy of these reforms is the combat training centers with resident opposing force (OPFOR) units. If I concentrate on the National Training Center (NTC) at Fort Irwin, it is because of my greater familiarity with it. But I believe that what I have to say is true of all the combat training centers, as well as the air combat equivalents at Nellis Air Force Base and Fallon Naval Air Station.

The visiting units are typically thoroughly whipped by the highly skilled—*but low-tech-equipped*—opposing forces (OPFORs).

Colonel John Rosenberger, recent commander of the 11th Armored Cavalry Regiment, the OPFOR at the National Training Center, rhetorically asks:

> How does OPFOR develop and sustain its ability to fight and defeat its opponents in almost every battle at the National Training Center? How does the regiment, fighting with 1960s–1970s technology, routinely defeat brigade task forces equipped with the most modern weapon systems and technology our Army can provide?[48]

His answer is mainly in terms of the training that the 11th ACR troopers receive at all levels, from private to colonel.

As with cohesion, I do not make cheap hyperbole when I call training a combat strength *multiplier.* Excellent training engages the whole person: mind, body, emotions, character, and spirit. It prepares for the demands and stresses of war and other situations with mortal stakes. Therefore, at all levels it must be "tough" and realistic.[49]

The particular content of training experience to which "toughness" applies varies with the technical content and military role the trainees are being prepared for and with rank. All roles need training to perform effectively in the face of physical danger and to perform ethically in the face of moral danger. The relative proportions of physical and moral danger may tend to change according to rank, but in the interconnected modern world no enlisted man or woman is too low to be released from moral strain or the need for moral understanding. Former Marine Corps Commandant Charles C. Krulak spoke of the "strategic corporal," whose "maturity, restraint, and judgment" can influence foreign policy outcomes at the strategic level.[50] And no officer is too high to be sheltered from the dangers of attack.

Training, from the Point of View of Ethics ...

It's not often that the words "ethics" and "training" show up in the same sentence, and similarly infrequent, the words "competence" and "ethics."

Mention of ethics puts us in a Sunday-go-to-church frame of mind, and competence is something for the workplace and the professions. Put "ethics" with "workplace," and the mind usually goes to sex, lies, and stealing money—still no thought of competence. I hope to persuade you that competence is an *ethical* imperative in military service.

The basic argument is simple: lives and devastating wounds are at stake in military performance, ranging from the private beside you who might not know how to handle a grenade safely, to millions of lives at risk from weapons of mass destruction. The mortal stakes of military service means that without competence there can be no trust—in peers, in subordinates, in seniors, in self. No more than a surgeon can be excused for failure to achieve and maintain skill and knowledge by simply meaning well, no service member of any rank can be excused from the responsibility to know his or her stuff.

Of course there are moments in war, in dangerous emergencies, and in exercises simulating war, when instant obedience is required. For example, fire fighting in a burning ship cannot be suspended for a chief petty officer to answer "why" questions, but those providing training in these essential activities must know why, and convey enough of this rationality to permit their sailors to build habits of obedience on well-founded trust. Obedience based on well-founded trust in the competence and integrity of the senior is much more reliable than the reflex of blind obedience based on fear. Integrity also means that institutional powers to reward or punish are only employed for the good of the training or the good of the trainees, never for the private personal interests of the trainer. If a trainer uses power to coerce a private gain, be it sexual, financial, or careerist, the whole body of trainees—sometimes the whole service—is injured. *There are no private wrongs in the abuse of military authority.* In some instances the moral fabric of the whole service is damaged, and the trust and respect of the nation are impaired. In training no less than in military operations, all personnel watch the trustworthiness of those who wield power over them.

What service members need at every level is moral knowledge, as well as technical knowledge.

Every atrocity strengthens the enemy and potentially disables the service member who commits it. The distinction between lawful combatant (who may thus be legally and morally attacked) and protected person is the bright line between soldier and murderer. The overwhelming majority of people who volunteer for our armed services are not psychopaths; they are good people who will be seared by knowing themselves to be murderers. You do not "support our service men" by mocking the law of land warfare and calling it a joke.

Francis Lieber's 1863 "Instructions for the Government of Armies of the United States in the Field" (the Lieber Code) expressed what I believe to be the continuing consensus of serious military professionals: "Men who take up arms against one another in public war do not cease on this account to be moral beings, responsible to one another and to God." Even tough-guy gunslingers in the ground forces, and all those whose ideals includes "supporting our troops," have good reason, based on national self-interest, to respect and support the rules of war. Everyone who thinks that repeating "there are no rules" demonstrates patriotic support for the troops should think again.

LEADERSHIP

It's easy to make the case that excellence in military leadership is a combat strength multiplier. Proving that such excellence protects the troops from psychological injury is harder, especially since this is the least studied of the three protective components—cohesion, training, leadership. Because of the powerful correlation between the rates of psychiatric casualties with physical casualties, it's plausible to expect that data connecting leadership performance with physical casualties can be generalized to mind wounds:

> Data from the Vietnam war covering 34 maneuver battalions in 5 Army divisions and separate brigades in the years 1965 and 1966 indicate that, "maneuver battalions under experienced commanders (6 months or more in command) suffered battle deaths in sizeable skirmishes at only 2/3 the rate of units under battalion commanders with less than 6 months in command."[51]

The scarcity of empirical studies on the relationship between leadership and psychological injury is startling. Reuven Gal, former chief psychologist of the Israel Defense Forces, and his U.S. Army co-author, Colonel Franklin Jones, could do little more than assert their intuition in this, because the data connecting leadership performance and psychological injury rates have never been systematically gathered:

> The soldier's confidence in the commander is also critical in protecting him from overwhelming battle stress. . . . [This confidence derives from] (1) belief in the professional competence of the commander, (2) belief in

his credibility, and (3) the perception that he cares about his troops. While in garrison all three components are equally important; in combat trust in the commander's professional competence becomes primary.[52]

These authors visualize the commander as a giant lens that focuses battlefield, unit, and individual factors into the soldier's appraisal of the combat situation, which in turn determines the soldier's success or failure in coping.

During the period of military self-reform described above, the Army Chief of Staff, Edward "Shy" Meyer, attempted to implant a culture of leadership that he called "positive leadership":[53]

- Make it safe to tell the truth.
- Support subordinate leaders' professional growth.
- Trust them and work hard to assure their success.
- Assign missions without prescribing the means to accomplish them.
- Provide situations in which subordinate leaders practice what they've learned.
- Build their competence to assess situations and take the initiative to develop adaptive solutions.
- Mentor, rather than intimidate, subordinate leaders.
- Refrain from meddling in their spheres of responsibility.
- Require subordinate leaders to study their profession.
- Take responsibility for setting mission and priorities, not assigning every task as "highest priority, to be done immediately."
- Listen to subordinate leaders' feedback on time budgets and resources, supporting realistic time management.
- Support self-maintenance, rather than defeat it.

In a painful historical irony, General Meyer was trying to undo the de facto leadership culture that came out of World War II: expectation of instant, blind obedience from subordinates. While demanding blind obedience and micromanaging their subordinates, American leaders were fond of making speeches to them and to the public about democracy and individual initiative. Here's the irony: the leadership practices listed above were brought to their fullest development by the Germans, who were *not* then practitioners of political democracy. The Israelis, who *do* practice political democracy, also follow these "German" leadership practices. In several important ways, the Communist Chinese in Korea also followed these practices at the small-unit level. My point is that there is *no* useful correlation between the leadership culture of a military organization and the large-scale political culture of the nation that creates it. Conventional wisdom holds that military organizations mirror the culture of the nations that create them. This is like the truth pronounced by the Oracle of Delphi in ancient Greece: it may not mean what you think it means. The culturally prestigious ideas that the U.S. armed services imported from the civilian sector were the ideas of "scientific management," not empowering subordinates or the "democratic" spirit of valuing the insight and collective wisdom of the lowly NCOs.

The leadership culture that both protects the troops from psychological injury and makes them militarily effective is well understood: *it is the constellation of leadership culture described above.* It's what I mean by "properly supported" leadership. These practices are neither anti-democracy because the Germans, Chinese, and North Vietnamese used them, nor military democracy, because they run counter to the authoritarian U.S. leadership culture that grew out of World War II—the use of the word "democracy" here is a red herring either way.

Leadership, from the Point of View of Ethics . . .

Thumos, character, is a living thing that flourishes or wilts according to the ways that those who hold power use power. Character is fluid throughout life, and imitative throughout life. In high-stakes situations, people learn about the use of power from the ways power is actually used in their environment, even if they are not "directly involved." Moral learning continues throughout life.

As Aristotle famously says in the *Rhetoric* I.ii.3, it is the *ethos,* the character of the leader, that is most compelling and persuasive. Listen again to Aristotle's explanation of *thumos* in the *Politics* VII.6.1327b39ff. He says, "*Thumos* is the faculty of our souls which issues in love and friendship. . . . *It is also the source . . . of any power of commanding* and any feeling for freedom."[54] The spirited self-respect that Homer called *thumos* becomes particularly critical to leadership in a combat situation. To trust a leader, the troops need to feel that the leader is his or her "own person," not a slave. In combat, trust goes to the leaders who give critical obedience, rather than blind obedience, to their own bosses. A leader giving blind obedience to an irrational or illegal order gets the troops killed without purpose ["wasted"] or irretrievably tainted by commission of atrocities.[55] The "charismatic" impact of a leader being his "own person" doesn't come from a rational calculation that such a leader would not obey uselessly suicidal or atrocious orders. When Aristotle spoke of *thumos* as the source of any power to command, he was speaking of its direct emotional impact.

Tell the truth and make it safe to tell the truth. In military organizations, the core reason for truth-telling is the maintenance of *trust,* both up and down the chain of command. In the long run, neither punitive sanctions, nor the Ten Commandments, nor the finest system for selecting officers of good character can guarantee truthfulness. Consistent, reliable truth telling is only possible when power is deployed in such a way that it is safe to tell the truth. Only then do subordinates air their doubts and problems, tell bad news, own up to failures. This is not coddling, because truthfulness in leadership also calls for vigorous criticism of subordinates' shortcomings. The trust created by the practices of positive leadership given above is the main reason they are combat multipliers, while mistrust among peers and along the chain of command is a potent self-generated source of "friction."[56] Leadership truthfulness at all levels means eliminating perverse incentives to look good at the expense of *being* good. Unit "readiness" reporting has been laced with institutionalized fraud for decades.[57] This is where personnel evaluation and promotion policy must converge with ethics and good leadership practices. But so far, every attempt to reform this policy area has gone on the rocks.

Use power in accordance with "what's right." Nothing destroys trust in the chain of command so quickly as a leader's exploitation of institutional power to coerce a private gain from subordinates, be it sexual, financial, or careerist. Of these, careerist exploitation is the most frequent and the most damaging. The whole unit—sometimes the whole service—is injured. As I have said, there are no *private* wrongs in the abuse of military authority. The target of the abuse of power is not alone in being injured. *That* service member's trust in the chain of command is going to be impaired or destroyed, of course, but in addition everyone that learns of the violation of "what's right" also suffers injury to the capacity for social trust. The competence, consideration, and moral integrity with which leaders deploy institutional power are central to vertical cohesion. Everyone watches the trustworthiness of those who wield power above them; and this "fishbowl factor" is far-reaching.

A cartoon titled *"Promotion Surgeries,"*[58] which appeared a few years ago in the *Navy Times*—it could have been in any of the services—showed three pictures of a mid-career officer stripped to his shorts, and in each frame a different sewn-up surgical incision. The first frame, referring to the rank of lieutenant commander (major in ground and air forces), showed an incision running across his forehead and was captioned, "Brain

Removal." The second frame, a back view referring to the rank of commander (lieutenant colonel), showed an incision running down the middle of his back, and was captioned, "Backbone Removal." The last frame, again from the front, referring to the rank of captain (colonel), showed an incision on the left side of his chest, captioned, "Heart Removal." A well-led force needs all of its officers to have all of their literal and figurative organs.[59]

The technological advances that have taken place since the end of World War II do not change the basic need for cohesion, training, and leadership. Today, a few privileged military formations get these good resources. The veterans I serve demand that *every* American service member who can be sent into harm's way shall have them. There is no reason, other than cultural and institutional inertia, that this should not be done.

Trust is the master concept that links cohesion, leadership, and training.[60] In fact, they are the things that build trust, forming and strengthening character throughout a military career.

Ethics, leadership, and policy are not distinct realms of function in military institutions—even though the current American institutions treat them separately. They are simply different refractions of the same beam of light, its culture. Recently, Lieutenant General Walter Ulmer, Jr., USA, retired, wrote, "Changing the culture of any organization is a leadership task, yet there appears to be no strategic design for how to change Army culture."[61] I propose that we make *creation and preservation of trust* across all ranks and between the armed services and the nation as the "vision statement" for such a strategic design, with cohesion, leadership, and training as its embodiments. We have known for more than a century that cohesion, leadership, and training are combat strength multipliers. In contrast, personnel turbulence, individual-based (rather than unit-based) manning, replacement, and rotation policies, training to check all the boxes and looking good rather than robust military competence, a climate of fear among officers, making them averse to decision, responsibility, and truthfulness—these are combat strength hemorrhages.

Some specific policy proposals to nourish the reader's imagination are found in Appendix III.

You, the American people, are the ultimate commander of the armed services. Caring about these things and *informing yourself*—so that your caring can be effective—are basic to democratic citizenship.[62] If you make trust—founded in cohesion, training, and leadership—your "commander's intent," the specific reforms in Appendix III may be the best way to fulfill that intent. Or there may be other, better ways. That doesn't matter. What counts is that the civilian and uniformed leadership of the armed services faithfully and intelligently carry out your intent. To both the public and the military leadership, the veterans I serve say: Do it!

21

Odysseus As a Military Leader

So many of Odysseus' grim and despicable failures of leadership responsibility have already been pointed out in this book that it is time to
remind ourselves of his strengths and positive contributions to the Greek
war effort. Odysseus was extremely productive in all of those military
endeavors that involve *mētis*—cunning intelligence, deception, reconnaissance, manipulation, secrecy, spying, and strategy.[1] It's hard to overstate
the military value of these capacities. Good reconnaissance and intelligence allow the soldier to evade the enemy's traps and to lay his own. Both
are keys to winning fights with minimum casualties, good reasons for
Athena's moniker as "The Soldier's Friend." She was the goddess of *mētis*.

The ancient Chinese military philosopher Sun Tzu sings the praises of
reconnaissance and spying in the final chapter of *The Art of War*:

> So what enables an intelligent government and wise military leadership to
> overcome others and achieve extraordinary accomplishment is foreknowl-
> edge. Foreknowledge cannot be gotten from ghosts and spirits, cannot be
> had by analogy, cannot be found out by calculation. It must be obtained
> from people, people who know the conditions of the enemy.[2]

Odysseus was also a spy. During Telemachus' visit with Menelaus in
Sparta, Helen describes Odysseus' daring solo penetration into Troy
(*Odyssey* 4:274, Fagles). We never hear what Odysseus learned, or
whether it was of any value, but his solo mission is consistent with his
courage and crafty intelligence.

Iliad 10 reports his night reconnaissance with Diomedes behind Trojan lines. During this exceedingly dangerous mission, he discovers the Trojan order of battle (*Iliad* 10:471ff, Fitzgerald), but his boss, Agamemnon,
the "consumer" of this intelligence, never makes any use of it, in keeping
with his general incompetence. Odysseus and Diomedes also learn that
Hector and his top commanders are conferring *unguarded* by the tomb of

Ilos (10:458ff). We know that Odysseus is armed with a bow (10:287) and that he is capable of aimed rapid fire of great accuracy. So why do they not decapitate the Trojan leadership or even try? Greed for personal gain gets in the way. Odysseus and Diomedes have just learned that a newly arrived and travel-weary Thracian contingent is camped in an isolated and vulnerable spot with

> Horses most royal . . .
> whiter than snow and swift as the seawind.
> [The king's] chariot is a masterwork in gold and silver.
> (*Iliad* 10:481ff, Fitzgerald)

Homer puts the idea to go after this booty in Diomedes' mouth, but Odysseus never says, "Whoa! Let's keep our eye on the ball," and wholeheartedly goes for the booty.[3] I'm trying to give a fair account of Odysseus' military virtues, but everywhere I turn I stub my toe on the defects of his character—in this case he has lost sight of the military purpose of the night reconnaissance. There's a fair chance that in the next morning's battle the Greeks would be thrown out of their beachhead and all slaughtered. Nestor had said, just before he proposed the night reconnaissance,

> Terrible pressure is on us. . . .
> The issue teeters on a razor's edge
> for all [Greeks]—whether we live or perish.
> (*Iliad* 10:191ff, Fitzgerald)

Odysseus and Diomedes find the Thracian camp, kill the Thracian king and a lot of sleeping soldiers, and race away with the prize team and chariot, outrunning the hue and cry. They drive their prize into the Greek beachhead. Amidst all the crowing and congratulations on their flashy prize, amid the relief that both Odysseus and Diomedes have returned safely, nobody remembers to debrief them. *Iliad* 10 ends with the two warriors having a hot bath and a stiff drink.

The Greeks are saved the next day, not by Odysseus, but by Achilles' releasing his fresh troops under Patroclus' command to take the Trojans on the flank by surprise.

THE TROJAN HORSE

The towering achievement, the one that secures Odysseus' place in the pantheon of military imagination, is the ruse of the Horse. This deception, conceived and carried out by Odysseus, turned Greek defeat into victory.[4]

We hear about the Horse twice in the *Odyssey*, first when Menelaos describes Helen's attempt to smoke out the Greek fighters concealed inside by imitating their wives' voices (4:307ff, Fagles), and second when Odysseus tips the singer Demodocus and requests that he sing about the Horse (8:552ff, Fagles). There's no taking this accomplishment away from Odysseus—he did it. The basic story is a familiar one: The Greeks build a large hollow wooden horse big enough to hold a force of picked fighters. The army then embarks, pretending to give up, and the ships sail away, but they only withdraw out of sight behind the offshore island of Tenedos. The Trojans celebrate their victory and the lifting of the siege, and are deceived into bringing the Horse inside the city walls. That night while the city sleeps, the Greek ships return, while the troops inside the Horse spread out, killing Trojans and opening the gates.

The most detailed account, based on Epic Cycle texts that have not survived to the present, except as summaries, is in Virgil's *Aeneid*. Because Virgil's analysis is so penetrating and still relevant to military surprise today, I shall rely upon it.

The deception of the so-called Trojan Horse was complex and subtle, and deserves to be rescued from the trivializing presentation it usually receives. The Horse, according to Virgil, was "too big for the gate, *not* to be hauled inside!"[5] Successful deception requires a dynamic falsehood, an untruth with beauty and appeal.[6]

The key figure is Sinon, ingenious liar, who persuades the Trojans that he's a Greek traitor, by scarring himself as Odysseus had done to penetrate Troy. He points out a thing that would not have been obvious on the beach some distance from the walls: *the Horse was too big to be taken into the city*. This endowed the deception with the innocence and certainty of truth. Sinon proclaims that if anyone violates the Horse, which he says is an offering to Athena, all of Troy will suffer. On the other hand, if they contrive to bring it up into the citadel—which on the face of it was impossible because it was too big—it would more than replace the stolen Palladium as a talisman of the city's safety. The Palladium was a miraculous guardian statue of Athena previously stolen from the citadel of Troy by Odysseus and Diomedes.[7]

The leading Trojans were dead set against having anything to with the Horse, fearing that it was a trick or a siege engine. They wanted to build a bonfire under it or throw it into the sea, and one of them, Laocoön, was so angered by the sight of it that he hurled his spear at its side.

The response of the Trojans was not, as our schools usually teach it, "Look at the beautiful gift the Greeks left us!"

The Trojans would probably have kept it on the beach where it was built, if the gods had not lent horrifying credence to Sinon's claim that Athena would punish desecration of her offering—thus lending credence to the whole deception. Laocoön drew the lot as priest for that day's sacrifice to Poseidon, and just as he was about to slaughter the bull by the water's edge, two giant snakes crawled out of the sea and ate Laocoön's sons and then tangled him in their coils. Almost everyone in Troy saw this as his punishment for violating Athena's offering with his spear, and the cry went up to bring the Horse inside. It was irresistible. They even had to tear down part of the wall and dismantle the gate to get the Horse through. The false idea had taken root. Cassandra's warnings could not dissuade them. Even the testimony of the senses could not get through: four times the Horse lurched with such force that the soldiers inside were thrown against one another, making a great clatter of their arms.

Students at all levels of education will profit if the Trojan Horse is rescued from the children's book treatment that it now receives, and is taught as something from which we can learn valuable lessons about the dynamic of *self*-deception.

A study by James J. Wirtz, *The Tet Offensive: Intelligence Failure in War*,[8] provides examples of how successful military deception is mostly *self*-deception by the target. The most prominent and appealing untruth that the Americans fell for was the Repeat-the-Glorious-Victory-of-Dien-Bien-Phu narrative. The Vietnamese had broken the French will to continue fighting in 1954 by successfully attacking and forcing the surrender of a high-profile sixteen-thousand-man French force at Dien Bien Phu. Historian Wirtz describes the grip that this appealing, but false, analysis had on the American leadership:

> Dien Bien Phu exerted a powerful influence on [American] intelligence analysts and commanders more than a year before the onset of the Tet attacks. Intelligence analysts believed that, given General Giap's earlier victory and the devastating impact it had on French public opinion, the North Vietnamese would attempt to inflict another "Dien Bien Phu" on the United States [at Khe Sanh]. U.S. Commanders . . . [welcomed] the

prospect of engaging the communists in a set piece battle. . . . U.S. commanders hoped that the communists would attempt to repeat their earlier victory, thereby allowing U.S. firepower to be fully utilized. As the siege of Khe Sanh materialized on the eve of the Tet offensive, it appeared that these hopes would finally be realized.[9]

The North Vietnamese created the impression that their main effort in what is now remembered as the Tet Offensive was the Marine Combat Base at Khe Sanh. The siege of Khe Sanh successfully riveted and deceived American attention—the main effort was elsewhere. The senior American leadership had congratulated itself that the Khe Sanh Marine Combat Base worked a tether-the-goat-to-lure-the-tiger-out-of-the-mountains strategy, drawing the North Vietnamese into a position where they would be destroyed by American firepower.

Americans endured persistent, multilayered mental assaults by their skillful and tenacious Vietnamese enemy. Booby traps, camouflage, ambush, and unexpected appearances and disappearances play with the mind. As common as the mind games of *mētis* are in the *Odyssey,* they are rare in the *Iliad*.[10] However, the reader should not imagine that somehow the war crafts of *mētis*—deception, concealment, cunning, ambush, and surprise—were in general abhorrent to the warrior ethos of the noble gentlemen fighting at Troy.[11] However, the *Iliad* is dominated by the figure of Achilles, whose *personal* understanding of a noble character rejected everything deceitful and devious. In his famous reply, looking straight at Odysseus, after the latter has conveyed Agamemnon's buyout offer to him, he says,

> Odysseus, master soldier and mariner,
> I owe you a straight answer. . . .
>   I hate
> as I hate Hell's own gate that man who hides
> one thought within him while he speaks another.
>   (*Iliad* 9:377ff, Fitzgerald)

Duplicity was not unheroic per se in the Homeric world, but was personally hateful to Achilles, Homer's antithesis to Odysseus. Centuries later Achilles' enormous prestige in classical Athens made "openness [the opposite of guile]" into "the largest part of noble character " for that culture.[12] Athenian contempt for secrecy and deceit was a theme in Pericles' famous funeral oration in Thucydides:

And then we are different . . . [from the Spartans] with regard to military preparations. Our city is open to the world, and we have no periodic deportations of foreigners in order to prevent people seeing or learning our secrets which might be of military advantage to the enemy. This is because we rely, not on . . . deceits but on our own real courage. . . . The Spartans, from boyhood are submitted to the most laborious training in courage, whereas we pass our lives without such restrictions but we are no less ready to face the same dangers as they are.

(Thucydides 2.39.1)[13]

Pericles connects deception with fear, a lack of manly courage. A character in one of Euripides' plays says, "No brave man would choose to kill an enemy by stealth rather than confront him face on."[14] Our own culture has adopted many of the Athenian ideals. I believe that when President George W. Bush called the men who flew to their own deaths by crashing airplanes into the New York World Trade Center "cowards," he voiced this aspect of the American classical inheritance, connecting military deception with fear and thus "cowardice."

SUMMARY OF THE CHARGES AGAINST CAPTAIN ODYSSEUS

In Part One I laid out the evidence that warranted at the very least a court of inquiry if not a court-martial:
Overall:

- The loss of twelve ships and crews, in excess of six hundred of the youth of Ithaca and environs, who accompanied Odysseus to Troy.

Specifically:

- Unable to control his troops in a relatively simple situation, seventy-two lost unnecessarily at Ismarus.[15]
- Takes troops into needless danger on a selfish or irresponsible impulse, six lost in the Cyclops' cave.
- Protects himself when he could have protected everyone, approximately 480 lost in the Laestrygonian fjord.
- Fails to muster his crew in an orderly way for first departure from Circe's island, one lost.
- Unable to control his crew with regard to the Sun god's beef, all the remaining, approximately forty, lost.

The following would generally not give rise to charges, but reflect badly on his qualities as a leader:

- Rarely disagrees with his boss, Agamemnon, even when the latter is disastrously wrong.
- Doesn't tell his men the truth: lies of both commission and omission.
- Doesn't trust them to do even the simplest things right, staying awake nine days and nights manning the tiller from Aeolia to Ithaca. Had this leadership failure not occurred, he would have arrived at Ithaca with approximately 530 of his crew within months of leaving Troy.
- Indulges his own pleasures at the expense of the mission of bringing his troops home, lingering with Circe.

And in the name of giving the defense an even break, I repeat items in Odysseus' favor:

- A talented and brave warrior who takes initiative and personal risks on behalf of others in a fight.
- Brilliant in the construction of deception plans.
- Brave, resourceful, self-sacrificing as a solo spy and as a reconnaissance leader.
- Loyal and resourceful in carrying out his boss's wishes.

Odysseus seems to get into trouble when he is responsible for others. Scholars can rightly point out that applying standards for a modern military officer to Odysseus is an anachronism. For one thing, Odysseus was the independent political chief, the king if you like, of the men in his command, with arbitrary and ill-defined powers. His fiduciary duties, if any, to these men arose from a likewise ill-defined mix of personal obligations to each man and his father individually, and the very real sanction of blood revenge when he got home, if he seriously violated the town's moral consensus.

ACHILLES, ODYSSEUS, AND AGAMEMNON[16]

These three Homeric leaders are alike in being courageous and effective fighters in their form of warfare. Achilles was a standout in speed, stamina, and spear-work. Odysseus was a brilliant archer, but also good with a spear. Agamemnon didn't stand out in any particular military skill, but was personally brave and competent enough to win some duels.[17]

But in every *other* dimension of leadership and military practice they contrast sharply with each other:

The *Iliad* portrays Achilles as having broad, other-regarding care for *all* the troops, not just his own. He is famous among them for his skill and interest in treating wounds. When a plague ravages the army, it is Achilles

who steps in to end it, both by obtaining a correct diagnosis and prescribing treatment. He leads by example and is lavish in his generosity to
both peers and subordinates. He shows moral courage, standing up to
Agamemnon, as well as great physical courage.[18] As the commander of the
Greek maneuver force, he has taken twelve cities by sea and eleven by
land, making him the most admired fighter and troop commander in the
Greek army. He is habitually blunt and truthful to the point of being tact-
less. What you see is what you get; he speaks the same to everyone.
When angry, his language gets ungrammatical and somewhat coarse. [19] He
is idealistic, passionate, and energetic, letting his emotions show. He is also
perfectionistic and given to self-righteousness, which makes other people
not want to upset him.

Achilles died in the final year of the war, so we know nothing of how he
would have conducted himself during the homeward trip with the Myrmidons, the contingent he brought with him to Troy. We have watched
Odysseus and his men on their way home. But earlier, during the war (in
the *Iliad*), we hardly saw him with his men at all. Unlike the tongue-tied
Ajax and the unadorned Achilles, Odysseus in the *Iliad* was eloquent in
his persuasion and artistically scathing in his ridicule. He was mainly on
stage as Agamemnon's principal staff officer, or as a fighter on the battlefield where he related almost exclusively to other Greek leaders or to
Trojan adversaries, but hardly at all to his own men. Agamemnon gave
him the task of returning the captive woman Chryseis to her father in
Iliad 1; Odysseus stopped the stampede to the ships in *Iliad* 2, which
Agamemnon caused, saving his neck. In *Iliad* 2, Odysseus took the initiative as Agamemnon's deputy to humiliate the critic Thersites and to
give him a public beating. Odysseus functioned as Agamemnon's representative where "the general's" presence was not required, such as pacing
off the dueling ground with Hector in *Iliad* 3. In the "Embassy" to buy
out Achilles in *Iliad* 9, Odysseus was clearly Agamemnon's negotiator,
with Ajax and old Phoenix along to soften Achilles up. In *Iliad* 14, we find
the only occasion where Odysseus did anything but agree with Agamemnon. With his boss in a terminal funk, ready to bolt for his ship, Odysseus
said to him,

> Hell's misery! . . .
>   Would you, then,
> quit and abandon forever the fine town
> of Troy that we have fought for all these years,
> taking our losses? Quiet! or some other

[Greeks] may get wind of this. No man
 . . . could ever
allow that thought to pass his lips—no man
who bore a staff, whom army corps obeyed,
as [Greeks] owe obedience to you.
Contempt, no less, is what I feel for you
after the sneaking thing that you propose.
While the two armies are in desperate combat,
haul our ships into the sea? . . .
As for ourselves, sheer ruin is what it means.
While our long ships are hauled down, will the soldiers
hold the line? Will they not look seaward
and lose their appetite for battle? There,
commander, is your way to wreck us all."

(Iliad 14:95ff, Fitzgerald)

Agamemnon was as much a failure as the commander of the static siege force around Troy as Achilles was a success as the commander of the mobile strike force.[20] The whole tragedy of the *Iliad* was kicked off by Agamemnon's breathtaking twin violations of his army's moral order, first by impiously refusing to ransom the captive girl Chryseis to her father, the Priest of Apollo, and then by publicly dishonoring his most esteemed, most effective subordinate commander, Achilles. The next day, Agamemnon was so obtuse that he demanded the following bizarre demonstration of the army's loyalty:

Agamemnon tells his officers he's going to *pretend* to give up the war. It's the day after he has dishonored Achilles in front of the troops by seizing his *geras,* Achilles' Medal of Honor.[21] Agamemnon does one of the nuttiest things in the annals of military leadership, real or fictional. He says to his officers—

We'd better move if we're going to get the men [ready].
But I'm going to test them first with a little speech,
The usual drill—order them to beat a retreat in their ships.
It's up to each one of you [officers] to persuade them to stay.

(Iliad 2:77ff, Lombardo, trans.; emphasis added)

Apparently he has done this before enough times that it seems normal, and nobody says to him, "That's a *really* bad idea!" Odysseus never says, "Boss, you *sure* you want to do that?" Then, with the whole army mustered, Agamemnon stands before them and says that even though they came ashore with a ten-to-one advantage over the Trojans, Zeus has decreed their failure after so much struggle and sacrifice:

> Now this is what I say, and I want us all to obey:
> Let's clear out with our ships and head for home.
> There's no more hope we will take Troy's . . . town.
> (2:150ff, Lombardo)

There's a stampede for the ships, a mad rush that takes everyone by surprise. Apparently in the past, when Agamemnon had pulled this dumb trick, the troops had stood fast and said, "Hey, we're here for the duration." Agamemnon is surprised; the Greek officers are surprised—even the gods are surprised—when the army bolts for the ships.

But should *we* be surprised? No, we should not be—because this is the predictable result of Agamemnon's betrayals of "what's right" the previous day with Achilles and with the priest.[22] Motivation, loyalty, and perseverance go whooshing out of the troops like air from a balloon. In the modern world they desert psychologically, even if they can't desert physically. This scene in *Iliad* 2, the stampede to the ships, carries one of the *Iliad*'s most important lessons for military leaders. "Command climate" is not the weather report of atmospherics and mood; it is the observed trustworthiness of how power is employed. What Agamemnon did to Achilles was no private wrong. As I said before, everyone is watching the trustworthiness of those who wield power above them. If any dared to ask, Agamemnon would have said that what went between him and Achilles was none of their business. But when a military leader violates "what's right" in the use of power, the injury afflicts everyone. Agamemnon caused Achilles' desertion and the next day caused the stampede to the ships, the desertion of his whole army.

When I speak of prevention of moral injury in military service, this Homeric episode is an example of what I want to prevent: betrayal of "what's right" in a high-stakes situation by someone who holds power. The consequences for those still on active duty range from a loss of motivation and enjoyment, resulting in attrition from the service at the next available moment, to passive obstructionism, goldbricking, and petty theft, to outright desertion, sabotage, fragging, or treason. In a war, the consequences are catastrophic.

Agamemnon's main motivational tools were shame, humiliation, and pitting one subordinate against another. He was weak, inconsistent, driven by self-gratification, and demonstrated egregiously bad judgment.

Heaven help a military force of any size with this kind of leadership!

Achilles stands out as a paragon of leadership, up to the point when Agamemnon's disastrous misuse of power destroys him. Achilles was an almost perfectly good leader; Agamemnon was an almost perfectly bad leader. Odysseus was a mixture of extremely good and extremely bad military traits. Don't laugh: Homer may have given us a basic message on military personnel management—"Put the right person in the right place. In the wrong place, he'll do harm."[23] As a staff officer, strategist, independent intelligence operative, and solo fighter, Odysseus was brilliant. As a troop leader, he was a catastrophe. Homer's great epics show him in full depth and perspective.

22

Conclusion

If you have read this far, you have found me an unashamed moralist. The reason for that is also plain: I regard the ethical use of power to be one key to prevention of psychological injury, particularly of complex PTSD and deformed *thumos*. Simply, ethics and justice *are* preventive psychiatry. But I trust that it's also clear that I am not what scholar W. B. Stanford called a "moralistic enemy of poetry" seeking to censor the *Odyssey* or dismiss it as childish, because it is so marvelously entertaining.[1] I reject the view that the arts are intrinsically harmless, benign, or irrelevant. While we no longer believe that the arts can command physical nature, as in mimetic magical dances commanding the weather or the herds, they are undoubtedly a commanding force of nature where *human* nature is concerned. No soldier ever threw himself on a grenade for the laws of thermodynamics or even the categorical imperative, but has done so for a story. I stand with Aristotle, and against his teacher, Plato, in seeing the arts as essential to the moral education of citizens, even when the subject of the art is as slippery as Odysseus.

Epic heroes of the Homeric poems, Odysseus and Achilles, were both "men of pain," suffering greatly, but also causing great pain and destruction to others.[2] The ancient Greeks venerated them like gods, composing prayers to them, bringing offerings at their tombs and shrines, marking them as sacred, holy. One of the veterans quoted in *Achilles in Vietnam* described the memories that he wanted to—and feared to—narrate as "sacred stuff."

When we use the word "hero" today, we want it to mean only good and benign. In the same way we also want "holy" to mean only good and benign. The original meanings of both "hero" and "holy" included dark, destructive sides. Both hero and holy fascinate and rivet the attention, to be sure, but they are *dangerous*.[3] They explode out of any container we hope to put them in, burst any chains of agreed rules and reciprocity we hope will bind them.

Homeric heroes inflict trauma, but it is just as true to say that trauma creates heroes. Achilles suffered the one-two blows of Agamemnon's betrayal and the death of his closest comrade, Patroclus, which together powered his epic rampage in the *Iliad*. Odysseus' multiple traumas, starting in childhood, powered his epic rampage in the *Odyssey*. They both had a giant *thumos*. Whether giant *thumos* manifests as *biē* or as *mētis*, it is impossible to found civil society or for that matter a "well-regulated militia" on giant *thumos*.[4] Very early in the development of democratic politics, giant *thumos* was recognized as a source of danger and disorder, a source of moves to tyrannize the entire populace.[5] Equal citizen respect does not preclude vigorous competitive struggles among citizens in politics and economics, but does require that the struggle restrain *biē* and *mē tis* to create a trustworthy setting in which no one ends up a slave. Ever since its origin, democratic struggle has been scorned as unheroic, because it renounces the fight to the death and the making of slaves. The rowdy and contentious Funeral Games for Patroclus in *Iliad* 23, which are Achilles' great step back into human society, might be taken as an early metaphor for the rowdy and messy, but ultimately safe, struggle of equal citizens. If either safety or struggle is lost, democratic process ceases.

Democracy is deeply related to the healing and prevention of trauma. Healing requires voice. The circle of communalization of trauma, which is essential to the healing of trauma, is much aided by the arts. Sometimes these are highly cultivated arts, as in the Homeric poems or Athenian tragedies, but human groups engage in the arts in many other ways when grappling with trauma. This book and *Achilles in Vietnam* are about the arts, especially the narrative arts, as social responses to trauma.

Prevention of trauma lies squarely in the realm of justice, ethics, and recognition of one another's humanness, recognition that we are in this together and part of one another's future. As such, prevention is intrinsic to the goals of our own polity and of any future world polity based on democracy.

THE CIRCLE OF COMMUNALIZATION OF TRAUMA

Judith Herman eloquently pointed out in *Trauma and Recovery*[6] that the trauma survivor must be permitted and empowered to voice his or her experience; the listener(s) must be allowed to listen, believe, and remember; the listener(s) must be allowed to repeat what they have heard to others. Each of these steps is forbidden in a tyranny, whether it is a public, official tyranny, like the "Republic" of Iraq, or private tyrannies like those created by domestic batterers, incest perpetrators, or on prison tiers. When trauma survivors hear that enough of the truth of their experience has been understood, remembered, and retold with enough fidelity to carry *some* of this truth—no one who did not experience their trauma can ever grasp *all* of the truth—then the circle of communalization is complete.[7]

The arts can and usually do play vital roles at each one of these steps. Often the artist is the trauma survivor himself or herself—but this is not essential. The Muses can implant the truth of experience in the imagination of artists who have never "been there," so long as the artist is able to listen to trauma survivors. Professional artists are *not* required for this. It is impossible to overstate the importance of the arts in creating the supportive social movements that permit trauma to have voice and the voice to be heard, believed, remembered, and respoken.

While I have couched this in terms of the verbal, narrative arts of poetry, narrative history, narrative fiction, theater, and film, I trust the reader has already understood that this applies equally to the visual arts and the arts of music and movement. Often with trauma survivors themselves, the non-verbal arts are the door that is most readily opened.[8] Creating art has far greater potential for healing trauma than consuming art as a reader, listener, or viewer—as valuable as these are. I believe that a trauma survivor gets more out of composing and performing his own poem, which may not be a masterpiece, than he would hearing Homer himself perform his masterpiece.

Part of the genius of the Vietnam Veterans Memorial in Washington—the Wall—is that it invites both active doing and passive viewing. Walking down the gentle slope next to the panels is an act of entering the sacred space. Many people leave letters and poems. As fine as the many books on the Wall are, they are very different from physically entering its precinct, making rubbings, watching the Three Fighting Men statuary group gaze at the Wall with their stunned look.

PURIFICATION AFTER BATTLE

I have appealed for renovation in our military institutions to protect service members from psychological and moral injury. In addition to political demands for such renovation, the American citizenry has other work to do. As a society we have found ourselves unable to offer purification to those who do the terrible acts of war on our behalf. I believe this is something to be done jointly by people from all our religions, from the arts, from the mental health professions, and from the ranks of combat veterans—*not* from the government. What I have in mind is a communal ritual with religious force[9] that recognizes that *everyone* who has shed blood, no matter how blamelessly, is in need of purification. Those who have done something blameworthy require additional purification and penance, if their religious tradition provides for it. The community as a whole, which sent these young people to train in the profession of arms and to use those arms, is no less in need of purification. Such rituals *must* be communal with the returning veterans, not something done to or for them before they return to civilian life. This new cultural creation also must stay free of the taint of sectarian, political, and ideological partisanship, which would willingly kidnap such a ritual. All modern soldiers go into battle under constraint—they have enough to carry without being blamed or credited with the political decision to fight that battle.

I do not know how the creation of a new and widely accepted cultural practice can be accomplished, but I do know that we need it.

WHAT DOES IT MEAN TO "BE HOME"?

What have we learned from Vietnam veterans and from Odysseus about being home? So much resonates in the one syllable, "home," that we should not be surprised if unpacking the idea makes quite a heap. Reach into the heap and pull something out, and you discover it's tangled with almost everything else.

Safety: Neither Odysseus nor the Vietnam combat veterans with complex PTSD found safety in the place that was supposed to be their home. In Ithaca, Odysseus was literally surrounded by young men who would kill him if they were given the chance. Danger was what PTSD veterans expected. The expectation of harm was itself a result of their psychological injuries, but subjective or objective, it wasn't home.

Acceptance: Can Odysseus or the veterans say who they are without fear? Vietnam veterans experienced everything, from others feeling awkward to outright abuse.

Value and respect: Odysseus was told, "Get away from my table" by one of the suitors (in Odysseus' own home!). An airline stewardess moved one of my patients, in uniform, because the person in the next seat didn't want to sit beside "the likes of him." Returning infantrymen found their hard-won skills without value and they were pigeonholed as "unskilled labor." What value will this veteran's contribution have? Odysseus returned disguised as a beggar, whose social value was seen as a net negative.

Knowing one's way: Odysseus spent ten years completely lost, metaphorically speaking. When he finally returned to Ithaca, he couldn't recognize the place at first. Through a combination of the changes that had taken place in themselves and taken place in American society during their years of military service, many Vietnam veterans could not "get around" socially and economically.

According to pattern: Odysseus' hope that the expected pattern of his domestic life—symbolized by the immovable olive tree bed—was terrifyingly shaken by Penelope's test of his identity. Many Vietnam veterans were deeply shaken by the economic changes that made it impossible for them to own their homes and provide for their families in the way their World War II fathers had.

Part of each other's future: Vietnam combat veterans sometimes came to feel that the country had discarded them, that they were not the nation's honored elite as they had been led to expect. They rarely felt that their fellow citizens looked them in the eye and said, "We are part of each other's future." Odysseus got to Ithaca, had to pretend to be someone else, killed a lot of his fellow citizens, and then had to leave again, with only a ghost's promise of any future there at all.

Comfort: Home is where you *can* sleep, where you can soothe and comfort yourself and find things familiar and in place, where you find peace when you want it. Vietnam combat veterans with complex PTSD still find no rest, no restorative sleep. Odysseus' first nights in his own home were troubled, uncomfortable, endangered.

TRAUMA STUDIES AND OTHER FIELDS OF KNOWLEDGE

I forecast that trauma studies will be as influential in the other fields of knowledge as psychoanalysis was fifty and a hundred years ago. For me, this is an annoying parallel, because I am no great friend of Freudianism. However, the field of trauma studies is the only new thing emerging from psychiatry since psychoanalysis that is likely to have as sweeping an effect in philosophy, literary and other arts criticism, history, political science (including especially democratic theory), economic development studies, anthropology, sociology (including especially criminology), education, organizational studies, government, military science, human evolutionary biology, and on and on.

One of the pervasive philosophic-cultural questions that pops up in many disciplines is whether there is such a thing as "human nature" or whether everything that matters to and about humans is historically and culturally constructed, and thus can only be understood and judged relative to the local time and place that created these people. University of Texas classicist Professor Erwin Cook, one of several who generously agreed to review the manuscript of this book for "howlers"—flubs by an amateur classicist that make the pros howl with laughter—did me the honor of going beyond finding howlers and gave forthright, vigorous criticism as he might to a colleague. He commented that I took an ahistorical and universalizing approach to Homer's epics, contrasting it to historical and cultural research. Because of my gratitude toward and respect for this scholar, I want to address this question of a universal "human nature" head-on.

Let us look at the ethical and value systems of human culture in the same way that we look at language: to use language is a human universal. Language is no less a biological trait than our breathing—but the vocabulary and syntax are culturally constructed through historical social practice. In this book I have asked readers to adopt a modern definition of the juicy Homeric word *thumos* as the human universal trait of commitment to people, groups, ideals, and ambitions, and of emotional upheaval when these are threatened. Like the sentences we speak, the content of *thumos* is historically and culturally constructed. If I use Homer's word in this effort, it is not because I believe that the ancient Greeks were present at the Creation, but because Homer and his admirers, such as Aristotle, were profoundly interested in *thumos,* and we can still learn from what they said about it. They were the inventors of some political concepts and practices that we still inhabit today.

I am a physician by trade and my Ph.D. is in one of the laboratory neurosciences, so you may suspect me of being a physical reductionist—someone who believes that only the material body is "real." You might expect me to believe that anything psychological, social, and cultural is just an imaginary will-o'-the-wisp, a shadow on the wall, or a shining bubble on the stream. Not so! This big, expensive[10] brain of ours *coevolved* with mind, society, and culture. We are just one being—physical, psychological, social, cultural at every instant. These are not reducible to one another, none is "real" with the others mere shadowy epiphenomena. Nor do they represent a ladder of value or importance. Culture is not "above" the mind; the body is not more "real" than society. Like the hummingbird's beak and the deep-throated blossom, they evolved at the same time through interaction with each other. At best, the distinctions among brain, mind, society, and culture are throwaways—temporary guides to perception and communication, temporary artifacts of the philosophical, institutional, and methodological history of the West.[11]

Themis (Homer's word for the social code of "what's right") has many language-like properties. The subjective experience of being "fluent" in a moral code is that it seems natural, inevitable, necessary, and good. The subjective experience of ethical *un*intelligibility is moral indignation, *nemesis*, aversion, and hatred—"strong evaluation." Detection of cheaters, slackers, liars, and spies is deeply embedded in our cognitive and emotional machinery[12]

So when I say that it is our animal nature to be social—to live in relation to moral codes and to social dispositions of value and power—I am saying nothing different from Aristotle's famous line that the human is *politikon zōon,* the animal of the community (*Politics* I.1.9, 1253a). He was speaking as a zoologist.

Two momentous human universals flow from our large, language-capable brain. The first is so obvious you may laugh out loud: *Children are born at a very young age.*[13] Before you go, "Yes, and what color was Washington's white horse?" and dismiss this as an empty tautology, stop to consider the prolonged helplessness and absolute life-and-death dependency that human babies have compared to other species. Many plains animals are up and moving with the herd within minutes of being freed of the placenta.

Every human being has had the experience of powerlessness, and of his or her absolute dependence on beings much larger and more powerful. This is universal and momentous. When these powers are benign and nurturing the baby gets through it. The adult equivalent of the benign caregivers of infancy is the encompassing deployments of social power in accordance with "what's right," the adult's cloak of security. Any objective situation in adulthood, which reproduces the absolute helplessness and powerlessness of the infant, can cause psychological injury especially if intentionally inflicted by other people in violation of "what's right." Severe trauma in adulthood can damage *thumos* in the absence of any weakness in the genes or childhood abuse or neglect.[14]

The second Great Obvious Truth is: *The death rate is 100 percent of all live births.* We are mortal, and because of our large, language-using brains, we know it and we talk about it. These two facts about human existence, helplessness in infancy and awareness of mortality, are human universals that span all cultures and historical eras. We are truly one species in every sense that matters. Together these form a basis for universalizing quests in philosophy and the arts. Psychologizing, universalizing approaches to great art have merit side by side with historical, anthropological, stylistic, and linguistic investigations of the particularity of such works. The particular and the universal are like breathing in and breathing out. We can only reach the universal through the particular; and the intelligibility of the particular depends upon the universal.

A NEW ABOLITIONISM

The Vietnam veterans that I have worked with were treated shabbily by both the political right—who scorned them as "losers," lacking the war-winning sterner stuff of the World War II generation—and by the political left, who held them responsible for everything vile or wrongheaded that led us into the war, was done during the war, or came out of the war. The New Abolitionism that I advocate will undoubtedly annoy both the traditional political left, because of my respect for the military profession, and annoy the traditional political right, because of my hostility to war itself and a practical call for its abolition.

Aristotle's formula, that a *philos* is "another myself," is the key to most socially organized human violence. In the modern world, the state has acquired the quality of a *philos*. Except in our slums, we no longer fight to the death for recognition as individuals, but nations continue violently to compel deference, violently demand acknowledgment.

Economic historian and social philosopher Francis Fukuyama, formerly at the American defense think tank RAND, has seriously raised the question of whether the spread of liberal republics that extend equal citizen recognition can bring Hegel's historical dynamism of war to an end—the "end of history," or in the words of the title of Kant's famous essay, "To Perpetual Peace."[15] At stake here is whether equal citizen honor and the overlapping intermediate attachments that we speak of as "civil society " (or in the Catholic Church's jargon, the "principle of subsidiarity") can bring an end to giant *thumos*. Does equal citizen honor and the civil web of plural attachments create a new human psyche, a new human altogether who no longer hungers for domination, who no longer schemes and labors for the triumphal moment when he can see fear in the eyes of his enemy and witness his annihilation? These ideological and social-structural dimensions are staples of democratic theory. Trauma studies can contribute the insight that the Horsemen of the Apocalypse trample the psychic "middle" so essential to the democratic process. The trampled soul may be so broken as to be unable to imagine a future and unable to struggle for it; or the trampled soul may be so bloated with vengeance and the determination never again to be helpless that nothing short of domination is tolerable. In the last two hundred years the sewer and the railroad have magnificently hobbled two of the Horsemen: plague and famine.

To stabilize a republic, it may indeed be necessary to have a critical mass and right mix of people with middling *isothumos*—for whom equal citizen honor is not only good enough, but loved and celebrated. Probably societies do not have to rid themselves entirely of individuals with giant *thumos* in order to end war. There are excesses of *thumos* that may be tolerable in some individuals, but to which a *nation* must not extend even its little finger. A boring lawfulness in the conduct of nations is the best that can be hoped for; and if this lawfulness reliably allows free development of individuals, then it is very good indeed.

Historian of ancient societies Hans van Wees, in his study *Status Warriors*,[16] has connected the violence of the *Iliad* to the ways its "heroic" culture constructed the emblems and evidence of honor. Iliadic culture persistently measured honor in the quantity of deference by others. Because deference, and thus honor, could be compelled through violence and the threat of violence, we see much more violence in that setting than in a culture where the evidence of honor is, for example, a financial net worth of $10 million, or lineal descent from King Edward III, neither of which can be compelled by violence. In sixteenth-century Brescia in Italy, numerous deaths resulted from duels over who deferred to whom in the town's narrow alleys. Many of the deaths among poor teenagers in American slums today appear to be similarly based on deference as the only currency of honor. They have reasons to think that equal citizen honor is a lie and a sham, and have been stripped bare of the warming garments of civil society.[17]

People who are personally modest, self-controlled, and forgiving— apparently without a shred of giant *thumos*—may act like bloodthirsty lunatics when they believe that their national honor has been debased, or their religious group insulted. It works the other way, too. People who daily suffer the oppressions and humiliations of poverty and disprized social identities may become euphoric when "their" athletic team or nation has done something glorious. A magazine cover photo[18] shows a crowd of sari-clad young Indian women demonstrating with a banner crudely lettered "WE PROUD ON OUR NUCLEAR TEST"—what makes my blood run cold is the transported look of ecstasy on their faces. Nationalism and xenophobia are the most seductive music of the demonic, full of uplift and power.

We are rightfully suspicious of statements of the form: "It's human nature to do this . . . It's just the way it is." So with reluctance and trepidation I shall make such a statement: "High-stakes threat of destruction to *thumos*—to attachments, ideals, ambitions—triggers killing rage against the human source of this threat. It's in our species nature."

So does that mean that war—which is state-practiced violence against another state—is an inevitable, permanent, irremovable feature of human life? No . . . It may mean that *evil* can never be eradicated; it may mean that it is not possible to eliminate individual human violence—but war, a state activity, is like chattel slavery—this we can end.

In our ancestral environment, where the human brain evolved to its present size and structure, the maximum size of a society was probably no more than 150 souls. They probably warred with one another, perhaps in the way chimpanzee bands make war.[19] Within these Paleolithic bands we may reasonably conjecture that there was some sort of internal peace, as there is in chimpanzee bands. It was in this setting that modern *Homo sapiens* evolved. If any societal practice of peace and war can be said to be biologically "natural" for the human animal, it is probably that this small community shared food within itself and violently defended its own against all others. But then whatever evolved in the brain that permitted human attachment to societies of five thousand, permitting internal peace in such a large group—this is the same brain capacity that permits societies of 5 million or 500 million to have internal peace. The tiny population of Iceland is unimaginably large compared to the ancestral bands in which our modern brain evolved. So when we think about ending war, we must conclude with William of Ockham in the fourteenth century, "What is—is possible!" The human brain presents no fundamental barrier to a world without war. From the biological point of view of 150-person ancestral bands in which the modern human brain evolved, "perpetual peace" has already happened!

Like ending chattel slavery, ending the social practice of war will be the work and struggle of centuries. Clausewitz famously said, "War is a continuation of politics by other means." Tyranny is Clausewitz on his head: tyranny is the prosecution of war by means of political institutions. When a state declares war on a segment of its own population, we call it genocide. As a practical matter, if we wish to end wars *between* states, we must also end the wars that states wage against their own people, as the events in the

Balkans show so clearly. Destruction of an ethnic minority in one country becomes a casus belli in a neighboring country where that minority is the majority. It simply doesn't work to turn one's back and say, "That's an internal affair."

How do we do this? You will be disappointed to hear that the answer is already so familiar that it may seem tedious: trustworthy collective security. To end war, every nation and every population within every nation must have well-founded confidence in their own safety. This was essentially Kant's argument two centuries ago. In liberal republics, citizens do not fear being killed or enslaved by their own governments, so there is the first echelon of protection for their populations. The second layer of protection would be—and Kant necessarily argued this without historical evidence—that a universal regime of collective security among republics would end wars among themselves.[20]

An enduring sense of surprise—a heartening surprise—in my work with American military professionals on prevention of psychological and moral injury in military service is that *they* are not the obstacles to the elimination of war. Those who have been in it hate it with more passion than I am ever likely to match.

The service of the soldier will still be needed in the collective security regime that Kant envisioned. International peace, according to Kant, is domestic peace writ large. So we have a paradox: to have peace we need soldiers—whose main task is making war.

Even if the United States cannot and should not be the only policeman for the world, this does not mean the world does not need soldiers—the international equivalent of the police in a collective security regime—nor mean that the United States shouldn't actively support the police. As freelance military and paramilitary organizations, such as al-Qaeda, acquire more powerful weapons and communications technology,[21] it should be doubly evident that the world needs people with the *thumos* to be soldiers.

Those who sacrifice in military service rightly enjoy profound honor. They sacrifice their lives and body parts, sometimes their sanity, and according to my analysis, they sacrifice their freedom when plunged into war. In a peace-ensuring system of trustworthy collective security, those who offer to do the soldier's work, to risk all that, and sacrifice all that for peace, truly deserve our honor. These paradoxical strains are part of what we must take on in ending the human practice of war.

The original Abolitionists understood that their work would take more than one lifetime. They passed it as a heritage to their children. In the words of the Talmud, "You are not expected to finish the job, but neither are you free to lay it down."

SEPTEMBER 11, 2001

The shared experience and aftermath of the attack on the New York World Trade Center and on the Pentagon produced bittersweet reactions among the veterans of VIP. On the one hand, they were flooded with sensory-reliving symptoms: the smell of burning jet fuel, the stench of dead bodies, rage, the gut-twisting sense that another attack is coming—but where?—the hunger to personally hit back. On the other hand, one veteran after another reported seeing the light of comprehension coming on in the eyes of family members, neighbors, employers. "I *get* it! This is what it's been for you . . ." Like combat vets with PTSD, ordinary Americans had nightmares, intrusive memories, constant, obsessive thoughts about airplane and anthrax attacks. Like combat vets with PTSD, they lost interest in many things they had previously thought very important. Sex? Forget it. Laughter? Forget it. They became jumpy and hypervigilant.

The country as a whole rediscovered a great many lessons about cohesion and how it controls fear. I hope readers will see the connection—between the courage-making power of solidarity and the moves I have advocated in this book to protect and strengthen our troops.

APPENDIX I:

A POCKET GUIDE TO HOMER'S *ODYSSEY*[1]

Part One (Books 1–4):
A Home Without Husband or Father

Odysseus' wife, Penelope, and son, Telemachus, have lived for ten years knowing that the Trojan War is over, and that Odysseus made it out of Troy alive. But where is he? Penelope is still beautiful (and rich, *if* Odysseus *and* Telemachus are dead), and surrounded by all the ambitious and aggressive young men in the area, competing for the widow's hand. Not satisfied simply to pay her court, the suitors carouse in Odysseus' manor house on the island of Ithaca, feasting from his herds and storerooms, drinking his wine, and taking their pleasures with his maidservants. The suitors press Penelope to quit stalling and choose one of them to replace her missing-and-presumed-dead husband. The boy Telemachus is an adolescent with an absent father, who has heard how great his dad was, but his mother's candidate husbands are the only men on the scene now. Desperate to know whether he is really an orphan as he fears, he leaves home to visit his father's comrades on the mainland who have already made it back from Troy. The suitors secretly plot to assassinate Telemachus on his way back. This will give them control of Odysseus' wealth and lands, once Penelope picks one of them as her new husband.

Part Two (Books 5–8):
Odysseus Starts the Last Lap for Home

Not too flattering for Odysseus, we find him alive and bedded down with the lovely sea goddess Calypso on her distant island where he's a castaway. But the gods on Mount Olympus tell her to let him go; even though she's beautiful and has been very nice to him, after seven years, he's tired of her and wants to get home. The trouble is, he's lost his whole squadron and his own ship. With her reluctant help he builds a raft and sets out across the sea, only to be shipwrecked again, and washed up naked and half dead in a river inlet on the island of Phaeacia. With a nudge from his patron goddess, Athena, Princess Nausicaa goes to this very same river, and they meet. Odysseus is nothing if not charming to beautiful young girls, and he persuades Nausicaa to give him clothes and entrée to her parents' court and its hospitality. He does not reveal who he is. He fills his hungry belly and hears the great court poet sing true stories of the Trojan War. This bard is the genuine article. The complacent Phaeacian nobles are hugely entertained by these stories of the war—but when Odysseus hears them he weeps and weeps. The king notices and presses him to say who he is.

Part Three (Books 9–12):
Odysseus Tells of His Adventures in Wonderland

Odysseus reveals his identity and agrees to tell his story: (1) Shortly after leaving Troy, his squadron sacks the city of Ismarus, escaping with serious losses during a counterattack. The squadron then is blown off course to the (2) Land of the Lotus Eaters, who offer the men an addicting drug, and then to (3) the island inhabited by the Cyclopes (plural of Cyclops), one of whom eats several of his crew. Escaping from there, the squadron fetches up on (4) a floating island ruled by King Aeolus, who can control the sea winds and who helps Odysseus and his squadron get straight home to Ithaca. After screwing this up within sight of home and losing Aeolus' further help, Odysseus' exhausted squadron pulls into (5) the peaceful fjord of the Laestrygonians, which looks like a safe place to rest. The inhabitants surprise and sink all the ships in the squadron, except Odysseus' own ship, which alone was moored outside the fjord. Terrified and bereaved, they row away from the slaughter and land on (6) the island of the beautiful witch, Circe, who turns all her guests but Odysseus into pigs. After getting the upper hand, Odysseus persuades her to restore his crew. She gives him sailing instructions from there that lead through (7) the Land of the Dead. Here he meets the ghosts of his dead comrades Achilles, Agamemnon, and Ajax and of others, including his mother, who has died while he was away at the Trojan War. He learns from the ghost of Teiresias that if he reaches home alive, he then must leave again to complete one last trial. Returning to Circe for more instructions, he continues on past the dangers of (8) the island of the Sirens, and (9) the many-headed monster Scylla and the nearby whirlpool Charybdis, to (10) the island where the sun god keeps his cattle. There, Odysseus' crew disobeys him by killing and eating some of the sacred cattle and brings down the god's destruction of the last ship and crew. Odysseus rides some flotsam past (11) the giant whirlpool of Charybdis. Odysseus alone survives and washes up on (12) the island of Calypso, where we found him at the beginning of Part Two.

PART FOUR (BOOKS 13–16):
FATHER AND SON RETURN TO ITHACA AND ARE REUNITED

The Phaeacian king and queen are deeply impressed by the truth and glory of Odysseus' story and give him a pile of valuable gifts and a free ride home to Ithaca. Disoriented on the beach at Ithaca and unable to recognize his homeland, Odysseus meets his patron, the goddess Athena, who tells him where he is and disguises him as an old beggar so the people of his homeland won't recognize him. She tells him of the dangerous situation with the suitors, and assures him his son is safe. She instructs Odysseus to go to the hut of his loyal servant, the pig farmer Eumaeus, rather than head straight home. Athena then flies off to tell Telemachus to hurry back, but only to Eumaeus' hut, avoiding the ambush laid by the suitors. Odysseus cannot immediately enlist Eumaeus, because there's been a steady stream of con artists passing through Ithaca. It's been twenty years since he left, and who knows what he looks like? When Odysseus says he knows that Odysseus is close by, Eumaeus politely calls him a liar. Odysseus tells a heartrending life story—which *is* a complete pack of lies—and in response, Eumaeus tells his equally heartrending, but true, life story. They weep together. Then Telemachus arrives and son and father are reunited. They test each other, and after Odysseus reveals himself, discuss their common enemy, the mob of suitors.

PART FIVE: (BOOKS 17–20):
STRANGER AT HOME

Telemachus and Odysseus make their way separately to the palace. In his beggar's disguise, Odysseus appears at the door, where his son, playing along with the beggar ruse, piously and charitably admits him to the palace. The suitors again show themselves to be disgusting hooligans, just "asking for it," punishment from the gods. Taking Odysseus as a penniless bum, they abuse him in various ways, even though he now enjoys the religious and political protection of the manor's hospitality. There are more than a hundred suitors, and Odysseus has to be very careful not to tip his hand and get himself killed. Apart from Telemachus, no one knows who he is, and given all the scammers who have shown up, who is going to believe the kid if he tells them? After the suitors clear out for the night, Odysseus remains behind and gets an audience with Penelope on the pretext that he has news of Odysseus. Both because Penelope has had her hopes raised and dashed by con men and because the goddess Athena guarantees his disguise, she does not recognize him. However, his childhood nurse, Eurycleia, does, and almost blows his disguise. But maybe because of the subliminal effect of his actual presence, Penelope sets the next day, a feast day to Apollo the Archer God, for the trial of Odysseus' bow. To win her in marriage a suitor must string it and shoot an arrow through the lined-up holes of twelve axe-head sockets—one of Odysseus' favorite stunts before he went off to war. After prayers and omens before dawn, Odysseus arises to prepare himself, his son, and two loyal servants for the coming feast, trial, and battle with the suitors, who crowd back into the hall to resume their rowdy binge.

PART SIX (BOOKS 21–24):
VETERAN TRIUMPHANT

Penelope fetches the bow, a stiff, powerful hunting bow that few men are strong enough to string, much less shoot straight. She carries it to the hall where the suitors are drinking and abusing the disguised Odysseus. She announces the contest for her hand in marriage and leaves. They try to string it and fail. Telemachus, who of course knows the beggar's identity, fakes an argument with Eumaeus to get the bow into his father's hands without tipping off the suitors. Odysseus quickly strings the bow, and puts arrow after arrow into the suitors. When his arrows are gone, he and his son and two comrades battle with spears against the still superior number of living suitors, but after killing some in a pitched battle they panic the rest and slaughter them as they try to flee the locked house. Odysseus has identified all the maidservants who had been sluts with the suitors and orders them to drag the corpses from the hall and wash up the suitors' blood and their terror-loosed shit; then he has Telemachus kill the maids.

Penelope, alone in her bedroom, does not believe the news that Odysseus has returned. When the long-awaited reunion takes place, they are distracted, mistrustful, and reserved. Odysseus expects revenge from the relatives of the young bloods he has just killed. To buy time, he arranges lights and music for a fake wedding celebration in the locked house. Penelope is still mistrustful of another charlatan. She tests him with secret knowledge of the construction of their marital bed that he alone knows. At last they embrace in their bed. He tells her he must leave again soon; they make love; they tell each other what has happened in the twenty years of their separation; they sleep. At sunup Odysseus, Telemachus, and their loyal retainers slip out of town to the orchard in the hills where Odysseus' aged father, Laertes, has been living in ineffectual, depressed retirement. After Odysseus reveals himself to his father in a somewhat cruel manner, the three generations prepare themselves to fight off the posse of relatives carrying out the law of vendetta. The mob appears. After an opening skirmish, in which old Laertes is rejuvenated and Telemachus acquits himself bravely, Zeus stuns them all with a thunderbolt and Athena compels them to make peace. Odysseus is restored to his rightful place. Even though he must still complete his final trip away from home, he—and we—have been authoritatively promised that he and Penelope will end their lives in contented, peaceful, well-tended old age.

APPENDIX II:

INFORMATION RESOURCES

FOR VIETNAM VETERANS AND THEIR FAMILIES

Some of the resources listed below have Vietnam veterans themselves in mind, some almost entirely veterans' wives and families in mind. Some are general trauma sites. Veterans will benefit enormously by using resources listed for spouses and families, and vice versa. Most resources are focused on Vietnam veterans, but the following site has links to veterans and military unit associations from other conflicts as well: Veterans' Associations Links Page: http://members.tripod.com/flavets/linkpage.htm.

www.vwip.org   A site edited by John Tegtmeier, with information resources listed in a glossary-type format. Has many fine narratives.

www.vietvet.org   A site edited by Bill McBride, with links to the World Wide Web Vietnam Veteran Location Service. Has many fine narratives.

www.themovingwall.org   The Web site for the organization that carries half-sized replicas of the Wall to public places around the country for week-long stays. This profound program lowers the financial and psychological barriers that many veterans face in visiting the Wall in Washington. The schedule of locations and dates is posted on this site.

www.virtualwall.org   The Virtual Wall, maintained by Jim Schueckler. "The Virtual Wall contains virtual memorials to the men and women named on the Vietnam Veterans Memorial. Each name or photo on our index pages links to a personal memorial. If you do not find a name here, you may *request* a memorial; no fee, no donations, no commercials." A database of American military deaths in the Vietnam War is at www.no-quarter.org.

www.va.gov/rcs   The Vet Centers (officially the Readjustment Counseling Service, or RCS) do excellent work out of storefront centers
around the country. They are usually listed in the telephone book
under "Vet Center," and a complete directory is available through the
RCS Web site. The heart of the Vet Center concept is peer counseling. Many of the counselors are veterans, although today a great many
who started as uncredentialed peer counselors have taken training in
one or another of the mental health professions.

www.trauma-pages.com   A site edited by psychologist David Baldwin,
devoted to all aspects of trauma, including combat trauma.

www.ncptsd.org   The official web site of the National Center for PTSD,
with a link to search the PILOTS database of scientific and scholarly
literature on trauma.

www.dr-bob.org/tips/ptsd.html   My pamphlet called "About Medications for Combat PTSD." It needs updating, but the philosophy of
informed partnership will never go out of date.

www.patiencepress.com   For access to *The Posttraumatic Gazette*, a
newsletter with a wealth of resources and wisdom for veterans and their
families. I strongly recommend purchase of the complete set of back
issues and subscription to the *Gazette*.[1]

Two excellent books for spouses and families of veterans:

Mason, Patience C. H. *Recovering from the War: A Woman's Guide to
Helping Your Vietnam Veteran, Your Family, and Yourself.* New York:
Viking, 1990.

Matsakis, Aphrodite. *Vietnam Wives: Facing the Challenges of Life with
Veterans Suffering Post-Traumatic Stress Disorder.* 2nd ed. Lutherville,
Md.: Sidran Press, 1996.

APPENDIX III:

SOME PROPOSALS

"You Americans spend so *much*, and get *so little* for it."
—Martin van Creveld, Jerusalem, 1999[1]

Completely renovate the military personnel system, so that it reliably produces skilled, cohesive units, and competent, ethical leaders at all levels. The three touchstones—cohesion, leadership, and training—are the *desired end state* that this renovated personnel system should achieve and support. Everything that currently exists in the way of policy, practice, and assumption should be tested against this end state, and likewise everything that is proposed.

Here are some assumptions about American military service that are so familiar they have become invisible. Every one needs to be critically reexamined and most of them discarded:

OBSOLETE ASSUMPTIONS
BUILT INTO THE CURRENT MILITARY PERSONNEL SYSTEM[2]

- Military fighting formations on any scale can best be thought of as machines. Machines run best and can be best maintained using identical, standardized parts. Service members must be interchangeable.
- War is an industrial process.
- Only *individual* training and skill credentials matter.
- The only costs of moving a service member from one unit to another are the financial costs of the move and the administrative paperwork. Like-credentialed troops are fungible.
- Personnel turbulence is a fact of life.

- There's no way to replace casualties, except individual by individual. Units should be kept up to strength on the battlefield by the constant flow of individual replacements.
- Too much cohesion in small units is dangerous to the chain of command.
- Among units of like kind, uniform readiness and uniform capability are best.
- Weapons matter more than skill.
- Enlisted service members are a "free good," either conscripted or motivated to enlist by conscription.
- Under all circumstances, a unit that has been "filled" to or beyond its table of organization is more ready than one that is not.
- Only officers can make decisions or think of better ways to do things.
- Success in the military is measured by the rank you achieve.
- Everyone wants to get ahead, to move higher in the table of organization; conversely, anyone who is motivated by anything other than advancement in rank is deficient in either "attitude" or "motivation" and is "complacent."
- Officership is a form of general management, requiring only the ability to organize, motivate, communicate, and set goals and priorities. Officers are "generalists" not "specialists."
- The only motivations that count are "tangible incentives" appealing to the service member's self-interest.
- Opportunities for advancement in rank have to be uniform.
- Career equity must trump other considerations. "When stabilization [of the unit] conflicts with the concept of equity in fulfilling personnel assignments, equity will prevail" (A[rmy] R[egulation] 614–5).
- Individuals must be managed by a centralized personnel system.
- If allowed to remain in roles they excel at, enjoy, and consider important, service members will stagnate.
- If allowed to form strong bonds with other service members, they will engage in favoritism, cronyism, and prejudice.
- Our military services are scientifically managed and organized. Military history and comparative study of military institutions contribute little to the development of successful military organizations
- The Department of Defense must organize itself around the requirement for total mobilization.
- No one can remain mentally and physically fit ("young and vigorous") for military service beyond the age of fifty.

- There is no way reliably to measure mental and physical fitness, vigor, and competence.
- Job security makes people slack.
- Relentless competition in everything—"running scared"—floats the best people to the top and gets the most out of everyone.
- Enlisted military service is unskilled manual labor and should be compensated at that rate.
- Only tangible incentives matter.

SOME SPECIFIC RECOMMENDATIONS

- "Flatten" the services—reduce the number of operational echelons and headquarters.
- Replace trickle-in-trickle-out individual manning with life-cycle unit manning.
- Give every service member a home unit and every unit a home base and a lifetime unit association membership for him/herself and his/her family.
- Make unit stability the rule, with turbulence the exception, rather than turbulence the rule and stability the exception.
- Replace up-or-out with up-or-stay-if-still-performing.
- Significantly reduce the numbers in the O-1 to O-6 grades.
- Replace specific branches with combined arms, logistics, and specialists.
- Decentralize officer management.
- Link promotion of tactical officers to decision-making ability and performance in repeated force-on-force free-play field exercises and repeated true competitive war games
- Reform military education and training—introduce true competitive war gaming as a core educational and cultural practice for tactical personnel at all levels and beginning with entry-level training.
- Do away with "all or nothing" twenty-year retirement system; vest pensions at seven to ten years.
- Require *all* officers to serve in enlisted ranks prior to commissioning (including those on their way to or graduating from the service academies).
- Reconceptualize the skills, compensation, and training of the enlisted ranks of the combat arms in terms of professional athletes or musicians, rather than unskilled manual labor.

- Renovate the enlisted and officer personnel systems together, so that they harmonize.

The above list is my own, but it overlaps considerably with the recommendations found in Major Donald Vandergriff's *Path to Victory: America's Army and the Revolution in Human Affairs*.[3] Major Vandergriff's excellent book documents the cultural and institutional history of the U.S. military personnel system, as well as its persistent result of *reducing* military capability.

How We Get There from Here[4]

My mission from the veterans I serve is one of democratic persuasion in the military services, the Congress, and the public. The agenda is open, not concealed: with a three- to five-year horizon, an omnibus military personnel act in Congress that:

- is bipartisan, and nonideological (this is neither a Republican thing nor a Democrat thing, neither liberal nor conservative);
- has been openly and thoroughly debated within the military services and the Department of Defense, and the changes contemplated have been *requested* by the services;
- is adaptable to each service's distinctive traditions, technologies, and force structure, eliminating "one size fits all" in personnel policy, practice, and culture; and
- treats service members decently in the face of inevitable changes to their career expectations, through an intelligent ten-year implementation plan.

———

**OUR WORST PROBLEMS ARE SOLVABLE
WITHOUT SPENDING MORE MONEY!
OUR WORST PROBLEMS ARE SELF-INFLICTED!**

———

NOTES

Frontispiece

1. Attic red figure stamnos by the Siren Painter, ca. 500–450 B.C.E. *Odysseus and the Sirens*. London E440, from Vulci. *ARV* 289.1 (J. D. Beazley, *Attic Red-Figure Vase-Painters*, 2nd ed. [Oxford: Oxford University Press, 1963]. After A. Furtwängler and K. Reichhold, *Greichische Vasenmalerei: Auswahl Hervorragender Vasenbilder* [München: Verlagsanstalt F. Bruckmann, 1900–1925], pl. 124.) Image courtesy of the Perseus Digital Library, www.perseus.tufts.edu.

Preface

1. Taking Homer at his word was the approach *Achilles in Vietnam* took to the *Iliad*, the Achilles epic: The *Iliad* opens with a thunderclap, when Achilles' commander Agamemnon betrays the moral order of his army by wrongfully seizing Achilles' prize of honor, his *geras*. Agamemnon had no more right to do that than a modern colonel taking the Medal of Honor ribbon off the tunic of a sergeant under his command. Achilles' rage at this degrading treatment leads him to withdraw physically from the battle, something that he could do legally but a modern soldier can only do psychologically. When an inspiring and effective combat leader pulls out, the result is loss upon loss to his comrades as the enemy moves in, just what happened to the Greeks. Achilles then lets his foster brother Patroclus, his closest comrade and second in command, go back into the fight. Patroclus saves the Greeks from being thrown into the sea from their beachhead, but is killed doing it. Achilles suffers profound grief and guilt, goes berserk and commits outrage after outrage in the course of winning the war for the Greeks by bringing down Hector. This is the surface story of the *Iliad*, about combat soldiers and what matters to them: the moral and social world they inhabit. This surface story *means* something in the real world.
2. *Parameters: US Army War College Quarterly*, vol. 25, no. 3, Autumn 1995, p. 133.

I. Introduction

1. Citations are to Robert Fagles's *Odyssey* translation (New York: Viking Penguin, 1996) or to Robert Fitzgerald's *Odyssey* translation (New York: Vintage Classics, 1990). They are in the form book number: line number(s), translator's name. Where other translations are quoted, the source is identified in the same manner and referenced in the notes. Line numbers refer to the translations' numberings; where the line numbers refer to the original Greek, this is noted as "orig." rather than with a translator's name. The Loeb Classical Library editions of Homer provide the sources

for the original Greek, respectively the *Iliad,* ed. A. T. Murray (Cambridge, Mass.: Harvard University Press, 1924), and the *Odyssey,* ed. A. T. Murray, as revised by George E. Dimock (Cambridge, Mass.: Harvard University Press, 1995).

A note on English representation of Greek words and proper names: I have followed the spelling conventions used by Professor Robert Fagles, whose *Odyssey* translation is most frequently quoted in this book. Where other translations have been quoted I have retained the spelling used in the quoted source. I have refrained from using accents when I transliterate Greek words that are not proper names, with the exception of the eta and omega, which are shown as *ē* and *ō,* respectively. I have also substituted "Greek" for Achaian, Argive, and Danaan, where they have appeared in the Homeric quotations.

2. The words in this epigraph were written in 1996, and Jim Shelby gave me permission to use them the same year. After I recontacted him this year to make certain that I still had his permission, he wrote, "I would be doing a disservice to say that I still felt that way. I am part of a community now, go to church, work a regular job, and am fortunate to have a wife and daughter. There are moments when I actually experience being alive, being vulnerable." He credited the Kansas City Vet Center, various mental health professionals, and the community of VWAR (see Chapter 18) for assisting in his "return" to life.

3. Voice-over in Mick Hurbis-Cherrier and Catherine Hurbis-Cherrier, *History Lessons.* Video, 1992.

4. George E. Dimock, Jr., "The Name of Odysseus," *Hudson Review* 9:52–70 (1956) and "The Man of Pain" in that author's *The Unity of the Odyssey* (Amherst: University of Massachusetts Press, 1989), pp. 246–63. John Peradotto, in *Man in the Middle Voice: Name and Narration in the Odyssey* (Princeton: Princeton University Press, 1990), p. 128, gives it simply as "Hate."

5. Gregory Nagy, *The Best of the Achaeans: Concepts of the Hero in Archaic Greek Poetry* (Baltimore: Johns Hopkins University Press, 1979), p. 69. For an overview of Greek heroism as dangerous to the people, see Johannes Haubold, *Homer's People* (Cambridge: Cambridge University Press, 2000). Erwin Cook, "'Active' and 'Passive' Heroics in the *Odyssey,*" *Classical World* 93:2 (1999), pp. 149–67, shows how Odysseus is a man of pain because he is a man of hatred, and how he uses the pain he causes and suffers to identify himself, even to members of his own household.

6. Cook, "'Active' and 'Passive' Heroics in the *Odyssey.*" See also Donna Wilson's "Lion Kings: Heroes in the Epic Mirrors," *Colby Quarterly,* in press, 2002, and Haubold, *Homer's People.*

7. We've been offered allegorical readings of Homer at least since the sixth century B.C.E. with Theagenes of Regium and the first century C.E. with the Stoic Heraclitus. But also, I acknowledge that I have text-based problems with a strict allegorical interpretation of Books 9–12—the worst of which is the narrator's several mentions of Odysseus' marvels outside that framework. For example, *Odyssey* 20:19, where Odysseus privately thinks of the Cyclops inside his own head during a snatch of interior monologue. These outside-the-frame mentions put these adventures at the same level of narrative reality as the swineherd, the gods, the Trojan War, the bow, and so on. See Hugh Parry, "The *Apologos* of Odysseus: Lies, All Lies?," *Phoenix* 48 (1994), pp. 1–20; Scott Richardson, "Truth in the Tales of the Odyssey," *Mnemosyne* 49 (1996), pp. 393–402.

8. Jenny Strauss Clay, *The Wrath of Athena: Gods and Men in the Odyssey* (Princeton: Princeton University Press, 1983), p. 198.

9. The Homeric way of grieving and memorialization were explored in *Achilles in Vietnam,* Chapter 3.

10. Novato, Calif.: Presidio Press, 2002.
11. New York: Atheneum/Macmillan, 1994; New York: Touchstone, 1995.
12. Homer's picture in the *Iliad* of the love that arises between comrades (cohesion) was fully discussed in *Achilles in Vietnam*—see index entries there under *"philia"* and "Comrades, special." For the relationship between military cohesion and love, see "Cohesion" from the *Commandant of the Marine Corps Trust Study*, available on the Web at www.belisarius.com/author_index.htm.
13. I thank Colonel Charles J. Dunlap, Jr. (USAF), an Air Force staff judge advocate, for his comments on Odysseus from a military justice perspective. Any errors in the legal analysis of Odysseus' conduct are entirely my own.
14. W. B. Stanford, *The Ulysses Theme: A Study in the Adaptability of a Traditional Hero* (New York: Barnes & Noble, 1968), p. 5.
15. Thomas G. Palaima, "To Be a Citizen or an Idiot: The Choice Is Ours," *Austin American-Statesman*, October 9, 2001, four weeks exactly after September 11.

2. Odysseus Among the Rich Civilians

1. This all but unknown sequel to *All Quiet on the Western Front* follows the surviving men in that unit back to their hometown through their demobilization and their attempts to readjust to civilian society. Published in Germany in 1931 and then suppressed by the Nazis, it was first translated into English by A. W. Wheen, and published the same year in the United States, but forgotten. Fortunately this masterpiece was reprinted in a trade paperback by Fawcett in 1998 and is now for the first time widely available. The epigraph is from pages 115–17.
2. Pietro Pucci's *Odysseus Polutropos* (Ithaca: Cornell University Press, 1987) introduced me to the Homeric contrast between *gastēr* and *thumos*. His whole Chapter 14 is devoted to exploring this contrast. See also Charles Segal, *Singers, Heroes, and Gods in the Odyssey* (Ithaca: Cornell University Press, 1994), index entries under *gastēr*, belly, and *thumos*.
3. All these citations are to the Fitzgerald translation.
4. An ancient commentary on this passage in *Odyssey* 8 makes this point explaining why they are at each other's throats. See Nagy, *The Best of the Achaeans*, p. 45ff. See also Erwin Cook, *The Odyssey in Athens: Myths of Cultural Origins* (Ithaca: Cornell University Press, 1995), and Wilson, "Lion Kings: Heroes in the Epic Mirrors."
5. Professor Erwin Cook disagrees: Odysseus' not-quite-concealed tears engineer his identification as a "man of pain," i.e., a hero.
6. Charles Segal, *Singers, Heroes, and Gods in the Odyssey*, p. 90, says Homer's words in Greek could equally well mean, "I am Odysseus son of Laertes, who am a subject in song to men by all my wiles."

3. Pirate Raid: Staying in Combat Mode

1. Translated from Latin by R. M. Adams (New York: W. W. Norton, 1975), p. 13.
2. *Political Writings*, trans. and ed. Biancamaria Fontana (Cambridge: Cambridge University Press, 1988), p. 61. Thanks to Professor Eugene Garver for this quotation.
3. *Now It Can Be Told* (New York: Harper, 1920), p. 547f, quoted in Willard Waller, *The Veteran Comes Back* (New York: Dryden, 1944), p. 118.
4. Odysseus begins his yarn in Book 9. The Ciconians, as the inhabitants of Ismarus were called, were Trojan allies (Iliad 2:846, 7:73, orig.). My calling it a pirate raid may be disputed because of this, saying it was simply a continuation of the war. However, Troy has fallen, and Odysseus offers no political justification for the attack. The booty of an undefended town is apparently all the justification needed. W. B. Stanford, *The*

Odyssey of Homer, 2nd ed. (New York: St. Martin's Press, 1965), commentary to 9:39f. See note 8, below, to this chapter.

5. Waller, *The Veteran Comes Back,* p. 109.
6. Ibid., p. 143ff.
7. Hill & Wang, 1994.
8. The modern sensibility is shocked by what appears to be a gratuitous raid, but according to the standards of the day, they may have been seen as a legitimate target. In Odysseus' eyes, if he needs to explain anything, it is failing to pull out with the booty in time to evade the Ciconians' counterattack. Ancient audiences probably had a less critical reaction to this raid than we do. Piracy was a respectable occupation even into sixth century B.C.E. Athens, when Solon's law declared that "If . . . cult followers of heroes, or members of a clan, or messmates, or funerary associates . . . or pirates, or traders make arrangements among themselves, these shall be binding unless forbidden by public texts [laws]." Justinian's *Digest* 47.22.4, quoted in W. R. Connor, "Civil Society, Dionysiac Festival, and the Athenian Democracy," in J. Ober and C. Hedrick, *Dēmokratia: A Conversation on Democracies, Ancient and Modern* (Princeton: Princeton University Press, 1996), p. 219. Thucydides I.5 gives the following picture:

> For the Hellenes in early times . . . turned to piracy as soon as they increased their contacts by sea, some of the most powerful men leading the way for their own profit and to support the needy. Falling on unwalled cities consisting of villages, they plundered them and made their main living from this, the practice not yet bringing disgrace but even conferring a certain prestige; witness those mainlanders even of the present who glory in successful raiding, also the request everywhere in early poetry that men arriving by sea say whether they are pirates, as though those questioned would not deny the practice nor would those who wanted to know blame them. (*The Peloponnesian War,* trans. Steven Lattimore [Indianapolis: Hackett, 1998], p. 5.)

9. Richard Kulka et al., *National Vietnam Veterans Readjustment Study* (hereinafter *NVVRS*) (New York: Brunner/Mazel, 1990), p. VII-21-1.
10. L. P. Croker, *Army Officer's Guide,* 45th ed. (Harrisburg: Stackpole, 1989), p. 410.
11. Emphasis added. Tennyson's *Ulysses* is widely anthologized. The edition I have used is *The Works of Alfred Lord Tennyson* (Ware, U.K.: Wordsworth Editions, 1994), p. 147f.
12. *Good-bye to All That,* revised 2nd ed. (Anchor, 1957), p. 287.
13. Remarque, *The Road Back,* pp. 252–53.
14. Mick Hurbis-Cherrier and Katherine Hurbis-Cherrier, *History Lessons.* Video, 1992.

4. Lotus Land: The Flight from Pain

1. Homer calls the inhabitants of the town Ciconians. For ancient Ismarus, see F. H. Stubbings, "The Recession of Mycenaean Civilization," in *The Cambridge Ancient History,* 3rd ed., Vol. 3, Part 2, ed. I. E. S. Edwards et al. (Cambridge: Cambridge University Press, 1975), p. 351.
2. The word that Fitzgerald translates here as "browsing" is the same as used elsewhere for cows and horses grazing. Scholar Erwin Cook takes this to be a Homeric suggestion that the crewmen who ate the lotus reduced themselves to animals, i.e., dehumanized themselves. See Cook, "'Active' and 'Passive' Heroics," p. 57. He finds the whole theme of demeaning or forbidden eating, crystallized by the eating of the sacred cattle of the sun god by the remnant of the flotilla, as the overall ethi-

cal fault requiring their destruction. They yield to physical appetites. Of course, Odysseus yields to his sexual appetites and to the luxury comforts of the nymphs' homes. Are we supposed to see a scale of merit here, that yielding to sex is morally superior (in the world of Odysseus) to yielding to hunger?

3. *NVVRS*, VI-13-1f, VI-15-1f. Data showing substance abuse rates in combat vets with and without current PTSD and civilian counterparts with and without current PTSD have not been published, to my knowledge. The data mentioned here are for all combat vets, lumped together whether they have current PTSD or not, and for all veterans with current PTSD, whether or not they were exposed to high levels of combat stressors.

4. In this I follow Judith Herman's *Trauma and Recovery: The Aftermath of Violence—From Domestic Abuse to Political Terror* (New York: Basic, 1992, Part 2, "Stages of Recovery."

5. Self-mutilation, a not uncommon addiction among survivors of childhood sexual and physical torture, is relatively rare among combat veterans. I have had only one patient who used to engage in self-mutilation, and he had a history of being repeatedly raped in childhood by his father. The frequency of severe childhood sexual and/or physical abuse among the combat veterans in our program appears no greater than in the nonveteran population.

6. Aphrodite Matsakis, *Vietnam Wives: Facing the Challenges of Life with Veterans Suffering Post-Traumatic Stress Disorder,* 2nd ed. (Lutherville, Md.: Sidran Press, 1006).

7. With the same demographic characteristics as the in-country Vietnam veterans sampled by the *NVVRS*.

5. Cyclops: The Flight from Boredom

1. Jeremy Wilson, *Lawrence of Arabia: The Authorized Biography of T. E. Lawrence* (London: Heinemann, 1989), p. 771f of Minerva paperback reprint. Lawrence died after six days in a coma from a head injury after being thrown from his motorcycle in 1935, at the apparently sedate speed of 40 miles per hour, but almost certainly too fast to safely deal with the unexpected in the undulations of the country lane (p. 934).

2. See van Wees, *Status Warriors,* for estimates of the number of people on each ship. Odysseus has a dozen vessels at 9:176, Fagles.

3. At what point did Odysseus realize that he was dealing with giants? The whole story is told by Odysseus in retrospect, so clearly at the time he is telling the story he knows they were giants, but did he know it at the time he decided to take the potent wine? The text says that the caves of the Cyclopes were visible across the water on the goat island, but doesn't mention seeing the giants themselves. But he does not decide to take the wine until 9:219 (Fagles) when Odysseus and his crew have already crossed over the water. From the shore he can see that the cave above is a giant's lair. This prompts Odysseus to take the wine, which in retelling he describes as being on a hunch. Hardly a prudent decision by a responsible leader. Why not turn around and leave? A few lines later, at 237, he retells the decision to take the wine, speaking of his "foreboding" that they would shortly meet a giant. Is this Odysseus trying to bury the evidence of leadership malpractice by claiming fame for prescience? Then they enter the cave and there's no more doubt than if we were to enter a house with fifty-foot ceilings and chair seats and tabletops above our heads.

4. Stanford, *The Ulysses Theme,* Chapter 5. Homer's epics abound with these precious luxury items that custom required a host to give to a guest according to the respective ranks of the host and the guest.

5. Cook, *The Odyssey in Athens.* Cook marshals all the examples of forbidden banquets

and illegal feasting in the Odyssey. See his index entries under "Dietary code" and "Feasting." The audience for the irony created by the parallel between Odysseus and his men and the suitors would have been Homer's audience, of course, not the internal audience for Odysseus' tales, the Phaeacians.

6. 9:272f, Fitzgerald; emphasis added.

7. A. Dane and R. Gardner, "Violent Acts and Violent Times: A Comparative Approach to Postwar Homicide Rates," *American Sociological Review* 41:937–63 (1976).

8. This is the same word that Odysseus uses to introduce himself to the Phaeacian court, and frequently a synonym for, or illustration of, *mētis*.

9. I thank Professor Erwin Cook for explaining that *mē tis* and *mētis* were not exact homophones, but close enough to make the pun. In the context of oral performance there would have been no sight gag of the words in close proximity.

10. A few lines later Odysseus attributes it all to Zeus, "Zeus was still obsessed with plans to destroy my entire oarswept fleet and loyal crew of comrades" (9:618f). In the epic's prologue, the narrator blames his comrades' offense against the sun god, "the recklessness of their own ways destroyed them all, the blind fools, they devoured the cattle of the Sun and the Sungod blotted out the day of their return" (1:9ff). The narrator of the prologue seems to have forgotten that eleven out of twelve of Odysseus' flotilla had already been sunk before his one remaining ship reached the island where the sun god pastured his cattle. And when the god Hermes visits Calypso to tell her that she must let Odysseus go, he recites yet a different god's-eye history of the events: "But voyaging back they outraged Queen Athena. . . . / There all the rest of his loyal shipmates died" (5:121ff).

So who's responsible for the holocaust of Odysseus' military contingent of more than six hundred of the flower of Ithaca's youth? Athena? The sun god? Zeus? Poseidon? And who brought down each god's wrath? The Greek commanders? The sailors themselves? Odysseus? Or was it just Zeus' arbitrary will, possibly holding a war to thin the humans who were overpopulating the earth?

11. Cook, *The Odyssey in Athens*, p. 16.

12. The text "overdetermines" the divine antagonisms that are in play: not only Poseidon, but also Athena is mad at Odysseus as an individual, with all the dangers that implies about the safety of his men, and Helios the sun god and Zeus also want their hides. How unjust divine justice is in the *Odyssey* has been remarked on many times. The multiple sources of divine enmity are marshaled by Jenny Clay in *The Wrath of Athena*.

13. Cook, "'Active' and 'Passive' Heroics in the *Odyssey*." Professor Cook would not agree with my connecting "living on the edge" with heroics.

6. Odysseus Gets a Leg Up—and Falls on His Face: The Workplace

1. For a fascinating picture of a blood-feuding culture quite distant from the Homeric world, but amazingly similar, i.e., the society of the Icelandic sagas, see William I. Miller, *Humiliation and Other Essays on Honor, Social Discomfort, and Violence* (Ithaca: Cornell University Press, 1993). Such societies unmistakably have mechanisms of social control, but cannot be said to have a "government" except by stretching the meaning of the word to include all social control sanctioned by the culture.

2. It's not as though there is no competent helmsman. The nymph/witch Circe also gives them a perfect following wind to take them to the Underworld, and Odysseus trusts the helmsman to stay on course (11:10, orig.)-presumably the same helmsman who would have been aboard, unused, when they sailed for Ithaca from Aeolia.

3. A good example of this is Patroclus, Achilles' foster brother and second-in-command in the *Iliad*.

> Menoitios [Patroclus' father]
> ... had brought me, under a cloud,
> a boy still, on the day I killed the son
> of Lord Amphídamas—though I wished it not—
> in childish anger over a game of dice.
> Peleus [Achilles' father] ... adopted me
> and reared me kindly, naming me your squire.
>   (Iliad 23:100ff, Fitzgerald)

4. Jonathan Shay, *Achill in Vietnam. Kampftrauma und Persönlichkeitsverlust*, trans. Klaus Kochmann (Hamburg: Hamburger Edition, 1998).
5. As with so many themes in this book, Willard Waller's 1944 recommendations on the occupational reintegration of returning war veterans in *The Veteran Comes Back* are still worth reading and taking to heart today. For the specific area of occupational readjustment and pensions, see the final sections of the book. However, it should be evident by now that I hope as many people as possible will want to read that book in its entirety. It is still in many libraries and quite findable on the used book market.

7. A Peaceful Harbor: No Safe Place

1. As given above in note 2 to Chapter 4 and note 5 to Chapter 5, Homer scholar Erwin Cook sees Odysseus' men as bringing on their own destruction by yielding to physical appetites.
2. John Gardner, in *The Art of Fiction* (New York: Vintage, 1985), calls frigidity "a fault of soul," rather than of writing technique. But whose soul here—Homer's or Odysseus'? "Strictly speaking, frigidity characterizes the writer who presents serious material, then . . . fails to treat it with the attention and seriousness it deserves" (p. 118). Gardner attributes this formulation to Longinus.
3. Twelve ships in the *Iliad*, 2:636f, orig. Karl Reinhardt, "The Adventures in the Odyssey" (1948), trans. H. I. Flower, in Seth Schein, *Reading the Odyssey. Selected Interpretive Essays* (Princeton: Princeton University Press, 1996), pp. 69–73. Also Ralph Hexter, "[The episode] provides the narrator a dramatic and economical way to dispatch most of Odysseus' companions and all but one of his ships in one fell swoop, a move that the narrative shape of the Odyssey requires." *A Guide to the Odyssey* (New York: Vintage, 1993).
4. Morally and politically, the storyteller's art can be as explosive as nitroglycerine—witness the power of the nationalistic stab-in-the-back/revenge/rebirth story that the Serbians tell of their fourteenth-century defeat by the Turks in Kosovo, or the power that the stab-in-the-back rhetoric of the German defeat in World War I had in propelling Hitler to power. I believe it's time we gave up the sentimental notion that art is always beneficent. Human art, like human language, is a phenomenon of nature, neither intrinsically good nor intrinsically bad.
5. Scholar Erwin Cook interprets Odysseus' decision to tie up outside in exactly the opposite sense that I do here. He says, "Odysseus begins heroically enough by taking up a 'wing position' at the mouth of the Laistrygonian harbor analogous to the positions of Akhilleus and Aias at Troy." Professor Cook sees this as Odysseus taking up the dangerous position on the exposed flank-thus protecting, rather than neglecting, the safety of his command. "'Active' and 'Passive' Heroics in the *Odyssey*," pp. 149–67.

8. Witches, Goddesses, Queens, Wives—Dangerous Women

1. Odysseus fears that Calypso plans this in Book 5; Clytemnestra as accessory to Agamemnon's murder, 4:101f and 11:462ff; Penelope as possible threat, see Chapter 15 below; Helen spotting Odysseus when he infiltrates Troy in disguise 4:281ff; the old nurse Eurycleia identifies him from the distinctive scar on his thigh 19:528ff; the danger to Odysseus from Phaeacian toughs at Nausicaa's beck and call, if she chooses 7:35ff (by inference); Circe—this chapter; Sirens 12:44ff; Scylla 12:94ff; Helen—the whole Trojan War. (All line numbers to Fagles translation.)
2. The portrait of the loyal swineherd, Eumaeus, and the various mentions of livestock and those who tend it suggest the following hierarchy of prestige in the world of Odysseus: beef cattle and horses at the top, pigs next, with sheep and goats at the bottom.
3. In some traditions Odysseus is descended from the god Hermes, through his grandfather Autolycus.
4. Copyright © 2002 by Dennis Spector, all rights reserved. Reprinted by permission. From *The Exorcism of Vietnam* [working title], mixed nonfiction history and interviews and pseudonymous autobiography, in preparation.
5. Copyright © 2002 by Dennis Spector. All rights reserved. Used by permission.

9. Among the Dead: Memory and Guilt

1. Large parts of Odysseus' story of Hades are devoted to working his agendas to get his hosts to take him home, to pump up his own image, and to get more and more guest-gifts. Valuable guest-gifts, and "gift exchange," are perennial subjects of scholarship on the ancient Mediterranean. They apparently represented a significant component of the ancient economy. These so-called prestige goods could be extremely, even obscenely valuable. The long list of famous women Odysseus says he met in the Underworld seems crafted to excite and please Queen Arete. In this he's startlingly successful. When he finishes and says it's time for sleep, she's the first to speak up and mousetraps her noble guests into each bringing guest-gifts for Odysseus. But she still keeps his ride home dangling.

    King Alcinous finally awakens to the fact that Odysseus has not told him what he asked—Odysseus' story of the Trojan War. The king skates on the thin edge of calling him a liar:

    > "Ah Odysseus . . . one look at you
    > and we know that you are no one who would cheat us—
    > no fraud, such as the dark soul breeds and spreads
    > across the face of the earth. . . . Crowds of vagabonds
    > frame their lies so tightly none can test them. But you,
    > what grace you give your words. . . .
    > You have told your story with all a singer's skill. . . .
    > But come now, tell me truly: your . . . comrades—
    > did you see . . . down in the House of Death,
    > any *who sailed with you and met their doom at Troy?*
    > The night's still young.
    > (11:411ff, Fagles; emphasis added)

    Is he setting a trap for Odysseus, hoping to show him up as a scammer? The *Iliad* is the definitive text on the war, which Demodocus, the court bard, knows all about and has sung about for the king. But by this point in Odysseus' story, King Alcinous already knows that more than eleven out of twelve Ithacans have died on the way home in the charge of their captain—who has survived, but not arrived with even one shipmate from the remaining vessel. Where are they?

Odysseus pretends to misunderstand and replies with an account of the senior Greek officers he met in Hades, starting with Agamemnon, and moving on to Achilles and Ajax. In doing so, he not only gives the impression of being their equals at Troy, but also subtly one-ups each of them. If all we had was the *Iliad,* we might remember Odysseus this way: "Mmmm, let me think . . . Odysseus . . . oh, yes, he was one of Agamemnon's staff officers, a pretty good one, as I recall." Nobody would have to stop and think who Agamemnon, Achilles, or Ajax were.

2. *Achilles in Vietnam,* "Guilt and Wrongful Substitution" chapter.

3. This is essentially Sophocles' version in the Ajax. In case you are thinking that Odysseus received the arms of Achilles as an apt reward for the ruse of the Trojan Horse, Achilles' death and the award of his arms occurred before the war's sudden end in victory for the Greeks. In some respects this play about Ajax's suicide presents one of the most sympathetic pictures of Odysseus in all of Athenian tragedy. See Charles Segal, *Tragedy and Civilization: An Interpretation of Sophocles* (Cambridge, Mass.: Harvard University Press, 1981), pp. 148–50. Sophocles' *Philoctetes* is more representative in that it foregrounds Odysseus' manipulativeness and deceit toward the noble-spirited son of Achilles, Neoptolemus.

4. Sometime around the beginning of the fourth century B.C.E., an associate of Socrates named Antisthenes "wrote a pair of speeches as if they had been delivered by Ajax and Odysseus during the infamous dispute over which of them should inherit . . . the armour." Jon Hesk, *Deception and Democracy in Classical Athens* (Cambridge: Cambridge University Press, 2000), pp. 118–21, gives a fascinating summary and analysis of these speeches.

5. William Mullen, "Pindar and Athens," *Arion* New Series 1/3,1974. I thank Professor Mullen for drawing this to my attention and supplying the quotation.

6. Gregory Nagy, Introduction to the Knopf edition of Fitzgerald's *Iliad* translation, p. xv.

7. Nemean 3:48ff (deer and lions); Isthmian 5:38ff (combat kills).

8. Stanford, *The Ulysses Theme,* pp. 102–17.

9. Ibid., p. 110.

10. Ibid. p. 111. Classicist Charles Segal describes Odysseus' religious views thus: "His gods are simply the appendage of his own purposes." *Sophocles' Tragic World,* p. 100.

11. John P. A. Gould, "Sophocles," *Oxford Classical Dictionary,* 3rd ed., ed. Simon Hornblower and Anthony Spawforth (Oxford: Oxford University Press, 1996), p. 1423. For the military background of Athenian tragic theater see J. Shay, "The Birth of Tragedy—Out of the Needs of Democracy," *Didaskalia: Ancient Theater Today,* vol. 2, no. 2, April 1995. Online: didaskalia.berkeley.edu/issues/vol2no2/Shay. html.

12. The ellipses are Mary Garvey's. E-mail of December 10, 2001. Quoted by permission. "Hierarchies of suffering" were discussed in *Achilles in Vietnam,* pp. 192 and 239n10.

13. See pp. 65–75 and 192.

14. The text leans in the direction of Odysseus being aware of the death, but being unwilling to take the time to perform the death rites. Nothing in what Circe says to him suggests that he would have to return to her island after the trip to Hades, so at the time he left, he could not have been thinking, "We'll do this when we get back." This is either another example of Odysseus' indifference to the welfare of those serving under him, or of his being so "fried" that he just says, "Don' mean nothing, drive on."

15. Perhaps Odysseus was responding to the threat "or my curse may draw god's fury

on your head" (11:81, Fagles), which Elpenor also said. Who knows what the dead are capable of?

16. 7th Annual Meeting, International Society for Traumatic Stress Studies, Washington, D.C., 1991.

17. *Achilles in Vietnam,* p. 198ff.

18. Ibid., p. 71.

19. Frederick Ahl and Hanna Roisman in their book *The Odyssey Re-Formed* (Ithaca: Cornell University Press, 1996), p. 131.

20. Ibid. I owe this insight, slapping my forehead with my hand, to the classical scholars Frederick Ahl and Hanna Roisman in *The Odyssey Re-Formed.* At 15:399f the loyal swineherd Eumaeus confirms this, saying Anticleia "died of grief for her boy."

21. While some veterans with complex PTSD seem devoid of conscience, others seem to suffer an excess of it. Their conscience stands in the way of their getting help from people who both want to help and have demonstrated ability to help. These veterans *know* about "secondary trauma," psychological injury to mental health professionals working with them. Because the veterans know, they keep silent about their worst demons, until they have observed the therapist and his or her setting long enough to know that it is safe—for themselves and for the therapist.

   About ten years ago, when I had only three years experience and was still quite green, I was sitting eating a sandwich in a group therapy room a quarter hour before a therapy group I was to conduct. Because our program is based on the concept that the veterans heal one another through the power of their community together, they are encouraged to consider the rooms "theirs" and to come early and stay late. One veteran came with some photographs of enemy soldiers he had blown apart with his M-79 Thumper, the shotgun-style grenade launcher. Out of respect for the dead, I put down my sandwich, but made the error of not explaining why I put down my sandwich. The veteran grabbed back the pictures looking stricken, fearing he had made me sick to my stomach. These photographs were intensely meaningful, important, and also probably harmful for him to dwell on privately, without anyone to "process" the feelings, memories, and thoughts that they evoked. His fear of hurting me shut down his chance at that bit of recovery. He never brought the pictures to the clinic again, despite offers to structure the encounter any way he felt safe.

   The subject of clinician self-care and prevention of secondary trauma in the mental health workplace is a large one. Dealing with secondary trauma is not a secondary issue to the success of the treatment enterprise. See J. Shay and J. Munroe, "Group and Milieu Therapy for Veterans with Complex Posttraumatic Stress Disorder," in *Posttraumatic Stress Disorder: A Comprehensive Text,* ed. Philip A. Saigh and J. Douglas Bremner (Boston: Allyn & Bacon, 1999), pp. 391–413. Access to the literature of secondary trauma as an occupational exposure in many fields of work can be found in the bibliography to the second edition of *Secondary Traumatic Stress,* ed. Beth Hudnall-Stamm (Lutherville, Md.: Sidran Press, 1999).

22. Yael Danieli, *International Handbook of Multigenerational Legacies of Trauma* (New York: Plenum, 1998).

23. Lawrence A. Tritle, *From Melos to My Lai: War and Survival* (London and New York: Routledge, 2000), p. 184.

10. What Was the Sirens' Song?: Truth As Deadly Addiction

1. George Hoffman and a number of other veterans who have never been my patients speak in their own names and have generously allowed me to use their words here. This is excerpted from the complete "War Story," which can be found in a collection

of George "Sonny" Hoffman's writings on the Web at www.vietvet.org/sonny.htm. George Hoffman reserves all rights.

2. In fairness to those who recall the songs' appeal as sexual, there are strong sexual associations to the grassy meadow (lēimon was also used to refer to the female genitals) on which they sing and the "enchanting" (thelgousin) effect of their songs. See Jean-Pierre Vernant, "The Refusal of Odysseus," trans. V. Farenga, in Schein, *Reading the Odyssey,* p. 186n9.

3. Pietro Pucci, "The Song of the Sirens," in Schein, *Reading the Odyssey,* p. 191.

4. Ibid. This is one of the main points of Pucci's paper.

5. The Sirens, in a line not quoted above, speak of veterans "delighting in" (terpsamenos) their song, 12:188, orig.

6. Willy Peter: white phosphorus incendiary.

7. Ahl and Roisman, *The Odyssey Re-formed,* p. 147. Elsewhere, I have tried to put the Homeric word *thumos* back into current circulation as a less pathologizing and prejudicial term than "narcissism." See Shay and Munroe, "Group and Milieu Therapy for Veterans," pp. 391–413, especially the section "Destruction of Normal Narcissism." See also J. Shay, "Killing Rage: *Physis* or *Nomos*—or Both?," in *War and Violence in Ancient Greece,* ed. Hans van Wees (London: Duckworth and Classical Press of Wales, 2000), pp. 31–56, especially the section "Honor, Narcissism, and *Thumos.*"

8. Pucci, *Odysseus Polutropos,* p. 212n7.

9. J. Shay, "Achilles: Paragon, Flawed Character, or Tragic Soldier Figure?" *Classical Bulletin* 71:117–24 (1995).

10. *Republic* X 621c.

11. 2.583.

12. Translated by Janet Lloyd (New York: Zone Books, 1999), p. 87.

13. Segal, *Singers, Heroes, and Gods in the Odyssey,* p. 103.

14. In the eyes of bureaucracies, more syllables is always better: Is there any substantive difference in meaning between the four-syllable verb "adjudicate" and the one-syllable verb "judge"?

15. My esteemed colleague in *Commandant of the Marine Corps Trust Study* Bruce Gudmundsson, a world-class military historian, gives the following comments on the *"Dolchstoss von hinten."* First, many soldiers from the front felt that they had not been beaten—much like many American Vietnam veterans say "we won every battle"—and thus were baffled and humiliated by the surrender. Second, the phrase was not originally a nationalist, right-wing coinage, but actually first used by Friedrich Ebert, a Social Democrat, the first chancellor of the Weimar Republic, to some army troops. When I asked Gudmundsson what Ebert had in mind, he said it probably referred to (a) the British blockade, which Germany saw as a violation of international law and illegitimate, and (b) Germany's geographical "back," which was exposed to the knife by the collapse of Bulgaria and the Austro-Hungarian Empire after the Battle of Salonica. The phrase was subsequently appropriated and exploited to great effect by ultranationalist groups such as the Nazis.

11. Scylla and Charybdis: Enemies Up, Down, and Sideways

1. 12:113, Fagles.

2. Lieutenant General Harold G. Moore and Joseph L. Galloway, *We Were Soldiers Once . . . and Young* (New York: Random House, 1992), p. 345.

3. More dangerous women! Both Scylla and Charybdis are gendered female.

4. Cook, 1999, p. 157.

5. The text is not crystal clear as to whether Circe's instruction to put everything into

speed was aimed at avoiding Scylla's jaws altogether, not veering into the whirlpool, or at limiting her catch to six, not giving her a shot at another six by hanging around to fight. Heubeck and a number of other scholars come down squarely that Circe's warning is that Scylla "may sally forth a *second* time . . . with six heads, and attack you *again*." See his commentary to 12:122–23, orig.

6. A. Heubeck and A. Hoekstra, *A Commentary on Homer's Odyssey,* vol. 2. (Oxford: Oxford University Press, 1989), p. 130.

12. The Sun God's Beef: The Blame Game

1. 12:298, Fagles.
2. Cattle rustling was apparently a major sideline for Greek warriors. I imagine their society being much like the present-day herding society in the horn of Africa, where herdsman and warrior are called by the same word and where men are *always* armed to the teeth when they tend their cattle. When Achilles and Agamemnon blow up in the opening book of the *Iliad,* Achilles sneers,

> You thick-skinned, shameless, greedy fool!
> Can any [Greek] care for you, or obey you,
> after this on marches or in battle?
> As for myself, when I came here to fight,
> I had no quarrel with Troy or Trojan spearmen:
> *they never stole my cattle or my horses.*
> (*Iliad* 1:175ff, Fitzgerald; emphasis added)

This is an insight into the world of these Greek warriors of the Archaic Period. Achilles doesn't say "the Trojans never burned our town or raided our shipping," but "they never stole my cattle."

3. Scholars Ahl and Roisman comment, "Eurylochus usually spots Odysseus' intent to endanger his comrades or treat them unfairly."
4. Homer scholar Erwin Cook disagrees with my finding irony here and says that here "Zeus" simply means "the gods" and that the sun god's island and the gale are simply workings out of the divine plan set in train by the Cyclops' curse (personal communication).
5. 24:468ff, Fitzgerald.
6. See Segal, *Singers, Heroes and Gods in the Odyssey,* p. 217.
7. We can recall that the other time Odysseus fell asleep, on the way from the island of the King of the Winds straight home to Ithaca, it didn't come out well.
8. Ahl and Roisman, *The Odyssey Re-Formed,* p. 151.
9. Ibid., p. 150.
10. Ex. 32. Homeric scholar Donna Wilson: "a traditional theme common to Homer and Israelite tradition alike that the people fail to restrain themselves in the long absence of a leader; the suitors do the same thing" (e-mail, December 18, 2001).
11. See *Dereliction of Duty* by U.S. Army armored cavalry Major H. R. McMaster (New York: HarperCollins, 1998).
12. Apologies to "Longinus," the unknown, probably first-century author of *On the Sublime,* who first speculated that the *Iliad* = Homer's young maturity and the *Odyssey* = Homer's old age, based on considerations of the differing style and form of the two epics. See Howard Clarke, *Homer's Readers: A Historical Introduction to the* Iliad *and the* Odyssey (London and Toronto: Associated University Presses, 1981), p. 207. As much as I am temperamentally drawn to Longinus' account, I don't need to see "Homer" as one person.

13. The dichotomy between achieved and ascribed status is a staple of sociological analysis.

14. See Ian Morris, "The Strong Principle of Equality and the Archaic Origins of Greek Democracy," in Ober and Hedrick, *Dēmokratia*, pp. 19–48.

15. Donna Wilson, in *Ransom, Revenge, and Heroic Identity* (Cambridge: Cambridge University Press, 2002), argues persuasively that the clash between Achilles and Agamemnon in the *Iliad* is fundamentally the clash between the meritocratic and aristocratic bases of legitimation of power.

16. See Hans van Wees, *Status Warriors* (Amsterdam: Gieben, 1992), for the Iliadic context and William I. Miller, *Humiliation and Other Essays on Honor, Social Discomfort, and Violence* (Ithaca: Cornell University Press, 1993), for the very *Iliad*-like setting of saga Iceland.

17. Especially with regard to their love of luxury and creature comforts. Ibid., pp. 32–33.

18. See John F. Lazenby, "Mercenaries," in Hornblower and Spawforth, eds., *The Oxford Classical Dictionary*, p. 961f. A post-Homeric example is Xenophon, who hired out to the Spartan king Agesilaus and the Persian prince Cyrus the Younger. See Jon Hesk, *Deception and Democracy in Classical Athens*, p. 127.

19. The tensions between the "achieved" meritocracy and "ascribed" nobility never evaporated in ancient Greece nor have they since. However, once the Homeric poems got to Athens and the balance in Athens shifted in favor of meritocracy, the stock of Achilles soared and that of Odysseus crashed. The story of how the Homeric poems took up ritual and political residence in Athens is a complex and fascinating one. See Gregory Nagy, *Poetry as Performance: Homer and Beyond* (Cambridge: Cambridge University Press, 1996), and Cook, *The Odyssey in Athens*. My thanks to a half-dozen classicists for helping me think this through. I have accepted many of their criticisms, but stubbornly resisted others. Credit for *any* merit in this conjecture belongs to them and to the cited works. Any defects of fact or reasoning are my private property.

13. Above the Whirlpool

1. The full text of "The Dodger Song" can be found on the Web at www.geocities.com/Nashville/3448/dodger.html.

2. Portions of this section appeared in "Guilt and Good Character," *Religion and Ethics Newsweekly* (online), June 1, 2001, www.thirteen.org/religionandethics/week440/vietnam.htm, where the full commentary can be found.

3. Gregory L. Vistica, "What Happened in Thanh Phong," *The New York Times Magazine*, April 29, 2001, pp. 50–57, 66–68, 133. Kerrey was awarded the Medal of Honor for an act of heroism during a later action unconnected to the mission at Thanh Phong.

4. Ibid., p. 66.

5. Thomas E. Ricks, "Kerrey Team Takes Issue with Report: 6 of 7 SEALs Meet on Vietnam Killings," *The Washington Post*, April 29, 2001.

14. Calypso: Odysseus the Sexaholic

1. *The Veteran Comes Back*, p. 140.

2. 1:16ff and 5:1–160, Fagles.

3. Aphrodite Matsakis, *Vietnam Wives* (Kensington, Md.: Woodbine House, 1988). This book is currently available from the Sidran Press in a second edition, 1996. This citation is to the first edition.

15. Odysseus at Home

1. I do not respond quite so positively to Odysseus' warmth and truthfulness toward his son, because his son, Telemachus, is not in any sense a separate being from Odysseus. He literally lives or dies with Odysseus. If he errs or falls short, it is akin to Odysseus' throwing arm missing the mark with a spear. Penelope, despite the housebound existence of the well-born Mediterranean wife, is very much her own person, not a mere product of Odysseus' imagination and agendas.

2. Clay, *The Wrath of Athena*, p. 196f.

3. Donald Lateiner, *Sardonic Smile: Nonverbal Behavior in Homeric Epic* (Ann Arbor: University of Michigan Press, 1995), p. 245.

4. Clay, *The Wrath of Athena*, explores what's behind this abandonment.

5. Some scholars reject the notice of the suitors in the Underworld as a later insertion in the text, and claim that Odysseus hears about the suitors for the first time from Athena on the beach.

6. W. B. Stanford's *Enemies of Poetry* (London: Routledge & Kegan Paul, 1980), p. 131ff, warns against "stereotype fallacies" in imagining what ancient poets could or could not do. This subject, however, is vigorously debated among scholars.

7. See Mark W. Edwards, *Homer: Poet of the* Iliad (Baltimore: Johns Hopkins University Press, 1987). "Double motivation" and "overdetermination" are the terms critics have used. Peradotto, in *Man in the Middle Voice*, pp. 60–67, adds an additional dimension to the critical theme of multiple motivations. Segal, *Singers, Heroes, and Gods in the Odyssey*, p. 217, refers to "double determination" as a "common Homeric device."

8. See *Achilles in Vietnam*, pp. 32f and 82f, for more of this tank veteran's words.

9. When Odysseus and Telemachus meet at the swineherd's hut, Odysseus levels with his son because they live or die together. He is a useful ally, but he cannot reside absolute trust in anyone else but his son. They have an identity of interests not shared by Penelope. If the suitors take down Odysseus, Telemachus is dead or exiled. Penelope survives as the new wife of the leading suitor, not the enslaved spoil of war.

10. The translator here uses the word "palace," but we should not imagine an enormous structure built over generations by a hereditary monarchy. It is more apt to imagine a hacienda, walled for defense and with little refinement.

11. The story of two angels visiting Sodom in Genesis 19 is one well-known example.

12. Odysseus actually declines an invitation to visit her immediately, as she asks when she hears that there is a stranger from abroad in the house. He subtly puts himself on an equal footing with the suitors by telling Eumaeus that his going to see her might further anger the suitors (17:629).

13. Unwittingly, when they send out their pages—thus sending out the news that Penelope is finally going to make her choice and be wed—the suitors also set up Odysseus' final strategic deception, when he has killed off all the suitors behind locked doors. Odysseus tells the harper to strike up wedding songs and dances to buy time before the townspeople figure out what Odysseus has done and that they want his blood.

14. 1:149f, Fagles, describes the row on row of spears in a rack (or jar) by the entrance of Odysseus' hall.

15. Neil Sheehan, *A Bright Shining Lie: John Paul Vann and America in Vietnam* (New York: Random House, 1988), p. 308.

16. Eurybates is mentioned in Book 2 of the *Iliad* as Odysseus' lieutenant, so he has survived the first nine years of the war.

17. After she awakens, she looks around for her geese and sees that they are not dead,

subtly hinting that she is relieved and likes having them around. This is but one of several hints that Penelope is on the verge of defecting. Athena's warning to Telemachus in Sparta is one, an even subtler one is the parallel between the jaw-gripped fawn on the brooch she gave to Odysseus and the jaw-gripped fawn in Menelaus' simile for what Odysseus would do to the suitors—and to Penelope, who is the doe! Telemachus repeats this as a subtle warning to his mother on his return. See Nancy Felson-Rubin, *Regarding Penelope* (Princeton: Princeton University Press, 1994), p. 21f. Elsewhere in this book Professor Felson-Rubin assembles the did she/didn't she evidence on whether and when she recognized Odysseus.

18. Waller, *The Veteran Comes Back*, p. 98.
19. *NVVRS*, p. II-45-1, and Richard A. Kulka et al., *Trauma and the Vietnam War Generation* (New York: Brunner/Mazel, 1990), p. 28, citing U.S. Bureau of the Census, 1987.
20. Matsakis, *Vietnam Wives*, p. 33.
21. Patience C. H. Mason, *Recovering from the War: A Woman's Guide to Helping Your Vietnam Veteran, Your Family, and Yourself* (New York: Viking, 1990), p. 241. Robert Mason wrote *Chickenhawk* (New York: Viking Penguin, 1983) and *Chickenhawk: Back in the World* (New York: Viking Penguin, 1993).
22. Mason, *Recovering from the War*, p. 248.
23. *The Collected Poems of Wilfred Owen*, ed. C. Day Lewis (New York: New Directions, 1965), p. 37.
24. PTSD clinicians and researchers Lizabeth Roemer, Brett T. Lidz, Susan M. Orsillo, and Amy W. Wagner have investigated this intentional withholding of emotion in "A Preliminary Investigation of the Role of Strategic Withholding of Emotion in PTSD," *Journal of Traumatic Stress* 14:149–56 (2001).
25. Leukos is not identified by his place of origin, and ten years into the war, could have come from anywhere, not necessarily Ithaca or the nearby towns. Based on the *Iliad* alone, it would appear that the casualties *at Troy* among Odysseus' original Ithacan contingent appear to be few to none! A search using the names of places, such as Ithaca, Neritos, and Korkyleia, contributing to his battalion in the Muster of the Ships in *Iliad* 2, does not turn up a single death identified with these "hometowns" anywhere else in the *Iliad*.
26. In the episode with the King of the Winds, Odysseus (who was asleep, you recall) reports his crew as saying, "'Heaps of lovely plunder he hauls home from Troy, while we who went through slogging just as hard, we go home empty-handed'" (10:45ff, Fagles). Despite this mention of plunder, I find the otherwise total absence of mention of booty in Odysseus' ships—and particularly of captive women—quite a noteworthy silence.
27. Criterion A:2 of Code 309.81 Posttraumatic Stress Disorder. In *Diagnostic and Statistical Manual of Mental Disorders*, 4th ed. (DSM-IV) (Washington: American Psychiatric Association Press, 1994), pp. 424–29. The three symptom clusters (criteria B, C, D) are reexperiencing symptoms, withdrawal and numbing symptoms, and symptoms of increased psychological and physiological mobilization ("arousal"). The detailed DSM-IV descriptive criteria can be found on literally hundreds of places on the World Wide Web, and do not require reproduction here.

    In the Cyclops and Scylla episodes, Odysseus has a hard time owning fear and horror. When he admits to them at all, he usually uses "we," including himself in the fear of his men, which he then rises above, contrasting his own subsequent responses.
28. This is typical of Homer's fictional method—to salt the essential information on the motivation of character and action throughout the narrative, rather than in the chronological, case-history manner found in some modern fiction. For example, Homer salts the full picture of Achilles' good character prior to the thunderbolt open-

ing of *Iliad* 1 in little data packets throughout the *Iliad*. This is discussed in Shay, "Achilles: Paragon, Flawed Character, or Tragic Soldier Figure?"

29. Nancy Felson-Rubin, *Regarding Penelope,* p. 70f. Astonishingly, Autolycus surfaces in *Iliad* 10 in connection with the boar-tusk helmet (lines 261ff, orig.) that Odysseus puts on for the night reconnaissance with Diomedes. The text gives the helmet's provenance with its theft by housebreaker Autolycus, then passing through various hands, presumably as guest-gifts finally to his grandson Odysseus. See Brian Hainsworth, *The Iliad: A Commentary,* Vol. 3 (Cambridge: Cambridge University Press, 1993), p. 179ff, particularly the commentary to line 10:267.

30. Erwin F. Cook, *The Odyssey in Athens,* p. 85.

31. Dimock, "The Name of Odysseus"; also "The Man of Pain" in that author's *The Unity of the Odyssey,* pp. 246–63. John Peradotto gives it simply as "Hate" in *Man in the Middle Voice,* p. 128.

32. Nancy Sultan, *Exile and the Poetics of Loss in Greek Tradition* (Lanham, Md.: Rowman & Littlefield, 1999), p. 43. I have no inclination to entangle myself in the controversy that rages to this day as to whether a disposition to criminal behavior is inherited or learned, nature or nurture, *physis* or *nomos.* You can see that I lean to the latter. Homer does not make us privy to the stages of "violentization" laid out by Lonnie H. Athens in *The Creation of Dangerous Violent Criminals.*

33. Personal communication, March 2002.

34. Vengeance is "payback," taken by the avenger and involuntarily given by its target in compensation for the damage done to body, possessions, or honor (which in that world encompasses the first two). The thinking and ideology underlying the Homeric honor concepts of compensation, so clearly voiced here by Eupithes, are laid out in the *Iliad.* See Donna F. Wilson's brilliant University of Texas doctoral dissertation (1997), now reworked into *Ransom, Revenge, and Heroic Identity* (Cambridge: Cambridge University Press, 2002).

16. Introduction

1. Portions of this chapter and the next are reedited by permission from Shay and Munroe, "Group and Milieu Therapy for Veterans," pp. 391–413, and from Shay, "Killing Rage," pp. 31–56, available online at www.belisarius.com/author_index.htm.

2. See note 27 to the previous chapter for access to the full APA criteria for PTSD.
   The implicit idea of "normal" in the official diagnostic system of the American Psychiatric Association derives from the historically and cross-nationally *not* typical psychology of someone who has been spared—who has never been ridden down by any of the Horsemen of the Apocalypse. "Normal" means: never been in war, never in famine, never in pandemic, never been raped or tortured, never lived in a tyranny. Mr. American Normal may even mean that neither of Normal's parents were ever trampled either, nor even his grandparents! I do not praise the Apocalypse and say it's good for us to be trampled by its Horsemen. I want nothing more fervently than the elimination of famine, plague—and war.

3. J. Douglas Bremner, Steven M. Southwick, and Dennis S. Charney, "The Neurobiology of Posttraumatic Stress Disorder: An Integration of Animal and Human Research," in Saigh and Bremner, *Posttraumatic Stress Disorder,* pp. 103–43. See also R. K. Pitman, L. M. Shin, and S. L. Rauch, "Investigating the Pathogenesis of Post-Traumatic Stress Disorder with Neuroimaging," *Journal of Clinical Psychiatry* 62S17:47–54 (2001), for the remarkable pace of scientific progress that the new, noninvasive, *in vivo* imaging methods permit. The two years between these two reviews showed palpable progress.

4. I believe that I am referring to the same phenomenon that Judith Herman described under this name in *Trauma and Recovery* and "Complex PTSD: A Syndrome in Survivors of Prolonged and Repeated Trauma," *Journal of Traumatic Stress,* 5:377–92 (1992).
5. *Odyssey* 9:20f, Fitzgerald.
6. Bernard J. Verkamp, *The Moral Treatment of Returning Warriors in Early Medieval and Modern Times* (Cranbury, N.J.: Associated University Presses, 1993). Cf. Numbers 31:19ff.
7. See Leon Golden's excellent monograph, *Aristotle on Tragic and Comic Mimesis,* American Philological Association, American Classical Studies monograph No. 29, 1992.
8. Georges Dumézil, *The Destiny of the Warrior,* trans. Alf Hiltebeitel (Chicago: University of Chicago Press, 1970), p. 23f.
9. Every atrocity strengthens the enemy. There were not enough officers in the U.S. Army in Vietnam who saw this clearly at the time. Returning to the situation of young Lieutenant Kerrey, the way SEAL teams were employed in the Mekong Delta was an advantage to the enemy and a setup for harm to the SEALs. One officer who saw this was Colonel Carl Bernard, an Army infantry officer who fought in both Korea and Vietnam. During part of his time in Vietnam, Colonel Bernard was a province senior adviser in the Delta, working for John Paul Vann, the career Army officer and critic of the war who was the subject of Neil Sheehan's book about Vietnam, *A Bright Shining Lie.* A few days after the Kerrey story broke, Bernard wrote:

> This episode proves again the very old conclusion about how little Americans knew about the "people's war" that Kerrey and the rest of us were in. Simply stated, we did not know how to fight such a conflict at its beginning, and we learned very little during its course, in significant part because of the constant transfer of personnel [causing their knowledge and experience to be lost]. We were hurt even more by bringing the wrong lessons from Korea, and our dedicated, enduring refusal to learn anything at all from the French experience. We knew almost nothing of our enemy; we knew very little more of our supposed allies beyond our assumption of common goals. And we knew far too little of our own forces and those who manned them.
>
> The SEAL teams had no more capability to accomplish their so-called counterinsurgency missions one month (!) after they arrived in country than I have of doing brain surgery. The difference is that I know that I do not have these exotic skills, and I stay out of hospital operating rooms.
>
> I was damned unkind a couple of months after Than Phong in restricting the activities of the SEAL team in Vinh Binh, the province below the one in which [Kerrey was] operating. As I told them in some dudgeon, their activities were sustaining the Viet Cong's recruiting effort even better than the Air Force's activities. (Personal communication, e-mail, May 10, 2001.)

In a "people's war," the enemy recruits the uncommitted and unmotivated in the civilian population to its side when they can entice us to respond indiscriminately or massively against the civilian population.

Second, every atrocity potentially disables the service member who commits it. When I speak here of atrocity disabling the service member, I am not pointing to that person's distant future as a guilt-ridden veteran, as important as that may be. I refer to the immediate question of whether he or she is lost to the force *today* because of the psychological injury incurred by committing atrocities. Sober and responsible troop leaders and trainers, who have personally "seen the elephant" and

cannot be painted as cravenly "PC," are concerned about prevention of psychological injury as a readiness issue. An injured service member is lost to the force,
whether the injury is physical or psychological.

10. R. Severo and L. Milford, *The Wages of War: When America's Soldiers Came Home—From Valley Forge to Vietnam* (New York: Simon & Schuster, 1989). See also the fascinating study by John P. Resch, *Suffering Soldiers: Revolutionary War Veterans, Moral Sentiment, and Political Culture in the Early Republic* (Amherst: University of Massachusetts Press, 1999).

11. An excellent summary of the Platonic view of this is found in Martha Nussbaum, "Tragedy and Self-Sufficiency: Plato and Aristotle on Fear and Pity," in A. O. Rorty, *Essays on Aristotle's Poetics* (Princeton: Princeton University Press, 1992).

12. The numbers are somewhat distorted by one quite wealthy Continental Army vet who brought up the average at the beginning of the period, but then brought it down by his departure or death. Removing him from the analysis makes the decline less dramatic and the starting disparity in wealth more marked. But even with this one rich patriot removed, the decade-by-decade decline in wealth of the long-service veterans compared to the stability of the other two groups is still significant. See Resch, *Suffering Soldiers*, p. 210.

13. Personal communication. Swedish Sanskrit scholar Ernst Arbman probably offered the best German equivalent for *thumos* in 1927 as *"die Ichseele,"* the "I-soul," which captures its narcissistic dimension. Conventionally, it is translated as *"das Gemüt,"* which is as opaque in German as the conventional English equivalent, "spirit." While I like Arbman's coinage for *thumos* I do not subscribe to the rest of his critical approach.

14. Francis Fukuyama, author of *The End of History and the Last Man* (New York: Free Press, 1992), has tried to put *thumos* back into circulation, transliterating the word as *thymos*. See pp. 162ff and other places indexed under *thymos*.

15. *Phenomenology of Spirit* IV.A, and elsewhere. Transition from citizen to slave was the most salient image and vivid fear in the ancient Greek world. Loss of a battle or of a war could convert citizen to slave in a day.

16. A particularly useful overview of the psychoanalytic usage can be found in Sydney Pulver, "Narcissism: The Term and Concept," in A. P. Morrison, ed., *Essential Papers on Narcissism* (New York: New York University Press, 1986). Heinz Kohut's most influential work, and the source of my emphasis on ideals and ambitions as content for *thumos*, is *The Analysis of the Self: A Systematic Approach to the Psychoanalytic Treatment of Narcissistic Personality Disorders* (Madison: International Universities Press, 1971).

17. I discuss the biological significance of social trust and speculate on how war in the upper Paleolithic shaped human psychology in "Killing Rage."

18. Or "another myself." Quoted from *Nicomachean Ethics* IX.9.1170b6 (trans. Irwin). Aristotle's account of friendship is rich, complex, and laced with surprises. See particularly A. W. Price, *Love and Friendship in Plato and Aristotle* (Oxford: Oxford University Press, 1990), Chapter 4.

19. Martha C. Nussbaum, *The Fragility of Goodness* (Cambridge: Cambridge University Press, 1986), p. 354. Citations of the word *philos* and related words in the *Iliad* and *Odyssey* fill a whole page of R. J. Cunliffe's *A Lexicon of the Homeric Dialect* (Norman: University of Oklahoma Press, 1963; reprint of Blackie and Son, London, 1924), pp. 408–9.

20. *Achilles in Vietnam,* pp. 35–37.

21. The first and second items on this list seem to me to connect to Circe's description of what she saw:

Now you are burnt-out husks, your spirits haggard, sere,
always brooding . . .
your hearts never lifting with any joy—
(10:502ff, Fagles)

22. "Nostalgia" was the term going back to the seventeenth century that military medicine gave to the often fatal collapse of the will to live and of all self-care among soldiers. It was still in official use in the Union Army in the Civil War. Eric Dean gives
an excellent account of this history in pp. 128–31 of *Shook Over Hell: Post-Traumatic Stress, Vietnam, and the Civil War* (Cambridge, Mass.: Harvard University
Press, 1997). "Musselman" was concentration camp slang for this same phenomenon. Because the Nazis murdered inmates who could no longer work, it was *always*
fatal.

23. Whether Hitler or bin Laden or both had awful traumatic backgrounds is not excul-
patory. Despite many requests, I have never testified as an expert witness to get
someone off on a PTSD defense. While it may seem contradictory, I have lobbied
the governor of my state for better services to incarcerated veterans with PTSD.

24. There has been a burst of scholarship in this area, for example, *Understanding the
Political Spirit: Philosophical Investigations from Socrates to Nietzsche,* ed. Catherine H. Zuckert (New Haven: Yale University Press, 1988); James F. McGlew,
Tyranny and Political Culture in Ancient Greece (Ithaca: Cornell University Press,
1993); Ober and Hedrick, eds., *Dēmokratia;* Barbara Koziak, *Retrieving Political
Emotion: Thumos, Aristotle and Gender* (University Park: Pennsylvania State University Press, 2000); Martha Nussbaum, *Upheavals of Thought: The Intelligence of
Emotions* (Cambridge: Cambridge University Press, 2001)—inquiry into equal
political respect is woven throughout this large book.

25. John Hesk, *Deception and Democracy* (Cambridge: Cambridge University Press,
2000). I thank Professor Josiah Ober for his patience in discussing Athenian legal
restraints on *biē* and *mētis* with me.

26. It is possible that veterans who have remained stable in only *one* of these states in the
above list (pages 160–61) would never come to our attention in a specialized combat
PTSD program because they would be dead, incarcerated, hidden in the woods and
not coming out, famous and powerful on a small or large scale, or diagnosed elsewhere as schizophrenic or physically ill. If complex PTSD after combat appears to be
defined by repetitive cycling, that may be because the veterans themselves or the
social system sends those who do *not* cycle somewhere else, rather than to us.

17. From the Clinic to the Wall

1. I was too busy trying to survive. Within the five years after the end of my psychiatry
training, I had to take major responsibility in a family business with extremely serious problems, had a stroke (age forty!), my marriage disintegrated, and I was slan-
dered by a senior colleague, derailing an attempt to get back on my feet at Harvard
Medical School, where I had been on the faculty because of my research. I would not
voluntarily undergo any of these experiences again, but I embrace them as my life,
and as my second education.

2. Throughout this book I have used the word "patient" rather than "client." The non-
medical disciplines in mental health have embraced the word "client," apparently
making the cultural connection to the client of a law, accounting, or business firm. Perhaps because of the suggestion that the client is free to take his business elsewhere,
this appears to confer more dignity on the individual than "patient," which is thought
to confer a less powerful image, especially when contrasted to "the doctor." No one

will be surprised that I have something to say about these usages based on the origins of the words in classical antiquity. A "patient" is one who suffers, the word being derived from Latin *patī*, to suffer. The "Passion" of Jesus on the Cross has the same etymology. "Client," on the other hand, comes from Latin *cliens*, the dependent or hanger-on of a patron. A *cliens* hears the orders of his patron and jumps to please him. I ask you, which suggests greater dignity? I use the word "patient" not because I am a doctor and wish to assert my authority; instead I recommend it to *all* mental health professionals, psychologists, nurses, social workers, and counselors, because it reflects the ethical basis of what we do—the alleviation of suffering.

3. Treatment outcome studies of the intensive inpatient VA specialized treatment units have shown a marked and persistent reduction of violence and an equally marked and persistent improvement in the veterans' quality of life. Not surprisingly, the symptoms of simple combat PTSD—the symptoms most measured by most studies, because of their official enunciation by the American Psychiatric Association—were little changed. They may represent irreversible brain changes, or at least irreversible with present knowledge.

4. Dr. Munroe recently received the Sarah Haley Award for Clinical Innovation of the International Society for Traumatic Stress Studies, the main professional organization in the trauma field. He and I have published a detailed description of the VIP treatment approach in "Group and Milieu Therapy of Veterans," pp. 391–413.

5. Many of our professional colleagues—whom we love and respect—disagree vociferously with us, because they accept the cultural model of the scientist-professional laid out in its classic analysis by the great mid-century sociologist Talcott Parsons (who was my senior tutor in college). Readers familiar with Parsons's work will recognize the influence of the "pattern variables" in my critique. Explanation of the value pattern of the professional and how it leads to failure with complex PTSD is given in Shay and Munroe, "Group and Milieu Therapy of Veterans," based on Parsons's *The Social System* (New York: Free Press, 1951). I agree that treatment of simple PTSD may not require any more trust than is required to receive treatment for a ruptured appendix. Reliance on credentials and institutional position suffices and personal trust isn't needed.

Functional specificity (division of labor among different occupational specialties) is deeply institutionalized in licensure, departmental organization of medical facilities, and career paths in the professions. For many combat veterans with complex PTSD, the careerism of officers and the career management systems of the military services (manifested then as six-month rotations in troop command positions) were the visible sources of their betrayals. Also, the division of labor is a key element in the processes that support state-authorized *atrocities and torture*. Veterans who had the misfortune of witnessing or participating in these were told, "none of your business" or "not my job" or "just do your job" if they raised objections. Many of those who crossed into the heart of darkness and executed those orders are now dead by their own hand. Herbert C. Kelman, "The Social Context of Torture," in *The Politics of Pain: Torturers and their Masters,* ed. Ronald D. Crelinsten and Alex P. Schmid (Boulder: Westview Press, 1994).

6. James F. Munroe, "Therapist Traumatization from Exposure to Patients with Combat-Related Post-Traumatic Stress Disorder: Implications for Administration and Supervision" (Ann Arbor, Michigan: Dissertation Abstracts).

7. My own vanity has laid seductive traps. I got into trouble a couple times after the publication of *Achilles in Vietnam* from no longer listening to the particularity of a veteran's experience, but rather I fit his words into schemes of my own invention. This is just as bad as fitting it into schemes read in textbooks.

8. Herman, *Trauma and Recovery,* Chapter 8.

9. For further details of our Stage One approach, see Shay and Munroe, "Group and Milieu Therapy of Veterans."
10. An educational pamphlet "On Medications for Combat PTSD" gives my philosophy and some specific experience on this subject. It is found on the Web at www.dr-bob.org/tips/ptsd.html.
11. F. Kirkland, R. R. Halverson, and P. D. Bliese, "Stress and Psychological Readiness in Post-Cold-War Operations," *Parameters* 26:79–91 (1996), p. 86.
12. Kirkland et al.'s prescriptions are explicitly and implicitly incorporated in the Army's current doctrine on combat stress control, *FM 22–51: Leader's Manual for Combat Stress Control,* about which more in Part Three.
13. A vast and unexplored subject is the ways that trauma generates the human experience of the holy. I hasten to add that "holy" does not automatically mean good, or beneficent—it is "daunting awfulness and majesty" and "something uniquely attractive and fascinating," according to Rudolf Otto's classic phenomenological exploration, *The Idea of the Holy,* trans. John W. Harvey (Oxford: Oxford University Press, 1923; 2nd ed., 1950). The sacred is—first and foremost—powerful.
14. As of May, 3, 2001: www.vietnamwall.org/news/namesadded.html.
15. Inscribing the names of all the soldier-citizen dead was first practiced by the Athenians in their *"demosion sema,* or National Cemetery, in the Kerameikos district" of the city. Tritle, *From Melos to My Lai,* p. 166. A photo of fragments of these "casualty lists" is on p. 167 of Professor Tritle's book.
16. From Lydia Fish e-mail to VWAR-L, October 28, 1995. Copyright © Joan Duffy Newberry, May 1987. By permission.
17. "Mental Cases," in *The Collected Poems of Wilfred Owen,* p. 69.
18. The comparison to Odysseus and his crew visiting the Underworld is inviting, but leads nowhere that I am able to see.
19. 11.170ff, Fagles.
20. M. R. Ancharoff, J. F. Munroe, and L. M. Fisher, "The Legacy of Combat Trauma: Clinical Implications of Intergenerational Transmission," in Yael Danieli, ed., *International Handbook of Multigenerational Legacies of Trauma* (New York: Plenum, 1998).
21. M. R. Harvey, "An Ecological View of Psychological Trauma and Trauma Recovery," *Journal of Traumatic Stress* 9:3–23 (1996). See also Shay and Munroe, "Group and Milieu Therapy for Veterans," pp. 391–413.
22. This should help justify the claim that considerations of social trust are human universals, and not purely an invention of the modern state or market economies. However, trust is dramatically more important in the modern setting than in small, face-to-face ("primitive") societies. Paper money and banking rest almost entirely on trust.
23. James Munroe prefers the term "basic trust" to "social trust." He also refers to what we foster in VIP as a family of reorigin where the veteran can relearn social trust. He is drawn to metaphors drawn from the family; I am drawn to metaphors from the *polis.* J. F. Munroe, J. Shay, C. Makary, M. Clopper, and M. Wattenberg, *Creating a Family of Re-Origin: A Long-Term Outpatient PTSD Unit,* training "institute" at the Fifth Annual Meeting of the Society for Traumatic Stress Studies, San Francisco, 1989.
24. Understanding and responding to these tests of trust is a huge subject beyond the scope of this chapter. It is, however, addressed in Shay and Munroe, "Group and Milieu Therapy for Veterans."
25. A key word in Aristotle's Rhetoric is *"pistis,"* to which scholars have given all sorts of tortured translations, e.g., "the available means of persuasion." However, in the everyday language of Aristotle's time, the word simply meant "trust." See Christopher

Carey, "Rhetorical Means of Persuasion," in Amélie Oksenberg Rorty, ed., *Essays on Aristotle's Rhetoric* (Berkeley: University of California Press, 1996), pp. 399–415. I have summarized the Rhetoric for military use as a text on leadership in the handout to a visiting lecture in ethics at the U.S. Naval Academy. This handout is available online at www.d-n-i.net/fcs/aristotle.htm.

26. I have pointed this out in my one small foray on the subject of Athenian tragic theater: "The Birth of Tragedy—Out of the Needs of Democracy."
27. Aristotle, *Rhetoric*, I.ii.3.
28. Copyright © Michael Viehman, by permission. See biographical sketch on pages 184–85.

18. Lew Puller Ain't on the Wall

1. "Lydia Fish Vita," *The Vietnam Veterans Oral History and Folklore Project,* online at faculty.buffalostate.edu/fishlm/folksongs/vita.htm.

VWAR-L was the subject of Richard R. Rohde, "Identity, Self, and Disorder Among Vietnam Veterans: PTSD and the Emergence of an Electronic Community," Ph.D. dissertation (Anthropology), University of Hawaii, 1995. On p. 253, Dr. Rohde says, "My central criticism of the medical model of PTSD is that it locates the source of the problem within the individual, with little or no emphasis on the social-relational aspects of PTSD." It should be evident to the reader that I heartily agree with this criticism as it applies to complex PTSD. I suspect that if we understood better how social recognition plays out in brain physiology, we would also see that he might be correct with regard to simple PTSD also.

2. I have pursued a two-stage permission process with the members of VWAR. In the first stage (mostly in 1997) I requested their permission to use the message at all. In the second, I sent them this complete chapter, so that they could see how I had edited their message and how I had contextualized it. In every case I received Stage One permission. No messages here are from members who *refused* Stage Two permission; their wishes are respected, of course. However, that leaves the members who gave Stage One permission, but whom I have been unable to reach. I have sent e-mail to their last known e-mail address in the VWAR directory, and called their last known telephone number from the same source. These few messages are identified only by their nickname or first name to protect their identities should they not wish to be associated with the words.

3. E-mail, December 21, 2001.
4. E-mail, December 8, 2001.
5. This information supplied by Tom Sykes at my request.
6. New York: Facts on File, 1985, pp. 144–45.
7. E-mail, December 11, 2001.
8. E-mail, December 10, 2001. My heart aches when I read this message.
9. E-mail, December 5, 2001.
10. Information provided by Jack Mallory at my request.
11. A Jarai ["Montagnard"] with whom the author fought against the NVA. Mike McCombs's tribute to Weet is found in the story "Blood Brother" in the superb collection on the Web at www.vietvet.org/namvet99.htm.
12. A few additional pieces can be found at www.vietvet.org/mcmike.htm.
13. About five years later a flame war (an angry exchange of e-mail, with or without insults) flared briefly when Palmer Hall posted "A Valentine's Card for Those Who Were Not There: Ode for the Really-Cares." After evoking the experience of privation, fear, and grief of combat, the poem ends with the following lines:

Four words are all that count:
(1) YOU
(2) WERE
(3) NOT
(4) THERE!
It doesn't matter
that you reallycare.

—Palmer

This brought an immediate and furiously obscene reply from a woman member who had been intensely connected to a veteran before, during, and after the Vietnam War. In a December 5, 2001, e-mail message to me, Palmer Hall called this poem "satire." He was exploring and gently criticizing the stay-the-fuck-away-from-me mentality of some combat veterans. (See page 194 for more by and about Palmer Hall.) A day after the "satire" was posted, it brought this quiet, more-in-sorrow response from Judee Strott:

"REALLYCARE" [excerpts]
by Judee Strott

They say that it hurt them deeply,
that nobody wanted to hear
of the horrors of war they went through
when they came home from Vietnam, that year. . . .

Well, there were many people who tried to help,
who just were pushed away,
many who have always cared
and will till their dying day.

It just doesn't seem to matter to some
that we were always here,
they only want to hurt us,
when they call us "ReallyCares."

It seems they're intent on making us feel
just like they felt back then—
wounded in spirit and an object of scorn
unwanted by countrymen. . . .

When the ReallyCares are gone my friends,
what will there be left?
VVets with the cynical mistrust they have,
alone again, bereft. . . .

14. Online: lists.village.virginia.edu/sixties/HTML_docs/Texts/Humor/Weptronics/wep_product.html.
15. E-mail, December 8, 2001.
16. E-mail, December 16, 2001.
17. Used by permission. Published previously in H. Palmer Hall, *From the Periphery: Poems and Essays* (San Antonio: Chili Verde Press, 1994).

18. E-mail, December 4, 2001. James Byrd, Jr., was an African-American who was murdered in Texas on June 7, 1998, by two white men who may or may not have cut his throat, but then chained him by the ankles to their pickup truck and dragged him to pieces while still alive. (Source: Roy Bragg, "Jasper Trial Defendant Says Byrd's Throat Was Cut," *San Antonio Express-News,* Friday, September 17, 1999.)

19. Some material in Part III originated in the *Commandant of the Marine Corps Trust Study,* which can be found on the Web at www.belisarius.com/modern_business_strategy/shay/cohesion.doc. For a detailed refutation of the belief that emotion and reason are in all ways antithetical, see Antonio R. Damasio, *Decartes' Error: Emotion, Reason, and the Human Brain* (New York: Grosset/Putnam, 1994). The philosophic controversy, dating back to Plato's time, has been taken up with great cogency and power by philosopher Martha Nussbaum in *The Fragility of Goodness.* The footprints of Professor Nussbaum's philosophizing are all over my own work. In my view she has nailed the emotion-reason controversy once and for all in *Upheavals of Thought.*

20. E-mail, December 13, 2001.

21. E-mail, December 12, 2001.

22. You would not believe the vehemence of the controversy that this subject has aroused. Veterans have reacted as though their personal honor hinges on the empirical question of whether the suicide rate among veterans is smaller, the same as, or greater than the rate among demographically matched civilians. John Tegtmeier has assembled a specialized bibliography of publications related to suicide and mortality from all causes of American Vietnam vets: www.vwip.org/articles/T/Tegtmeier-John_USVeteranPost-ServiceMortalityAndSuicidesBibliography.htm. Readers should be aware of the following, not included in Tegtmeier's bibliography: *Mortality of Vietnam Veterans—The Veteran Cohort Study 1997,* Australian Department of Veterans Affairs, 1997, on the Web at www.dva.gov.au/media/publicat/mortal1.htm; T. A. Bullman and H. K. Kang, "Posttraumatic Stress Disorder and the Risk of Traumatic Deaths Among Vietnam Veterans," *Journal of Nervous and Mental Disease* 182:604–10 (1994); and P. Arhaud, L. Weisaeth, L. Mehlum, and S. Larsenn, *The UNIFIL Study 1991–1992, Report: I. Results and Recommendations* (Oslo: HQ Defense Command Norway, Joint Medical Service, 1993). The definitive methodology applied in the Australian mortality study has never been tried in the United States. The Australian study found a cumulative mortality from all causes of the Australian Vietnam Veteran cohort as of December 31, 1994, to be 6.5 percent, including combat deaths. I share the widespread belief that there has been a very large number of suicides among Vietnam veterans. Michael Kelley, a vocal critic of this belief, estimates the cumulative mortality from all causes among American Vietnam theater vets to be 10.16 percent (Michael Kelley, "The Three Walls Behind the Wall: The Myth of Vietnam Veteran Suicide," www.vwam.com/vets/suicide.html). Kelley proclaimed the Australian study to be "perhaps the most important study of Vietnam veteran mortality to date." When it suits his rhetorical purpose, he cites and applies the Australian estimates. But apparently he is neither shocked nor curious that the cumulative mortality from all causes was 56 percent higher among American Vietnam Vets than among Australian Vietnam Vets, according to his own numbers. He sets up an estimate of "150,000 [American Vietnam vet] suicides" as a straw man to knock down and ridicule the whole idea that there was a significant "excess" of suicides. The most commonly heard guess, "as many [suicides] as there are [KIAs] on the Wall," is one I readily believe. This number would not be astonishing in the total 300,000 cumulative, all-causes cohort deaths by 1994 that Kelley uses, especially in light of being more than twice the Australian mortality. I believe that until the

definitive methodology used by the Australians is used in the United States, we simply will not know how many Vietnam vets have killed themselves.

23. My colleague Dr. James Munroe, whom we met in the last chapter, calls this the four Vs offered by communities of veterans: validation, venting, value, and views. "The loss and Restoration of Community: The Treatment of Severe War Trauma," *Journal of Personal and Interpersonal Loss* 1:393–409 (1996).

24. faculty.buffalostate.edu/fishlm/folksongs/nvrleave.htm.

25. Discussion list courtesies call for members to indicate in the "subject" line what the new subject is that's on their mind, rather than just hit the "reply" button with the old subject line and start writing about the new one.

26. The other members of the VIP team are well aware that the veterans are resourceful and have most likely gotten their home phone numbers anyway.

19. Introduction

1. F. D. Jones, "Psychiatric Lessons of War," in Jones et al., eds., *War Psychiatry* (a volume of the new *Textbook of Military Medicine*) (Washington: Office of the Surgeon General, Borden Institute, Walter Reed Army Institute of Research, 1995), p. 13. These graphs are extremely faint and require strong light and close inspection to see the two curves on each chart. Reuven Gal, *A Portrait of the Israeli Soldier* (Westport: Greenwood, 1986), p. 214.

2. I examine the reasons that trust is a combat strength multiplier in "Trust: Touchstone for a Practical Military Ethos," in Donald Vandergriff, ed., *Spirit, Blood, and Treasure: The American Cost of Battle in the 21st Century* (Novato, Calif.: Presidio, 2001). These reasons can be summarized into two headings: Trust reduces the impact of "external" or Clausewitzian "friction," and lubricates the "internal" or self-generated forms of friction analyzed by the late Colonel John R. Boyd, USAF, in his famous Observation-Orientation-Decision-Action formulation. For a comprehensive introduction to Boyd's thought, see his writings, commentaries, and links to published and forthcoming books on Boyd in www.belisarius.com.

3. The two traditional topics in military ethics, *jus ad bellum* (rightness in the aims and circumstances of war) and *jus in bello* (rightness in the conduct of war), are much in need of enhancement by a third, *jus in militaribus* (rightness in the policies and practices of military institutions), which interacts in numerous ways with the first two.

4. Possibly in response to the chorus of criticism, the Department of Defense has adopted for 2000 and 2001 images that do include service members. In 2002, however, the Department of Defense reverted to type. See www.d-n-i.net/fcs/comments/c443.htm#afd for images of the 1987–2002 Armed Forces Day posters

20. Preventing Psychological and Moral Injury in Military Service

1. This chapter is greatly indebted to and inspired by the late Faris R. Kirkland, Ph.D., a Korean War and Vietnam War combat officer, who in retirement from the U.S. Army made himself the leading historian of Army leadership doctrine and practice. As a senior social scientist at the Walter Reed Army Institute of Research, he played key roles in the field studies of COHORT (COHesion, Operational Readiness, Training) in the 1980s and was lead author on many of the reports of this effort. He was a generous mentor and teacher on military institutions and became a treasured friend and critic. His last completed work will appear posthumously as "Honor, Combat Ethics, and Military Culture" in T. E. Beam et al., eds. *Military Medical Ethics*, vol 1, in *Textbook of Military Medicine* (Washington: Office of the Surgeon General,

U.S. Department of the Army and Borden Institute, 2001), Chapter 6. In press. His friends, fellow reformers, co-workers, and admirers are working to bring to publication a small fraction of the innovative and valuable work he left unfinished when he died at the age of sixty-eight.

This chapter is a shortened version of a paper by the same title, which formed part of the *Commandant of the Marine Corps Trust Study, 2000,* and is available in its entirety on the Web at www.belisarius.com/author_index.htm.

2. E-mail, January 21 and 22, 2002. Dennis Spector writes further about himself: "I did nothing to be ashamed of in Vietnam and I was not going to be condemned by people who knew nothing about it and I had become against the war myself. So I buried everything deeply and got on with my life. The trauma eventually won. Ten years later, I had to be treated to understand and overcome it. When I read 'Odysseus in America' [in manuscript], I finally understood the universally unavoidable human call combat made on my psyche. Trust was broken, no matter what, and we have trouble ever again trusting and relaxing—our ready-to-fight level of awareness is always there. I have seen from the story told in your book, how so many of my characteristics and beliefs center around 'TRUST,' the search for 'TRUST,' the need for 'TRUST,' the refusal to live my life without 'TRUST,' and the violent reactions and hatred I develop for those who 'BREAK TRUST.'" Quoted by permission.

3. One fine officer, who is currently an important armored cavalry commander, recalled a joint exercise in which the company he commanded received a radio message from a Marine unit maneuvering "jointly" with his own. He passed the message around to his staff— Can anyone make this out? The language was surely English, but no one could decipher its meaning. Perhaps the Army and Marine generals were making jointness work, he said, but the troops and subordinate leaders who actually have to achieve a common purpose were not exercising together enough to understand each other's language.

4. I give a more comprehensive account of cohesion in my "deliverable" for the *Commandant of the Marine Corps Trust Study,* available on the Web at www. belisarius.com/author_index.htm. The heading here is taken from the title of Colonel William Darryl Henderson's book, *Cohesion, the Human Element in Combat: Leadership and Societal Influence in the Armies of the Soviet Union, the United States, North Vietnam, and Israel* (Washington: National Defense University Press, 1985). At the time of its writing, Colonel Henderson was at the U.S. Army Research Institute for Behavioral and Social Sciences.

5. Ardant DuPicq, *Battle Studies,* trans. J. N. Greely and R. C. Cotton, in *Roots of Strategy, Book 2, 3 Military Classics* (Harrisburg: Stackpole, 1987), p. 136.

6. Samuel Haber, *Efficiency and Uplift: Scientific Management in the Progressive Era, 1890–1920* (Chicago: University of Chicago Press, 1964), pp. 68–69. See Major Donald Vandergriff, *Path to Victory: America's Army and the Revolution in Human Affairs* (Novato, Calif.: Presidio Press, 2002).

7. Martin van Creveld, *Fighting Power: German and U.S. Army Performance, 1939–1945* (Westport: Greenwood Press, 1982), pp. 78–79. For a detailed and sophisticated comparison of U.S. and German performance in World War II, see Appendix E of Colonel Trevor N. Dupuy's *A Genius for War: The German Army and General Staff, 1807–1945* (McLean, Va.: Nova Publications, 1984).

8. Stephen E. Ambrose, *Citizen Soldiers: The U.S. Army from the Normandy Beaches to the Bulge to the Surrender of Germany, June 7,1944–May 7, 1945* (New York: Simon & Schuster, 1997), pp. 285–86.

9. Jones, "Psychiatric Lessons of War," pp. 13–14.

10. Personal communication.

11. Nora Kinzer Stewart, *Mates and Muchachos: Unit Cohesion in the Falklands/ Malvinas War* (Washington: Brassey's [U.S.], 1991), Chapter 2.
12. Albert J. Glass, *Neuropsychiatry in World War II*, vol. 2 (Washington: Surgeon General of the U.S. Army, 1973), p. 995.
13. See Jones, "Psychiatric Lessons of War," and Reuven Gal and Franklin D. Jones, "A Psychological Model of Combat Stress," in Jones et al., eds., *War Psychiatry*, pp. 133–48; Reuven Gal, *A Portrait of the Israeli Soldier* (Westport: Greenwood, 1986).
14. William Ian Miller, *The Mystery of Courage* (Cambridge, Mass.: Harvard University Press, 2000), reached me too recently for me to do more than scan the table of contents. I hope to turn my parts of the *Commandant of the Marine Corps Trust Study* into a short book, and shall have a chance to digest it then.
15. Steven Pressfield, *Gates of Fire* (New York: Doubleday, 1998), p. 380. A real Spartan Dienikes (or Dionikes) is mentioned in ancient stories as having fallen at Thermopylae.
16. First Friday Defense Lunch, March 1, 2002. Quoted by permission.
17. For a detailed refutation of the belief that emotion and reason are in all ways antithetical, see Damasio, *Decartes' Error*.
18. "Cohesion," *Commandant of the Marine Corps Trust Study*, p. E 5.
19. *When leadership is good,* otherwise the cohesion may turn the group's motivation and attitude against the chain of command. Cohesion and esprit de corps are related, but different, phenomena, the former being a purely face-to-face phenomenon, the latter being possible between people who have never met. See my "Cohesion" paper for the *Commandant of the Marine Corps Trust Study* for more extended discussion and references to the social science literature online at www.belisarius.com/author_index.htm.
20. 1 John 4:18 (KJV).
21. Elite formations tend to be firm believers in the "right stuff" theory. They tend to overlook the fact that elite formations get the right resources—of stability, competent leadership, and prolonged, cumulative, realistic (state-dependent) training. My personal fire-in-the-belly mission is to see these good resources provided to *every* combat arms and direct combat support service member in *all* parts of the U.S. armed services.
22. Gerald F. Linderman, *The World Within War: America's Combat Experience in World War II* (New York: Free Press, 1997), p. 45, emphasis added.
23. Henderson "was there" and fought and suffered, and earned the right to speak about winning or losing that war. Henderson speaks in his Preface of "the U.S. loss in Vietnam." And yet, with some reason, many American Vietnam vets say we "won every battle." See *Achilles in Vietnam*, p. 7ff, for a veteran becoming enraged with me for referring to the Vietnam War as a defeat.
24. Retired marine H. John Poole has just brought out an enormously illuminating and valuable book that addresses this very question, *Phantom Soldier: The Enemy's Answer to U.S. Firepower* (Emerald Isle, N.C.: Posterity Press, 2001).
25. The classic discussion of this paradoxical dynamic is Edward Luttwak's *Strategy: The Logic of War and Peace* (Cambridge, Mass.: Harvard University Press, 1987).
26. Van Creveld, *Fighting Power*, p. 95.
27. I am using the acronym COHORT to stand for the whole range of Army policies and practices aimed at stabilizing soldiers in their units. Sometimes these were called the "New Manning System," sometimes the "Unit Manning System," sometimes "OSUT" (One Station Unit Training), and sometimes COHORT. Each different name applied to a slightly different set of policies and practices, but all with the same overall objective.

28. Explaining *why* the services do things this way is far beyond the scope of this book, but is thoroughly covered in Major Donald Vandergriff's magisterial history of the American military personnel system, *Path to Victory*.

29. Faris R. Kirkland et al., *Unit Manning System Field Evaluation: Technical Report No. 5* (Washington: Walter Reed Army Institute of Research, September 1987), p. 24.

30. The 11th ACR is now the dreaded OPFOR (Opposing Force) at the National Training Center at Fort Irwin.

31. A retired U.S. Army lieutenant colonel.

32. John C. F. Tillson and Steven L. Canby, *Alternative Approaches to Organizing, Training, and Assessing Army and Marine Corps Units, Part I: The Active Component*. Report C-MDA 909 89 C 0003/T-L6-1057 for the Assistant Secretary of Defense (Force Management and Personnel) (Alexandria: Institute for Defense Analysis, November 1992), p. III-8.

33. Former Army Chief of Staff General Edward "Shy" Meyer, at First Friday Defense Lunch, May 7, 1999. Other guests at First Friday Defense Lunch from the Army's reform era have been Lieutenant General Bob Elton, Lieutenant General Dick Trefry, and General Donn Starry. The leading spirit of the reforms, General Max Thurman, is no longer living. Faris Kirkland was working on a biography of Thurman at the time of his death, and faithfully attended First Friday until he was no longer physically able.

34. The Army's ferocious unwillingness to report any unit as unready is curiously not shared by the Navy, which unblinkingly "reports ships as unready when they return from an overseas deployment and large numbers of sailors are reassigned." HQ U.S. Army Training and Doctrine Command, *Assessment of the Unit Manning System,* Fort Monroe, Va., March 1981, p. 1. Quoted in Tillson and Canby, *Alternative Approaches,* p. A-3. Confirmed as still true by Captain Michael Dunaway, USN, at First Friday Defense Lunch, May 7, 1999.

    The current Status of Resources and Training System (SORTS) and the unit's condition rating (C-rating), the basic documents used by management to assess the readiness of units and thus the performance of their leaders, continue to be mainly matters of counting equipment, counting bodies ("fill") and credentials, but blind to the stability, cohesion, and collective proficiency of the unit. Richard K. Betts, *Military Readiness: Concepts, Choices, Consequences* (Washington: Brookings Institution, 1995), pp. 136–39.

35. As of 1992, when Tillson and Canby did their study, "company-sized units in the Army face turbulence of 8 to 10% per month for enlisted men, 6 to 10% for NCOs and 10% for officers. This means that the average unit changes over 100% of its personnel each year and must commence its training cycle on an annual basis." Tillson and Canby describe the impact of the individual replacement system:

    The [individual replacement] system has a devastating impact on Army units in wartime. The wartime system treated soldiers as anonymous spare parts from the day they arrived in their replacement training centers, through their training and deployment to a combat theater, to their assignment to a unit on the line (often in contact with the enemy), during their treatment by the medical system once they became a casualty, and in reassigning them to a different unit when they returned to the combat theater.

    These concepts have been at the heart of Army planning since World War I . . . the time when large-scale casualties caused by attrition warfare and the novelty of the assembly line exercised a heavy influence on planners. In this system, men became spare parts to be produced on an assembly line. Once trained, they were to be inserted in combat units as needed. But assignment to a unit did not mean that the soldier would have the time to learn about that unit or that the unit would have the time to build its collective skills. . . . This system and the unanticipated demands of the war conspired to produce units of semi-trained individuals barely adequate to conduct the relatively simple tactics called for in that war. . . .

The replacement system designed for WWII was built on the principles developed for WWI. Once again soldiers were considered interchangeable spare parts and replacements became a class of supply to be managed in the same way as any other class of supply. General Marshall believed that the success of the American Army in World War II lay in its ability to keep divisions "up to strength daily by trained men from the replacement pool." It was this concept that led to the fundamental organizational and operational decisions that still dominate today.

Tillson and Canby,
Alternative Approaches, pp. III-17, III-9f.

36. A book with great, but to my knowledge unrecognized, relevance to the profession of arms is *The Logic of Practice*, by French anthropologist Pierre Bourdieu, trans. R. Nice (Stanford: Stanford University Press, 1980).
37. Tillson and Canby, *Alternative Approaches*, p. III-8.
38. Gal, *A Portrait of the Israeli Soldier*, p. 217.
39. Ibid.
40. The Reichsheer (German army), which had a total strength of about 400,000 in the spring of 1919, was reduced to 100,000 by March 1920. We must weep that the German army got *better* during the Weimar Republic, through its concentration on the human dimension of military organizations—cohesion, leadership, training— even though the Versailles Treaty forbade virtually every aspect of technological modernization. Dupuy, *A Genius for War*, pp. 192–93.
41. Charles E. Heller and William A. Stofft, *America's First Battles: 1776–1965* (Lawrence: University Press of Kansas, 1986). According to historian John Shy, the defeats were Long Island (Revolutionary War), Queenston Heights (War of 1812), Bull Run (American Civil War), Kasserine Pass (World War II—European theater), and Osan/Naktong (Korean War). The unnecessarily costly victories were San Juan (Spanish-American War), Cantigny (World War I), Buna (World War II—Pacific theater, but Bataan maybe should count here), and Ia Drang (Vietnam War—against the NVA).
42. *Human, All Too Human*, trans. R. J. Hollingdale (Cambridge: Cambridge University Press, 1986), p. 163.
43. An Army lieutenant general recently pointed out to me that Army Special Forces is in many respects a traditional regiment, referring to its unit stability, its esprit, and its training rigor.
44. Bruce I. Gudmundsson, "The German Army in World War I: The Contingents," *Tactical Notebook*, November 1991. He writes:

The final service rendered to the German nation by the system of regional recruiting was, ironically, to help ensure a quiet demobilization. When, in November of 1918, the regiments of the German Army marched home, they marched, in good order, to their local barracks. There the regiments were demobilized and the soldiers freed to walk the few miles that separated them from their homes.

Units that lacked a regional character, however, resisted demobilization. Men of the Assault Battalions, the Guard Divisions, or the Marine units formed by sailors who had volunteered for duty at the front, faced the hard choice between returning home to the loved ones of half-forgotten pre-war lives or remaining with the "families" that had sustained them in hard months and years of combat. Many opted for the latter, forming the hard nucleus of the Freikorps.

These latter units had an ethos that was essentially different from that of regionally based units. The latter, however misinformed they might have been about the relationship to Germany's aims in the First World War to the defense of their loved ones, were clearly fighting for hearth and home. The Freikorps, however, developed a nihilistic ethos that celebrated violence for its own sake. One of the symptoms of this was the resurrection of the cult of the Landesknechte, the 16th and 17th century German freebooters who ravaged Europe in search of booty and adventure. (By permission of the author.)

45. Waller's chapter "Objectives and Principles of a Veterans' Program," *The Veteran Comes Back*, pp. 259–83, pulls no punches and has never been surpassed as a picture of what's needed.

46. New York: Simon & Schuster, 1995.

47. There are ominous signs of "dumbing down" and hemorrhaging from our combat training centers. See Mark Lewis, "Lewis Report: Why Stopping the Exodus of Junior Officers Is Important, September 7, 2001," www.d-n-i.net/FCS_Folder/comments/c426.htm. Mark Lewis is currently an analyst at the Institute for Defense Analyses, a federally funded research and development center for the office of the Secretary of Defense.

48. Colonel John D. Rosenberger, "Reaching Our Army's Full Combat Potential in the 21st Century," *Landpower Essay Series* No. 99–2, February 1999, p. 1.

49. Evidence for these assertions can be found in my paper for the *Commandant of the Marine Corps Trust Study*, online at www.belisarius.com/modern_business_strategy/shay/shay_prevent_psy_injury.htm. Many important points, such as what "toughness" in training is, and why it is ethically required, are covered there, and are beyond the scope of this book.

50. General Charles C. Krulak, "The Strategic Corporal: Leadership in the Three Block War," *Marine Corps Gazette* 83:18–22 (January 1999).

51. Tillson and Canby, *Alternative Approaches*, p. III-4, quoting Thomas C. Thayer, ed., *A Systems Analysis View of the Vietnam War, 1965–1972*, vol. 8, *Casualties and Losses*, Office of the Assistant Secretary of Defense for Program Analysis and Evaluation, Defense Technical Information Center, 1975, DTIC #ADA051613, p. 225.

52. Gal and Jones, "A Psychological Model of Combat Stress."

53. This cluster of leadership practices has been called various things at various times and places: *Auftragstaktik*, "Positive Leadership," "Power Down," empowerment, decentralization, and others.

Both the benefits from these practices and the catastrophic consequences of the familiar rule-by-fear and manage-in-detail-from-the-top alternatives are lucidly documented in Faris Kirkland's publications in professional military journals and textbooks, a partial selection of which can be found in the Bibliography.

54. Quoted uncut above on page 157. This time I use Garver's translation.

55. U. F. Zwygart, "How Much Obedience Does an Officer Need?," U.S. Army Command and General Staff College pamphlet, 1993.

56. I have explored the role of trust in lubricating both the external (Clausewitzian) and internal (self-generated) sources of friction in military operations in "Trust."

57. See for example Major Donald Vandergriff, "truth@readiness.mil," *Proceedings of the U.S. Naval Institute*, June 1999.

58. *Broadside* by Jeff Davis, *Navy Times Almanac*, 1998.

59. To return to the matter of leadership responsibility in atrocities, Colonel Bernard's judgment on the Kerrey affair is that employment of the SEAL team in the Mekong Delta's densely populated area was wrongheaded from the start, and that the blame lies with the ignorance, negligence, and arrogance of the higher-ups who ordered these young Americans into morally impossible situations. The difference between an accident in the dark and a tragic us-or-them decision is thus a difference without a moral or legal distinction.

60. Current U.S. Marine Corps doctrine, Marine Corps Doctrinal Publication No. 6— *Command and Control*, places great and explicit emphasis on trust. For excerpts from this doctrinal publication see my piece "Preventing Psychological and Moral Injury in Military Service" from the *Commandant of the Marine Corps Trust Study*, available online at www.belisarius.com/author_index.htm. Also found in the same piece is a discussion that relates the work of comparative economic historian Francis Fukuyama (*Trust: The Social Virtues and the Creation of Prosperity* [New York: Free Press, 1995]) on trust in the civilian economy to the analysis of internal or self-generated "friction" in military operations.

61. "Military Leadership into the 21st Century: Another 'Bridge Too Far'?" *Parameters* 28:4–26 (Spring 1998).

62. Readers who are hungry for information on our military institutions that is of high quality, trustworthy, nonpartisan, nonideological, and economically untainted by military contracting money should start by immersing themselves in the Web site *Defense and the National Interest*, www.d-n-i.net, edited by Chet and Ginger Richards. It carries Franklin C. Spinney's famous "blasters" (e-mail circular letters), both current and archived.

21. Odysseus As a Military Leader

1. Very rarely is his *mētis* simply "good counsel"—good practical advice without legerdemain, without any "wow, how did he ever think of that!" The semantic range of *mētis* eventually extends to simply being expert at something, such as wood chopping, fishing, sailing, chariot driving. Not being a classical philologist myself, I must rely on secondary sources. The impression I gain from the main work on the subject, Marcel Detienne and Jean-Pierre Vernant's *Cunning Intelligence in Greek Culture and Society*, trans. Janet Lloyd (Chicago: University of Chicago Press, 1991), is that the marker that indicates the border between everyday skill and *mētis* is the "wow!" response evoked in the witness. "Such an astonishing sight leaves the spectator dumbfounded and makes him feel dizzy," p. 303.

2. Chester W. Richards, *A Swift, Elusive Sword. What if Sun Tzu and John Boyd Did a National Defense Review?*, Center for Defense Information, 2001, p. 15, quoting the Cleary translation. Richards's short, clear, and illuminating book is available on the Web in its entirety at www.cdi.org/mrp/swift_elusive_sword.pdf. Within Chinese culture many of the same struggles erupted over the value and dangers of *mētis*, cunning intelligence, as were fought out in the Greek world. Scholar Lisa Raphals has given a fascinating account of these parallels in *Knowing Words: Wisdom and Cunning in the Classical Traditions of China and Greece* (Ithaca: Cornell University Press, 1992).

3. Scholars, with some justice, will object that the whole hyperindividualistic culture of epic Greek heroism placed the acquisition of the tokens and emblems of personal prowess far above the common good. Their enormous economic value made a major if subsidiary contribution to the *kleos*-is-everything mentality of the epic hero. (*Kleos* means "fame.") However, as the contrast with Achilles shows, other-regarding motivation was available even in this epic world.

4. In keeping with "dual motivation," Athena is equally credited with the ruse. Epios is mentioned as the actual builder of the wooden Horse.

The Greeks overcame defeat in *two* forms. One was catastrophic failure of the amphibious expedition, leading to its destruction, as visualized in *Iliad* 10. This was *almost* turned into victory by Patroclus' surprise attack on the Trojans' flank with the fresh troops that Achilles had released to him. The other was the kind of defeat suffered by the English in the American colonies, or the Americans in Vietnam—realizing they could not win, they gave up and went home. The trick of the Horse turned stalemate, which would have resulted in the second sort of defeat, into victory for the Greeks.

5. Virgil [Publius Virgilius Maro], *Aeneid,* Book 2, line 258, trans. Robert Fitzgerald (New York: Vintage, 1981). Line numbering is to the translation. Emphasis added.

6. The classic treatment of the psychology of the leaders and bureaucrats of the side that is successfully surprised by its enemy is Richard K. Betts, *Surprise Attack* (Washington: Brookings Institution, 1982).

7. *Little Iliad* 1, in Hesiod, *The Homeric Hymns and Homerica,* trans. H. G. Evelyn-White (Cambridge, Mass.: Harvard University Press Loeb Library, 1914), p. 511.

8. Ithaca: Cornell University Press, 1991.

9. James J. Wirtz, *The Tet Offensive: Intelligence Failure in War* (Ithaca: Cornell University Press, 1991), p. 133.

10. Both instances of Trojan deception somehow involve Paris, first in *Iliad* 3, where he slips away from the single combat with Menelaus, designed to end the war in a political settlement, and second when the Trojan Pandarus, a political ally of Paris, is egged on by Athena to break the truce. He shoots an arrow at Menelaus from a hidden position in *Iliad* 4. The Greeks also make two deceptions in the *Iliad:* first was the defensive surprise sprung by the Greeks in *Iliad* 7, when they threw up a rampart on top of the funerary mound of those killed in the battle after the truce was broken in *Iliad* 4. This was Nestor's idea. The second was the offensive surprise (also Nestor's idea) achieved by Patroclus, disguised in Achilles' armor, when he and the Myrmidons took the Trojans on the flank.

11. Nagy, *The Best of the Achaeans,* pp. 47, 145. Homer pays great attention to Odysseus in the *Iliad,* who is often called "equal to Zeus in artifice." Achilles, a guileless embodiment of the straightforward fighter, is repeatedly contrasted to Odysseus, who is called "master of stratagems" (*Iliad* 3:321, Fitzgerald). On the battlefield the Trojan Skôdos addresses him, "Odysseus, great in all men's eyes, unwearied master of guile . . ." (*Iliad* 11:490f, Fitzgerald). His divine patron and inspiration, Athena, is daughter by Zeus of Mētis, the Olympian personification of *mētis* (Hesiod, *Theogony* 886, p. 511).

12. Thucydides III.82–83. See Martha Nussbaum, *The Fragility of Goodness,* pp. 404, 507n24.

13. Hesk translation. Hesk, *Deception and Democracy in Classical Athens,* p. 26. Hesk further demonstrates that the Athenian Hoplite ideology scorned military deception as a sign of fear or cowardice. See his section "Honest Hoplites and Tricky Spartans," pp. 23–40.

14. Rhesus 510–11; Hesk, *Deception and Democracy in Classical Athens,* p. 113n. Hesk expands this theme in his section "Deceit, Fear and Hoplite Courage," pp. 107–22.

15. While the troops were certainly undisciplined, the current ethos of the American officer corps finds the commander culpable when his troops run riot, unless he has demonstrated every reasonable effort to prevent such loss of control and to restore order in his command, once it has broken down.

16. Parts of this discussion are taken from *The Secretary of the Navy's Guest Lecture,*

"Achilles, Odysseus, Agamemnon: Homer on Military Leadership," Pentagon, Naval Command Center Auditorium, February 23, 2000. Available in its entirety on the Web at www.belisarius.com/author_index.htm with the handouts distributed at the talk.

17. Homer shows Agamemnon's courage by having him *pray* to be chosen by lot to duel with Hector in *Iliad* 7 and gives him center stage in the big battle in Book 11.

18. The story of Achilles' invulnerability, except for his heel, was either unknown to Homer or suppressed by him as out of keeping with his picture of Achilles' heroism, which *requires* that he be mortal and vulnerable, that is, human.

19. See Richard P. Martin, *The Language of Heroes: Speech and Performance in the Iliad* (Ithaca: Cornell University Press, 1989), pp. 146–205, "The Language of Achilles."

20. See Shay, "Achilles: Paragon, Flawed Character, or Tragic Soldier Figure?," for a discussion of the purely military background of the conflict between Achilles and Agamemnon.

21. In response to this dishonor, Achilles pulled himself and his troops, the Myrmidons, out of the war. As the independent leader of a national contingent, Achilles was free to withdraw. No one could arrest Achilles for desertion, any more than Westmoreland could have arrested the head of the Australian contingent in Vietnam.

22. Erwin Cook, "Agamemnon's Test of the Army in *Iliad* Book 2 and the Function of Homeric Akhos," *American Journal of Philology,* in press, notes these same two betrayals of the army's moral order, and their probable destruction of the army's morale, but credits Agamemnon with recognizing the impact of his own actions, and with ultimately restoring the army's loyalty and morale by his "paradoxical" test.

23. American military assignment officers insist that this is exactly what they do. However, many constraining concepts, practices, and policies make this illusory.

22. Conclusion

1. Stanford, *Enemies of Poetry,* p. 5.

2. See Gregory Nagy, *Greek Mythology and Poetics* (Ithaca: Cornell University Press, 1990), p. 13, giving Herakles as the early Greek pattern of the hero who both suffers and causes great pain; and see Cook, *The Odyssey in Athens,* pp. 29–32.

3. Otto, *The Idea of the Holy.*

4. Fukuyama, *The End of History and the Last Man.* Fukuyama coins the word "megalothymia" for this inflammation and aggrandizement of the *thumos.*

5. There has been a burst of scholarship in this area, for example, *Understanding the Political Spirit,* ed. Zuckert; McGlew, *Tyranny and Political Culture in Ancient Greece; Dēmokratia,* ed. Ober and Hedrick; Koziak, *Retrieving Political Emotion;* Nussbaum, *Upheavals of Thought.* Inquiry into equal political respect is woven throughout Nussbaum's large book.

6. Pp.7–32.

7. I hope it is clear from Part II that I do not believe this is all that is required for recovery, but some form of the circle of communalization of trauma seems to be essential to the second stage of recovery.

8. Homer's contemporary Hesiod speaks of the Muses in his work on the history of the gods, *Theogony.* He describes therapy of suffering by these goddesses of the arts in terms of forgetting, which I do not endorse:

> Happy is the man
> Whom the Muses love. Sweet flows the voice from his mouth.
> For if anyone is grieved, if his heart is sore

> With fresh sorrow, if he is troubled, and a singer
> Who serves the Muses chants . . .
> He soon forgets his heartache, and of all his cares
> He remembers none: the goddesses' gifts turn them aside.
>> Hesiod, *Theogony,* lines 96ff, in Hesiod,
>> *Works and Days and Theogony,*
>> trans. Stanley Lombardo
>> (Indianapolis: Hackett, 1993), p. 63f.

9. I have no desire to get tangled up in legalistic "what ifs" that would be raised by any governmental participation in such rites of purification. What I have in mind has nothing to do with "impunity" or "immunity" or "amnesty" for military crimes that should be prosecuted. A secular variant should be available for those who have no religion or have left the one they were born into, as many of my patients have done.

10. Our brain *is* expensive to feed. It is only 2 percent of our body weight but burns 20 percent of our calories. In an evolutionary perspective, that is a tip-off that something very special is going on. To invest the effort and take the risks for food to feed this hungry brain, it has got to be worth it or natural selection would not have grown it. What makes it worth the cost and the risk is precisely that it is a social and cultural brain. The communicative powers of language and symbol and the capacity to internalize the moral codes of a society provide the adaptive advantage that makes the human brain worth its keep.

11. I give a much more extensive treatment of this subject in "Killing Rage: *Physis* or *Nomos*—Or Both?," in *War and Violence in Ancient Greece,* ed. Hans van Wees (London: Duckworth and the Classical Press of Wales, 2000). Available online at www.belisarius.com/author_index.htm. That chapter explains a resolution to the controversy over how military self-sacrificial altruism that benefits nonkin could have evolved, based on the theoretical breakthrough of E. Sober and D. S. Wilson, *Unto Others: The Evolution and Psychology of Unselfish Behavior* (Cambridge, Mass.: Harvard University Press, 1998).

    Our physical brain size exploded by 50 percent with lightning rapidity a short time ago in evolutionary time. This began roughly 250,000 years ago and was completed by the beginning of the Upper Paleolithic, about fifty thousand to seventy thousand years ago, when highly specialized and artistically flaked flint tool kits, as well as the first bone and antler tools, appeared. Unlike their stereotyped predecessors, these tool kits varied dramatically from place to place, often within only fifty miles, and they became unfrozen in time. Astonishing prehistoric cave art was first created then; and for the first time the dead were buried with grave goods and we find the first evidence of clothing. In short, *culture* had appeared, probably with full human language. Our modern brain had *coevolved* with it. See Richard Leakey, *The Origin of Humankind* (New York: Basic, 1994), p. 125f. A useful time line is found in the frontispiece to his book. Also useful are the charts on p. 136, summarizing the differing chronologies coming out of the different methods that various scientific disciplines use to measure and mark periods. Robin Dunbar, *Grooming, Gossip, and the Evolution of Language* (Cambridge, Mass.: Harvard University Press, 1996), gives somewhat different brain volumes and dates. It is important to recognize how sparse the fossil record is for most of the periods we find interesting, and also to recognize that cranial volume, even if perfectly measurable from a few skull fragments, tells us nothing about the evolution of the microscopic architecture of the brain, particularly in critical structures such as the hippocampus that make up only a tiny fraction of total brain volume.

12. Leda Cosmides and John Tooby, "Cognitive Adaptations for Social Exchange," in

The Adapted Mind: Evolutionary Psychology and the Generation of Culture, ed. J. H. Barkow, L. Cosmides, and J. Tooby (New York: Oxford University Press, 1992), pp. 163–228.

13. The connection between human brain size and the long period of post-natal help-lessness apparently lies in the design constraints of the female pelvis. To give passage to a baby with a fully developed brain at birth would require an unworkably large pelvis. The evolutionary compromise was to push birth earlier in the developmental process, and allow the brain to mature in prolonged—and dangerously dependant—post-natal development.

14. Martha Nussbaum's new and major philosophic work, *Upheavals of Thought,* makes interesting and extensive use of child psychoanalysts, such as the still wise and fresh D. H. Winnicott. However, the psychoanalytic movement essentially followed Freud in adopting the Platonic, Stoic, and Kantian position that once good character was formed by good birth and good breeding, no bad thing in adulthood could shake it. The climactic chapter of Nussbaum's *The Fragility of Goodness,* "The Betrayal of Convention: A Reading of Euripides' Hecuba," made exactly the point that bad-enough experience *in adulthood* can wreck even the noblest character. Unfortunately this is never mentioned in *Upheavals of Thought,* and a reader could readily come away from the book with the Platonic/Stoic/Kantian no-bad-thing-can-harm-adult-good-character idea unchallenged.

15. Fukuyama, *The End of History and the Last Man,* especially Part Three and Chapter 26. Immanuel Kant's important essays "To Perpetual Peace: A Philosophical Sketch" and "Idea for a Universal History with a Cosmopolitan Intent" have been collected with other essays in *Perpetual Peace and Other Essays.*

16. Amsterdam: Gieben, 1992.

17. William Julius Wilson, *When Work Disappears: The World of the New Urban Poor* (New York: Alfred A. Knopf, 1996).

18. *Harvard Magazine,* September–October 1998.

19. Found in detail in Jane Goodall, *The Chimpanzees of Gombe: Patterns of Behavior* (Cambridge, Mass.: Harvard University Press, 1986), pp. 488–534, particularly pp. 503–14.

20. As Fukuyama and others have pointed out, the modern attempts to carry out Kant's program never followed his advice. While tipping their hats to Kant's prestige, both the League of Nations and the United Nations extended the principle of sovereign honor to all nations that met the least-common-denominator criteria for state-hood—regardless of how they stood internally with their inhabitants.

   History gives us no warrant to think there is something inherently peaceful about democracies per se. Ancient Athenian democracy was a dismal example: Athens's foreign policy reminded its enemies and even Athenians themselves of tyranny. Athens's most famous leaders, Pericles and Cleon, freely admitted that Athens was a tyrant to its neighbors. It is a humbling caution to notice how many nations in history have overthrown internal tyrannies only to play tyrant to their neighbors.

21. And when such nonstate actors have the resources to buy out failed states and turn them into wholly owned subsidiaries, as al-Qaeda did with Afghanistan. We have learned at a bitter price that failed states anywhere in the world cannot safely be treated as a matter of indifference.

Appendix I. A Pocket Guide to Homer's *Odyssey*

1. Any defects in this film synopsis presentation of the *Odyssey* belong entirely to me. Whatever strengths it has are owed to Stephen V. Tracy's *The Story of the Odyssey* (Princeton: Princeton University Press, 1990).

Appendix II. Information Resources
for Vietnam Veterans and Their Families

1. I have no financial relationship of any kind with Patience Mason or Patience Press.

Appendix III. Some Proposals

1. Personal communication.
2. Handout from *Secretary of the Navy's Guest Lecture,* "Achilles, Odysseus, Agamemnon: Homer on Military Leadership." Thanks to John Tillson of the Institute for Defense Analyses. A number of these points are documented in his IDA Document D-2290, "Reducing the Impact of Tempo," October 30, 1999.
3. Novato, Calif.: Presidio Press, 2002.
4. Excerpted from handout for J. Shay, "Causing Change," RAND Seminar Series, *Military Personnel Policy,* commissioned by VADM Pat Tracey, USN, Deputy Assistant Secretary of Defense for Military Personnel Policy, November 30, 1999.

BIBLIOGRAPHY

Ahl, Frederick, and Hanna Roisman. *The Odyssey Re-Formed*. Ithaca: Cornell University Press, 1996.

Ambrose, Stephen E. *Citizen Soldiers: The U.S. Army from the Normandy Beaches to the Bulge to the Surrender of Germany, June 7, 1944–May 7, 1945*. New York: Simon & Schuster, 1997.

American Psychiatric Association. *Diagnostic and Statistical Manual of Mental Disorders*. 4th ed. (DSM-IV). Washington: American Psychiatric Association Press, 1994.

Ancharoff, Michelle R., James F. Munroe, and Lisa M. Fisher. "The Legacy of Combat Trauma: Clinical Implications of Intergenerational Transmission." In Yael Danieli, ed., *International Handbook of Multigenerational Legacies of Trauma*. New York: Plenum, 1998.

Arhaug, P., L. Weisaeth, L. Mehlum, and S. Larsen. *The UNIFIL Study 1991–1992, Report: I. Results and Recommendations*. Oslo: HQ Defense Command Norway, Joint Medical Service, 1993.

Aristotle. *Nicomachean Ethics*. Trans. Terence Irwin. Indianapolis: Hackett, 1985.

———. *On Rhetoric*. Trans. George A. Kennedy. Oxford: Oxford University Press, 1991.

Athens, Lonnie H. *The Creation of Dangerous Violent Criminals*. Urbana: University of Illinois Press, 1992.

Australian Department of Veterans Affairs. *Mortality of Vietnam Veterans—The Veteran Cohort Study 1997*. Online: www.dva.gov.au/media/publicat/mortal1.htm.

Beam, T. E., A. E. Hartle, E. D. Pellegrino, and L. R. Sparacino, eds. *Military Medical Ethics*, vol. 1. In *Textbook of Military Medicine*. Washington: Office of the Surgeon General, U.S. Department of the Army and Borden Institute, 2002. In press.

Bellamy, Ronald F., and Russ Zajtchuk, eds. *Conventional Warfare: Ballistic, Blast, and Burn Injuries*. This volume is Surgeon General of the U.S. Army, *Textbook of Military Medicine*, part I, vol. 5. Washington: Walter Reed Army Medical Center, 1990.

Betts, Richard K. *Military Readiness: Concepts, Choices, Consequences*. Washington: Brookings Institution, 1995.

———. *Surprise Attack*. Washington: Brookings Institution, 1982.

Bourdieu, Pierre. *The Logic of Practice*. Trans. R. Nice. Stanford: Stanford University Press, 1980.

Bremner, J. Douglas, Steven M. Southwick, and Dennis S. Charney. "The Neurobiology of Posttraumatic Stress Disorder: An Integration of Animal and Human Research." In Philip A. Saigh and J. Douglas Bremner, eds. *Posttraumatic Stress Disorder: A Comprehensive Text*. Boston: Allyn and Bacon, 1999.

Bullman, T. A., and H. K. Kang. "Posttraumatic Stress Disorder and the Risk of Traumatic Deaths Among Vietnam Veterans." *Journal of Nervous and Mental Disease* 182:604–10 (1994).

Carey, Christopher. "Rhetorical Means of Persuasion." In Amélie Oksenberg Rorty, ed. *Essays on Aristotle's Rhetoric.* Berkeley: University of California Press, 1996.

Chandler, Alfred D. *The Visible Hand: The Managerial Revolution in American Business.* Cambridge: Harvard University Press, 1977.

Clarke, Howard W. *The Art of the Odyssey.* Wauconda: Bolchazy-Carducci, 1989.

———. *Homer's Readers: A Historical Introduction to the* Iliad *and the* Odyssey. London and Toronto: Associated University Presses, 1981.

Clay, Jenny Strauss. *The Wrath of Athena: Gods and Men in the Odyssey.* Princeton: Princeton University Press, 1983.

Connor, W. R. "Civil Society, Dionysiac Festival, and the Athenian Democracy." In J. Ober and C. Hedrick. *Dēmokratia: A Conversation on Democracies, Ancient and Modern.* Princeton: Princeton University Press, 1996.

Constant, Benjamin. *Political Writings.* Trans. and ed., B. Fontana. Cambridge: Cambridge University Press, 1988.

Cook, Erwin F. "'Active' and 'Passive' Heroics in the Odyssey." *Classical World* 93(2):149–67 (1999).

———. *The Odyssey in Athens: Myths of Cultural Origin.* Ithaca: Cornell University Press, 1995.

Cosmides, Leda, and John Tooby. "Cognitive Adaptations for Social Exchange." In *The Adapted Mind: Evolutionary Psychology and the Generation of Culture.* Jerome H. Barkow, Leda Cosmides, and John Tooby, eds. New York: Oxford University Press, 1992.

Crelinsten, Ronald D., and Alex P. Schmid, eds. *The Politics of Pain: Torturers and Their Masters.* Boulder: Westview Press, 1994.

Croker, L. P. *Army Officer's Guide.* 45th ed. Harrisburg: Stackpole, 1989.

Cunliffe, R. J. *A Lexicon of the Homeric Dialect.* Norman: University of Oklahoma Press, 1963.

Damasio, Antonio R. *Decartes' Error: Emotion, Reason, and the Human Brain.* New York: Grosset/Putnam, 1994.

Dane, A., and R. Gardner. "Violent Acts and Violent Times: A Comparative Approach to Postwar Homicide Rates." *American Sociological Review* 41:937–63 (1976).

Danieli, Yael. *International Handbook of Multigenerational Legacies of Trauma.* New York: Plenum, 1998.

Dean, Eric T., Jr. *Shook Over Hell: Post-Traumatic Stress, Vietnam, and the Civil War.* Cambridge, Mass.: Harvard University Press, 1997.

Detienne, Marcel. *The Masters of Truth in Archaic Greece.* Trans. Janet Lloyd. New York: Zone Books, 1999.

Detienne, Marcel, and Jean-Pierre Vernant. *Cunning Intelligence in Greek Culture and Society.* Trans. Janet Lloyd. Chicago: University of Chicago Press, 1991.

Dimock, George E., Jr. "The Name of Odysseus." *Hudson Review* 9:52–70 (1956).

———. *The Unity of the* Odyssey. Amherst: University of Massachusetts Press, 1989.

DSM-IV: see American Psychiatric Association.

Dumézel, Georges. *The Destiny of the Warrior.* Trans. Alf Hiltebeitel. Chicago: University of Chicago Press, 1970.

Dunbar, Robin. *Grooming, Gossip, and the Evolution of Language.* Cambridge, Mass.: Harvard University Press, 1996.

du Picq, Ardant. *Battle Studies.* Trans. J. N. Greely and R. C. Cotton. In *Roots of Strategy,* Book 2. Harrisburg: Stackpole, 1987.

Dupuy, Colonel Trevor N. *A Genius for War: The German Army and General Staff, 1807–1945.* McLean, Va.: Nova Publications, 1984.

Edmonds, W. T., Jr. "Lewis Puller Ain't on the Wall." Unpublished poem.

Edwards, Mark W. *Homer: Poet of the Iliad*. Baltimore: Johns Hopkins University Press, 1987.

Farley, Melissa. "Prostitution: Psychological and Social Death of Women." In *Calling Slavery by Its Name*, Symposium, 13th Annual Meeting International Society for Traumatic Stress Studies, Montreal, November 8, 1997.

Felson-Rubin, Nancy. *Regarding Penelope: From Character to Poetics*. Princeton: Princeton University Press, 1994.

Fish, Lydia. "Lydia Fish Vita." The Vietnam Veterans Oral History and Folklore Project. Online: faculty.buffalostate.edu/fishlm/folksongs/vita.htm.

Fukuyama, Francis. *The End of History and the Last Man*. New York: Free Press, 1992.

———. *Trust: The Social Virtues and the Creation of Prosperity*. New York: Free Press, 1995.

Gal, Reuven. *A Portrait of the Israeli Soldier*. Westport: Greenwood, 1986.

Gal, Reuven, and Franklin D. Jones. "A Psychological Model of Combat Stress," in Jones et al., eds. *War Psychiatry*. Washington: Office of the Surgeon General, Borden Institute, Walter Reed Army Institute of Research, 1995.

Gardner, John. *The Art of Fiction*. New York: Vintage, 1985.

Garver, Eugene. *Aristotle's Rhetoric: An Art of Character*. Chicago: University of Chicago Press, 1994.

Gibbs, Philip. *Now It Can Be Told*. New York: Harper, 1920.

Gibson, James W. *Warrior Dreams: Violence and Manhood in Post-Vietnam America*. New York: Hill & Wang, 1994.

Gilligan, James. *Violence: Reflections on a National Epidemic*. New York: Vintage, 1996.

Glass, Albert J. *Neuropsychiatry in World War II*. Vol. 2. Washington: Surgeon General of the U.S. Army, 1973.

Goetsch, Sallie. "Review of Achilles in Vietnam." *Bryn Mawr Classical Review* 94.3.21.

Golden, Leon. *Aristotle on Tragic and Comic Mimesis*. American Philological Association, American Classical Studies monograph No. 29, 1992.

Goodall, Jane. *The Chimpanzees of Gombe: Patterns of Behavior*. Cambridge, Mass.: Harvard University Press, 1986.

Graves, Robert. *Good-bye to All That*. Rev. 2nd ed. New York: Anchor, 1957.

Gudmundsson, Bruce I. "The German Army in World War I: The Contingents." *Tactical Notebook*, November 1991.

Haber, Samuel. *Efficiency and Uplift: Scientific Management in the Progressive Era, 1890–1920*. Chicago: University of Chicago Press, 1964.

Hainsworth, Brian. *The Iliad: A Commentary*. Vol. 3. Cambridge: Cambridge University Press, 1993.

Hall, H. Palmer. *From the Periphery: Poems and Essays*. San Antonio: Chili Verde Press, 1994.

———. "A Valentine's Card for Those Who Were Not There." Unpublished poem. Undated.

Harvey, Mary R. "An Ecological View of Psychological Trauma and Trauma Recovery." *Journal of Traumatic Stress* 9:3–23 (1996).

Haubold, Johannes. *Homer's People: Epic Poetry and Social Formation*. Cambridge: Cambridge University Press, 2000.

Headquarters, Department of the Army. *FM 22–51: Leader's Manual for Combat Stress Control*. Washington, D.C., September 29, 1994.

Headquarters, U.S. Army Training and Doctrine Command. *Assessment of the Unit Manning System*. Fort Monroe, Va., March 1981.

Headquarters, United States Marine Corps. *Commandant of the Marine Corps Trust Study, Final Report*. Contract N00421-00-PR-WL054, September 30, 2000.

————. *Marine Corps Doctrinal Publication 6—Command and Control,* 1996.

Hegel, Georg Wilhelm Friedrich. *Phenomenology of Spirit.* Trans. A. V. Miller. Oxford: Oxford University Press, 1977.

Heller, Charles E., and William A. Stofft. *America's First Battles: 1776–1965.* Lawrence: University Press of Kansas, 1986.

Henderson, Colonel William Darryl. *Cohesion, the Human Element in Combat: Leadership and Societal Influence in the Armies of the Soviet Union, the United States, North Vietnam, and Israel.* Washington: National Defense University Press, 1985.

Herman, Judith Lewis. "Complex PTSD: A Syndrome in Survivors of Prolonged and Repeated Trauma." *Journal of Traumatic Stress* 5:377–92 (1992).

————. *Trauma and Recovery: The Aftermath of Violence from Domestic Abuse to Political Terror.* New York: Basic, 1992.

Hesiod. *Theogony.* In Hesiod, *The Homeric Hymns and Homerica.* Trans. H. G. Evelyn-White. Cambridge, Mass.: Harvard University Press Loeb Library, 1914.

————. *Works and Days and Theogony.* Trans. Stanley Lombardo. Indianapolis: Hackett, 1993.

Hesk, John. *Deception and Democracy.* Cambridge: Cambridge University Press, 2000.

Heubeck, A., and A. Hoekstra. *A Commentary on Homer's* Odyssey. Vol. 2. Oxford: Oxford University Press, 1989.

Hexter, Ralph. *A Guide to the* Odyssey. New York: Vintage, 1993.

Hoffman, George "Sonny." "Sonny Reflections." Online: www.vietvet.org/sonny.htm.

Hoffman, Piotr. *The Human Self and the Life and Death Struggle.* Gainsville: University of Florida/University of South Florida Press, 1983.

Homer. *Iliad.* Trans. Robert Fagles. New York: Viking Penguin, 1990.

————. *Iliad.* Trans. Robert Fitzgerald. New York: Anchor Doubleday, 1975.

————. *Iliad.* Trans. Stanley Lombardo. Cambridge: Hackett, 1997.

————. *Iliad.* [In ancient Greek.] Trans. and ed. A. T. Murray. Cambridge, Mass.: Harvard University Press, 1924.

————. *Odyssey.* Trans. Robert Fagles. New York: Viking Penguin, 1996.

————. *Odyssey.* Trans. Robert Fitzgerald. New York: Vintage Classics, 1990.

————. *Odyssey.* [In ancient Greek.] Trans. and ed. A. T. Murray; rev. George E. Dimock. Cambridge, Mass.: Harvard University Press, 1995.

Hornblower, Simon, and Anthony Spawforth, eds. *The Oxford Classical Dictionary.* 3rd ed. Oxford: Oxford University Press, 1996.

Hudnall-Stamm, Beth, ed. *Secondary Traumatic Stress.* 2nd ed. Lutherville, Md.: Sidran Press, 1999.

Hurbis-Cherrier, Mick, and Catherine Hurbis-Cherrier. *History Lessons.* Video. 1992.

Johnson, Douglas V. "Review of Achilles in Vietnam." *Parameters* 25:133–35 (1995).

Jones, Franklin D. "Psychiatric Lessons of War." In Franklin D. Jones et al., eds. *War Psychiatry.* Surgeon General of the United States Army, *Textbook of Military Medicine,* part 1, vol. 4. Washington: Borden Institute, Walter Reed Army Institute of Research, 1995.

Kant, Immanuel. "To Perpetual Peace: A Philosophical Sketch" and "Idea for a Universal History with a Cosmopolitan Intent." In *Perpetual Peace and Other Essays,* trans. Ted Humphrey. Cambridge: Hackett, 1983.

Kelley, Michael. "The Three Walls Behind the Wall: The Myth of Vietnam Veteran Suicide." Online: www.vwam.com/vets/suicide.html.

Kelman, Herbert C. "The Social Context of Torture." In *The Politics of Pain: Torturers and Their Masters,* ed. Ronald D. Crelinsten and Alex P. Schmid. Boulder: Westview Press, 1994.

Kirkland, Faris R. "Combat Leadership Styles: Empowerment Versus Authoritarianism." *Parameters* 20(4): 61ff (1990).

———. "The Gap Between Leadership Policy and Practice: A Historical Perspective." *Parameters* 20(3): 50ff (1990).

———. "Honor, Combat Ethics, and Military Culture." In T. E. Beam, A. E. Hartle, E. D. Pellegrino, and L. R. Sparacino, eds. *Military Medical Ethics,* vol. 1. In *Textbook of Military Medicine.* Washington: Office of the Surgeon General, U.S. Department of the Army and Borden Institute, 2002. In press.

———. "Self-Care, Psychological Integrity, and Auftragstaktik." Proceedings of the Joint Services Conference on Professional Ethics—XIX. National Defense University Press, January 1997. Online: www.usafa.af.mil/jscope/jscope97.html.

———. "Soldiers and Marines at Chosin Reservoir: Criteria for Assignment to Combat Command." *Armed Forces and Society* 19:257ff (1996).

Kirkland, Faris R., et al. *Unit Manning System Field Evaluation: Technical Report No. 5.* Washington: Walter Reed Army Institute of Research, September 1987.

Kirkland, Faris R., R. R. Halverson, and P. D. Bliese. "Stress and Psychological Readiness in Post-Cold-War Operations." *Parameters* 26:79–91 (1996).

Kirkland, Faris R., and Pearl Katz. "Combat Readiness and the Army Family." *U.S. Army Military Review* 69:63ff (1989).

Kitfield, James. *Prodigal Soldiers: How the Generation of Officers Born of Vietnam Revolutionized the American Style of War.* New York: Simon & Schuster, 1995.

Kohut, Heinz. *The Analysis of the Self: A Systematic Approach to the Psychoanalytic Treatment of Narcissistic Personality Disorders.* Madison: International University Press, 1971.

Koziak, Barbara. *Retrieving Political Emotion: Thumos, Aristotle and Gender.* University Park: Pennsylvania State University Press, 2000.

Krulak, General Charles C. "The Strategic Corporal: Leadership in the Three Block War." *Marine Corps Gazette* 83:18–22 (1999).

Kulka, Richard A., et al. *The National Vietnam Veterans Readjustment Study: Tables of Findings and Technical Appendices.* New York: Brunner/Mazel, 1990.

———. *Trauma and the Vietnam War Generation.* New York: Brunner/Mazel, 1990.

Lateiner, Donald. *Sardonic Smile: Nonverbal Behavior in Homeric Epic.* Ann Arbor: University of Michigan Press, 1995.

Lazenby, John F. "Mercenaries." In Simon Hornblower and Anthony Spawforth, eds., *The Oxford Classical Dictionary.* 3rd ed. Oxford: Oxford University Press, 1996, pp. 961ff.

Leakey, Richard. *The Origin of Humankind.* New York: Basic Books, 1994.

Lewis, Mark. "Lewis Report: Why Stopping the Exodus of Junior Officers Is Important, September 7, 2001." Online: www.d-n-i.net/FCS_Folder/comments/c426.htm.

Linderman, Gerald F. *The World Within War: America's Combat Experience in World War II.* New York: Free Press, 1997.

Little Iliad. In Hesiod, *The Homeric Hymns and Homerica,* trans. H. G. Evelyn-White. Cambridge, Mass.: Harvard University Press Loeb Library, 1914.

Luttwak, Edward. *Strategy: The Logic of War and Peace.* Cambridge: Harvard University Press, 1987.

Martin, Richard P. *The Language of Heroes: Speech and Performance in the Iliad.* Ithaca: Cornell University Press, 1989.

Mason, Patience C. H. *Recovering from the War: A Woman's Guide to Helping Your Vietnam Veteran, Your Family, and Yourself.* New York: Viking, 1990.

Mason, Robert. *Chickenhawk.* New York: Viking Penguin, 1983.

———. *Chickenhawk: Back in the World.* New York: Viking Penguin, 1993.

Matsakis, Aphrodite. *Vietnam Wives.* Kensington, Md.: Woodbine House, 1988.

———. *Vietnam Wives: Facing the Challenges of Life with Veterans Suffering Post-Traumatic Stress Disorder.* 2nd ed. Lutherville, Md.: Sidran Press, 1996.

McCombs, Michael, Sr. "Blood Brother." In Michael McCombs, Sr. *Fading Photographs from My Mind's Own Album.* Online: www.vietvet.org/namvet99.htm.

McGlew, James F. *Tyranny and Political Culture in Ancient Greece.* Ithaca: Cornell University Press, 1993.

McMaster, Major H. R. *Dereliction of Duty.* New York: HarperCollins, 1998.

Miller, William I. *Humiliation and Other Essays on Honor, Social Discomfort, and Violence.* Ithaca: Cornell University Press, 1993.

———. *The Mystery of Courage.* Cambridge, Mass.: Harvard University Press, 2000.

Moore, Lieutenant General Harold G., and Joseph L. Galloway. *We Were Soldiers Once . . . and Young.* New York: Random House, 1992.

More, Sir Thomas. *Utopia.* Ed. R. M. Adams. New York: W. W. Norton, 1975.

Morris, Ian. "The Strong Principle of Equality and the Archaic Origins of Greek Democracy." In Josiah Ober and Charles Hedrick, eds. *Dēmokratia.*

Mullen, William. "Pindar and Athens." *Arion* New Series 1/3,1974.

Munroe, James F. "The Loss and Restoration of Community: The Treatment of Severe War Trauma." *Journal of Personal and Interpersonal Loss* 1:393–409 (1996).

———. "Therapist Traumatization from Exposure to Patients with Combat-Related Post-Traumatic Stress Disorder: Implications for Administration and Supervision." Unpublished doctoral dissertation. Ann Arbor: Dissertation Abstracts, 1991.

Munroe, James F., Jonathan Shay, Christine Makary, Michelle Clopper, and Melissa Wattenberg. *Creating a Family of Re-Origin: A Long-Term Outpatient PTSD Unit.* Training "Institute" at the Fifth Annual Meeting of the Society for Traumatic Stress Studies, San Francisco, 1989.

Nagy, Gregory. *The Best of the Achaeans: Concepts of the Hero in Archaic Greek Poetry.* Baltimore: Johns Hopkins University Press, 1979.

———. *Greek Mythology and Poetics.* Ithaca: Cornell University Press, 1990.

———. "Introduction," *Iliad.* Trans. Robert Fitzgerald. New York: Alfred A. Knopf, 1992.

———. *Poetry as Performance: Homer and Beyond.* Cambridge: Cambridge University Press, 1996.

Nietzsche, Friedrich. *Human, All Too Human.* Trans. R. J. Hollingdale. Cambridge: Cambridge University Press, 1986.

Nussbaum, Martha C. *The Fragility of Goodness.* Cambridge: Cambridge University Press, 1986.

———. "Tragedy and Self-Sufficiency: Plato and Aristotle on Fear and Pity." In A. O. Rorty, *Essays on Aristotle's Poetics.* Princeton: Princeton University Press, 1992.

———. *Upheavals of Thought: The Intelligence of Emotions.* Cambridge: Cambridge University Press, 2001.

NVVRS. See Kulka et al. *The National Vietnam Veterans Readjustment Study: Tables of Findings and Technical Appendices.*

Ober, Josiah, and Charles Hedrick, eds. *Dēmokratia: A Conversation on Democracies, Ancient and Modern.* Princeton: Princeton University Press, 1996.

Otto, Rudolf. *The Idea of the Holy.* 2nd ed. Trans. John W. Harvey. Oxford: Oxford University Press, 1923; 1950.

Owen, Wilfred. *The Collected Poems of Wilfred Owen.* New York: New Directions, 1965.

Palaima, Thomas G. "To Be a Citizen or an Idiot: The Choice Is Ours." *Austin American-Statesman,* October 9, 2001.

Parry, Hugh. "The Apologos of Odysseus: Lies, All Lies?" *Phoenix* 48 (1994), pp. 1–20.

Parsons, Talcott. *The Social System.* New York: Free Press, 1951.

Patterson, Orlando. *Slavery and Social Death: A Comparative Study*. Cambridge, Mass.: Harvard University Press, 1982.

Peradotto, John. *Man in the Middle Voice: Name and Narration in the Odyssey*. Princeton: Princeton University Press, 1990.

Pitman R. K., L. M. Shin, and S. L. Rauch. "Investigating the Pathogenesis of Post-Traumatic Stress Disorder with Neuroimaging." *Journal of Clinical Psychiatry* 62S17:47–54 (2001).

Plato. *Republic*. Trans. Paul Shorey. In Edith Hamilton and Huntington Cairns, *Plato: The Collected Dialogues*. Princeton: Princeton University Press, 1963.

Poole, H. John. *Phantom Soldier: The Enemy's Answer to U.S. Firepower*. Emerald Isle, N.C.: Posterity Press, 2001.

Pressfield, Steven. *Gates of Fire*. New York: Doubleday, 1998.

Price, A. W. *Love and Friendship in Plato and Aristotle*. Oxford: Oxford University Press, 1990.

Pucci, Pietro. *Odysseus Polutropos: Intertextual Readings in the* Odyssey *and the* Iliad. Ithaca: Cornell University Press, 1987; 1995.

———. "The Song of the Sirens." In Seth Schein, *Reading the Odyssey*.

Pulver, Sydney. "Narcissism: The Term and Concept." In A. P. Morrison, ed., *Essential Papers on Narcissism*. New York: New York University Press, 1986.

Raphals, Lisa. *Knowing Words: Wisdom and Cunning in the Classical Traditions of China and Greece*. Ithaca: Cornell University Press, 1992.

Reinhardt, Karl. "The Adventures in the Odyssey" (1948). Trans. H. I. Flower. In Seth Schein, *Reading the Odyssey*.

Remarque, Erich Maria. *The Road Back*. Trans. A. W. Wheen. New York: Little, Brown, 1931; rpt., New York: Fawcett Columbine, 1998.

Resch, John P. *Suffering Soldiers: Revolutionary War Veterans, Moral Sentiment, and Political Culture in the Early Republic*. Amherst: University of Massachusetts Press, 1999.

Richards, Chester W. *A Swift, Elusive Sword: What if Sun Tzu and John Boyd Did a National Defense Review?* Center for Defense Information, 2001. Online: www.cdi.org/mrp/swift_elusive_sword.pdf.

Richardson, Scott. "Truth in the Tales of the Odyssey." *Mnemosyne* 49:393–402 (1996).

Ricks, Thomas E. "Kerrey Team Takes Issue with Report: 6 of 7 SEALs Meet on Vietnam Killings." *The Washington Post,* April 29, 2001.

Rodriguez, Michael W. "The Lounge: We Can Never Leave." Poem. Online: faculty.buffalostate.edu/fishlm/folksongs/nvrleave.htm.

Roemer, Lizabeth, Brett T. Lidz, Susan M. Orsillo, and Amy W. Wagner. "A Preliminary Investigation of the Role of Strategic Withholding of Emotion in PTSD." *Journal of Traumatic Stress* 14:149–56 (2001).

Rohde, Richard R. "Identity, Self, and Disorder Among Vietnam Veterans: PTSD and the Emergence of an Electronic Community." Unpublished dissertation. Ann Arbor: Dissertation Abstracts, 1995.

Rorty, Amélie Oksenberg. *Essays on Aristotle's Poetics*. Princeton: Princeton University Press, 1992.

———. *Essays on Aristotle's Rhetoric*. Princeton: Princeton University Press, 1996.

Rosenberger, Colonel John D. "Reaching Our Army's Full Combat Potential in the 21st Century." *Landpower Essay Series* No. 99–2, February 1999.

Saigh, Philip A., and J. Douglas Bremner, eds. *Posttraumatic Stress Disorder: A Comprehensive Text*. Boston: Allyn & Bacon, 1999.

Schein, Seth. *Reading the Odyssey: Selected Interpretive Essays*. Princeton: Princeton University Press, 1996.

Segal, Charles. *Singers, Heroes, and Gods in the* Odyssey. Ithaca: Cornell University Press, 1994.

———. *Sophocles' Tragic World: Divinity, Nature, Society*. Cambridge, Mass.: Harvard University Press, 1995.

———. *Tragedy and Civilization: An Interpretation of Sophocles*. Cambridge, Mass.: Harvard University Press, 1981.

Severo, R., and L. Milford. *The Wages of War: When American's Soldiers Came Home—From Valley Forge to Vietnam*. New York: Simon & Schuster, 1989.

Shay, Jonathan. *Achill in Vietnam. Kampftrauma und Persönlichkeitsverlust*. German translation by Klaus Kochmann. Hamburg: Hamburger Edition, 1998.

———. *Achilles in Vietnam: Combat Trauma and the Undoing of Character*. New York: Atheneum, 1994; Touchstone, 1995.

———. "Achilles, Odysseus, Agamemnon: Homer on Military Leadership." The Secretary of the Navy's Guest Lecture. Naval Command Center Auditorium, Pentagon, February 23, 2000. Online: www.belisarius.com/author_index.htm.

———. "Achilles: Paragon, Flawed Character, or Tragic Soldier Figure?" *Classical Bulletin* 71:117–24 (1995).

———. "The Birth of Tragedy—Out of the Needs of Democracy." *Didaskalia: Ancient Theater Today*, vol. 2, no. 2 (April 1995) Online: http://didaskalia.berkeley.edu/issues/vol2no2/Shay.html.

———. "Causing Change." *Military Personnel Policy*. RAND Seminar Series. November 30, 1999.

———. "Cohesion." In *Commandant of the Marine Corps Trust Study 2000*. Online: www.belisarius.com/author_index.htm.

———. "Guilt and Good Character." *Religion and Ethics Newsweekly*, June 1, 2001. Online: www.thirteen.org/religionandethics/week440/vietnam.htm.

———. "The Invisible Gap: Ethical Standing for Commander Self-Care." *Parameters* 28:93–105, Summer 1998. Online: carlisle-www.army.mil/usawc/parameters/98summer/shay.htm.

———. "Killing Rage: *Physis* or *Nomos*—or Both?" In *War and Violence in Ancient Greece*, ed. Hans van Wees. London: Duckworth and Classical Press of Wales, 2000. Online: www.belisarius.com/author_index.htm.

———. "On Medications for Combat PTSD." In Robert Hsiung, ed., The Virtual Enpsych-lopedia by Dr. Bob 1995. Online: www.dr-bob.org/tips/ptsd.html.

———. "Preventing Psychological and Moral Injury in Military Service." *Commandant of the Marine Corps Trust Study 2000*. Online: www.belisarius.com/author_index.htm.

———. "Trust: Touchstone for a Practical Military Ethos." In Major Donald Vandergriff, *Spirit, Blood, and Treasure*.

Shay, Jonathan, and James Munroe. "Group and Milieu Therapy for Veterans with Complex Posttraumatic Stress Disorder." In Philip A. Saigh and J. Douglas Bremner, eds., *Posttraumatic Stress Disorder: A Comprehensive Text*. Boston: Allyn & Bacon, 1999.

Shay, Jonathan, Steven Canby, and Bruce I. Gudmundsson. *Commandant of theMarine Corps Trust Study*. Quantico, Va.: United States Marine Corps, 2000. Contract N00421-00-PR-WL054 with ACS Defense Industries.

Sheehan, Neil. *A Bright Shining Lie: John Paul Vann and America in Vietnam*. New York: Random House, 1988.

Sober, Elliott, and David Sloan Wilson. *Unto Others: The Evolution and Psychology of Unselfish Behavior*. Cambridge, Mass.: Harvard University Press, 1998.

Spinney, Franklin C. "Indexed Comments," *Defense and the National Interest*. Online: www.d-n-i.net.

Stanford, W. B. *Enemies of Poetry*. London: Routledge & Kegan Paul, 1980.

———. *The Odyssey of Homer*. 2nd ed. 2 vols. New York: St. Martin's Press, 1965.

———. *The Ulysses Theme: A Study in the Adaptability of a Traditional Hero*. 2nd ed. New York: Barnes & Noble, 1968.

Stewart, Nora Kinzer, *Mates and Muchachos: Unit Cohesion in the Falklands/Malvinas War*. Washington: Brassey's (U.S.), 1991.

Strott, Judee. "A Prayer for Death and Life." Unpublished poem.

———. "ReallyCare." Unpublished poem.

Stubbings, F. H. "The Recession of Mycenaean Civilization." In *The Cambridge Ancient History*, 3rd ed., vol. 3, part 2, ed. I. E. S. Edwards et al. Cambridge: Cambridge University Press, 1975.

Sultan, Nancy. *Exile and the Poetics of Loss in Greek Tradition*. Lanham, Md.: Rowman & Littlefield, 1999.

Summers, Harry G. *Vietnam War Almanac*. New York: Facts on File, 1985.

Tegtmeier, John. "US Veteran Post-Service Mortality and Suicides: A Selected Specialized Bibliography." Online: www.vwip.org/articles/T/TegtmeierJohn_USVeteranPost-ServiceMortalityAndSuicidesBibliography.htm.

Tennyson, Alfred Lord. *The Works of Alfred Lord Tennyson*. Ware, U.K.: Wordsworth Editions, 1994.

Thayer, Thomas C., ed. *A Systems Analysis View of the Vietnam War, 1965–1972*. Vol. 8: *Casualties and Losses*. Office of the Assistant Secretary of Defense for Program Analysis and Evaluation, Defense Technical Information Center #ADA051613, 1975.

Thucydides. *The Peloponnesian War*. Trans. Steven Lattimore. Indianapolis: Hackett, 1998.

Tillson, John C. F. *Reducing the Impact of Tempo*. Alexandria: Institute for Defense Analyses, IDA Document D-2290, October 30, 1999.

Tillson, John C. F., and Steven L. Canby. *Alternative Approaches to Organizing, Training, and Assessing Army and Marine Corps Units, Part I: The Active Component*. Report C-MDA 909 89 C 0003/1 L6-1067 for the Assistant Secretary of Defense (Force Management and Personnel). Alexandria: Institute for Defense Analysis, November 1992.

Tracy, Stephen V. *The Story of the Odyssey*. Princeton: Princeton University Press, 1990.

Tritle, Lawrence A. *From Melos to My Lai: War and Survival*. London and New York: Routledge, 2000.

Ulmer, Walter F., Jr. "Military Leadership into the 21st Century: Another 'Bridge Too Far'?" *Parameters* 28:4–26 (Spring 1998).

van Creveld, Martin *Fighting Power: German and U.S. Army Performance, 1939–1945*. Westport: Greenwood Press, 1982.

van Wees, Hans. *Status Warriors*. Amsterdam: Gieben, 1992.

———, ed. *War and Violence in Ancient Greece*. London: Duckworth and the Classical Press of Wales, 2000.

Vandergriff, Major Donald. *Path to Victory: America's Army and the Revolution in Human Affairs*. Novato, Calif.: Presidio Press, 2002.

———. "truth@readiness.mil." *Proceedings of the U.S. Naval Institute*, June 1999.

———, ed. *Spirit, Blood, and Treasure: The American Cost of Battle in the 21st Century*. Novato, Calif.: Presidio Press, 2001.

Verkamp, Bernard J. *The Moral Treatment of Returning Warriors in Early Medieval and Modern Times*. Cranbury, N.J.: Associated University Presses, 1993.

Vernant, Jean-Pierre. "The Refusal of Odysseus." Trans. V. Farenga. In Seth Schein, *Reading the Odyssey*.

Virgil [Publius Virgilius Maro]. *Aeneid*. Trans. Robert Fitzgerald. New York: Vintage, 1981.

Vistica, Gregory L. "What Happened at Thanh Phong." *The New York Times Magazine,*
    April 29, 2001, pp. 50–57, 66–68, 133.
Waller, Willard. *The Veteran Comes Back.* New York: Dryden, 1944.
Wilson, Donna. "Lion Kings: Heroes in the Epic Mirrors." *Colby Quarterly,* 2002. In
    press.
———. *Ransom, Revenge, and Heroic Identity.* Cambridge: Cambridge University
    Press, 2002.
Wilson, Jeremy. *Lawrence of Arabia: The Authorized Biography of T. E. Lawrence.* Lon-
    don: Heinemann, 1989.
Wilson, William Julius. *When Work Disappears: The World of the New Urban Poor.* New
    York: Alfred A. Knopf, 1996.
Wirtz, James J. *The Tet Offensive: Intelligence Failure in War.* Ithaca: Cornell University
    Press, 1991.
Zuckert, Catherine H., ed. *Understanding the Political Spirit: Philosophical Investiga-
    tions from Socrates to Nietzsche.* New Haven: Yale University Press, 1988.
Zwygart, U. F. "How Much Obedience Does an Officer Need?" U.S. Army Command
    and General Staff College pamphlet, 1993.

INDEX

PERMISSIONS ACKNOWLEDGMENTS

"Clearly one of the most original and most important scholarly works to have emerged from the Vietnam War. Beyond that, it is also an intensely moving work, intensely passionate, reaching back through the centuries to touch and heal."

—TIM O'BRIEN, author of
The Things They Carried and *July, July*

"A transcendent literary adventure."

—HERBERT MITGANG, *The New York Times*

"...CLEARLY ONE OF THE MOST ORIGINAL AND MOST IMPORTANT SCHOLARLY WORKS TO HAVE EMERGED FROM THE VIETNAM WAR. BEYOND THAT, IT IS ALSO AN INTENSELY MOVING WORK, INTENSELY PASSIONATE, REACHING BACK THROUGH THE CENTURIES TO TOUCH AND HEAL."
—TIM O'BRIEN, AUTHOR OF *GOING AFTER CACCIATO* AND *THE THINGS THEY CARRIED*

ACHILLES IN VIETNAM
COMBAT TRAUMA AND THE UNDOING OF CHARACTER

JONATHAN SHAY, M.D., Ph.D.

0-684-81321-1 · $13.00/$19.25 Can.

SCRIBNER
A Division of Simon & Schuster
A VIACOM COMPANY